Course	Creating Value: Selling
Course Number	**MKT 405**
	Patrick Lindsay
	MARKETING

http://create.mheducation.com

ISBN-10: 1308413262   ISBN-13: 9781308413266

Contents

Credits

chapter 1

SELLING AND SALESPEOPLE

SOME QUESTIONS ANSWERED IN THIS CHAPTER ARE

- What is selling?
- Why should you learn about selling even if you do not plan to be a salesperson?
- What is the role of personal selling in a firm?
- What are the different types of salespeople?
- What are the rewards of a selling career?

PROFILE

> *"Your customers, whether they are internal, end users or distributors, are relying on you to help them get their job done."*
>
> *Amber Fischer, Rehrig Pacific*

PROFILE My name is Amber Fischer, and I am a 2004 graduate of the St. Catherine University (formerly known at College of St. Catherine) business-to-business sales program. I began my college career as a sociology major. I was fascinated by observing what factors influence people's decisions and behaviors as they relate to their surroundings and teachings. As I approached my junior year, it became evident that a career in the field of business was the right path for me. Lynn Schleeter, Marge Matheson-Hance, Mary Henderson, and Greg Dinovis did a great job of showing me that the sales program was a perfect fit, as it combined my love of understanding and interacting with people with my appreciation for commerce. I was fortunate enough to be selected at 3M Frontline sales intern for the summer of 2003. Throughout that summer and the subsequent school year, I was responsible for working with 3M sales reps throughout the organization and in a variety of industries to build customer-focused organization "maps" in an effort to increase sales through cross selling. In order to be successful, I needed to sell the 3M reps on giving me the time and exposure to Fortune 500 customers so that I could construct accurate maps that I would then present to a large number of reps. I then needed to sell them on using my maps to get in deeper with their customers and share their contacts with other 3Mers.

Over my postcollege career, I have been fortunate enough to work in sales in a variety of capacities. I have worked for a nationwide distributor, Interline Brands, to sell directly to end users. In this role, I had to learn to sell my ability to solve urgent customer problems as well as sell my capabilities to manufacturer reps so that they would entrust me with the best training and leads in order to grow my business. I was also fortunate enough to work for 3M as a manufacturer's rep. In this role, I sold through distributor reps to end users. Distributors sell a variety of lines, so I had to sell them on the reasons why they should focus on my products and promote them to the end user. I also needed to influence end users to request 3M products.

I currently work for Rehrig Pacific selling transport packaging to large retail and food and beverage customers (Walmart, Pepsi, and Target are a few key customers). In this role, I am responsible for influencing and directly selling our products to the end user. I must also sell internally, as I work directly with production to get my product manufactured and delivered quickly. We also have a great design team that I can work with to bring innovative solutions to our customers. Of course, I must sell my business case plan to our executives in order to get a design budget.

While I have had a variety of sales experiences in my career, there are some significant consistencies I can identify. Your customers, whether they are internal, end users, or distributors, are relying on you to help them get their job done. Understanding the business pressures that result in needs is vital to effectively communicating your value to the customer. This does not happen overnight. You must put in the time and hard work to really understand your customers. You must be reactive in responding to their needs, proactive in bringing creative ideas to their challenges, and consistent in your message that you are the person they should be relying on to meet their goals.

Visit our Web site at: rehrigpacific.com

WHY LEARN ABOUT PERSONAL SELLING?

What's the first thing that pops into your mind when you hear the phrase "personal selling"? Do you conjure up images of fast-talking, nonlistening, pushy guys who won't take no for an answer? How about this definition: "Personal selling is the craft of persuading people to buy what they do not want and do not need for more than it is worth.[1]"

If that is your view of selling, we encourage you to study this book carefully. You're going to learn things about selling that you never knew before. Let's start with a more accurate definition of a professional salesperson, which is quite different from the one just mentioned. **Personal selling** is "the phenomenon of human-driven interaction between and within individuals/organizations in order to bring about economic exchange within a value-creation context."[2] Let's look at the definition more closely:

- It is more than just a set of sequential steps that a salesperson goes through with each buyer in order to get the order. It's not just about what a seller does but rather the *interaction* between sellers and buyers that makes selling work today. We will talk about steps in the selling process in this book, but remember that they are not necessarily sequential or all needed for all buying situations.

- It can often involve multiple people and organizations (not just one seller and one buyer, for example).

- Selling is all about creating **value**, which is the total benefit that the seller's products and services provide to the buyer. When describing this to prospects, the seller often refers to the collection of buyer-specific benefits as the **customer value proposition** (CVP), described more fully in Chapter 9. Just as our definition implies, this CVP is dynamic, evolving as time goes on and depends on the context of the situation.[3] In fact, success in future business often depends on enhancements to the original CVP.[4] Exhibit 1.1 provides examples of ways that salespeople create value.

- The goal of selling is to create economic exchange, not merely to promote the product or service. Customers today are very technology savvy and search enabled and no longer rely on salespeople alone to learn about products and services. Selling recognizes this fact and provides needed services to create the exchange that is in the best interests of both parties.

Exhibit 1.1

Examples of Ways That Salespeople Can Add Value in a Selling Situation

Provide an interface between the buying and selling companies.

Identify networks of key players in both the buying and the selling companies and then help to activate them to the task of cocreating value.

Encourage two-way communication and help to create effective bonds between people.

Help to create a climate of coleadership in the meetings rather than having the seller always take the leadership role.

Encourage both sides to learn from and understand each other.

Facilitate truly useful meetings and conversations between all parties.

Help to manage any situations that arise to bring everyone back to a value-adding perspective.

Help to foster conditions of trust and commitment between parties.

Be attuned to activities that increase value adding and help facilitate more of them.

Help key players to understand their own perceptions of what value is to them.

Create meaning out of situations that arise and conversations that occur.

Help to provide closure on solutions that provide value to all parties.

Source: Adapted from information found in Alexander Haas, Ivan Snehota, and Daniela Corsaro, "Creating Value in Business Relationships: The Role of Sales," *Industrial Marketing Management* 41, no. 1 (2012), pp. 94–105.

This economic exchange involves what we call profit for both parties. Everyone knows that sellers sell to make a profit. Why do buyers buy? Typically a student will say, "To satisfy a need or a want," and that is a good basic answer. More helpful is to recognize that buyers also buy to make a profit. But they calculate profit differently. A seller's profit is selling price minus cost of goods sold and selling costs. A buyer's profit, or value, is the benefit received minus the selling price and costs and hassles of buying, or time and effort, as noted in this equation:

$$\text{Personal Value Equation} = \text{Benefits received} - (\text{Selling price} + \text{Time and effort to purchase})$$

For example, when someone buys a product from a salesperson, the buyer's profit may be higher than that obtained by buying on the Internet due to the benefits received (expert knowledge in determining the appropriate product to purchase, assistance with installation, resolution of concerns, creation of new offerings based on the buyer's specific needs, and so forth). We'll explain more about benefits in Chapter 8.

EVERYONE SELLS

This text focuses on personal selling as a business activity undertaken by salespeople. But keep in mind that the principles of selling are useful to everyone, not just people with the title of salesperson. Developing mutually beneficial, long-term relationships is vital to all of us. In fact, the author team has taught the principles in this book to many groups of nonsalespeople. Let's look at some examples of how nonsalespeople sell ideas.

As a college student, you might use selling techniques when you ask a professor to let you enroll in a course that is closed out. When you near graduation, you will certainly confront a very important sales job: selling yourself to an employer.

To get a job after graduation, you will go through the same steps used in the sales process (discussed in Part 2, Chapters 6 through 14). First you will identify some potential employers (customers). On the basis of an analysis of each employer's needs, you will develop a presentation (as well as answers to questions you might encounter) to demonstrate your ability to satisfy those needs. You might even create a video resume, as Sales Technology 1.1 describes. During the interview you will listen to what the recruiter says, ask and answer questions, and perhaps alter your presentation based on the new information you receive during the interview. At some point you might negotiate with the employer over starting salary or other issues. Eventually you will try to secure a commitment from the employer to hire you. This process is selling at a very personal level. Chapter 17 reviews the steps you need to undertake to get a sales job.

Nonsalespeople in business use selling principles all the time. Engineers convince managers to support their R&D projects, industrial relations executives use selling approaches when negotiating with unions, and aspiring management trainees sell themselves to associates, superiors, and subordinates to get raises and promotions.

It's not just businesspeople who practice the art of selling. Presidents encourage politicians in Congress to support certain programs, charities solicit contributions and volunteers to run organizations, scientists try to convince foundations and government agencies to fund research, and doctors try to get their patients to adopt more healthful lifestyles. People skilled at selling value, influencing others, and developing long-term relationships are usually leaders in our society.

VIDEO RESUMES—THE NEW WAY TO SET YOURSELF APART

Employers receive hundreds of resumes for each sales position. You may meet all of the qualifications for the job and be a great candidate, but when it comes down to it, the people who review resumes and decide who will even get a call for an interview do not have the time to read through every aspect of each individual resume. You need to set yourself apart from the rest of the competition

With a video resume, you have the chance to instill your face in their minds. And why take the risk of having your resume read a way in which you did not intend for it to be read when you can verbally tell them your qualifications and why you are a great fit for the position; this limits the chance of communication errors. Here are some tips:

Do's of Video Resumes

- Practice and prepare what you are going to say.
- Dress professionally as if you were going in for an interview.
- Envision the camera as the eyes of the person viewing your video and maintain eye contact.
- Smile, smile, smile—your nonverbal cues can send a stronger message than you think.
- Ensure that the lighting in the room is as best as possible—dim lighting can lead to poor quality and also shows lack of preparedness.

- Edit your video, this is your opportunity to make it perfect. If you're not skilled with editing, check your campus for services that may be able to help you out.
- Keep the area that is being taped to no more than a head to waist shot.
- Film against a solid color—this will help to reduce "noise."
- Make sure that you are in a quiet area and free of distractions.

Don't of Video Resumes

- Get ahead of yourself and begin speaking too fast— you are talking to your computer, you have nothing to be nervous about.
- Chew gum—again, try to treat this entire process as if you are going in to the hiring manager's office for an interview.
- Avoid filler words, such as "umm," "ahh," "like," and "you know"—these words are a waste of time and show nervousness and lack of preparation, and if "they know," why would you have to tell them?

Source: Personal experience plus "Do's and Don'ts," *Internships.com*, http://www.internships.com/student/resources/prep/videointro/tips, August 30, 2012.

CREATING VALUE: THE ROLE OF SALESPEOPLE IN A BUSINESS

Companies exist only when their products and services are sold. It takes skill for salespeople to uncover exactly what a customer is looking for and how a potential product or service could add such value. Because this is so critical, this topic is covered in great detail in many chapters in this book.

Companies have many options in how they can approach customers as they add value, and the various methods are sometimes called **go-to-market strategies.** Strategies include selling through the Internet, field sales representatives, business partners, resellers, manufacturer agents, franchises, telemarketers, and others. Selling firms determine which strategy to use for each customer based on such factors as the estimated value of the customer over the lifetime of the relationship, often called **customer lifetime value.**[5] (Because this concept is so important, it is more fully discussed in Chapter 14.) Organizations whose go-to-market strategies rely heavily on salespeople are called **sales force–intensive organizations.**

Exhibit 1.2
Communication
Methods

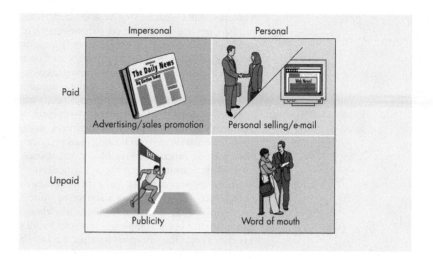

Naturally some firms use several strategies at the same time, and this is called **multichannel strategy.**[6] For example, Motorola uses the Internet for very small customers, telemarketers for midsized customers, and a field sales force for large, important customers.

Another way to view the role of salespeople in business is to realize that they are one element in the company's marketing communications program, as Exhibit 1.2 indicates.[7] Advertising uses impersonal mass media such as newspapers and TV to give information to customers, while sales promotions offer incentives to customers to purchase products during a specific period. Salespeople provide paid personal communication to customers, whereas publicity is communication through significant unpaid presentations about the firm (usually a news story). Finally, communication also occurs at no cost through word of mouth (communication among buyers about the selling firm).

Each of the communication methods in Exhibit 1.2 has strengths and weaknesses. For example, firms have more control when using paid versus unpaid methods. However, because publicity and word of mouth are communicated by independent sources, their information is usually perceived as more credible than information from paid communication sources. When using advertising, Internet sites, and sales promotions, companies can determine the message's exact content and the time of its delivery. They have less control over the communication delivered by salespeople and have very little control over the content or timing of publicity and word-of-mouth communication. Personal selling comes out on top in flexibility because salespeople can talk with each customer, discover the customer's specific needs, and develop unique presentations for that customer. Not surprisingly, personal selling is the most costly method of communication. The average cost of a sales call can be 10,000 times more expensive than exposing that single customer to a newspaper, radio, or TV ad.

Because each communication vehicle in Exhibit 1.2 has strengths and weaknesses, firms often use **integrated marketing communications,** which are communication programs that coordinate the use of various vehicles to maximize the total impact of the programs on customers.

For example, when Stouffer's introduced its new Spa Cuisine Classics, dinners that were inspired by chefs from wellness spas across the country, it used integrated marketing communications. Salespeople called on supermarkets and wholesale clubs. Advertising was created to generate awareness in consumers' minds. Coupons were offered to consumers to create interest and spur more rapid sales. Taste tests in stores were offered to build excitement and word of mouth. Publicity was generated that focused on the dinners' balance of great taste combined with the nutrition of whole grains. Although using salespeople in this example was an expensive part of the communication mix, it was important to do so to ensure that customers' precise needs were met.

Many students think—incorrectly—that advertising is the most important part of a firm's promotion program. However, many industrial companies place far more emphasis on personal selling than on advertising. Even in consumer product firms such as Procter & Gamble, which spends more than billions annually on advertising, personal selling plays a critical role.[8]

Students sometimes also have the mistaken notion that the growing world of e-commerce and the Web as a source of information are causing the demise of salespeople. While the Web has drastically changed the life of a salesperson, salespeople are not being completely replaced by all of the new technology. However, it is critical that the salesperson actually add value in this new reality.

Let's look at this from another perspective—your own life. Have you purchased anything from the Internet? Probably every student has—travel, music, clothing, books, and more. Have you noticed that, other than Internet services, everything you purchased on the Web existed in some form before the Web? Why, then, has the Web become such a ubiquitous place for commerce? Simple. The Internet makes information as well as products and services available the way the consumer wants them. Those who sell via the Web gain competitive advantage by selling the way the buyers (or at least some buyers in some situations) want to buy.

If salespeople want to sell effectively, they have to recognize that the buyer has needs that are met not only by the product but also by the selling process itself. These needs include time savings, shopping costs such as gas if they drive around, and others. Part of the salesperson's responsibility is to sell the way the buyer wants to buy.

WHAT DO SALESPEOPLE DO?

The activities of salespeople depend on the type of selling job they choose. The responsibilities of salespeople selling financial services for General Electric differ greatly from those of salespeople selling pharmaceuticals for Merck or paper products for Georgia-Pacific. Salespeople often have multiple roles to play, including client relationship manager, account team manager, vendor and channel manager, and information provider for their firms.[9] Studies have shown that when a salesperson's role encompasses more than simply the selling function, the seller's firm has more overall value.[10]

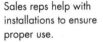

Sales reps help with installations to ensure proper use.

CLIENT RELATIONSHIP MANAGER

Sales jobs involve prospecting for new customers, making sales presentations, demonstrating products, negotiating price and delivery terms, writing orders, and increasing sales to existing customers. But these sales-generating activities (discussed in Chapters 6 through 14) are only part of the job. Although the numbers would vary greatly depending on the type of sales job, salespeople generally spend less than 50 percent of their time on-site in face-to-face meetings with customers and prospects. The rest of salespeople's time is spent in meetings, working with support people in their companies (internal selling), traveling, waiting for a sales interview, doing paperwork, and servicing customers.

Rather than buying from the lowest-cost suppliers, many buyers now are building competitive advantages by developing and maintaining close, cooperative relationships with a select set of suppliers, and salespeople play a key role in these relationships. Salespeople help customers identify problems, offering information about potential solutions and providing after-sale service to ensure long-term satisfaction. The phrase often used to describe this is **customer-centric**, which means making the customer the center of everything the salesperson does.[11] And buyers are demanding **24/7 service** (which means they expect a selling firm to be available for them 24 hours a day, 7 days a week). When salespeople fail in maintaining these relationships, the results are catastrophic. Research indicates that buyers worldwide are deserting firms they used to do business with in record numbers when their expectations are not met. For example, two-thirds of consumers surveyed cited poor service as the reason they left a provider in the last 12 months.[12]

The salesperson's job does not end when the customer places an order. Sales representatives must make sure customers get the benefits they expect from the product. Thus, salespeople work with other company employees to ensure that deliveries are made on time, equipment is properly installed, operators are trained to use the equipment, and questions or complaints are resolved quickly. Progressive selling firms like Standard Register and Johnson & Johnson's Ortho-Clinical Diagnostics are beginning to implement **six sigma selling programs,** which are designed to reduce errors introduced by the selling system to practically zero. Chapter 14 provides more insights on developing ongoing relationships through customer service.

ACCOUNT TEAM MANAGER

Salespeople also coordinate the activities within their firms to solve customer problems.[13] Many sales situations call for team selling, and studies show that salespeople who attempt to go it alone (sometimes called being "lone wolves") perform poorly, have lower job satisfaction, and have higher turnover intentions.[14] An example of team selling occurred when Dick Holder, president of Reynolds Metal Company, spent five years "selling" Campbell Soup Company on using aluminum cans for its tomato juice products. He coordinated a team of graphic designers, marketing people, and engineers that educated and convinced Campbell to use a packaging material it had never used before. Approaches for improving efficiency by working closely with other functional units in the firm are fully discussed in Chapter 16.

SUPPLY CHAIN LOGISTICS AND CHANNEL MANAGER

Sometimes it is necessary to interact with other partners and vendors to meet a customer's needs, and salespeople are often the key managers of these many relationships. With regard to **supply chain logistics,** the management of the supply chain, if a customer buys a new jet from Boeing, with features that will be added by a third-party vendor, the salesperson will need to coordinate the efforts of the vendor with Boeing. Glenn Price, who sells life and disability insurance with Northwestern Mutual, realizes the importance of working with channel partners. "Today the financial services industry is very complex, as are the needs of my clients, and I can't be all things to all people. I can, however, create a team of specialists. For areas outside of my expertise, all I have to do is identify which specialists are needed and bring them in. This approach allows me to operate at maximum efficiency while providing the highest level of expertise and service to my clients."[15]

INFORMATION PROVIDER TO THEIR FIRM

Salespeople are the eyes and ears of the company in the marketplace. For example, when Bob Meyer, a salesperson at Ballard Medical Products, was demonstrating a medical device, a surgeon commented that he could not tell whether the device was working properly because the tube was opaque. Meyer relayed this information to the vice president of engineering, and the product was redesigned, substituting a clear tube for the opaque tube.

To truly have effective impact on their organization, salespeople need to be skillful at disseminating the knowledge they have acquired from customers to

other people in their companies. In their reporting activities, salespeople provide information to their firms about expenses, calls made, future calls scheduled, sales forecasts, competitor activities,[16] business conditions, and unsatisfied customer needs. It's not surprising, therefore, that the vice presidents of finance and manufacturing in most firms, for example, care greatly about the work and information provided by salespeople. Much of this information is now transmitted electronically to the company, its salespeople, and its customers and is contained in a **customer relationship management (CRM)** system. For example, each night salespeople at Curtin Matheson Scientific, a distributor of clinical and laboratory supplies, enter call report information and download all the ordering and shipping information for their customers from the company mainframe to their laptop computers. Chapter 16 discusses the relationship between salespeople and their companies in great detail.[17]

Salespeople share important market information with their boss and others in the firm.

TYPES OF SALESPEOPLE

Almost everyone is familiar with people who sell products and services to consumers in retail outlets. Behind these retail salespeople is an army of salespeople working for commercial firms. Consider an iPad or MP3 player you might purchase in a store. To make the player, the manufacturer bought processed material, such as plastic and electronic components, from various salespeople. In addition, it purchased capital equipment from other salespeople to mold the plastic, assemble the components, and test the player. Finally, the player manufacturer bought services such as an employment agency to hire people and an accounting firm to audit the company's financial statements. The manufacturer's salespeople then sold the players to a wholesaler. The wholesaler purchased transportation services and warehouse space from other salespeople. Then the wholesaler's salespeople sold the players to a retailer.

SELLING AND DISTRIBUTION CHANNELS

As the MP3 player example shows, salespeople work for different types of firms and call on different types of customers. These differences in sales positions come from the many roles salespeople play in a firm's distribution channel. A **distribution channel** is a set of people and organizations responsible for the flow of products and services from the producer to the ultimate user. Exhibit 1.3

Exhibit 1.3
Sales Jobs and the
Distribution Channel

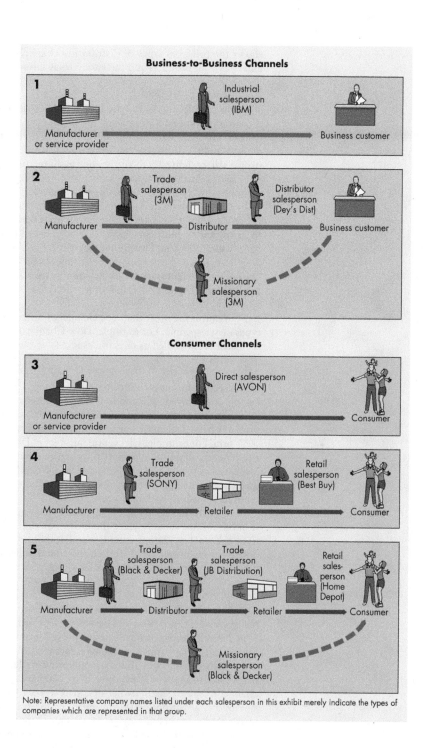

Business-to-Business Channels

1. Manufacturer or service provider → Industrial salesperson (IBM) → Business customer

2. Manufacturer → Trade salesperson (3M) → Distributor → Distributor salesperson (Dey's Dist) → Business customer; Missionary salesperson (3M)

Consumer Channels

3. Manufacturer or service provider → Direct salesperson (AVON) → Consumer

4. Manufacturer → Trade salesperson (SONY) → Retailer → Retail salesperson (Best Buy) → Consumer

5. Manufacturer → Trade salesperson (Black & Decker) → Distributor → Trade salesperson (JB Distribution) → Retailer → Retail salesperson (Home Depot) → Consumer; Missionary salesperson (Black & Decker)

Note: Representative company names listed under each salesperson in this exhibit merely indicate the types of companies which are represented in that group.

shows the principal types of distribution channels used for business-to-business and consumer products and the varied roles salespeople play.

Business-to-Business Channels

The two main channels for producers and providers of business-to-business, or industrial, products, and services, are (1) direct sales to a business customer and (2) sales through distributors. In the direct channel, salespeople working for the manufacturer call directly on other manufacturers. For example, Nucor salespeople sell steel directly to automobile manufacturers, Dow Chemical salespeople sell plastics directly to toy manufacturers, and Nielsen salespeople sell marketing research services directly to business customers.

In the distributor channel the manufacturer employs salespeople to sell to distributors. These salespeople are referred to as **trade salespeople** because they sell to firms that resell the products (that is, they sell to the trade) rather than using them within the firm. Distributor salespeople sell products made by a number of manufacturers to businesses. For example, some Intel salespeople sell microprocessors to distributors such as Arrow Electronics, and Arrow salespeople then resell the microprocessors and other electronic components to customers such as Dell.

Many firms use more than one channel of distribution and thus employ several types of salespeople. For example, Dow Chemical has trade salespeople who call on distributors as well as direct salespeople who call on large companies.

Sales Jobs and the Distribution Channel

In the second business-to-business channel (see Exhibit 1.3), a missionary salesperson is employed. **Missionary salespeople** work for a manufacturer and promote the manufacturer's products to other firms. However, those firms buy the products from distributors or other manufacturers, not directly from the salesperson's firm. For example, sales representatives at Driltek, a manufacturer of mining equipment, call on mine owners to promote their products. The mines, however, place orders for drills with the local Driltek distributor rather than with Driltek directly. Normally missionary and local distributor salespeople work together to build relationships with customers.

Frequently missionary salespeople call on people who influence a buying decision but do not actually place the order. For example, Du Pont sales representatives call on Liz Claiborne and other clothing designers to encourage them to design garments made with Teflon, and Merck sales representatives call on physicians to encourage them to prescribe Merck pharmaceutical products.

Consumer Channels

The remaining channels shown in Exhibit 1.3 are used by producers and providers of consumer products and services. The third channel shows a firm, such as State Farm Insurance, whose salespeople sell insurance directly to consumers. The fourth and fifth channels show manufacturers that employ trade salespeople to sell to either retailers or distributors. For example, Revlon uses the fourth channel when its salespeople sell directly to Walmart. However, Revlon uses the fifth channel to sell to small, owner-operated stores through distributors. Missionary salespeople are also used in consumer channels. For example, a Black & Decker missionary salesperson may go to a Home Depot store to meet customers there and see how well Home Depot is serving its customers.

Some of the salespeople shown in Exhibit 1.3 may be manufacturers' agents. **Manufacturers' agents** are independent businesspeople who are paid a commission by a manufacturer for all products or services sold. Unlike distributors and retailers, agents never own the products. They simply perform the selling activities and then transmit the orders to the manufacturers.

DESCRIBING SALES JOBS

Descriptions of sales jobs often focus on six factors:

1. The stage of the buyer–seller relationship.
2. The salesperson's role.
3. The importance of the customer's purchase decision.
4. The location of salesperson–customer contact.
5. The nature of the offering sold by the salesperson.
6. The salesperson's role in securing customer commitment.

Stage of Buyer–Seller Relationship: New or Continuing

Some sales jobs emphasize finding and selling to new customers. Selling to prospects requires different skills than does selling to existing customers. To convince prospects to purchase a product they have never used before, salespeople need to be especially self-confident and must be able to deal with the inevitable rejections that occur when making initial contacts. On the other hand, salespeople responsible for existing customers place more emphasis on building relationships and servicing customers. For example, Lou Pritchett of Procter & Gamble, in a continuing relationship with Walmart, increased sales to Walmart from $400 million a year to over $6 billion a year by being creative and building partnerships. And the more important the buyer, the larger the group of sellers engaged in selling to that buyer. Hormel has a team of 50 who sell to Walmart in Bentonville, Arkansas.

Salesperson's Role: Taking Orders or Creating New Solutions

Some sales jobs focus primarily on taking orders. For example, most Frito-Lay salespeople go to grocery stores, check the stock, and prepare an order for the store manager to sign. However, some Frito-Lay salespeople sell only to buyers in the headquarters of supermarket chains. Headquarters selling requires a much higher level of skill and creativity. These salespeople work with buyers to develop new systems and methods and sometimes even new products to increase the retailer's sales and profits.[18] Some firms distinguish between salespeople who focus on one task versus another, as "Building Partnerships 1.1" describes.

Importance of the Purchase to the Customer

Consumers and businesses make many purchase decisions each year. Some decisions are important to them, such as purchasing a building or a computer Internet security system. Others are less crucial, such as buying candy or cleaning supplies. Sales jobs involving important decisions for customers differ greatly from sales jobs involving minor decisions. Consider a company that needs a computer-controlled drill press. Buying the drill press is a big decision. The drill press sales representative needs to be knowledgeable about the customer's needs and the features of drill presses. The salesperson will have to interact with a number of people involved in the purchase decision.

Even though many sales jobs do not involve building long-term partnerships, we stress the concept of developing partnering relationships throughout this textbook because the roles of salespeople in many companies are evolving toward a partnering orientation. As you'll see in Chapter 16, partnering orientations are important within one's own organization as well as with customers. Further, salespeople are called on to build partnerships with some accounts and other

BUILDING Partnerships   1.1

HUNTER AND GATHERERS

There are many different types of salespeople and count-less ways that they can be described. In our organization we like to classify our salespeople as either a hunter or a gatherer. A hunter can be thought of as one who is a high-energy salesperson that is the first contact with a potential customer. The hunter has skills and ability to set the foundation of a relationship for the gatherer. Once the foundation is set and the relationship has been established, the gatherer has the opportunity to go in. The gatherer's job is to now utilize the specifics that he or she knows about the potential customer and to cultivate the relationship in preparation to make sales. The gatherers ensure that they maintain a high service level with the customer and continue to build and strengthen the day-to-day relationship that they have.

Hunters in our company are expert at gaining new busi-ness leads that often come about unintentionally. For example, Philip, one of our hunters, was at a sporting event and struck up a conversation with the man sitting next to him. The conversation, naturally, started out about the hockey game they were attending. But as the game progressed, both parties started talking more and more, eventually leading to what both of them do for a living. Philip stated that he was a salesperson of industrial sup-plies, and immediately the other man indicated that he was a plant manager of a big account that our company had been trying to land for a while. With the new found information, we sent one of our gatherers to this man a few months later, closing the business.

There are needs for a variety of selling skills in our organi-zation. We are glad to have both hunters and gatherers!

Source: Personal correspondence, used with permission, anonymous upon request.

Field salespeople go directly to the customer's place of business.

types of relationships with other accounts. The partnering orientation does not pre-vent salespeople from developing other types of relationships; rather, people who are good partners are likely to also be good at other types of relationships. Understand-ing partnerships is critical to understand-ing the professional selling process, as will become apparent as the book unfolds.

Location of Salesperson–Customer Contact: Field or Inside Sales

Field salespeople spend considerable time in the customer's place of business, communicating with the customer face-to-face. **Inside salespeople** work at their employer's location and typically communicate with customers by telephone or computer.

Field selling typically is more demanding than inside selling because the for-mer entails more intense interactions with customers. Field salespeople are more involved in problem solving with customers, whereas inside salespeople often respond to customer-initiated requests.

thinking **it** through   Which do you think you would prefer: an inside sales job or a field sales job? What makes one more attractive to you than the other?

The Nature of the Offering Sold by the Salesperson: Products or Services

The type of benefits provided by products and services affects the nature of the sales job. Products such as chemicals and trucks typically have tangible benefits: Customers can objectively measure a chemical's purity and a truck's payload. The benefits of services, such as business insurance or investment opportunities, are more intangible: Customers cannot easily measure the riskiness of an investment.

Intangible benefits are harder to sell than tangible benefits. It is much easier to show a customer the payload of a truck than the benefits of carrying insurance.

The Salesperson's Role in Securing Customer Commitment: Information or Placing an Order

Sales jobs differ by the types of commitments sought and the manner in which they are obtained. For example, the Du Pont missionary salesperson might encourage a clothing designer to use Du Pont Teflon fibers. The salesperson might ask the designer to consider using the fiber but does not undertake the more difficult task of asking the designer to place an order. If the designer decides to use Teflon fabric in a dress, the actual order for Teflon will be secured by the fabric manufacturer salesperson, not the Du Pont salesperson.

THE SALES JOBS CONTINUUM

Exhibit 1.4 uses the factors just discussed to illustrate the continuum of sales jobs in terms of creativity. Sales jobs described by the responses in the far right column require salespeople to go into the field, call on new customers who make important buying decisions, promote products or services with intangible benefits, and seek purchase commitments. These types of sales jobs require the most creativity and skill and, consequently, offer the highest pay.

The next section examines the responsibilities of specific types of salespeople in more detail.

EXAMPLES OF SALES JOBS

The following are brief examples of several of the thousands of sales jobs that exist today. As you read each example, notice the vast differences in the type of compensation, the number of accounts, the length of an average sales call, the length of the order cycle, the need to prospect, and so forth. All are based on real salespeople and the sales jobs they got when they first graduated from college. As you read the examples, think about which would be more attractive to you personally.

Chris is a salesperson for IBM Large Systems, selling mainframe computers to organizations. She has five clients, provided to her by her company, and does no

Exhibit 1.4
Creativity Level of Sales Jobs

Factors in Sales Jobs	Lower Creativity	Higher Creativity
1. Stage of the customer–firm relationship	Existing customer	New customer
2. The salesperson's role	Order taking	Creating new solutions
3. Importance of the customer's purchase decision	Low	High
4. Location of salesperson–customer contact	Inside company	Field customer
5. Nature of the offering sold by the salesperson	Products	Services
6. Salesperson's role in securing customer commitment	Limited role	Significant role

prospecting for new accounts. She is paid a straight salary and travels by plane three to five days each week. Each visit to an account is roughly three hours long. For the first three years she had no sales. In her third year she made the largest sale in the company's history.

Lauree works for Standard Register selling business forms and document management solutions. She has 200 clients and does a good bit of searching for new accounts. She is paid salary plus commission and gets orders essentially every single day, with no overnight travel. Each visit lasts about 45 minutes.

Scott works for Pfizer, a pharmaceutical company, calling on 100 doctors to tell them about his company's drugs. He is paid a salary plus a year-end bonus and as a missionary salesperson never gets an actual order from a doctor (the patients buy the Pfizer drugs). He does no overnight travel and never searches for new accounts, and each call is about five minutes long.

Jim sells Makita power tools and serves 75 dealers. He is paid a salary plus commission and does very limited searching for new accounts. He gets orders every day and has little overnight travel. Each call is about 30 minutes long.

Jeff works for Hormel, selling refrigerated meat products as well as pantry products like canned chili, and has about 100 accounts. He does no searching for new accounts and is paid a salary plus a year-end bonus. Each call lasts about 10 minutes, and he has no overnight travel.

Niki works for MetLife, selling life, auto, home owners, long-term care, and disability insurance as well as investments (IRAs, mutual funds, annuities, and so forth). She has 250 clients, has no overnight travel, and is paid straight salary. She does a good bit of searching for new accounts, and here average first in-person sales call to a new account lasts about 30 minutes.

The next section reviews some of the skills required to be effective in the sales positions just discussed.

CHARACTERISTICS OF SUCCESSFUL SALESPEOPLE

The market is full of books and articles discussing why some people are successful in selling and others are not. Yet no one has identified the profile of the "perfect" salesperson because sales jobs are so different, as the examples just provided illustrated. In addition, each customer is unique. However, the following traits are generally associated with successful salespeople.

SELF-MOTIVATED

Salespeople work in the field without direct supervision and may be tempted to get up late, take long lunch breaks, and stop work early. But successful salespeople are self-starters who do not need the fear of an angry supervisor to get them going in the morning or to keep them working hard all day. Furthermore, successful salespeople are motivated to learn, and they work at improving their skills by analyzing their performance and using their mistakes as learning opportunities.

DEPENDABILITY AND TRUSTWORTHINESS

Customers develop long-term relationships only with salespeople who are dependable and trustworthy.[19] When salespeople say the equipment will perform in a certain way, they had better make sure the equipment performs that way! If it doesn't, the customer will not rely on them again. And dependability and trustworthiness can't just be a false front: Salespeople who are genuine and come across as authentic are better-performing salespeople. From the Buyer's Seat 1.1 illustrates the importance of building and maintaining trust.

From the **BUYERS SEAT**

A TALE OF TWO SALESPERSONS: ONE GREAT, AND ONE...

For a salesperson to set him- or herself apart from the rest, it is crucial for one to prove to the buyer that he or she is a problem solver and is willing to be the buyer's front line with the seller's organization. Getting to know the buyer and the company is also an extremely important process for the salesperson to go through; he or she needs to know how to drill down and figure out the problem that the buyer's organization is facing and provide them with solutions to that problem. Honesty is huge when a salesperson is dealing with any buyer; any lie or false truth a salesperson may say to gain the business of the buyer will be uncovered at some point in time and will tarnish not only the relationship with that buyer but also the salesperson's credibility as a whole.

With the industry that I work in, it is essential for any salesperson to know who my end customer is. If a salesperson is able to really get to know who my end customer is and the trends that are hot in the industry, this is going to be a big factor when it comes to getting my company's business. Last but not least, to maintain a positive relationship with me as a buyer, follow-up skills are extremely important. Being able to check in and make sure that products have been received on time and that they are exactly what we had agreed on is huge. The following are two examples of recent situations I have encountered, one of which was over-the-top extraordinary and the other, well, you will find out.

First Example:

When getting ready to bring a new product in to our stores, we had all the dates set in stone for our marketing materials to be sent out to promote our new great product. We had strict terms with the manufacturer, and the product *had* to be delivered by a certain date. I received a phone call from the salesperson I had been working with, and when he said that a piece of the product had not been received at their manufacturing plant, all I could say was, "I don't care, it needs to be done; we agreed on the date, it needs to get done." Not knowing what was going to come of this, I was slightly worried. Little did I know that this salesperson went to his production manager and explained what was going on. He convinced his production manager to go to China to oversee the production of this product in order to do everything they could to get it done on time. This salesperson could have sat back and hoped that everything went alright, but he went above and beyond to do all in his power to make sure that we got our product on time—which we did!

Second Example:

Striving to carry products that consumers cannot find in other stores, we try to construct agreements with salespeople to ensure that we are the only store that will be selling certain products. When I was in a competitor's store and saw a product that I had just recently agreed to buy on their shelves, I was rather upset. I called my salesperson and asked her what was going on. She began by acting as though she had no clue what I was talking about, and finally, when we agreed that something needed to be done, I told her that I would work with her on product modifications to get the product the way I needed it to sell it in our stores. At the end of the conversation, she said, "Well, just let me know what you think we need to do." I could not believe that a salesperson would ask the buyer to solve a problem that the salesperson created in the first place. End result? No business!

Source: Personal correspondence, used with permission, anonymous upon request.

thinking **it** through

Take a minute and think about yourself. How dependable are you right now? Can people count on you to do what you say you will do? Or do they have to look you up and remind you of your promises? You don't start developing dependability when you graduate from college; it is something you should be working on right now. What can you do to start improving your dependability?

ETHICAL SALES BEHAVIOR

Honesty and integrity are critical for developing effective relationships. Over the long run, customers will find out who can be trusted and who cannot. Good ethics are good business.[20] Ethical sales behavior is such an important topic that much of Chapter 2 is devoted to it.

CUSTOMER AND PRODUCT KNOWLEDGE

Effective salespeople need to know how businesses make purchase decisions and how individuals evaluate product alternatives. In addition, effective salespeople need product knowledge—how their products work and how the products' features are related to the benefits customers are seeking. Chapter 3 reviews the buying process, and Chapter 5 discusses product knowledge.

ANALYTICAL SKILLS AND THE ABILITY TO USE INFORMATION TECHNOLOGY

Salespeople need to know how to analyze data and situations and use the Internet, databases, and software to effectively sell in today's marketplace.[21] **Selling analytics** is an attempt to gain insights into customers by using sophisticated data mining and analytic techniques.[22] Information technology will be discussed in every chapter in this book, and the use of analytical tools will be covered in Chapter 9 and other chapters.

COMMUNICATION SKILLS

The key to building strong long-term relationships is to be responsive to a customer's needs. To do that, the salesperson needs to be a good communicator. But talking is not enough; the salesperson must also listen to what the customer says, ask questions that uncover problems and needs, and pay attention to the responses.

To compete in world markets, salespeople need to learn how to communicate in international markets. Chapter 4 is devoted to developing communication skills, with considerable emphasis on communicating in other cultures.

FLEXIBILITY AND AGILITY

The successful salesperson realizes that the same sales approach does not work with all customers; it must be adapted to each selling situation. The salesperson must be sensitive to what is happening and agile enough to make those adaptations during the sales presentation.[23] Again, it is this flexibility that causes companies to spend so much money on personal selling instead of just advertising, which can't be tailored as easily or quickly to each individual.

CREATIVITY

Creativity is the trait of having imagination and inventiveness and using them to come up with new solutions and ideas. Sometimes it takes creativity to get an appointment with a prospect. It takes creativity to develop presentation that the buyer will long remember. It takes creativity to solve a sticky installation problem after the product is sold.

CONFIDENCE AND OPTIMISM

Successful salespeople tend to be confident about themselves, their company, and their products. They optimistically believe that their efforts will lead to success. Don't confuse confidence, however, with wishful thinking. According to research, truly confident people are willing to work hard to achieve their goals.

They are open to criticism, seek advice from others, and learn from their mistakes. They expect good things to happen, but they take personal responsibility for their fate. People who lack confidence, according to these same studies, are not honest about their own limits, react defensively when criticized, and set unrealistic goals.

Salespeople need emotional intelligence to be able to recognize customers' emotions.

EMOTIONAL INTELLIGENCE

Emotional intelligence (EI) is the ability to effectively understand and regulate one's own emotions and to read and respond to the emotions of others, and this is an important trait for salespeople.[24] EI has four aspects: (1) knowing one's own feelings and emotions as they are experienced, (2) controlling one's emotions to avoid acting impulsively, (3) recognizing customers' emotions (called empathy), and (4) using one's emotions to interact effectively with customers.[25] A recent study of over 6,000 people from a wide spectrum of industries found that good decision makers consistently score high in EI.[26] In marketing exchanges, EI is positively related to performance and retaining customers,[27] and TalentSmart notes that 90 percent of top performers have high EI.[28] Bad decisions result from a lack of EI, so it is not surprising that emotional immaturity plays a large role in many employee terminations.

What are some good first steps in improving your EI? Measure your own EI (see www.EIME-research.com) to learn where you currently stand. Learn to identify and understand your own emotions as they arise and recognize the fact that it is often in your best interest to step away from emotional situations and become more reflective. Engaging in most human interactions with just a keyboard (e.g., via texting or e-mailing) can reduce one's EI.[29]

Of course, one must realize that EI can be used in negative ways as well. People with high EI can use their skills to intimidate, manipulate, and spin outcomes to their own advantage.[30] We discuss aspects of EI as they relate to adaptive selling and effective verbal and nonverbal intelligence in Chapters 4 and 5.

ARE SALESPEOPLE BORN OR MADE?

On the basis of the preceding discussion, you can see that most of the skills required to be a successful salesperson can be learned. People can learn to work hard, plan their time, and adapt their sales approach to their customers' needs. In fact, companies show their faith in their ability to teach sales skills by spending billions of dollars each year on training programs. There is some evidence to suggest that students who take college courses in selling have higher placement rates in selling jobs.[31] The next section discusses the rewards you can realize if you develop the skills required for sales success.

REWARDS IN SELLING

Personal selling offers interesting and rewarding career opportunities. More than 8 million people in the United States currently work in sales positions, and the number of sales positions is growing. For the current number of salespeople in various types of sales jobs and to find average earnings, see the Occupational Outlook Handbook, created by the U.S. Department of Labor (www.bls.gov/ooh).

INDEPENDENCE AND RESPONSIBILITY

Many people do not want to spend long hours behind a desk, doing the same thing every day. They prefer to be outside, moving around, meeting people, and working on various problems. Selling ideally suits people with these interests. The typical salesperson interacts with dozens of people daily, and most of these contacts involve challenging new experiences.

Selling also offers unusual freedom and flexibility. It is not a nine-to-five job. Most salespeople decide how to spend their time; they do not have to report in. Long hours may be required on some days, and other days may bring fewer demands.

Because of this freedom, salespeople are like independent entrepreneurs. They have a territory to manage and few restrictions on how to do it. They are responsible for the sales and profits the territory generates. Thus, their success or failure rests largely on their own skills and efforts.[32]

ethics

FINANCIAL REWARDS

Salespeople tend to earn more money the longer they sell. Occasionally the top salespeople in a firm will even earn more than the sales executives in that firm. The average amount earned by salespeople depends somewhat on the annual revenues of the firm. Average starting salaries for students right out of college tend to range from $30,000 to $50,000, while experienced salespeople often make over $100,000 a year.[33]

The financial rewards of selling depend on the level of skill and sophistication needed to do the job. For example, salespeople who sell to businesses typically are paid more than retail salespeople. But salespeople usually don't earn overtime pay for working more than 40 hours.[34]

This young manager learned the ropes as a salesperson before moving into product management at his firm.

MANAGEMENT OPPORTUNITIES

Selling jobs provide a firm base for launching a business career. For example, Mark Alvarez started his sales career in the Medical Systems Division at General Electric (GE) selling diagnostic imaging equipment to hospitals in central Illinois. Over the years he held positions in the firm that included district and regional sales manager and product manager; at one point he had responsibility for all Medical Systems Division business in Latin America. Sixteen years later, he was in corporate marketing and was responsible for managing the relationships between GE's 39 divisions and key customers in the southeastern United States. These include such accounts as Federal Express, Disney, and Home Depot. Some of his businesses do more than $500 million worth of business with GE annually. His entry-level job in selling provided great experience for his current assignment. Many CEOs and chairmen of the board started their careers as salespeople.

THE BUILDING PARTNERSHIPS MODEL

This book is divided into three parts, as illustrated in Exhibit 1.5.

The knowledge and skills needed for successful partnerships are covered in Part 1. You will learn about the legal and ethical responsibilities of

Exhibit 1.5
The Building
Partnerships Model

1
Knowledge and
skills needed
for partnerships

2
The partnership
development
process

Building
Partnerships

3
The salesperson
as a manager

Exhibit 1.6

Steps in the Selling
Process

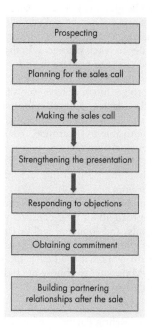

Prospecting

Planning for the sales call

Making the sales call

Strengthening the presentation

Responding to objections

Obtaining commitment

Building partnering
relationships after the sale

salespeople, the buying process, the principles for communicating effectively, and methods for adapting to the unique styles and needs of each customer.

In Part 2 you will explore the partnership development process and the activities needed for this to occur. After completing this section, you should have enhanced skills and understanding about prospecting, planning, discovering needs, using visual aids and conducting demonstrations effectively, responding to objections, obtaining commitment, formally negotiating, and providing excellent after-sale service. Exhibit 1.6 provides a chart that summarizes the selling process.

Finally, Part 3 discusses the role of the salesperson as a manager. You'll learn how you can improve your effectiveness as a salesperson by managing your time and territory and by managing the relationships within your own company. This section also discusses ways to manage your career.

SELLING YOURSELF

The "Selling Yourself" sections of this book are designed to help you see the connections of the chapter material with all aspects of your life right now. Of course we're all different, with different interests and activities, so some of the examples might better fit you than others. But read them all and try to make a connection with something in your life. Selling is something you do all the time, and the ideas found in this book can help you now, not just after you graduate!

In all areas of life, we are looking to gain something from the activities we participate in and interactions we have. Whether it be convincing the elementary students you mentor to compete in the local spelling bee because you get a lot of joy seeing them succeed in an area that they previously struggled with or convincing the local deli to give you an extra pickle with your sandwich because you really love pickles, you need to give others a compelling reason to help you reach your goal. In both cases, you are simply the influencer. You have no say in the final decision. While the needs (tangible vs. intangible in this example) may be different with every interaction, the key ways to achieve your goals remain the same.

You must undercover and understand why the other party would want to help you as well as reasons why they would hesitate to work with you. In the case of your mentees, they may be excited at the prospect of competing yet don't have the self-confidence to practice and compete on their own. The deli owner may want to make a customer happy in order to get repeat business (a key technique in being successful in sales) yet may feel the crunch of rising costs and hesitate to provide more than what the price of the sandwich covers.

Once you determine this, you can start building your case of educating your customers on why they would want to work with you. In the case of your mentees, helping them put together a practice schedule and providing coaching while discussing with them the positives of participating in such event and validating their concerns would be great ways to get them to commit. In the case of the deli owner, it may be as simple of asking politely while conveying your love of pickles or tipping the cashier. You have to be invested in the outcome and willing to give something in order to reach your goal. In the case of your mentees, you have to give your time and effort to prepare them for the challenge. You may have to be a little more outgoing and chatty with the sandwich artist than you normally would when rushing to get lunch or have to wait an extra minute for that pickle.

You need to be confident and, more important, positive in your message in order to meet your goal. People are more likely to respond to and to be influenced by people who are enjoyable to be around. Your reputation usually spans more than just that one person or interaction. Your mentees may share your idea with the activity director and ask for you to mentor more students for next year's event, or the next time you go into that deli, they may have that extra pickle ready and waiting for you.

The world of business is a small one. No matter what industry or capacity you work in, word will spread about your consistent and positive techniques to help others reach their goals, and soon you will be called on to share your refreshing and innovative ideas with others. Conversely, word will spread if you are unreliable and unpleasant to work with. Whether the goal is big or small, it will take some work to meet. Make sure to choose the right attitude to reach your goal as quickly and easily as possible.

Happy selling!

Source: Amber Fischer, Rehrig Pacific, used with permission.

SUMMARY

You should study personal selling because we all use selling techniques. If you want to work in business, you need to know about selling because salespeople play a vital role in business activities. Finally, you might become a salesperson. Selling jobs are inherently interesting because of the variety of people encountered and activities undertaken. In addition, selling offers opportunities for financial rewards and promotions.

Salespeople engage in a wide range of activities, including providing information about products and services to customers and employees within their firms. Most of us are not aware of many of these activities because the salespeople we meet most frequently work in retail stores. However, the most exciting, rewarding, and challenging sales positions involve building partnerships: long-term, win–win relationships with customers.

The specific duties and responsibilities of salespeople depend on the type of selling position. But most salespeople engage in various tasks in addition to influencing customers. These tasks include managing customer relations, serving as the account team manager for their firm, managing the relationships with vendor and channel members, and providing information to their firm.

Sales jobs can be classified by the roles salespeople and their firms play in the channel of distribution. The nature of the selling job is affected by whom salespeople work for and whether they sell to manufacturers, distributors, or retailers. Other factors affecting the nature of selling jobs are the customer's relationship to the salesperson's firm, the salesperson's duties, the importance of the buying decision to the customer, where the selling occurs, the tangibility of the benefits considered by the customer, and the degree to which the salesperson seeks a commitment from customers.

Research on the characteristics of effective salespeople indicates that many different personality types can be successful in sales. However, successful salespeople do share some common characteristics. They are self-motivated, dependable, ethical, knowledgeable, good communicators, flexible, creative, confident, and emotionally intelligent. They also have good analytical skills and aren't afraid of technology.

KEY TERMS

creativity 18
customer-centric 9
customer lifetime value (CLV) 6
customer relationship management (CRM) 10
customer value proposition 4
distribution channel 10
emotional intelligence (EI) 19
field salespeople 14
go-to-market strategies 6
inside salespeople 14
integrated marketing communications 7

manufacturers' agents 11
missionary salespeople 11
multichannel strategy 7
personal selling 4
sales force–intensive organization 6
selling analytics 18
six sigma selling programs 9
supply chain logistics 9
trade salespeople 11
24/7 service 9
value 4

ETHICS PROBLEMS

1. Let's say you have excellent emotional intelligence. How can you avoid using that to your advantage if it is detrimental to the buyer (e.g., if you manipulate the buyer based on your skills)?

2. The chapter says that selling jobs can be a great way to get your foot in the door at an employer. Let's say you really want to be in product development, not sales, yet the position that is being offered at the company is in sales. You hope that after doing the sales job for six months to a year you'll get promoted to the product development job. Should you be honest and tell the interviewer (the sales manager) that now? Or should you act as though you want to be a career salesperson?

QUESTIONS AND PROBLEMS

1. There are many different go-to-market strategies. For which of the following products and services do you think a sales force–intensive strategy would probably not be used? Why? Make any assumptions needed and list your assumptions in your answer.
   a. Movie rentals.
   b. Home air-conditioning maintenance service.
   c. Shredding service for sensitive documents.
   d. Solar-powered compactor garbage cans for city use on city streets (the specially designed cans actually compact the garbage that is thrown into the can four times a day, using energy from the sun, reducing the number of times the can needs to be emptied).

2. In "Building Partnerships 1.1" you read how the company has hunters and gatherers. Which type of position appeals to you the most? Why?

3. Comment on each of the following statements:
   a. Salespeople rip people off.
   b. Salespeople are born, not made.
   c. Selling is just a big bag of tricks.
   d. A salesperson should never take no for an answer.
   e. A good salesperson can sell anything to anybody.

4. Carly Anderson has been working as a receptionist at her father's business for two years since graduating from college. She is considering taking a selling job with a pharmaceutical company. The job involves calling on doctors and explaining the benefits of the firm's products. What are the similarities and differences between her receptionist job and the selling job she is considering?

5. Nick Chattaway worked his way through college by selling home theater systems at Best Buy. He has done well on the job and is one of the top salespeople in the home electronics department. Last week Safety Harness Inc. offered him a job selling seat belt kits to school bus manufacturers. Explain the differences between selling in a consumer electronics store and the Safety Harness Inc. sales job.

6. Poll at least five students who are not taking your selling course (and who, better yet, are outside the business school or program). What are their opinions about salespeople? How accurate are their opinions based on what you've read in this chapter?

7. Think about what you want in your first job out of college. Based on what you know so far from this chapter, how well does selling match your desires in a job?

8. According to the text, some sales jobs are located as inside sales instead of field sales. Why would anyone want to be an inside sales rep?

9. "Sales Technology 1.1" described the use of video resumes to set yourself apart. Create a video resume for yourself and make it available to your instructor.

10. Assume you are a sales manager and you need to recruit someone for the following sales positions. For each position, list the qualities you would want in the recruit:
    a. Salesperson selling custom signage to small businesses.
    b. Salesperson calling on college bookstores, selling university logo backpacks.
    c. Used tractor salesperson.
    d. Salesperson selling janitorial services to a small local restaurant.

CASE PROBLEMS

case 1.1

Chicago Blackhawks

Emily Hightower has been sales manager for Corporate Hospitality sales at the Chicago Blackhawks for the last three years. The Stanley Cup–winning Blackhawks are a National Hockey League franchise located in Chicago, Illinois. Blackhawks Corporate Hospitality is a unique way for businesses to entertain prospective clients or treat important customers to a special night out. The 20-person Executive Suites and 40- and 80-person Super Suites provide outstanding, panoramic views of the ice surface and can be rented on a per-game basis or a season basis. The all-inclusive packages (i.e., tickets to the event, parking passes, food and beverage, a private suite attendant, theater-style seating, easy access to elevators, multiple flat-screen televisions, and so on) make entertaining clients a breeze.

When Emily was promoted to the sales manager position, there were three full-time salespeople who called on businesses in the region. One quit right after she arrived, and Zach, a knowledgeable sports marketer with excellent connections in the business community, was hired as a replacement. Zach has been a real asset to the organization, building business in the financial and investment business community.

Emily thought everything was going smoothly until yesterday, when Chad, another salesperson, dropped a bombshell. He turned in his notice because he said he got a lucrative offer from the Chicago Bulls.

Emily sat in her office, mulling over the situation and halfheartedly working on the job description for Chad's position, when one of her most trusted administrative assistants, Amanda, walked in. After they chatted for a few minutes, the following conversation ensued:

Amanda: So why do you need a salesperson anyway? Why not just use our Web page to give prospective clients the information they need?

Emily: We have to have a salesperson, Amanda. I mean, there's always been three salespeople in our office.

Amanda: But I'm asking you to think outside the dots, Emily. Why do we need them? They cost the company a lot of money that we could save by just relying on Web advertising. Besides, the Chicago Blackhawks are already well known. There's no need for salespeople. The Blackhawks sell themselves!

The conversation continued in this vein for a few minutes, then Amanda left to work on some scheduling disputes. Emily sat there, thinking about what Amanda said. Who knows? Maybe Amanda had a good idea.

Questions

1. What impact would dropping one or more salespeople have on the Chicago Blackhawks Corporate Hospitality sales? You might want to review the section titled "What Do Salespeople Do?" as you answer this question.

2. If you were Emily, what would you do? Why?

case **1.2**

Motion Industries, Inc.

Brandon Williams is a salesperson for J. B. Hunt Trucking. For the past three or four months, he has tried to get in to see Chris Menton, a transportation specialist at Motion Industries, Inc. Motion Industries is a large distributor, specializing in the sales of bearings and power transmission products. They distribute industrial MRO (maintenance, repair, and operation replacement) parts and have access to more than 4.3 million parts through 501 locations. Motion Industries also has over 40 repair and service centers that are fully equipped to handle field services, repairs, and modifications. Parts are transported between the various Motion Industries locations as well as to the final customer, using trucking companies as well as UPS and the U.S. Postal Service.

Brandon knows that Motion Industries uses the services of a number of trucking companies, and he would like Chris to consider adding J. B. Hunt as one of its primary transportation suppliers. J. B. Hunt uses state-of-the-art technology that offers customers real-time data to help them make real-time decisions about transportation. J. B. Hunt has won a number of awards for its outstanding supply chain visibility and offers the same stellar service regardless of the size of the buying organization.

Brandon has never actually been able to talk to Chris, not even for a few seconds. His voice mail is all he has ever gotten when making phone calls to Chris. Visits in person have resulted in Chris's secretary just taking Brandon's card and telling him that Chris will call if he is interested. Brandon is now under pressure from his sales manager because Brandon has placed Motion Industries Valley on his prospect list for the last three months and has nothing to show for all his efforts.

Questions

1. One of the skills that salespeople should possess is creativity. Come up with three creative and totally ethical methods Brandon can use to get Chris's attention.

2. Assume that Brandon does get Chris's attention with one of the methods you've described and Chris is willing to speak with Brandon on the phone the next time he is called. What should Brandon plan on saying, assuming that he has just two or three minutes of phone time?

ROLE PLAY CASE

At the end of each chapter, beginning just below this paragraph, you'll find a short role play exercise that focuses on the product NetSuite. NetSuite is a leading contact management software package. Contact management software is a form of software designed to help salespeople increase their productivity by helping them keep track of the customers they call. In addition to a calendar that tells them when to call on an account, the software can track account information concerning what has been bought, when it was bought, the decision-making process, and even personal information about each person in the account. In addition, sales managers can generate reports automatically when reps upload information to the company network. Reps don't have to type as many reports as they would otherwise, such as sales forecasts and call reports. Further, the system can tie into the company's ordering system, which helps save the salesperson paperwork time. You can learn more about NetSuite from its Web page: www.netsuite.com.

Congratulations, you've just graduated from college! Unfortunately you focused so much on your studies that you have not interviewed for any jobs. You moved back home, but you keep in touch with the school's Career Services Center, where you saw a job posting for NetSuite. Apparently it is some sort of software for salespeople. You've not had any serious interviews, so you thought you'd sign up. Today is your interview. Be yourself; interview honestly as if you were truly talking with NetSuite. To help you prepare for this job interview role play, you may want to take some time to find out about NetSuite by visiting www.netsuite.com for more information.

To the instructor: Additional information needed to complete the role play is available in the Instructor's Manual.

ADDITIONAL REFERENCES

Barnes, Cindy, Helen Blake, and David Pinder. *Creating and Delivering Your Value Proposition: Managing Customer Experience for Profit*. Philadelphia, PA: Kogan Page, 2009.

Bosworth, Michael T., John R. Holland, and Frank Visgatis. *CustomerCentric Selling*. McGraw-Hill, 2009.

Bradberry, Travis. *Emotional Intelligence 2.0*. TalentSmart: Har/Dig En edition, 2009.

Chan, Kimmy Wa, Chi Kin (Bennett) Yim, and Simon S. K. Lam. "Is Customer Participation in Value Creation a Double-Edged Sword? Evidence from Professional Financial

Services across Cultures." *Journal of Marketing* 74, no. 3 (May 2010), pp. 48–64.

Fox, Jeffrey J. *How to Be a Fierce Competitor: What Winning Companies and Great Managers Do in Tough Times.* Hoboken, NJ: Jossey-Bass, 2010.

Geigenmüller, A., and L. Greschuchna. "How to Establish Trustworthiness in Initial Service Encounters." *Journal of Marketing Theory and Practice* 19, no. 4 (2011), pp. 391–406.

Guenzi, Paolo, Luigi M. De Luca, and Gabriele Troilo. "Organizational Drivers of Salespeople's Customer Orientation and Selling Orientation." *Journal of Personal Selling and Sales Management* 31, no. 3 (Summer 2011), pp. 269–85.

Hackett, Joshua, and Dana Tebow. *Emotional intelligence: Complete Guide to Improving Your Emotional Intelligence.* Blue Shift Publishing, 2012.

Hansen, John D., Tanuja Singh, Dan C. Weilbaker, and Rodrigo Guesalaga. "Cultural Intelligence in Cross-Cultural Selling: Propositions and Directions for Future Research." *Journal of Personal Selling and Sales Management* 31, no. 3 (Summer 2011), pp. 243–54.

Hasson, Gil. *Brilliant Emotional Intelligence.* Pearson Life, 2012.

Heilman, T. "Implementing 'Extreme' Customer Service." *Evaluation Engineering* 48, no. 11 (November 2009), pp. 14–19.

Hsieh, Ming-Huei, and Wen-Chiung Chou. "Managing Key Account Portfolios across the Process of Relationship Development: A Value Proposition-Desired Value Alignment Perspective." *Journal of Business-to-Business Marketing* 18, no. 1 (January 2011), pp. 83–119.

Jambulingam, T., R. Kathuria, and J. Nevin. "Fairness-Trust-Loyalty Relationship under Varying Conditions of Supplier-Buyer Interdependence." *Journal of Marketing Theory and Practice* 19, no. 1 (2011), pp. 39–56.

Jaramillo, Fernando, Douglas B. Grisaffe, Lawrence B. Chonko, and James A. Roberts. "Examining the Impact of Servant Leadership on Salesperson's Turnover Intention." *Journal of Personal Selling and Sales Management* 29, no. 4 (Fall 2009), pp. 351–66.

Jelinek, Ronald, and Michael Ahearne. "Be Careful What You Look For: The Effect of Trait Competitiveness and Long Hours on Salesperson Deviance and Whether Meaningfulness of Work Matters." *Journal of Marketing Theory and Practice* 18, no. 4 (2010), pp. 303–21.

Krasnikov, Alexander, Satish Jayachandran, and V. Kumar. "The Impact of Customer Relationship Management Implementation on Cost and Profit Efficiencies: Evidence from the U.S. Commercial Banking Industry." *Journal of Marketing* 73, no. 6 (2009), pp. 61–76.

Kumar, V., and Bharath Rajan. "Nurturing the Right Customers: By Measuring and Improving Customer Lifetime Value, You'll Be Able to Grow Your Most Profitable Customers." *Strategic Finance* 91, no. 3 (2009), pp. 27–33.

Le Meunier-FitzHugh, Kenneth, and Nigel F. Piercy. "Exploring the Relationship between Market Orientation and Sales and Marketing Collaboration." *Journal of Personal Selling and Sales Management* 31, no. 3 (Summer 2011), pp. 287–296.

Lytle, Chris. *The Accidental Salesperson: How to Take Control of Your Sales Career and Earn the Respect and Income You Deserve.* New York: AMACOM, 2012.

McKee, Judy. *The Sales Survival Guide: Your Powerful Interactive Guide to Sales Success and Financial Freedom.* Bloomington, IN: AuthorHouse, 2009.

Menguc, Bulent, Seigyoung Auh, and Young Chan Kim. "Salespeople's Knowledge-Sharing Behaviors with Coworkers outside the Sales Unit." *Journal of Personal Selling and Sales Management* 31, no. 2 (Spring 2011), pp. 103–22.

Newell, S., J. Belonax, M. McCardle, and R. Plank. "The Effect of Personal Relationship and Consultative Task Behaviors on Buyer Perceptions of Salesperson Trust, Expertise, and Loyalty." *Journal of Marketing Theory and Practice* 19, no. 3 (2011), pp. 307–16.

Piercy, Nigel F. "Strategic Relationships between Boundary-Spanning Functions: Aligning Customer Relationship Management with Supplier Relationship Management." *Industrial Marketing Management* 38, no. 8 (November 2009), pp. 857–64.

Poujol, F. Juliet, and John F. Tanner. "The Impact of Contests on Salespeople's Customer Orientation: An Application of Tournament Theory." *Journal of Personal Selling and Sales Management* 30, no. 1 (Winter 2010), pp. 33–46.

Rich, David. "Create Your Own Upturn: A Shift from Managing Volume to Managing Relationships." *CRM Magazine* 13, no. 10 (2009), pp. 14–15.

Rouzies, Dominique, et al. "Determinants of Pay Levels and Structures in Sales Organizations." *Journal of Marketing* 73, no. 6 (2009), pp. 92–104.

Rust, Roland T., Christine Moorman, and Gaurav Bhalla. "Rethinking Marketing." *Harvard Business Review* 88, no. 1 (2010), pp. 94–101.

Stanley, Colleen, and Jill Konrath. *Emotional Intelligence for Sales Success: Connect with Customers and Get Results.* AMACOM, 2012.

Stanton, Michael, Catherine Dixon, and Tanya Back. *The Graduate's Guide to Sales.* Lilburn, GA: Fairmont Publishing, 2012.

Stein, Steve, and Liam O'Brien. *The EQ Edge: Emotional Intelligence and Your Success.* Newark, NJ: Audible, Inc., 2012.

Tähtinen, Jaana, and Keith Blois. "The Involvement and Influence of Emotions in Problematic Business Relationships." *Industrial Marketing Management* 40, no. 6 (2011), pp. 907–18.

Taulli, T. "Three Steps to a Sound Business Model." *BusinessWeek Online* 19 (March 2, 2009).

Temkin, Bruce. "7 Keys to Customer Experience: Big-Picture Advice for How to Improve the Customer Experience over the Next Year." *CRM Magazine* 13, no. 12 (2009), p. 12.

Thomson, D. "Essential No. 2: Redefine Your Market." *BusinessWeek Online* 17 (November 16, 2009).

Thomson, D. "No. 1: The Breakthrough Value Proposition." *BusinessWeek Online* 7 (November 9, 2009).

Walton, David. *Introducing Emotional Intelligence: A Practical Guide.* London: Icon Books, 2013.

Weinstein, Art. *Superior Customer Value: Strategies for Winning and Retaining Customers.* 3rd ed. New York: CRC Press, 2012.

Weinstein, Luke, and Ryan Mullins. "Technology Usage and Sales Teams: A Multilevel Analysis of the Antecedents of Usage." *Journal of Personal Selling and Sales Management* 32, no. 2 (2012), pp. 245–60.

Wieseke, Jan, Florian Kraus, Michael Ahearne, and Sven Mikolon. "Multiple Identification Foci and Their Countervailing Effects on Salespeople's Negative Headquarters Stereotypes." *Journal of Marketing* 76, no. 3 (2012), pp. 1–20.

PART **3**

The Salesperson as Manager

chapter **17**

MANAGING YOUR CAREER

SOME QUESTIONS ANSWERED IN THIS CHAPTER ARE

- Which entry-level jobs are available to new college graduates?
- Where do I find these jobs?
- How should I go about getting interviews, and what should I do when I have an interview?
- What selection procedures besides interviews might I go through?
- Which career paths are available in sales?
- How can I prepare myself for a promotion into management?

"If you work just for money, you'll never make it. But if you love what you are doing and always put the customer first, success will be yours."

Spencer Ryan, Stryker

PROFILE

While in college, I knew exactly what I wanted to do and had a three-year goal after graduation: medical sales and a certain income level. I started with an entrepreneurial company specializing in a cancerous tumor treatment, related mainly to urology and interventional radiology. My lifelong mentor was a part of it and gave me a shot to become part of the team with the title Business Development/Clinical Applications. There were only seven of us in the company at the time, with four of us traveling to develop business and consult during operations.

The small business I experienced had both its ups and its downs. I was traveling 100 percent of the time throughout the western United States. In the winters, I was able to travel with my skis and stay the weekend somewhere instead of head home. As a company we had a passion to work hard and had fun in everything we did. It was like a family at times. A negative was the nightmare of figuring out how to grow a business on a low budget, pushing that boundary as long as possible until more assets could be acquired. The long, strenuous travel hours ended up being more expensive than desired.

Two years later, I decided to change paths. At that time we had 12 total employees, and the owner and I started a small company on the side in South Texas. My experience in the entrepreneurial world was great. I lived in California for a while, traveled all over, made some great connections, and learned a ton about the medical industry. But I had goals that this small company would not allow me to hit.

I moved to a large orthopedic company selling medical devices/implants specializing in trauma orthopedics. We take care of broken bones after traumatic events like car accidents or other accidents leading to fractures, joint replacements after a hip or shoulder fracture, and limb deformities on children and adults with a genetic deformity. I joined a sales team of three, and the trauma life began. I went from traveling 100 percent of the time to being on call in one city 100 percent of the time. I quickly picked up on the business and earned my own territory within a few months. I really began to

love what I do, and on top of that I hit my first financial goal.

Trauma life is crazy and cutthroat but fun: living on commission only with a pager and phone, no Caleber where you go, and getting called into surgery in the middle of the night and working 24/7. It's a way of life you have to commit to. Some people say you need a few screws loose to do trauma for more than a couple years and I agree. It's a passion.

I have been in trauma for four years with two large orthopedic companies, as I was recruited away by a competitor. My territory is my business. That is my only focus. Management has a sales team they focus on and are there to help you grow, support your growth, and act as sort of a buffer between you and corporate.

Are there more policies and procedures to go through with large corporations? Absolutely, but you have more resources to help you grow your own business/territory. The larger the company and more success you have, the more likely they are to invest in you, and move you up if desired. I don't prefer a larger company to a small company or vice versa; both have their pluses and minuses.

One mantra I've heard and lived by has worked well for me: "If you work just for money, you'll never make it. But if you love what you are doing and always put the customer first, success will be yours." I believe it is extremely important to find something you have a passion for and run. As a sales rep, service/customer support should be priority. To service and support something you love will drive even more success. Second, "You don't close a sale; you open a relationship if you want to build a long-term, successful enterprise." A sale needs to be looked at as a long-term relationship. Work yourself up to the top of the totem pole. Don't follow success; rather, be excellent, and success will follow you.

Visit our Web site at:
www.stryker.com

Landing that first career position is an exciting moment! However, the job search is just the first task in managing your career. Like the chess player who is thinking two or three moves ahead, you too must think about subsequent opportunities. Also like the chess player, you must maintain some flexibility so you do not checkmate your career if one strategy does not work.

Sales is a great place to begin a career. Just ask Mark Hurd, CEO of Oracle. Hurd started in sales with NCR and became president of the Teradata subsidiary and then president of NCR. From there, he took over Hewlett-Packard, leading a turnaround based on improving their sales force. At each step of the way, Hurd has grown each company by focusing attention on the sales function.

OPPORTUNITIES IN SELLING

Selling offers many opportunities.

Corporate executives clearly recognize the importance of selling experience in any career, as evidenced by people like Mark Hurd and Spencer Ryan (profiled at the start of this chapter). Many people, though, have also found career satisfaction by staying in sales throughout their working lives.

Whether the career is sales or any other field, similar questions apply when searching for a job. In this chapter the focus is on the search for a sales position and how to land the first job. We examine how companies make hiring decisions and offer tips on how to build selling and management skills while managing a career.

MAKING A GOOD MATCH

The keys to being successful and happy lie in finding a good match between what you need and desire in a position and the positions companies offer.[1] The first step, then, is to understand yourself, what you need, and what you have to offer. Then you must consider what each company needs and what each has to offer. As Exhibit 17.1 illustrates, a good match means your needs are satisfied by what the company offers and what you offer satisfies the company's needs.

Exhibit 17.1
A Good Match between Salesperson and Company

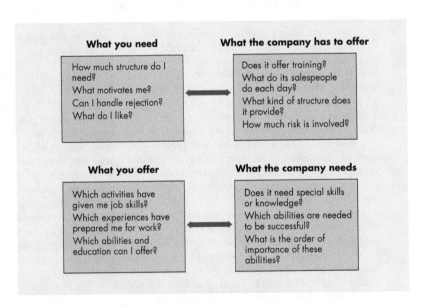

What you need

How much structure do I need?
What motivates me?
Can I handle rejection?
What do I like?

What the company has to offer

Does it offer training?
What do its salespeople do each day?
What kind of structure does it provide?
How much risk is involved?

What you offer

Which activities have given me job skills?
Which experiences have prepared me for work?
Which abilities and education can I offer?

What the company needs

Does it need special skills or knowledge?
Which abilities are needed to be successful?
What is the order of importance of these abilities?

Many companies, such as Konica-Minolta, Oracle, IBM, and others, use exotic trips as a reward for top performers.

UNDERSTANDING YOURSELF

Shakespeare said, "To thine own self be true," but to be true to yourself, you must know who you are, what you need, and what you can offer others.[2] Knowing these things about yourself requires substantial self-examination. We will pose some questions that can help you follow Shakespeare's suggestion.

Understanding Your Needs

The first step in making a good match between what you have to offer and a company's position is to determine what you need. Important questions to consider include the following:

1. *Structure:* Can you work well when assignments are ambiguous, or do you need a lot of instruction? Do you need deadlines that others set, or do you set your own deadlines? If you are uncomfortable when left on your own, you may need structure in your work life. Many sales positions, such as missionary and trade sales, are in a structured environment with well-defined procedures and routines. Other positions require the salesperson to operate with little guidance or structure.

2. *Motivation:* Will financial incentives, personal recognition, or simply job satisfaction get you going? Probably it will be some combination of the three, but try to determine the relative value of each to you. Then you can weigh compensation plans, recognition programs, and other factors when considering which sales position is right for you. You may want to review the section on compensation plan types in Chapter 16 to aid in determining which plan best suits your needs.

3. *Stress and rejection:* How much stress can you handle? Are you a risk taker, or do you prefer more secure activities? What do you do when faced with stress? With rejection? These are important questions in understanding what you need from a sales position. For example, capital equipment sales jobs can be high-stress positions because sales are few and far between. Other jobs may require you to wade through many rejections before landing a sale. If you thrive on that kind of challenge, the rewards can be gratifying. Some sales positions, though, involve working only with current customers, and salespeople incur little outright rejection. Every grocery store, for example, will carry at least some Procter & Gamble products so there is not the same stress placed on each individual sale.

4. *Interest:* What do you find interesting? Mechanical or technical topics? Merchandising? Art or fashion? You cannot sell something that bores you. You would just bore and annoy the customer.

Understanding What You Have to Offer

Other resources that can help you understand the person you are may be available through your college's placement center. You must also take inventory of what you bring to the job:

1. *Skills:* What activities and experiences taught you certain skills? What did you learn from those experiences and your education that you can apply to a career? Keep in mind that it is not the activities in which you

participated that matter to hiring companies; it is what you learned by participating that counts.

2. *Knowledge:* College has provided you with many areas of knowledge, but you have also probably learned much by participating in hobbies and other interests. For example, you may have special computer knowledge that would be useful in selling software, or you may have participated in a particular sport that makes you well suited to sell equipment to sporting goods stores. Kristen Scott, profiled at the start of Chapter 16, found that her course in CRM and her experience in selling NetSuite at the National Collegiate Sales Competition enabled her to compete against other salespeople with years of experience and win a sales position with Oracle straight out of college.

3. *Qualities and traits:* Every person has a unique personality. What parts of your personality add value for your potential employer? Are you detail oriented and systematic? Are you highly creative? In other words, what can you bring to the job that is uniquely you? Exhibit 17.2 lists traits of top salespeople, according to a study conducted for *Sales and Marketing Management* magazine.

Your answers to these questions will generate a list of what you have to offer companies. Then when you are in an interview, you can present features that make you a desirable candidate.

When to Ask These Questions

Unfortunately many students wait until just before graduation before seriously considering the type of career they desire. According to one career services director, students who start a search while in school will find a job three times faster than those who start after graduation. Although it is not always realistic to expect every student to map out a life plan prior to senior year, asking questions such as these as early as possible can guide a student to better course selection, better use of learning opportunities, and ultimately a better career decision. Then the student can begin actively searching for the job at the beginning of the senior year so that graduation signals the beginning of a career, not a career search.

Exhibit 17.2

Traits of Top Salespeople

1. Strong ego: able to handle rejection with healthy self-esteem.
2. Sense of urgency: getting it done now.
3. Ego driven: obsessive about being successful.
4. Assertive: being firm without being aggressive (see the discussion in Chapter 11).
5. Willing to take risks: willing to innovate.
6. Sociable: good at building relationships.
7. Abstract reasoner: able to handle complex selling situations and ideas.
8. Skeptical: a healthy bit of suspicion, not counting on commission until the sale is really a sale.
9. Creative: able to set oneself apart from the competition.
10. Empathic: able to place oneself in the buyer's shoes.

Source: Adapted from Erika Rasmusson, "The Ten Traits of Top Salespeople," *Sales and Marketing Management,* August 1999, pp. 34–37.

UNDERSTANDING THE COMPANY

While developing a good feel for who you are and what you have to offer companies, you should also explore what is available and which companies offer positions that appeal to you. As you can see in Exhibit 17.3, numerous sources provide information about positions and growth opportunities in various industries and specific companies. Don't forget, though, that the best sources are personal; be sure to talk over job opportunities with your friends, friends of your parents, and your professors. Use term papers as an excuse to call professionals in a field that interests you. Join trade and professional associations now because these offer great networking opportunities. As someone who has studied sales, you should use your prospecting skills too. Next let's discuss how to evaluate what you learn about the companies and their positions.

Exhibit 17.3
Sources of Job Information

Source	Example
Government	U.S. Industrial Outlook
Research services	Standard & Poor's Industry Surveys
Industry associations	Christian Booksellers' Association
Professional organizations	Sales and Marketing Executives International
General magazines	*BusinessWeek, Money*
Trade magazines	*Sales and Marketing Management, Selling Power*
Placement services	University placement office; nonfee private agencies such as Personnel One
Personal sources	Friends, relatives, industry association executives at trade shows, recruiters at career fairs
Web sites	marketingjobs.com

What the Company Has to Offer

When you meet a salesperson or sales manager, you should ask about compensation and recognition programs, training, career opportunities, and other information to determine whether the company truly offers benefits to satisfy your needs. You should also explore daily activities of the salesperson, likes and dislikes about the job, and what that person thinks it takes to succeed. This information will help you determine whether a match exists.

For example, if you need structure, you should look for a sales position in which your day is structured for you. Any industry that relies on repeated sales calls to the same accounts is likely to be highly structured. Industries with a structured sales day include consumer packaged goods sales (Procter & Gamble, Quaker Oats, and the like) and pharmaceutical sales (Novartis, Eli Lilly Company, and so forth). Even these sales positions offer some flexibility and independence. Office and industrial equipment sales provide much less structure when the emphasis is on getting new accounts.

Knowing your comfort level with risk and your need for incentives should help you pick a company with a compensation program that is right for you. If you need the security of a salary, look for companies in trade sales, equipment sales, pharmaceuticals, or consumer packaged goods. But if you like the risk of straight commission, which can often be matched with greater financial rewards for success, explore careers in areas such as convention sales, financial services, and other straight commission jobs.

Other factors to consider include the size of the company and its promotion policies, particularly if the company is foreign. Many companies have a "promote from within" policy, which means that whenever possible they fill positions with people who already are employees. One example is Worldwide Express, a company that sells shipping services in partnership with UPS. Alex BeMent was promoted after working at Worldwide Express for only six months to managing three salespeople, with responsibility for increasing the office to five or more. Such policies are very attractive if you seek career growth into management. A company that is foreign-owned, however, may prefer to staff certain positions with people from its home country.

Take advantage of interests you already have. If you are intrigued by medical science, seek a medical sales position. If merchandising excites you, a position selling to the trade would be appropriate. A bar of soap by itself is not exciting, but helping customers find ways to market that bar of soap is.

From the **BUYER'S SEAT**

17.1

WHAT THE RECRUITER SAYS

Dean Kyle, of Henry Schein, interviews dozens of graduating college students for sales jobs every year. Here's his advice to you if you're headed into sales.

"Probe, probe, probe. These three words may be some of the most important in my interviews. I have been interviewing hundreds of students for over 30 years. And they all make the same mistake. The funny thing is every candidate has been coached on it throughout his or her entire educational career.

I role-play with each one of my candidates in the interview; I tell them exactly what will happen. Students will immediately be met by an objection. Every time the buyer will shake his head and gruffly state, "Go away, we are already purchasing with company XYZ, we're happy, we don't need you." What would you say?

After I present this scenario, I lean over the desk and ask them that exact question. Ninety percent of my candidates answer the same way. After a little stuttering, stammering, and fidgeting, they product overload me. They spit fact after fact at me and go into a long, well-rehearsed list of product superiority.

This response is the opposite of what these students have been taught their whole sales education. Only 10 percent of students get it right—they probe! If I'm the buyer, I do not want to listen to a speech about product superiority; I want to be understood and heard. You accomplish this by asking questions. The 10 percent that impress me immediately calm their composure and ask probing questions. "I've heard good things about Company XYZ. Can you tell me more?" When my candidates begin to ask questions and dig deeper, they find pain points and opportunities to build a successful presentation and ultimately a successful interview.

What puts someone in that 10 percent during the interview? The number one trait I look for while interviewing is a level of maturity. These students are calm under pressure, confident in their speech, and natural in their role play with a good personality, effective communication skills, sales acumen, and a high level of energy. The best way to gain this level of maturity portrayed during an interview is through life experiences, which often come from internships. But even with the best of life experiences, don't leave all your training at the door when you walk into my office! Remember, probe, probe, probe."

Source: Brooke Borgias, used with permission.

What the Company Needs

At this point in your job search, you may have narrowed your selection to a group of industries or companies. At a minimum you have a good picture of what a company should offer to land you as a salesperson. The next step is to find a company that needs you. Finding out what a company needs will require some research, but you will find this step fun and rewarding. Dean Kyle, sales manager for Henry Schein who has recruited college students and others for sales positions, provides his perspective on how to impress recruiters in "From the Buyer's Seat 17.1."

In general, companies look for three qualities in salespeople: good communication skills, self-motivation, and a positive and enthusiastic attitude. One sales consultant says these are reflections of the personality traits ego drive, ego strength, and empathy.[3] Recall from Exhibit 17.2 that other characteristics are important, such as a sense of urgency.

Companies in certain industries may also desire related technical skills or knowledge, such as medical knowledge for the field of pharmaceutical sales or insurance knowledge to enter that field. All companies need salespeople with computer skills because computers are increasingly being used to track and manage accounts, communicate internally, and perform other important activities.

Career fairs, such as this one at a hotel during spring break, can be a great opportunity to find internships or permanent sales positions.

If you want to enter a field requiring specialized knowledge or skills, now is the time to begin acquiring that knowledge. Not only will you already have the knowledge when you begin to search for a position, but you will also have demonstrated self-motivation and the right kind of attitude by taking on the task of acquiring that knowledge and skill.

THE RECRUITING PROCESS

Early in this book we discussed the buying process so you would understand the purchase decision buyers make. Now we will look at the recruiting process so you will understand how companies will view you as a candidate for a sales job or any other position.

SELECTING SALESPEOPLE

In recent years companies have made considerable progress in screening and selecting salespeople. Most have discarded the myth that there is one single "sales type" who will be successful selling anything to anybody. Instead they seek people who match the requirements of a specific position, using various methods to gain information and determine whether a good match will be made.

APPLICANT INFORMATION SOURCES

To determine whether a match exists between the job requirements and the applicant's abilities, information about the applicant must be collected. Companies use five important sources of information: application forms, references, tests, personal interviews, and assessment centers. We describe these five sources from the perspective of the company so you can understand how they are used to make hiring decisions. We also explain how you should use these sources of information so you can present yourself accurately and positively.

The **application form** is a preprinted form that the candidate completes. You have probably already filled these out for part-time jobs you have had. The form should include factual questions concerning the profile the company established for the position. Responses on the form are also useful for structuring the personal interview. Résumés provide much of the same information application forms do but are often too individualized for easy comparison. For this and other reasons, companies must supplement résumés with an application form (we discuss résumés in greater detail later in this chapter).

Contacting **references,** or people who know the applicant, is a good way to validate information on the application form. References can also supplement the information with personal observations. The most frequently contacted references are former employers. Other references are coworkers, leaders of social or religious organizations, and professors. You should be aware that some organizations try to develop relationships with faculty so they can receive leads on excellent candidates before visiting the placement office. Professors recommend students who have demonstrated the qualities the recruiting companies desire.

When you select references, keep in mind that companies want references that can validate information about you. Choose references that provide different information, such as one character reference, one educational reference, and one work-related reference.

Experienced sales managers expect to hear favorable comments from an applicant's references. More useful information may be contained in unusual comments, gestures, faint praise, or hesitant responses that may indicate a problem. Before you offer someone's name as a reference, ask that person for permission. At that time you should be able to tell whether the person is willing to give you a good recommendation.

Intelligence, ability, personality, and interest **tests** provide information about a potential salesperson that cannot be obtained readily from other sources. Tests can also correct misjudgments made by sales managers who tend to act on "gut feelings." Although tests were widely criticized in the early 1980s for failing to predict success better than other sources did, recent studies indicate that assessment tests are growing in popularity once more, in part because of their improved predictive power.[4] The new assessment tests, however, are more accurate when they are specifically related to sales and the situations potential salespeople may encounter.

Several types of tests may be given. H. R. Challey Inc. designs tests to determine a person's psychological aptitude for different sales situations. BSRP offers a test that measures a salesperson's call reluctance, or fear of initiating contact. IBM requires sales candidates to demonstrate technical aptitude through a test, while Skyline (a company that sells exhibition equipment for trade shows and other displays) requires a test that indicates the individual's ability to handle details. Like many companies, KB Homes requires candidates to pass a math test because of the importance of calculating price correctly. Still other tests indicate a candidate's ethical nature. Companies may require candidates to take tests in all these categories.

The important point to remember about tests is to remain relaxed. If the test is a valid selection tool, you should be happy with the outcome no matter what it is. If you believe the test is not valid—that is, does not predict your ability to succeed in that job—you may want to present your feelings to the recruiter. Be prepared to back up your line of reasoning with facts and experiences that illustrate why you are a good candidate for the position.

Interviews, or personal interaction between recruiter and candidate, are an important source of information for recruiters. Companies now give more attention to conducting multiple interviews in the selection process because sometimes candidates show only slight differences. Multiple interviews can improve a recruiter's chances of observing the differences and selecting the best candidate. We cover interviews in more detail later in the chapter.

Companies sometimes evaluate candidates at centrally located **assessment centers.** In addition to being used for testing and personal interviews, these locations may simulate portions of the job. Simulating the job serves two purposes. First, the simulation lets managers see candidates respond to a joblike situation. Second, candidates can experience the job and determine whether it fits them. For example, Merrill Lynch sometimes places broker candidates in an office and simulates two hours of customer telephone calls. As many as half the candidates may then decide that being a stockbroker is not right for them, and Merrill Lynch can also evaluate the candidates' abilities in a lifelike setting.

Companies use many sources of information in making a hiring decision, perhaps even asking for a copy of a videotaped presentation you may make for this class. These sources are actually selling opportunities for you. You can present yourself and learn about the job at the same time, continuing your evaluation of the match.

SELLING YOUR CAPABILITIES

With an understanding of the recruiting process from the company's point of view, you can create a presentation that sells your capabilities and proves you have the skills and knowledge the company wants. Preparing the résumé, gaining an interview, and presenting your capabilities in the interview are important activities that require sound planning to present yourself effectively.

PREPARING THE RÉSUMÉ

The résumé is the brochure in your marketing plan. As such, it needs to tell the recruiter why you should be hired. Tom Day, sales manager for Hormel, says he literally gets hundreds of résumés for sales positions, whether he has a position available or not. His company prefers to hire inexperienced salespeople right out of college, as do many companies, so don't let a lack of experience create anxiety or lead to misrepresentation on your résumé.[5] There are two broadly accepted formats for résumés: a conventional format and a functional style. In some career centers or if you choose to use an online résumé service, such as LiveCareer.com, you can choose from as many as 1,400 templates, but most follow the conventional style. Whether you choose the conventional style or the functional style of résumé, the purpose is to sell your skills and experience.

Conventional Résumés
Conventional résumés are a form of life history, organized by type of experience. The three categories of experience most often used are education, work, and activities/hobbies (see the example in Exhibit 17.4). Although it is easy to create conventional résumés, it is also easy to fail to emphasize important points. To avoid making this mistake, follow this simple procedure:

- List education, work experience, and activities.
- Write out what you gained in each experience that will help you prove you have the desired qualities.
- Emphasize what you learned and that you have the desired qualities under each heading.

For example, the résumé in Exhibit 17.4 is designed for a student interested in a sales career. Note how skills gained in this class are emphasized in addition to GPA and major. The candidate has also chosen to focus on customer service skills gained as a camp counselor, a job that a recruiter would otherwise overlook. Rather than just listing herself as a member of the soccer team, the candidate highlights the leadership skills she gained as captain.

Exhibit 17.4
Conventional Résumé
Example

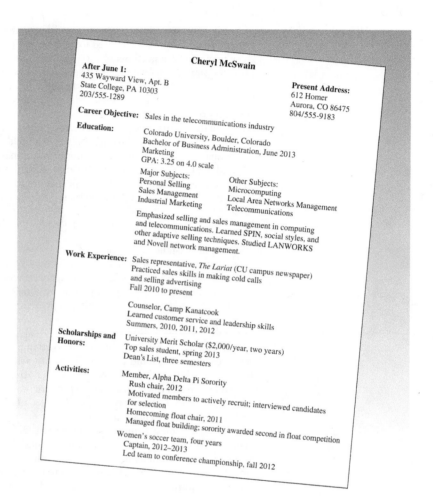

Cheryl McSwain

After June 1:
435 Wayward View, Apt. B
State College, PA 10303
203/555-1289

Present Address:
612 Homer
Aurora, CO 86475
804/555-9183

Career Objective: Sales in the telecommunications industry

Education:
Colorado University, Boulder, Colorado
Bachelor of Business Administration, June 2013
Marketing
GPA: 3.25 on 4.0 scale

Major Subjects: Other Subjects:
Personal Selling   Microcomputing
Sales Management   Local Area Networks Management
Industrial Marketing   Telecommunications

Emphasized selling and sales management in computing
and telecommunications. Learned SPIN, social styles, and
other adaptive selling techniques. Studied LANWORKS
and Novell network management.

Work Experience: Sales representative, *The Lariat* (CU campus newspaper)
Practiced sales skills in making cold calls
and selling advertising
Fall 2010 to present

Counselor, Camp Kanatcook
Learned customer service and leadership skills
Summers, 2010, 2011, 2012

**Scholarships and
Honors:**   University Merit Scholar ($2,000/year, two years)
Top sales student, spring 2013
Dean's List, three semesters

Activities: Member, Alpha Delta Pi Sorority
Rush chair, 2012
Motivated members to actively recruit; interviewed candidates
for selection
Homecoming float chair, 2011
Managed float building; sorority awarded second in float competition
Women's soccer team, four years
Captain, 2012–2013
Led team to conference championship, fall 2012

Functional Résumés

Functional résumés reverse the content and titles of the conventional résumé, organizing by what the candidate can do or has learned rather than by types of experience. As you can see in Exhibit 17.5, an advantage of this type of résumé is that it highlights more forcefully what the candidate can do.

When preparing a functional résumé, begin by listing the qualities you have that you think will help you get the job. Narrow this list to three or four qualities and then list activities and experiences to prove that you have those skills and abilities. The qualities are the headings for the résumé; the activities and experiences show that you have those qualities. One difficulty with this type of résumé is that one past job may relate to several qualities. If that is the case, emphasize the activity within the job that gave you the experience for each specific quality.

GAINING THE INTERVIEW

Students should begin examining different industries as early as possible, as we suggested earlier. As graduation looms closer and the time for serious job hunting arrives, your knowledge of the industries and companies that interest you will

Exhibit 17.5
Functional Résumé
Example

Cheryl McSwain

After June 1:
435 Wayward View, Apt. B
State College, PA 10303
203/555-1289

Present Address:
612 Homer
Aurora, CO 86475
804/555-9183

Career Objective: Sales in the telecommunications industry

Sales and Customer Service Experience:

Studied SPIN and adaptive selling techniques in personal selling.
Sold advertising in *The Lariat*, campus newspaper. Responsibilities included making cold calls, presenting advertising strategies, and closing sales.
Performed customer service tasks as camp counselor at Camp Kanatcook.
Served as the primary parent contact during drop-off and pick-up periods, answering parent queries, resolving parental concerns, and handling similar responsibilities.

Management and Leadership Experience:

Studied situational management in sales management.
Served as rush chair for sorority. Responsible for motivating members to recruit new members and developed and implemented a sales training seminar so members would present the sorority favorably within university guidelines.
Managed homecoming-float project. Sorority awarded second place in float competition.
Captained the women's varsity soccer team to a conference championship.

Telecommunications Skills and Experience:

Studied LANWORKS and Novell network management in telecommunications.
Designed, as a term project, a Novell-based LAN for a small manufacturing business.
Purchased and installed a six-computer network in a family-owned wholesaling business.

Scholarships and Honors:

University Merit Scholar ($2,000/year, two years)
Top sales student, spring 2013
Dean's List, three semesters

put you a step ahead. You will also understand the process the company will go through in searching for a new salesperson.

Using Personal Contacts

More important, you have already begun to make personal contacts in those fields—contacts you can now use to gain interviews. The same salespeople and sales managers who gave you information before to help you with term projects will usually be happy to introduce you to the person in charge of recruiting. Contacts you made at job fairs and trade shows can also be helpful.

thinking it through

Many students feel uncomfortable asking for favors from people they barely know, such as asking an acquaintance to forward a résumé to a decision maker or set up an interview. How can you overcome such feelings of discomfort? Why would someone want to help you find places to interview? What obligations do you have to people who give you the names of job contacts?

Using Employment Postings

Responding to Web postings or newspaper advertisements can also lead to job interviews. You will need to carefully interpret employment postings and then respond effectively to them.

All ads are designed to sell, and employment ads are no exception. But what sounds great may not be wonderful in reality. Here are some phrases often found in such ads and interpretations of them:

Independent contractor: You will work on straight commission with no employee benefits. You will probably receive no training and little, if any, support. Some experienced salespeople prefer this type of position, but it is probably not the best place to start.

Earn up to $ (or *unlimited income* or *our top rep made $500,000 last year*): You need to know what the average person makes and what the average first-year earnings are, not what the top rep made or the upper limit. The job could still be desirable, but you need to find out what reality is before accepting a position.

Sales manager trainee: This is another title for sales representative. Don't be put off or overly encouraged by high-sounding titles.

Bonuses paid weekly, daily commissions, or *weekly commissions:* These are high-pressure jobs and probably involve high-pressure sales.

Ten salespeople needed now! That's because everyone has quit. This company uses salespeople and then discards them.

You should look for two things in an ad: what the company needs and what it has to offer. The company should provide concrete information about training, compensation plan (although not necessarily the amount), amount of travel to expect, and type of product or service you will sell. You should also expect to find the qualifications the company desires, including experience and education. If this is a job you really want but you do not have the experience now, call and ask how to get it. Be specific: "What companies should I pursue that will give me the experience you are looking for?" If the ad requires e-mail response only, send an e-mail message and mention that you are a student. Many people are willing to help someone get started.

Responding to Postings

Many postings and ads will ask you to write or e-mail and may not list the company's name. A blind box number is given when the company name is not included in a newspaper ad; the box number is usually at the address of the newspaper. For example, the ad may say to send a résumé to Job Posting 943 at Monster.com. Don't be put off by the lack of company name; the posting or ad may be placed by a company such as IBM that would otherwise receive a large number of unqualified applicants. Companies use blind postings and blind box numbers for many legitimate reasons.

Writing the Cover Letter

When you write in response to a posting, you are writing a sales letter—even if you send it by e-mail. Like any sales letter, it should focus on what you can do for the company, not what you expect from it. The letter should start with an attention getter. Here is one example:

In today's economy, you need someone who can become productive quickly as a territory representative. Based on your posting at Monster.com, I believe that I am that person.

The Internet is a great source of leads for jobs; however, recruiters report receiving hundreds, and sometimes thousands, of résumés for every job they post. If you really want a job with a particular company, approach it like a sales opportunity and use your prospecting and relationship building skills.

This attention getter is direct, focuses on a probable need, and refers to the posting. The attention getter tells why you should be considered. The probability of getting a response to this e-mail is far greater than if you simply said,

> Please consider me for the territory representative position you posted at Monster.com.

The body of the letter should center on two or three reasons why you should be hired. For example, if you have the qualities of self-motivation and leadership, devote two paragraphs relating each to the position. Use your résumé as proof. For example:

> A territory representative position often requires self-motivation. As you can see from the attached résumé, I demonstrated self-motivation as a sales representative for the campus newspaper, as a volunteer for the local food bank, and as a member of the Dean's Honor Roll during two of the last four semesters.

The letter should close with a request for action. Ask for an interview and suggest times you are available. For example:

> Please call me to arrange an interview. My schedule allows me to meet with you on Tuesday or Thursday afternoon.

An alternative is to state that you will call:

> I will call you early next week to discuss my potential as a salesperson for XYZ Corporation.

No response does not necessarily mean you have been rejected; follow up with a phone call if you do not hear anything within a week. One former student got a job because he called to verify that the sales manager had received his résumé. She had never seen it but was impressed enough with the student's phone call to arrange an appointment. Sometimes e-mail is lost or delayed, goes to a junk mail file and gets deleted, or simply is deleted accidentally—and you would not want a company to miss out on the opportunity to hire you because of a computer glitch!

THE INTERVIEW

Many students do not realize how much competition exists for the best entry-level sales positions, or perhaps they do not know what companies look for in new employees. Students often act as though they are shopping for a job. Job shoppers, however, are not seriously considered by recruiters, who are usually astute enough to quickly pick up on the student's lack of interest. If the job shopper does become interested, it is probably too late because the recruiter has already discounted this applicant. Like it or not, you are really competing for a job. As in any competition, success requires preparation and practice.

Preparing for the Interview

Students who know something about the company and its industry lead the competition. You have already looked for company and industry information in the library, in business reference books, and in periodicals. You visited its Web site. You have also interviewed the company's customers, salespeople, and sales managers. You can use this knowledge to demonstrate your self-motivation and positive attitude—two of the top three characteristics sales managers look for in sales candidates. You will find it easier to demonstrate the third top characteristic, communication skills, with the confidence you gain from proper preparation.

In addition to building knowledge of the "customer," you must plan your responses to the questions you will be asked. Exhibit 17.6 lists standard interview questions.

Exhibit 17.6
Frequently Asked Interview Questions

1. What are your long-range and short-range goals and objectives? When and why did you establish these goals, and how are you preparing yourself to achieve them?
2. What do you consider to be your greatest strengths and weaknesses?
3. Why did you choose the career for which you are preparing?
4. How do you think a friend or professor who knows you well would describe you?
5. Why should I hire you?
6. In what ways do you think you can make a contribution to our company?
7. Do you think your grades are a good indication of your academic achievement?
8. What major problem have you encountered, and how did you deal with it?
9. What do you know about our company? Why are you seeking a position with us?
10. If you were hiring a graduate for this position, what qualities would you look for?

Scenario questions are popular with recruiters. These questions ask what the candidate would do in a certain situation involving actions of competitors. (For example, what would you do if a customer told you something negative about your product that you knew to be untrue, and the customer's source of information was your competitor?) Such questions test ethics regarding competitors and the ability to handle a delicate situation. Scenario questions also test the candidate's response to rejection, ability to plan, and other characteristics. You can best prepare for these types of questions with this class and by placing yourself in the situations described in the cases and exercises in this book. You may also want to review the questions at the ends of the chapters.

The sales field has several unusual characteristics, such as travel, that influence the type of questions asked. For example, if significant travel is part of the position, you may be asked, "Travel is an important part of this job, and you may be away from home about three nights per week. Would you be able and willing to travel as the job requires?" However, some questions are illegal, and you do not have to answer

Exhibit 17.7
Examples of Legal and
Illegal Questions

Subject	Legal Questions	Illegal Questions
Name	Have you ever used another name?	What is your maiden name?
Residence	Where do you live?	Do you own or rent your home?
Birthplace or national origin	Can you, after employment, verify your right to work in the United States?	Where were you born? Where were your parents born?
Marital or family status	Statement of company policy regarding assignment of work of employees who are related.	With whom do you reside? Are you married? Do you plan a family?
	Statement of company policy concerning travel: Can you accept this policy?	
Arrest or criminal record	Have you ever been convicted of a felony? (Such a question must be accompanied by a statement that a conviction will not necessarily disqualify the applicant.)	Have you ever been arrested?

Source: Baylor University Career Services Center.

them, such as "What is your marital status? Do you plan to have a family? Will that affect your ability to travel?" Exhibit 17.7 lists some questions that are illegal, as well as legal questions that you may have to answer.

So what do you do when you are asked an illegal question? One thing you should do is report the incident to your school's career services personnel if the interview is taking place on campus or as a result of the campus career services center. But when actually faced with the question, you have several choices. One is to ask, "Why do you ask? Is that important?" You may find that it is a question asked by an interviewer out of personal curiosity, and the interviewer may not have realized the question was inappropriate. Another response is to simply reply, "I'm sorry, I would prefer not to answer that question." If probed, you can state that you believe the question is not legal, but you will check with career services later; if the question is legal, you will answer it later. If the interviewer is simply ignorant, you will probably get an apology, and then the interview will move on. Otherwise you've identified a company where you may not wish to work. Your final option is, of course, to go ahead and answer the question.

At some point during the interview, the recruiter will ask whether you have any questions. In addition to using the standard questions concerning pay, training, and benefits, you should prepare questions that are unlikely to have been answered already. For example, suppose your research has uncovered the fact that the company was recently awarded the Malcolm Baldrige Award for Quality; you might plan to ask what the company did to win that award.

You may also want to plan questions about the interviewer's career, how it got started, and what positions he or she has held. These questions work best when you are truly interested in the response; otherwise you might sound insincere. Answers to these questions can give you a personal insight into the company. Also, you may often find yourself working for the interviewer, so the answers to your questions may help you decide whether you like and can work with this person.

Other important subjects to ask about are career advancement opportunities, typical first-year responsibilities, and corporate personality. You also need to know how financially stable the company is, but you can find this information for public firms in the library. If the firm is privately owned, ask about its financial stability.

Finally, it may seem trivial, but shine your shoes! You are interviewing for a professional position, so look professional. Recruiters have told us about students showing up for interviews dressed in cut off shorts and a T-shirt or looking hung over. Those interviews were over before they began. One interviewer even described how a student took a phone call from her mother during the interview. She told her mom that the interview was going great! Well, it was until she took the phone call. If you do not look the part now, an interviewer will not see you in the part.

During the Interview

The job interview is much like any other sales call. It includes an approach, needs identification, presentation, and gaining commitment. There are, however, several important differences because both parties are identifying needs and making presentations.

THE APPROACH Social amenities will begin the interview. You will not need the same type of attention getter that you would on a cold call. However, you may want to include an attention getter in your greeting. For example, use a compliment approach, such as "It must be very exciting to work for a Malcolm Baldrige award winner."

NEEDS IDENTIFICATION One difference between sales calls and job interviews is that both parties have needs they have individually defined before the meeting (in a sales call, SPIN helps you assist the buyer in defining needs). A question such as "Are you willing to relocate?" is used not to define needs so much as to determine whether the company's needs will be met. You should prepare questions that will help you learn whether the company's offer will meet your needs.

Take notes during the interview, especially when asking about the company, so you can evaluate whether your needs will be met. Carry a portfolio with extra résumés and blank paper and pens for note taking or use a pad computer, such as an iPad. You may want to ask, "Do you mind if I take notes? This information is important to me, and I don't want to forget anything."

Try to determine early whether your interviewer is a sales manager or a personnel manager. Personnel managers may have a difficult time telling you about the job itself, its daily activities, and so forth; they may be able to outline only things such as training and employee benefits. Sales managers can tell you a lot about the job, perhaps to the point of describing the actual territory you will work in.

Personnel managers do not like being asked about salary; you will find that many people will advise you not to ask about money on the first interview. On the other hand, you are making an important decision. Why waste your time or theirs if the salary is much lower than your other alternatives? Sales managers are less likely to object, but just in case, you may want to preface a question about earnings by saying, "Compensation is as important a consideration for me as training and other benefits when making a decision. Can you tell me the approximate earnings of a first-year salesperson?" You will probably get a range rather than a specific figure. You could also wait until a later meeting to ask about earnings.

People who prefer security desire compensation plans with an emphasis on salary. Other people like the potential rewards of straight commission. If either is important to you, ask about the type of compensation plan in the first meeting. For example, you should ask, "What type of compensation plan do you offer: salary, straight commission, or a combination of salary plus commission or bonus?"

PRESENTATION Features alone are not persuasive in interviews, just as features alone do not persuade buyers to purchase products. Recall the FEBA technique presented in Chapter 8, which stands for feature, evidence, benefit, agreement. Cheryl McSwain (see Exhibit 17.4) might say, "I was a camp counselor for two summers at Camp Kanatcook (*feature*), as you can see on my résumé (*evidence*). This experience taught me customer service skills that you will appreciate when I sell for you (*benefit*), don't you agree?"

If asked to describe yourself, use features to prove benefits. Recruiters will appreciate specific evidence that can back up your claims. For example, if you say you like people and that is why you think you would be a good salesperson, be prepared to demonstrate how your love of people has translated into action.

Many students carry portfolios into interviews. A **portfolio** is an organized collection of evidence of one's career.[6] For example, a portfolio might contain letters of reference, a résumé, thank-you letters from customers, a paper about an internship, a strategic plan created for a business policy class, or even photographs of the homecoming float for which you were chairperson. Some of our students offer videos of their sales calls from this class as part of their portfolios; these are often made available through YouTube to recruiters, along with digital portfolios that look like Web pages. Portfolios are one method of offering proof that you can deliver benefits.

thinking **it** through

How would you describe yourself in terms of features? What needs would be satisfied by those features so they could become benefits? What would go on your Web site or in your portfolio to prove your features? How could you use a Web site to market yourself?

Keep in mind that the interviewer also will be taking notes. Writing down answers takes the interviewer longer than it takes for you to speak. Once a question is answered sufficiently, stop and allow the interviewer time to write. Many applicants believe they should continue talking; the silence of waiting is too much to bear. Stay silent; otherwise, you may talk yourself out of a job.

GAINING COMMITMENT Because sales positions usually require skill at gaining commitment, sales managers will want to see whether the candidate has that skill. Be prepared to close the interview with some form of gaining commitment: "I'm very excited about this opportunity. What is our next step?"

Be sure to learn when you can expect to hear from the company, confirm that deadline, and write it down. You may want to say, "So I'll receive a call or a letter within the next two weeks. Let's see, that would be the 21st, right?"

Asking for commitment and confirming the information signal your professionalism and your organizational and selling skills.

SPECIAL TYPES OF INTERVIEWS

You can face many types of interviews: disguised interviews, stress interviews, and panel interviews, among others. **Disguised interviews,** or interviews in which the candidate is unaware that the interviewer is evaluating the candidate, are common at college placement offices. In the lobby you may meet a **greeter**, probably a recent graduate of your college, who will try to help you relax before a scheduled interview and offer you an opportunity to ask questions about the job and the company. Although you can obtain a lot of good information from a greeter, you may want to save some questions for the real interview. You may also want to repeat some questions in the interview to check for consistency. Keep in mind that the greeter is also interviewing you, even though the meeting seems like friendly conversation. Keep your enthusiasm high and your nerves low.

ethics

A **stress interview** is designed to place the candidate under severe stress to see how the candidate reacts. Stress interviews have been criticized as being unfair because the type of stress one experiences on a job interview often differs from the type of stress one would actually face on the job. Still, many reputable companies believe it is appropriate to try to determine how a candidate reacts to stress because stress is a real part of just about every sales position. One tactic is to ask three questions at once and see how the candidate answers; another is to ask, "How are you going to lose money for me?" (*translation*: What mistakes have you made in the past and what might you do in the future?) or other reversed versions of appropriate questions. Another strategy is to ask questions such as "What is 36 cubed?" or "What will the interest rates be on such and such a date (two years from now), to the exact one-hundredth please?"[7] While questionable in terms of measuring the appropriate form of stress, these methods are less questionable than the following: The interviewer asks the applicant to reveal something personal, such as a time when the person felt emotionally hurt. Once the situation has been described, the interviewer may mock the applicant, saying the situation wasn't that personal or that hurtful and surely the applicant can dig deeper. Another stress tactic is to ask the interviewee to sell something such as a pencil or a table; while this question is reasonable when used to observe selling style, being an unreasonable "customer" can turn the call into a stress interview.

You probably will not see stress interviews at a college placement office, but you could face one at some point in the job-hunting process. You may find it helpful to deal with a stress interview by treating it as a game (say to yourself, "She's just trying to stress me out; I wonder how far she will go if I don't react?"). Of course you may simply refuse to play the game, either by terminating the interview or by changing the subject. If you terminate the interview, you will probably not get the job.

In **panel interviews** you will encounter multiple interviewers. During a panel interview try to make eye contact with each interviewer. Focus on each person for at least three seconds at a time; anything less than that and you are simply sweeping the room. When asked a question, begin your answer by directing it to the questioner but then shift your attention to the group. By speaking to the group, you will keep all interviewers involved and avoid a two-person conversation. You may want to review how to sell to a group, described in Chapter 8.

Panel interviews require special tactics by the candidate to keep all interviewers involved. A focus on only the older gentleman may cost this young man a position.

Group interviews are similar to panel interviews, but they include several candidates as well as several interviewers. Group interviews may take place in a conference room or around a dinner table. If you find yourself in a group interview, avoid trying to top the stories of the other candidates.

Distinguish yourself by asking interviewers about their careers and what they find it takes to be successful.

Treat social occasions during office or plant visits as interviews, and avoid alcohol or overeating. As with stress interviews, the key is to maintain your cool while being yourself. You cannot do that if you overindulge. Remember that companies are still evaluating you during these "social" events.

FOLLOW-UP

Regardless of the type of interview, you should send a thank-you note shortly afterward. Send one to the greeter, if possible (thus, you will probably want to get this person's business card). If you had a panel interview, find out who the contact person is and write to that person. If you send a thank-you card, you'll stand out. Most people who write a follow-up will send an e-mail, which is the least you should do. If you send a card, thank the person in the first paragraph, then summarize the interview. Focus your summary on the reasons why you should be hired. In the final paragraph reiterate your thanks and end with an assumptive statement, such as "I look forward to seeing you again." Whether you send a card or an e-mail, it should be short and to the point.

If you do not hear by the target date, contact the person. One former student got his first job simply because he followed up. Sales managers will appreciate the saleslike perseverance; personnel managers may not so you may want to send them an e-mail. Within another week, call the personnel manager also. Simply ask for the status of your application rather than whether you got the job. The process of deciding may have taken longer than expected, or other situations may have caused delays. You need to know where you stand, however, so you can take advantage of alternatives, if possible.

INTERVIEWING NEVER ENDS

Even if you spend your entire career with one company, your job interviewing days are not over after you land that first job; you will interview for promotions as well. Some companies even interview candidates for admission to management development programs. The same techniques apply in all these cases. You will still need to prepare properly, conduct the interview professionally, close for some level of commitment, and follow up.

MANAGING YOUR CAREER GOALS

An important aspect of career management is to set life-based objectives and then use them to determine your career objectives. Balance between family and work goals is necessary, or one of several negative consequences could occur, such as divorce or success without fulfillment. One survey reported that a lack of work–life balance was one of the top reasons that managers resigned, were terminated, or were poorly evaluated.[8] Another study indicated that the recession of the late 2000s significantly impacted work–life balance for the worse. Nearly 50 percent of workers reported significant increases in stress due to work–life conflict.[9]

Balance, then, is important when setting career goals. Career decisions must be compatible with family and personal objectives. Keeping life goals in mind and remembering your reasons for setting those goals will help you map out a career with which you can be happy.

MAKING THE TRANSITION FROM COLLEGE TO CAREER

That first year after college is a unique and important time in anyone's life. How this transition is handled can have a big influence in whether you reach success

BUILDING Partnerships

17.1

PERSONAL BRANDING AND THE BUSINESS PROFESSIONAL

Do you think personal branding matters? No? Then ask "RG3" or "Johnny Football." Both of those nicknames were creations by athletic departments that realized that their athletes needed branding to help them in their Heisman quest. In fact, not only did Baylor's athletic marketing department create the nickname, they also created an RG3 logo. Going into his Heisman-winning season, the knock on Robert Griffin was that he was a running quarterback; after all, his ESPN Top 10 plays were all running plays. So to counter that misperception, the team created a logo of Robert about to pass.

True, no amount of marketing would have overcome bad seasons for either Robert Griffin or Johnny Manziel. Neither would have won the Heisman had they not also had outstanding years.

What do you need for a personal brand?

1. Decide what your brand will mean. For RG3, it meant emphasizing his passing skills; for Johnny Football, it was the "all things football," the quintessential player who overcame his youth (he was the first freshman to win the Heisman).

2. Create hooks. A hook is something that helps people remember who you are. During the dot-com boom, consultant Dave Schrader called himself e-Dave, somewhat as a joke because every company was adding an "e" before its name (think e-Harmony). He's gone back to just plain "Dave," but people still remember him because of that e-Dave brand. Jackie Sherr, a realtor, always wears something bright red. Jeff Tanner, a consultant, always wears cowboy boots, and because he races thoroughbred horses, he also incorporates horse-racing images into his speeches. These hooks help people remember who you are.

3. Tie the hook to the purpose. Schrader helps companies make money through technology; the "e-Dave" is for "e-commerce." Sherr promotes putting your style into your home; the red shows her personal style. Tanner consults on sales and marketing performance; horse racing is all about performance.

4. Create a message. Some call it an elevator speech, meaning you should be able to describe yourself and your brand in the time it takes to ride an elevator. Develop a one-sentence description of who you are and what you can do.

5. Perform. Branding is about making a promise, so don't make a promise you can't or won't keep.

Personal branding is something you can and should start now. While your own brand will morph over time as you develop new skills and interests, starting now will help you land that first position and give you time to hone your brand.

or experience disappointment. Although a life's work is not created or ruined in the first months, a poor start can take years to overcome. It is not just a matter of giving up student attitudes and behaviors; making the transition also requires taking the time to understand and earn the rights, responsibilities, and credibility of being a sales professional. You will make mistakes during that transition; everyone does. But as many successful salespeople have learned, it isn't whether you make mistakes but rather whether you learn from them.

Many new hires want to make a great first impression, so they charge ahead and fail to recognize that the organization was there long before they were and has already developed its own way of doing things. The first thing to do is learn the organization's culture, its values, and the way things are done there.

Another important aspect of the first year is that you are under a microscope. Your activities are watched closely as management and your peers try to decide whether you are someone they can depend on. Demonstrate a mature willingness to learn, plus respect for those with experience. Part of this mature willingness to learn means you hold your expectations in check and keep your

Exhibit 17.8
Sales Advancement at Schneider Electric

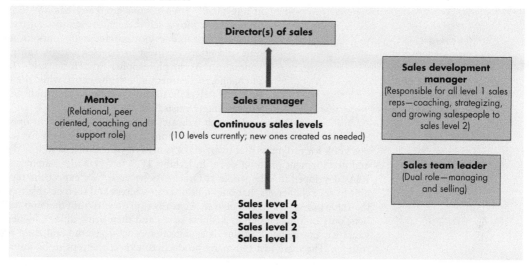

promotion hopes realistic. Remember that recruiters tend to engage in puffery when presenting the opportunities and benefits of a company. Although the recruiter said it may be possible to earn a promotion in six months, the average may be much longer.

Seek a partnership with your manager. Although partnership implies a peer-level relationship and you do not have the experience to be a true peer with your manager, use the same partnering skills with him or her that you would use with customers. Find out what your manager needs and wants and then do it. Every workday is a test day except that you sometimes write the questions. Just like your professor, your manager wants the answers, not the problems. Give your boss solutions, and you will be well on the way to a partnership.

DUAL CAREER PATH

When you start out in sales, many career options are open. Career paths can alternate between sales and marketing or follow a route entirely within sales or entirely within marketing. You may even wind up as chief executive officer of a major global corporation, like Mark Hurd at Oracle. Exemplifying how you might pursue various positions, Exhibit 17.8 depicts the various career paths for salespeople at Schneider Electric. In addition to sales management opportunities, many companies also have opportunities in marketing and product development that begin in sales.

CONTINUE TO DEVELOP YOUR KSAs

Knowledge, skills, and abilities, or **KSAs,** are the package that you offer your employer. You just spent four or five years and a lot of money developing a set of KSAs, but like any asset, your KSAs will begin to decay if you do not continue to invest in them. Because you are the person in your company to whom your career means the most, many companies, such as Cisco, have recognized that ownership of development belongs to the person, not to the company, and have turned training into self-directed development programs. In addition to

Exhibit 17.9
Soft Skills Developed at Oracle

Negotiation

Value messaging

Competitive positioning

Reference selling

Working with partners

Prospecting skills

Best practices for how to lead a good sales cycle

self-directed training, much of the company's training has also gone virtual, meaning salespeople can access it online at any time.[10] Even if your company has not formalized development into a self-directed program or if the development program does not provide many options, take the time and effort to invest in yourself so you can grow in your career. As the philosopher Eric Hoffer said, "In times of change, the learners inherit the earth, while the learned find themselves beautifully equipped to handle a world that no longer exists."[11]

Research indicates that career development opportunities vary widely among companies, especially for salespeople. Look for programs that involve assessment of your skills, as well as direction and development of those skills. In Exhibit 17.9 Jeffrey Bailey summarizes soft KSAs developed in salespeople at Oracle. As he says, "We expect the reps to be able to spot challenges that our solutions can address and then be able to explain the value our solutions can deliver. We really don't try to train them on the products, only on understanding business issues and then being able to highlight the value we can bring. It is our sales consultants who get the real deep product training. There are just too many products to expect the reps to be deep in any of them."

Lifelong learning is important in today's learning organization. Although many companies have downsized, it is the versatile, well-educated employee who not only keeps a job but also develops a career.

Lifelong learning can be an important factor in not only improving your position but also enjoying what you do. Once you have a position within an organization, your objective will be to develop yourself to get a promotion and then to be successful in that promotion. (To get the promotion after that, you will need to do well in the job you are seeking.) You should take several significant actions in each position along the way. The first action is to understand your options because sales can often lead to various positions.

Sources of Improvement

Most companies continue to train their salespeople after basic sales training, but most training of experienced salespeople is product related rather than sales skills related. If you want to improve your selling skills, you may have to actively seek assistance.

The first place to start is with the field sales manager. When that person works with you in your territory, solicit feedback after each call. During these curbside conferences, you can learn a great deal about what you are doing from an objective observer. One warning, however: Make sure your manager only observes during the sales call and does not try to get into the act! As we discussed in the previous chapter, many sales managers are former salespeople who get excited in the heat of battle and may try to take over the sales call.

Peers provide another source. Who is successful in the company? When gathered together for a sales meeting, many successful salespeople pick one another's brains for new ideas and strategies. Offer to work with them in their territories for a day or so in order to learn from them. In most situations they will be flattered and helpful. Noncompeting salespeople in professional organizations such as Sales and Marketing Executives, an international organization of salespeople and marketing managers, will also be flattered to share their tips with you.

Learning doesn't end at graduation. This team of salespeople at Mechanical Service Company is learning about a new product.

Bookstores offer a wealth of material for developing sales skills. Many good books remind salespeople of the basics of selling and present advanced methods of selling and negotiating. Be sure to keep this book, too, because you will want to refer to it when you are in the field.

Sales seminars—in-person, online, or on DVDs and CDs—are also available. Seminars, such as those offered by Zig Ziglar, Dale Carnegie, Wilson Learning, and Tom Hopkins, can be very motivating. However, many experienced salespeople desire more than just motivation; they look for seminars that also teach new ways to present and gain commitment, as well as other sales skills. Some even learn to play golf because that's what their customers do.[12]

Another source of improvement is an industry association. Many industries and professions offer certification programs, which not only require that you improve and update your knowledge and skills but also offer proof to your customers that you have made that effort. Francisco Limas, sales representative with National Restaurant Supply in El Paso, sought certification in food safety and is now pursuing certification as a Foodservice Equipment Distributors Association Certified Salesperson. Though he's been recognized by the industry's top salespeople, he realizes that the certification provides both education and an assurance of quality to customers.[13] Certification was one measure of service quality that these buyers used when comparing suppliers.

Industry associations, though, can and do provide many training opportunities that may not lead to certification. For example, the National Association of Insurance and Financial Advisors (NAIFA) offers a number of professional development courses, including one called the NAIFA Sales System. The program is primarily delivered online, though it also includes a book and access to NAIFA mentors who will coach students through challenges that arise in their regular sales calls.[14]

In this course you have begun to develop your interpersonal persuasion, or selling, skills. Whether or not you plan a career in sales, you owe it to yourself to continue to develop these skills.

Learn Your Current Job

Learn all you can about the job you have now. Many people want promotions as fast as they can get them, regardless of their readiness. But consider that you will probably be managing the people who will be holding your current job. To be truly effective as their manager, you should learn all you can about the job of the people you hope to manage while in the best position to do so: while you are one of them.

Learn the Job You Want Next

A manager once said, "In order to become a manager, you must first be a manager." He meant that promoting someone is easier when that person already has the characteristics the position requires—that is, already acts like a manager—rather than having only potential.

SELF-PROMOTION VIA TECHNOLOGY

Are you LinkedIn? Most students are on Facebook and Twitter but seem to be slow to get a profile on LinkedIn or to start using the Internet for professional purposes through blogging and other activities.

Not every business professional needs a blog, but every business professional should have a profile on LinkedIn. Jeffrey Bailey, sales manager for Oracle, stated that the company wouldn't even consider hiring a salesperson who hasn't used social media personally. "If a prospective salesperson isn't using LinkedIn professionally already, then they can't sell in today's environment," believes Bailey. Like a Facebook for professionals, LinkedIn allows you to record your professional experience (like a résumé, only with more detail), provide opportunities for others to write recommendations for you (ask your professors), and endorse your abilities (ask your friends). However, Bruce Hurwitz, a professional staffer, cautions against reciprocal endorsements, or endorsing someone just because they endorsed you. "I won't [reciprocate] because it would be meaningless," and he has had requests for more information on people he has endorsed.

Another way to network is to read and comment on others' blogs. Reading your customers' blogs (or, for now,

the companies you may want to work for) is a good idea to see what's on their minds. Lisa Gschwandtner suggests being strategic about when to comment on what you read, choosing media (Twitter, blogs, LinkedIn status, and so on) and opportunities that fit the brand you are trying to build (see "Building Partnerships 15.1" in Chapter 15 on building a personal brand). Don't comment on every blog your customer or prospective employer writes and don't respond to every tweet; rather, comment only when you have something to say that contributes to the conversation. As a student, feel free to also ask questions in response to what you read. People are always happy to help students, and this is a way for you to build your network.

While it's important to contribute to online dialogues in ways that build your personal brand, it's also important to be personal. You can comment or tweet about a Red Sox/Yankee game if that's your interest. But commenting on how long it took to recover from the party at a trade show is probably not a good idea.

Sources: Lisa Gschwandtner, "It's All about Strategy," *Selling Power*, January–February 2010, pp. 32–36; Debra Donston-Miller, "LinkedIn Profiles: Not Just for Resumes Anymore," *Informationweek Online*, October 18, 2012); Jeffrey Bailey, personal interview, November 8, 2012.

Several ways exist for you to learn about the job you desire. First, solicit the help of people who hold the job now. Many companies expect managers to develop their people. Take advantage of that fact; ask for the help of such managers. Find out what they did to prepare themselves and what you should do.

Second, volunteer to take on special projects that will demonstrate your leadership and organizational abilities. Taking projects off the hands of your manager can also let you see the manager's responsibilities. Look for ways you can contribute to the overall sales team to show your commitment to the organization, your ability to lead and develop others, and your management skills.

In addition to improving your skills, many sales professionals also recommend building a personal brand—a professional reputation that is not only strong and positive but also widely recognized. Social media offer one outlet for building that brand, as discussed in "Sales Technology 17.1."

MANAGING STRESS

Selling can be a stressful career. For example, with three days left in the month, Richard Langlotz, then a sales manager at Konica-Minolta but now a regional vice president, faced a sales team that lost $100,000 in business. One sale alone, worth $60,000, would have made the team's quota, but that account delayed its order for a few months. The other prospects decided to go with the competition. Suddenly it looked as though Langlotz was going to finish the month well below quota. To top it off, one of his salespeople quit. What did he do? "I took my sales team to a pizza place," Langlotz says. He thought about calling a meeting and getting tough with his team, but he realized they already had enough stress and didn't need any more from him. At the pizza parlor, without any prompting from him, each salesperson examined his or her prospect lists and determined how the team was going to move sales forecast for the next month into the current month. The team was successful, and Langlotz says he learned a valuable lesson. "When you have good people doing their best, they don't need more stress from their manager." Many salespeople liken sales to a roller-coaster ride, with great emotional highs when sales are good but emotional lows when sales are poor. Research shows that support from the sales manager, such as that offered by Langlotz, can go a long way to reduce stress among salespeople.[15]

For some people, coping with stress results in changing jobs. Changing jobs may be the right thing for some people to do. Others turn to less healthful releases, such as absenteeism, drugs, alcohol, and so forth.[16] All jobs have some stress; managing that stress is important to leading a happy and healthy life. However, managing stress does not always mean removing the cause of stress. Sometimes, as with the loss of a loved one, most people find they must manage stress because they cannot remove or change its cause. Two types of stress common to salespeople because of the unique nature of sales positions are situational stress and felt stress.

SITUATIONAL STRESS

Situational stress is short-term anxiety caused by a situational factor.[17] You may face situational stress when waiting to make a sales presentation for your class, for example. The best strategy to deal with situational stress is to leave the situation or remove the situational factor causing the stress, but that approach is not always possible. You cannot, for example, simply tell your instructor that you are too stressed to sell in class today, so you are leaving! One technique for managing situational stress is to imagine that the situational factor has been removed (see Exhibit 17.10 for more ideas). In class, imagine that you have already finished your role play. Mentally consider that feeling of relief you get when you

Exhibit 17.10
Coping with Situational Stress

Use imaging: Close your eyes and imagine yourself past the source of stress. Try to feel the actual sensation of what it will be like when the stress is gone.

Exercise: Exercise can moderate feelings of stress. When situational stress occurs over a period of time, set time aside for exercise breaks.

Take breaks: Take a walk, phone a friend, do something. If working on a stressful project, take regular stress breaks. Combine imaging techniques with breaks to increase the stress-reducing power of breaks.

Rest: In addition to breaks, be well rested when the situation arises. If you have a major presentation, get a good night's rest beforehand.

Prepare: If the situation involves future performance, prepare and practice. Prepare for every contingency, but don't let the tension build by thinking only of things going wrong.

Recover: Plan time for postsituation recovery before you charge into the next high-stress situation. Doing two major presentations in one day, for example, may not provide you with the recovery time you need to do well in the second presentation.

know you have done a job well. Sometimes imaging success can reduce feelings of stress.

In sales situational stress may be caused by impending presentations, deadlines for closing orders (as in Richard Langlotz's case), and similar situations. Situational stress can cause stage fright in even the most experienced salespeople. One price of success is that situational stress will continue to occur, but successful salespeople learn to control their feelings of situational stress.

FELT STRESS

Felt stress lasts longer than situational stress because the causes are more enduring. **Felt stress** is psychological distress or anxiety brought about by job demands or constraints encountered in the work environment. For example, one study showed that when salespeople felt obliged to use coercive sales tactics, their levels of felt stress increased because they knew they were engaging in ethically questionable techniques.[18] Perhaps the most common form of felt stress is role stress, or feelings of stress caused by the salesperson's role.

Role stress is brought about by role conflict, role overload, and/or role ambiguity. **Role conflict** occurs when two partners demand incompatible actions of the salesperson. A common such occurrence is when the customer wants something that seems reasonable but the company won't allow it. Ted Howell represents a training company and was selling an e-learning training program. A customer wanted to see previous work, especially because he didn't like the demo version the company offered. Ted knew that the demo version didn't represent the client's solution, but his manager kept telling him that the demo should be sufficient. Ted's frustration level hit the boiling point in one call, to the point where his manager asked what was wrong. How do you tell your manager that he's the problem? Ted didn't, but he also gave the client another demo that was more in line with his needs. Seeing the right demo was all the client needed, and Ted got the sale.[19] Conflict occurred with the salesperson caught in the middle. **Role ambiguity** occurs when the salesperson is not sure what actions are required. The salesperson may not be sure what is expected, how to achieve it, or how performance will be evaluated and rewarded. **Role overload** is what happens when the role demands more than the person can perform. Asking a new salesperson to make the same types of presentations to high-level accounts that a veteran would make could cause role overload.

In general, the best way to handle role stress is to increase role accuracy (see Exhibit 17.11 for specific ideas). When the problem is role ambiguity, simply asking for further instruction or reviewing training materials may be helpful. Coaching and other management support can also be requested. Role conflict and role ambiguity require prioritizing activities. In the example of the salesperson who feels stress due to conflict between the customer's and the manager's demands,

Exhibit 17.11
Reducing Role Stress

Prioritize: Set your own priorities so that when different people place conflicting expectations on you, your preset priorities determine where your actions will go.

Seek support: Enlist support of your priorities from your spouse, your manager, and other key people. By focusing on goals and priorities, you can reduce conflict over specific activities.

Reset expectations: By prioritizing and seeking support, you can reset expectations of various constituencies so that they are in harmony. Communicate and gain agreement on what you are capable of doing so that others' expectations of you are realistic.

Act and move on: Once you have made a decision to act, don't dwell on the conflict. Act and move on.

the salesperson must decide whose needs will be met. Once that decision is made, further stress can be avoided by refusing to dwell on the conflict. Note that the conflict is still there (both parties have conflicting demands), but the effect on the salesperson is minimized.

In either case a strong partnership with the sales manager can greatly aid in reducing stress. When a partnership is formed between a sales manager and a salesperson, the salesperson has a better understanding of the demands of the job, which activities should receive priority, and how the job should be performed. Partners also have access to more resources and more information, which can help remove some of the organizational constraints that can bring about stress.[20]

Strong sales skills can also reduce feelings of stress. Mastery of the job will reduce feelings of stress because the salesperson is in control of the situation.

SELLING YOURSELF

This entire chapter is about selling yourself throughout your career. Here we focus on some aspects specific to college students looking for a career.

College students may not realize the competition they face. That company is interviewing not only at your school, but also probably at three or four others. At each school it may talk to 15 students, or about 75 total, all for one position. In addition, recruiters get hundreds and sometimes thousand of résumés if they also post the job on the Internet. The key is to make yourself stand out and still be truthful.

Keeping the résumé simple is one way to get noticed. According to Eric Ruiz, CEO of SalesJobs.com, one mistake college students make is to put in too much detail. "All they want to know is if you can sell and what kind of numbers you've produced. For recent graduates, that's just a matter of putting the right spin on your part-time job at the local burger shack; instead of saying you 'worked the order window,' write that your shift had the highest sales numbers of any shift, or that you increased ice cream sales by 6 percent by suggesting a weekly 'buy one get one half-off' day."[21]

When responding to a posting on the Internet, don't just cut and paste your résumé into an online form. Special formatting may not come across properly when the recruiter looks at it online unless the file is saved as rich text. Similarly, don't use an uncommon software format that few recruiters may have. Your résumé may come across as dots, blocks, and zeroes.

Ruiz also suggests that you don't write a cover letter for each online posting. "Writing a cover letter does not help you in the sales industry. The people reading your résumé are HR professionals and sales recruiters; they're generally overworked, and find cover letters superfluous. Again, they're only interested in seeing hard data regarding what you've sold, whom you sold it to, and what numbers you produced. They are focused on your previous performance because being successful in sales requires such a specialized skill set," says Ruiz.

He suggests creating an individually tailored version of your résumé for each industry in which you're seeking employment, emphasizing knowledge and experience that would transfer to different industries. For example, if you're working in food and beverage sales but you want to get into medical equipment sales, write that you "have a large percentage of hospital accounts" and are "familiar with the purchasing staff at all the local hospitals" and that you've "sold to doctors before."

E-mail addresses like *myvixen* and *partystupid* may be fine in college but not when you're looking for a job. "E-mail addresses should be professional— first name, last name, and a number is fine," notes Ruiz. While Ruiz recognizes that many people apply for sales jobs, "It's the little things, like a follow-up e-mail address, that can help you get that dream job." Once you create a professional address, be sure to check it often, don't change it again (some companies report being unable to track down a good candidate), and don't let the mailbox fill up.

And clean up your Myspace and Facebook pages. Many companies regularly review these pages before making a hiring decision. Similarly, create a professional voice mail message. It's time to get professional!

SUMMARY

A sales career offers many opportunities for growth and personal development, but that career has to start somewhere. That is the purpose of the job search: to find a good match between what you need and have to offer and what a company needs and has to offer.

To achieve a match that results in mutual satisfaction, you must first understand who you are—specifically what you need and what you have to offer. You can ask yourself a number of questions to stimulate your thinking about the type of person you are and what you will need from a sales position. In addition, as you review your experiences in school, work, and other activities, you can identify the skills and characteristics that you have to offer.

Finding industries and companies with the characteristics you desire will require you to apply your marketing research skills. The library contains many sources of information that will help you. Personal sources can also be useful in providing information as well as leads for interviews, as can the Internet.

Sources for job interviews include the campus placement office, personal contacts, and advertisements. Résumés are personal brochures that help sell a candidate. Writing effective cover letters will help you get interviews off campus, while the interview itself is similar to a sales call. Plan questions that demonstrate your knowledge of and interest in the company. Also, plan to ask for information that will help you make your decision. Follow up after the interview to demonstrate your desire and perseverance.

You are the person in the company to whom your career means the most. Therefore, you must actively manage your own career. Set career goals that are compatible with family and personal objectives. Keeping the reasons for these career goals in front of you will enable you to make better decisions.

Learn the job you have now. You may someday manage people who have this job; the better you know it, the better you will be at managing it. To become a manager, you must first be a manager. Learn the manager's job as well and volunteer for activities and projects that will let you demonstrate your management ability.

Stress can occur in any job. Situational stress is short term, whereas felt stress is longer term. For many people, the key to managing stress is to reduce the influence of stressors because the causes of stress often cannot be eliminated.

Sales offers a challenging and exciting career. The opportunities are so varied that almost anyone can probably fit into some sales position. Even if you choose a career in another field, take advantage of the material in this chapter. You should find these job search and career management tips helpful in any field. Good luck!

KEY TERMS

application form   461
assessment center   463
conventional résumé   463
disguised interview   471
felt stress   480
functional résumé   464
greeter   472
group interview   472
interview   462
KSAs   475

panel interview   472
portfolio   471
references   462
role ambiguity   480
role conflict   480
role overload   480
role stress   480
situational stress   479
stress interview   472
tests   462

ETHICS PROBLEMS

1. You are interviewing for your dream job. Suddenly the interviewer notices your wedding ring and compliments you on it. But then he says, "You know, this job requires a lot of travel. What is your spouse going to say to that?" You answer the question, and he replies, "That's great, now, when you don't have kids. You don't have kids, do you? Because it is tough to be successful if you don't get the travel done." What do you do? What would you do if the interviewer said, "You know, handling conflict is an important part of this job. Describe a conflict you've had with your spouse and how you handled it."

2. Some people recommend signing up for as many interviews as possible, reasoning that the experience will be helpful when you find a company with a job you really want. (And who knows? You might find a job you like.) Is this practice ethical? Why or why not? If you answer that it depends, what does it depend on?

QUESTIONS AND PROBLEMS

1. What would you do differently if you were being interviewed by an amiable, a driver, an analytical, or an expressive? What about a panel interview with one driver and one amiable? One analytical and one expressive?

2. Spencer Ryan began his career in a small but rapidly growing company (look back at the opening profile). What were the advantages to his start? What do you think he may have missed out on by not working for a big, well-known company? Would you prefer to start out with a small or a large company, and why?

3. Now that you are at the end of the book, what traits do you have that would make you successful in sales? Are there specific industries or sales positions to which you are better suited? Why? Compare your list to that in Exhibit 17.2. How do you stack up? How would you prove that you have those traits?

4. Some interviews are conducted over the phone or by videoconference. What do you think is important and different about these types of interviews compared to face-to-face interviews? Do you think these difference carry over into selling by phone versus in person? Would you consider an inside sales position? Why or why not?

5. Reread "Building Partnerships 17.1." If a potential employer asked you today to describe your brand, what would it be? How do you make yourself memorable? What changes do you need to make to your social media presence to prepare for transitioning to a professional career and to build your personal brand?

6. Answer the questions in Exhibit 17.6 as you would in a sales job interview.

7. Your summer internship in a sales job was a bad experience. Your biggest complaint was that the sales manager seemed incompetent. Despite this negative experience, you like sales, so you are interviewing for a sales position. What would you say if asked why you do not seek full-time employment with the summer internship firm?

8. One recruiter called a professor to check on a student that the professor referred. The recruiter said, "You gave this student my name last Wednesday and now it is Tuesday. Does this delay signal a lack of interest?" How would you answer that if the recruiter was asking you the question and you were the student? Why would a recruiter comment on the time it took to call? (Note that this is based on an actual situation.)

9. You are in an interview, and you think this is your dream job. How would you secure commitment? What would you say different in the first interview if it is a screening interview on campus versus the fourth interview at company headquarters? Is securing commitment more or less important for sales positions than for other types of positions?

10. What stresses do you have now? How do you deal with stress? What healthy ways to handle stress do you use? What are some ways you respond to stress that may not be so healthy?

CASE PROBLEMS

case **17.1**

Choices, Choices!

While studying for the final exam for the sales class, a group of students began talking about jobs. "I just don't think I could do sales," said Amanda. "I just don't think I could either go cold calling or try to call people on the phone I don't know and try to sell them something. But I like working with people."

"I think I could," replied Bill. "I just don't know what I want to sell. It has to be something I believe in." Murmurs of agreement followed. "And I want to have something different every day—I don't think I could sit behind a desk with the same old routine."

"I'm more like Amanda," said Emily. "I don't think I could do a lot of cold calling, but I'd like to be in sales anyway. Maybe something where they come to me or I see the same people. I'm good with people once I get to know them."

"I heard a lot of companies start you out on the phones first," Roger noted. "Like IBM. You start out on the phones, and if you're good, then you get to go out into the field."

Questions

1. What kinds of jobs would Bill be suited for? Emily? Can Emily's fears be overcome, or should she just find a job that doesn't involve cold calling?

2. Using the Web, find a position for each student to apply for. Print the ad and then on the same sheet (write on the back if you need to) justify your choice.

3. Pick one of the four positions you used in question 2 for yourself. Why is that a good fit for you?

case **17.2**

Mandy Baker's Interview

At 8:45 a.m., Mandy Baker arrived at her campus placement center for a 9:00 interview. She was surprised to be greeted by Caleb Washington, whom she had known in a marketing class. This conversation followed:

CALEB: Mandy, good to see you! I see that you are interviewing with us today. [shakes Mandy's hand and offers her a chair in the lobby]

MANDY: Caleb! Hi, how are you? I didn't know you were with HealthSouth. I've got the 9:00 spot.

CALEB: Great! I started with HealthSouth right after graduation, and it has been a great six months. Tell me, are you interviewing with many medical firms or just with HealthSouth?

MANDY: I'm very interested in pharmaceuticals, but I know that HealthSouth is doing real well. So I thought that I should consider all medical companies. One of the physicians at a sports medicine center recommended

HealthSouth. She said that your company does a lot of the rehabilitation services for the NFL as well as here at the university.

CALEB: That's right, we do! I'm glad to hear that others agree we are one of the best. [leans a little closer] Look, just relax in the interview. HealthSouth really likes to get people from State, and I'm sure you will do well. [looks up at the entrance of an older woman] Oh, here's Erin Rogers, my sales manager. She'll be interviewing you today. Erin, here's an old friend of mine, Mandy Baker.

ERIN: [stepping forward and offering her hand]: Mandy, it's nice to meet you.

MANDY: [shaking her hand firmly]: It's nice to meet you, too, Ms. Rogers. [turning to Caleb] Caleb, it was good to see you again. Perhaps we'll talk some more later. [Mandy and Erin seat themselves in the interviewing room; Erin has her iPad open with a small keyboard]

ERIN: Tell me about yourself, Mandy.

MANDY: I'm the oldest of three children, and we were raised in a small town in the eastern part of the state. As a kid, I was very interested in soccer and wanted to be an Olympic soccer player. But an ankle injury ended my soccer career. Still, I learned a lot about self-discipline and the importance of hard work to achieve success, and I am still involved in soccer as a coach for a youth team. In fact, I rehabbed my ankle at a HealthSouth center. Anyway, I chose State because it offers a strong marketing program. Marketing, and sales especially, seems to me to be a place where your success is directly related to your efforts. And I believe that more strongly now that I have taken the sales class here at State.

ERIN [types "h"]: I see. [momentary silence as she finishes the notes, then looks up] Tell me about a time when you were the leader of a group and things were not going your way. Perhaps it looked as if the group wasn't going to meet your objectives. What did you do?

MANDY: Let's see. There was the time when we were working on a group project for my marketing research class. Understand, though, that we had not elected a formal leader or anything. But no one in the group really wanted to do the project; everyone thought that research was boring. So at a group meeting, I suggested we talk about what we liked to do in marketing. After all, we were all marketing majors. Each person talked about why he or she had chosen marketing. Then I framed the project around what they wanted out of marketing. When they looked at it as a marketing project instead of a research project, it became something they wanted to do.

ERIN: Did you get an A?

MANDY: No, we got a B+. But more important, we were the only group that had fun, and I think we learned more as a result.

ERIN: I see. [momentary silence as she types] Tell me about your sales class—have you had any opportunity to use what you learned, and, if so, how'd you do?

MANDY: You mean other than this interview? [Erin smiles] I found that I use the questioning skills to learn about potential sorority members. These skills really helped me understand what they wanted in a sorority and whether we were a good fit. And the presentation skills I use with every in-class presentation, but I've not had a sales job, if that's what you mean.

The interview went on for nearly 30 minutes. Mandy thought she had done fairly well. She stopped in the lobby to write down her impressions and record Erin's answers to questions about the company. She smiled at Caleb, who was talking to another applicant.

Questions

1. What did Mandy do right? Why was that right? What did she do wrong? Why was that wrong?
2. What was Caleb's purpose at the interview? What do you think Caleb could tell Erin about Mandy?
3. HealthSouth is a publicly traded company. What sources of information could Mandy use to learn about the company? What information should she expect to get from those sources?

ROLE PLAY CASE

Congratulations, you just got promoted! Now you have to replace yourself by hiring a college graduate to take over your sales territory. Given everything you've learned about NetSuite this semester and what you know about sales, take a few minutes to identify the three most important features a salesperson should bring to the job and the questions you'd ask to determine if the candidate had those features. Then take turns interviewing each other in your group. There is no candidate information to be provided—each student will portray himself or herself when playing the candidate role.

ADDITIONAL REFERENCES

Alkhateeb, Fadi M., Patricia Baidoo, Marija Mikulskis Cavana, Danielle Gill, and Amanda Howell. "Is Certification for Pharmaceutical Sales Representatives Necessary?" *International Journal of Pharmaceutical and Healthcare Marketing* 5, no. 3 (2011), pp. 222–33.

Briggs, Elten, Fernando Jaramillo, and William A. Weeks. "Perceived Barriers to Career Advancement and Organizational Commitment in Sales." *Journal of Business Research* 65, no. 7 (July 2012), pp. 937–49.

Bristow, Denny, Douglas Amyx, Stephen B. Castleberry, and James J. Cochran. "A Cross-Generational Comparison of Motivational Factors in a Sales Career among Gen-X and Gen-Y College Students." *Journal of Personal Selling and Sales Management* 31, no. 1 (Winter 2011), p. 77.

Eesley, Dale T., and Phani Tej Adidam. "Mavenness and Salespeople Success: An Empirical Investigation." *Journal of Applied Business Research* 28, no. 5 (September/October 2012), pp. 903–12.

Hamwi, G. Alexander, Brian N. Rutherford, and James S. Boles. "Reducing Emotional Exhaustion and Increasing Organizational Support." *Journal of Business and Industrial Marketing* 26, no. 1 (2011), pp. 4–13.

Hawass, Hisham Hamid. "Committed Salesforce: An Investigation into Personality Traits." *International Journal of Business and Management* 7, no. 6 (March 2012), pp. 147–60.

Joo, Baek-Kyoo (Brian), and Sunyoung Park. "Career Satisfaction, Organizational Commitment, and Turnover Intention: The Effects of Goal Orientation, Organizational Learning Culture and Developmental Feedback." *Leadership and Organization Development Journal* 31, no. 6 (2010), pp. 482–500.

Karakaya, Fahri, Charles Quigley, and Frank Bingham. "A Cross-National Investigation of Student Intentions to Pursue a Sales Career." *Journal of Marketing Education* 33, no. 1 (April 2011), p. 18.

Lewin, Jeffrey E., and Jeffrey K. Sager. "An Investigation of the Influence of Coping Resources in Salespersons' Emotional Exhaustion." *Industrial Marketing Management* 38, no. 7 (October 2009), pp. 796–811.

Mallin, Michael L., Edward O'Donnell, and Michael Y. Hu. "The Role of Uncertainty and Sales Control in the Development of Sales Manager Trust." *Journal of Business and Industrial Marketing* 25, no. 1 (2010), pp. 30–42.

Marschke, Eleanor, Robert Preziosi, and William J. Harrington. "How Sales Personnel View the Relationship between Job Satisfaction and Spirituality in the Workplace." *Journal of Organizational Culture, Communication and Conflict* 15, no. 2 (2011), pp. 71–110.

Mayo, Michael, and Michael L. Mallin. "The Impact of Sales Failure on Attributions Made by 'Resource-Challenged' and 'Resource-Secure' Salespeople." *Journal of Marketing Theory and Practice* 18, no. 3 (Summer 2010), pp. 233–47.

Murray, Lynn M., and Arthur K. Fischer. "Staffing a New Sales Force: A Human Resource Management Case Study." *Journal of Business Case Studies* 7, no. 4 (July/August 2011), pp. 1–7.

Onvernah, Vincent. "The Effects of Coaching on Salespeople's Attitudes and Behaviors: A Contingency Approach." *European Journal of Marketing* 43, no. 7/8 (2009), pp. 938–51.

Rutherford, Brian N., Yujie Wei, JungKun Park, and Won-Moo Hur. "Increasing Job Performance and Reducing Turnover: An Examination of Female Chinese Salespeople." *Journal* of *Marketing Theory and Practice* 20, no. 4 (Fall 2012), pp. 423–36.

Sarathy, P. Sanjay. "Salespeople's Performance and Change in Career in Their Maintenance Stage." *International Journal of Organizational Innovation (Online)* 4, no. 3 (Winter 2012), pp. 216–34.

Schultz, Roberta J., Charles H. Schwepker Jr., and David J. Good. "Social Media Usage: An Investigation of B2B Salespeople." *American Journal of Business* 27, no. 2 (2012), pp. 174–94.

Shannahan, Kirby L., Alan J. Bush, and Rachelle J. Shannahan. "Are Your Salespeople Coachable? How Salesperson Coachability, Trait Competitiveness, and Transformational Leadership Enhance Sales Performance." *Journal of the Academy of Marketing Science* 41, no. 1 (January 2013), pp. 40–54.

Spillan, John E., Jeff W. Totten, and Manmohan D. Chaubey. "Exploring Personal Selling as a Career Option: A Case Study of the Perceptions of African-American Students." *Academy of Marketing Studies Journal, Special Issue* 2, no. 15 (2011), pp. 93–106.

Valenzuela, Leslier M., Jay P. Mulki, and J. Fernando Jaramillo. "Impact of Customer Orientation, Inducements and Ethics on Loyalty to the Firm: Customers' Perspective." *Journal of Business Ethics* 93, no. 2 (May 2010) pp. 277–93.

The Partnership Process

chapter **6**

PROSPECTING

SOME QUESTIONS ANSWERED IN THIS CHAPTER ARE

- Why is prospecting important for effective selling?
- Are all sales leads good prospects? What are the characteristics of a qualified prospect?
- How can prospects be identified? How can social media be used?
- How can the organization's promotional program be used in prospecting?
- How can an effective lead qualification and management system aid a salesperson?
- How can a salesperson overcome a reluctance to prospect?

2

PART

PROFILE

PROFILE My name is Angela Bertero, and I graduated from Texas State University–San Marcos in 2008. I earned my master's in business administration and bachelor of business administration in marketing. While at Texas State University, I served as president of our national championship Students in Free Enterprise team and won quarter finalist at the National Collegiate Sales Competition, both of which were advised by Vicki West. Mrs. West introduced me to Liberty Mutual Insurance, which is where I was hired as a licensed sales representative.

Liberty Mutual offers a full line of high-quality insurance products and services. As the main contact for the company, it is my responsibility to develop and maintain client relationships as well as identify prospective customers and promote Liberty Mutual products.

While retention is key to a business's success, prospecting for new clients is crucial to growing my book of business. I have found success using the following methods of prospecting: referrals from satisfied clients and business partners, networking, and cross-selling to current clients. Referrals are by far the most important source of prospects.

Successful prospecting isn't about running around town and meeting everyone you can. It's about identifying your target market and knowing how to communicate that to your existing customers and referral partners. To do this, I often review the services I have provided for my clients and ask them if they know anyone in a similar situation that I may be able to help. I tell all of my clients that the greatest compliment I can receive is a referral from them.

I also work closely with a variety of referral partners to fill my pipeline with prospective new clients: mortgage brokers, realtors, financial advisors, auto dealerships, bankers, employers, school districts, and alumni associations, to name a few.

It is important that my referral partners know what a good prospect looks like to me so that the leads they send me are actually qualified referrals.

My networking group, Business Networking International (BNI), has given me the opportunity to give weekly educational moments to other professionals in different industries, or, as I like to call them, my marketing team. When I first joined BNI, I expected—or hoped for—immediate results. I have since learned that building personal relationships while becoming a trusted advisor to those around me is critical to building my network over time. After just a year, though, the partnerships I have made are a huge part of my weekly prospecting. We meet once a week to share ideas, help grow each other's businesses, and fill each other's pipelines with prospects. Then, we meet one to one to learn more about how we can work together for a mutually beneficial partnership.

To be a successful networker, make an effort to understand other people's businesses and connect with them on a personal level. Always follow up and thank your networking contact for the leads they send you and, if you can, send them leads as well.

Visit our Web site at:
www.libertymutual.com

An important activity for nearly all salespeople is locating qualified prospects. This chapter provides resources to help you prospect effectively and efficiently.

THE IMPORTANCE OF PROSPECTING

Prospecting, the process of locating potential customers for a product or service, is the most important activity that many salespeople do.[1]

Why is it so important? Salespeople must find new customers to replace those that switch to competitors, go bankrupt, move out of the territory, merge with noncustomers, or decide to do without a product or service. A salesperson often needs to prospect even in existing accounts because of downsizing, job changes, or retirements of buyers. Sales trainer Joe Girard uses a Ferris wheel metaphor to describe the important process of adding new customers (loading new accounts onto the Ferris wheel) to replace customers you lose (people getting off the Ferris wheel). Without replacing lost accounts, your Ferris wheel will soon be running with no one on board.

Of course, prospecting is more important in some selling fields than in others. For example, the office products salesperson, stockbroker, financial advisor, or real estate sales representative with no effective prospecting plan usually doesn't last long in the business. Sales positions such as these may require 100 contacts to get 10 prospects who will listen to presentations, out of which one person will buy. Each sale, then, represents a great deal of prospecting. It is also important in these fields to prospect continually. Some sales trainers relate this process to your car's gas tank: You don't wait until the gas gauge is on empty before you fill up!

Some sales positions require less emphasis on locating new contacts. For example, a Lockheed Martin salesperson assigned exclusively to sell the F-16 tactical fighter jet to Taiwan, South Korea, Greece, and Singapore would not spend any time trying to locate new governments to call on. For these types of sales positions, prospecting as we normally think of it (that is, looking for new leads) is not an important part of the sales process. Nevertheless, salespeople cannot ignore these obvious leads, as the next section discusses. Salespeople still have to assess whether leads are good prospects.[2]

CHARACTERISTICS OF A GOOD PROSPECT

Prospecting actually begins with locating a **lead** (sometimes called a "suspect")—a potential prospect that may or may not have what it takes to be a true prospect. Some salespeople mistakenly consider every lead a prospect without first taking the time to see whether these people really provide an opportunity to make a sale.

To avoid that mistake, the salesperson must **qualify the lead.** Qualifying is the process of determining whether a lead is in fact a **prospect.** If the salesperson determines that the lead is a good candidate for making a sale, that person or organization is no longer considered a lead and instead is called a prospect. Note that many leads do not become prospects. Exhibit 6.1 illustrates this process. One thousand leads might be needed, for example, to generate 200 prospects, of which only 15 might become prospects. Some companies break

Exhibit 6.1
The Sales Funnel

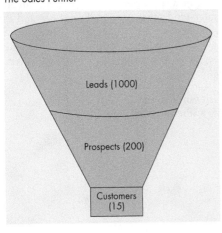

Leads (1000)

Prospects (200)

Customers (15)

down this **sales funnel** into more levels, depending on how complex the purchase process and sales cycle are.

The following five questions are used by many organizations to help qualify leads and pinpoint the good prospects:

DOES A WANT OR NEED EXIST?

Research has supplied no infallible answers to why customers buy, but it has found many reasons. As we pointed out in Chapter 3, customers buy to satisfy practical needs as well as intangible needs, such as prestige or aesthetics.

By using high-pressure tactics, sales attempts may be made to those who do not need or really want a product. Such sales benefit no one. The buyer will resent making the purchase, and a potential long-term customer will be lost.

DOES THE LEAD HAVE THE ABILITY TO PAY?

For example, the commercial real estate agent usually checks the financial status of each client to determine the price range of office buildings to show. A client with annual profits of $100,000 and cash resources of $75,000 may be a genuine prospect for office space in the $30,000 to $50,000 annual rental bracket. An agent would be wasting time, however, by showing this client space listed at $100,000 annual rent. The client may have a desire for the more expensive setting, but the client is still not a real prospect for the higher-priced office space if he or she doesn't have the resources to pay for it.

Ability to pay includes both cash and credit. Many companies subscribe to a credit-rating service offered by firms such as Dun & Bradstreet. Salespeople use information from these sources to determine the financial status and credit rating of a lead. They can also qualify leads with information obtained from local credit agencies, consumer credit agencies such as Experian, noncompetitive salespeople, and the Better Business Bureau. Salespeople are sometimes surprised at their leads' credit ratings. Some big-name firms have poor ratings.

DOES THE LEAD HAVE THE AUTHORITY TO BUY?

Knowing who has the authority to make a purchase saves the salesperson time and effort and results in a higher percentage of closed sales. As discussed in Chapter 3, many people can be involved in a purchase decision, and it can be unclear who has the authority to buy.

Because of downsizing, some firms are delegating their purchasing tasks to outside vendors. These service vendors, called **systems integrators,** have the authority to buy products and services on behalf of the delegating firm. Systems integrators usually assume complete responsibility for a project from its beginning to follow-up servicing. An example would be Lockheed Martin acting as a systems integrator for the complete mail-processing system of a new postal sorting facility in Germany. In that scenario every potential vendor would actually be selling to Lockheed Martin, not to the German government. When systems integrators are involved, salespeople need to delineate clearly who has the authority to purchase. Sometimes the overall buyer (the German government in this example) will retain veto power over potential vendors.

CAN THE LEAD BE APPROACHED FAVORABLY?

Some leads simply are not accessible to the salesperson. For example, the president of an international bank, a major executive of a large manufacturing company, or the senior partner in a well-established law firm normally would not normally be accessible to a young college graduate starting out as a financial advisor for Edward Jones. Getting an interview with these people may be so difficult and the chances of making a sale may be so small that the sales representative should eliminate them as possible prospects.

IS THE LEAD ELIGIBLE TO BUY?

Eligibility is an equally important factor in finding a genuine prospect. For example, a salesperson who works for a firm that requires a large minimum order should not call on leads that could never order in such volume. Likewise, a representative who sells exclusively to wholesalers should be certain the individuals he or she calls on are actually wholesalers, not retailers.

Another factor that may determine eligibility for a particular salesperson is the geographic location of the prospect. Most companies operate on the basis of **exclusive sales territories,** meaning that a particular salesperson can sell only to certain prospects (such as doctors in only a three-county area) and not to other prospects. A salesperson working for such a company must consider whether the prospect is eligible, based on location or customer type, to buy from him or her.

Salespeople should also avoid targeting leads already covered by their corporate headquarters. Large customers or potential customers that are handled exclusively by corporate executives are often called **house accounts.** For example, if Marriott Hotels considers Ingersoll Rand a house account, a Marriott Hotel salesperson (who sets up events and conventions at the hotel) located in New York City should not try to solicit business from one of Ingersoll Rand's divisions located in New York City. Instead all Ingersoll Rand business would be handled by a Marriott executive at Marriott corporate headquarters.

OTHER CRITERIA

Leads that meet the five criteria are generally considered excellent prospects by most companies. Some sellers, however, add other criteria. For example, DEI Management Group instructs its salespeople to classify leads by their likelihood of buying.

Some firms look at the timing of purchase to determine whether a lead is really a good prospect. Relevant questions to consider include these: When does the prospect's contract with our competitor expire? Is a purchase decision really pending? How do we know? Still other firms look at the long-term potential of developing a partnering relationship with a lead. Here are some questions to ponder: What is the climate at the organization—is it looking to develop partnering relationships with suppliers? Do any of our competitors already have a partnering relationship there?

The Corporate Executive Board takes an entirely different approach to prospecting and qualifying leads, which they term **insight selling.**[3] Under this approach, salespeople evaluate prospects who do not necessarily have a clear understanding of what they need but are in a state of flux and have been shown to be quite agile in making changes (that is, they are able and willing to act quickly when a compelling case is made to them). This approach also encourages salespeople to interact with people in the buying firm who are skeptical rather than friendly information providers and then coach these skeptical decision makers how to buy the seller's solution. Why this approach? Proponents claim that buyers today already know a great deal about the marketplace and understand many of their options and that salespeople who follow the proposed approach are more successful in gaining commitment.

HOW AND WHERE TO OBTAIN PROSPECTS

Prospecting sources and methods vary for different types of selling. A sales representative selling corrugated containers for Citation Box & Paper Company, for example, may use a system different from what banking or office products

Exhibit 6.2
Overview of Common
Sources of Leads

Source	How Used
Satisfied customers	Current and previous customers are contacted for additional business and leads.
Endless chain	Salesperson attempts to secure at least one additional lead from each person he or she interviews.
Networking	Salesperson uses personal relationships with those who are connected and cooperative to secure leads.
Center of influence	Salesperson cultivates well-known, influential people in the territory who are willing to supply lead information.
Social media	Salesperson uses online tools like LinkedIn, Facebook, and Twitter to prospect for new customers and maintain contact with existing customers.
Other Internet uses	Salesperson uses Web sites, e-mail, listservs, bulletin boards, forums, roundtables, and newsgroups to secure leads.
Ads, direct mail, catalogs, and publicity	Salespeople use these forms of promotional activities to generate leads.
Shows, fairs, and merchandise markets	Salespeople use trade shows, conventions, fairs, and merchandise markets for lead generation.
Webinars and seminars	Salespeople use seminars and online webinars to generate leads.
Lists and directories	Salesperson uses secondary data sources, which can be free or fee-based.
Databases and data mining	Salespeople use sophisticated data analysis software and the company's databases to generate leads.
Cold calling	Salesperson tries to generate leads by calling on totally unfamiliar organizations.
Spotters	Salesperson pays someone for lead information.
Telemarketing	Salesperson uses phone and/or telemarketing staff to generate leads.
Sales letters	Salesperson writes personal letters to potential leads.
Other sources	Salesperson uses noncompeting salespeople, people in his or her own firm, friends, and so on to secure information.

salespeople would use. Exhibit 6.2 presents an overview of some of the most common lead-generating methods. Note that there is some overlap among the methods.

SATISFIED CUSTOMERS

Satisfied customers, particularly those who are truly partners with the seller, are the most effective sources for leads. In fact some trainers argue that successful salespeople should be getting about 75 percent of their new business through referrals from customers, and firms are now encouraged to calculate **customer referral value,** which is the monetary value of the these referrals as well as the costs to get and maintain the referrals.[4] Referrals of leads in the same industry are particularly useful because the salesperson already understands the unique needs of this type of organization (If you have sold to a bank already, you have a better understanding of banks' needs). Referrals in some cultures, like Japan, are even more important than they are in North America.

To maximize the usefulness of satisfied customers, salespeople should follow several logical steps. First they should make a list of potential references (customers who might provide leads) from among their most satisfied customers. This task will be much easier if the salespeople have maintained an accurate and detailed database of customers. Some current customers could be called **promoters** or **evangelists**. These are your most loyal customers who not only keep buying from you but also urge their friends and associate to do the same.[5] Next

Salespeople use referral events to generate leads.

salespeople should decide what they would like each customer to do (such as have the customer write a personal letter or e-mail message of introduction to a specific prospect, see whether the customer would be willing to take phone inquiries, have the customer directly contact prospects, or have the customer provide a generic letter of reference or write a recommendation for you on LinkedIn). Finally salespeople should ask the customer for the names of leads and for the specific type of help she or he can provide.

Salespeople sometimes gather leads at **referral events,** which are gatherings designed to allow current customers to introduce prospects to the salesperson. For example, a Merrill Lynch financial advisor might invite a group of current clients to a ski resort for a weekend. The skiing weekend is free for clients who bring one or more prospects. Other events that salespeople use include sporting events, theater visits, dinner at a nice restaurant, a short cruise, or golf lessons by a pro. The key is that the gathering should be fun and sociable and a way for a salesperson to gather leads. The name of a lead provided by either a customer or a prospect, known as a **referred lead,** is generally considered the most successful type of lead.

Satisfied customers not only provide leads but also are usually prospects for additional sales. This situation is sometimes referred to as **selling deeper** to a current customer. Salespeople should never overlook this profitable opportunity. Sales to existing customers often result in more profits than do sales to new customers. For example, if a midsized company increased its customer retention by just 5 percent, its profits would double in only 10 years. Customers that buy a lot from the selling firm at a lower service cost are sometimes affectionately referred to as "star clients."[6] Chapter 15 explores selling deeper more fully. Of course it is also possible that a customer could be the other kind of a referrer—one who tells others about how poorly you or your product performed. This **negative referral** is not the kind of referral a salesperson likes to get, and every effort should be made to ensure that the customer is satisfied and stays satisfied with the solution offered by the salesperson. This also will be discussed in more detail in Chapter 14.

Finally, salespeople who leave one company can bring their sales clients with them to the new company for which they work. Phil Birt did that when he was laid off from Seagate Technology during the recent recession and went to work for Bell Micro. At Bell Micro, Birt grew the revenue of one customer by $400,000 in four months and that of another customer by $100,000 in a single month.[7] Of course salespeople who change jobs must always follow the agreements signed with their first employers before transferring such business.

ENDLESS-CHAIN METHOD

In the **endless-chain method** sales representatives attempt to get at least one additional lead from each person they interview. This method works best when the source is a satisfied customer and partner; however, it may also be used even when a prospect does not buy. Exhibit 6.3 illustrates how a sales representative successfully used the endless-chain method.

NETWORKING

Networking is the utilization of personal relationships by connected and cooperating individuals for the purpose of achieving goals. In selling, networking simply

Exhibit 6.3
Example of the Endless-Chain Method of Prospecting

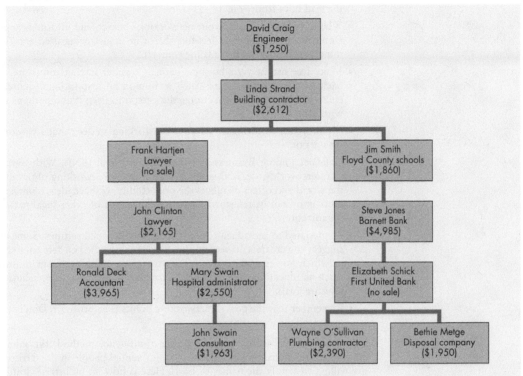

The sales representative used the endless-chain method to produce $25,690 in business (selling fax machines) within a 30-day period. All the sales resulted directly or indirectly from the first referral from an engineer to whom the sales rep had sold a mere $1,250 worth of equipment.

means establishing connections to other people and then using those networks to generate leads, gather information, generate sales, and so on. Networking can, and often does, include satisfied customers.

Networking is crucial in many selling situations.[8] For example, trying to sell in China without successful networking, called *guanxi* in China, would be disastrous.

Successful networkers offer a number of practical suggestions:[9]

- Call at least two people per day, and go to at least one networking event every week to increase your exposure and time with your contacts.

- Make a special effort to move outside your own comfort zone in a social setting. Learn to mingle with people you don't already know. One expert calls this behavior acting like a host instead of like a guest.

- Spend most of your initial conversation with a new contact talking about his or her business, not yours, and don't forget to learn about the person's nonbusiness interests.

- Follow up with your new contact on a regular basis with cards, notes of congratulations about awards or promotions, and articles and information that might help her or him.

- Whenever you receive a lead from your contact, send a handwritten, personal note thanking the person for the information, regardless of whether the lead buys from you.
- Whenever possible, send your networking contact lead information as well. Don't make your contact feel like she or he is just being used and the only thing you care about is leads for yourself.
- Make free use of your business cards. Consider having something on the back of your business card (such as humor, an inspirational quote, or an endorsement) that will encourage the person to keep it and perhaps share it with others.
- Monitor the performance of your networking to see what's working and what's not.
- Consider joining Business Network International (BNI). With over 3,600 chapters worldwide, BNI is the largest business networking organization in the world and offers members the opportunity to share ideas, contacts, and, most importantly, referrals. There are thousands of other local networking organizations.
- Be prepared to introduce yourself succinctly in social settings. Some experts suggest you create a 30-second commercial (also called an "elevator speech") in which you introduce yourself and provide some pertinent information (such as education, general work history, a significant accomplishment, and a future goal).[10]
- Remember that the goal of networking events is to prospect. Don't start trying to sell the lead at the event.

In one form of networking, the **center-of-influence method,** the salesperson cultivates a relationship with well-known, influential people in the territory who are willing to supply the names of leads. Here is how an industrial cleaning service salesperson used the center-of-influence method when meeting with a well-known and respected maintenance engineer:

Now that you've had the opportunity to learn more about me and my service, I wonder if you will do me a favor? You mentioned that it was probably the best-designed package you've ever seen. I know that as an engineer you wouldn't personally need my services, but can you think of any of your business associates who could benefit from such a plan? Does one come to mind?

thinking **it** through   Who is a center of influence for you right now? How could a salesperson who wanted to sell you something learn who your center of influence is?

In industrial sales situations the centers of influence are frequently people in important departments not directly involved in the purchase decision, such as quality control, equipment maintenance, and receiving. The salesperson keeps in close touch with these people over an extended period, solicits their help in a straightforward manner, and keeps them informed about sales that result from their aid.

The Roper Organization, which has studied centers of influence for more than 45 years, states that they are consistent in one aspect: their degree of activity. Centers of influence tend to be those who enjoy being very socially involved in their communities. And people in the community not only trust these individuals but also seek their advice.

GENERATING LEADS THROUGH SOCIAL MEDIA

With the enormous presence that social media has in today's society, it is important for salespeople to consider their use. Here are a few quick yet astonishing facts about social media:

- Facebook has more weekly traffic than Google.

- If Facebook were a country, it would be the third largest in the world.

- The Ford Explorer launch on Facebook generated more traffic than a Super Bowl ad.

- Ninety percent of consumers trust peer recommendations, and social media is key in this. Only 14 percent of consumers trust advertisements.

- There are close to a billion active monthly users of Facebook.

- There are more than 465 million Twitter accounts with 1 million more being added each day and 175 million tweets being tweeted daily.

- LinkedIn has two new members joining every second.

- There are over 57 million LinkedIn users in the United States alone.

When used correctly, social media has the potential to be an integral part of an organizations prospecting strategies.

Sources: Jake Bialer, "WATCH: Amazing Social Media Statistics," *Huffington Post*, August 6, 2011, http://www.huffingtonpost.com/2011/06/08/social-media-statistics-2011_n_873116.html, as viewed September 7, 2012; "Social Networking Watch: News on the Social Networking and Social Media Industry," All Social Networking Statistics, April 30, 2012, http://www.socialnetworkingwatch.com/all_social_networking_statistics, as viewed August 21, 2012.

One true story illustrates the method's use. A Xerox representative found that decision makers from several companies would get together from time to time. These accounts formed a **buying community**: a small, informal group of people in similar positions, often from several companies, who communicate regularly, both socially and professionally. The salesperson also found that one particular decision maker in that group, or community, would share the results of any sales call with the other members of the community. Thus a call on that account had the power of seven calls. By working carefully with this center of influence, the salesperson closed nine orders from the seven accounts, with sales that totaled more than $450,000.

SOCIAL MEDIA

Social media has been defined as "the technological component of the communication, transaction, and relationship building functions of a business that leverages the network of customers and prospects to promote value co-creation."[11] As described in Chapter 4, salespeople are using social media, like LinkedIn, Facebook, blogs, and Twitter, to communicate with buyers. Given the growing importance of these channels (see "Sales Technology 6.1"), these types of tools can also be used to prospect for new customers.

Salespeople should first determine their overall approach for using social media, involving either a push or a pull strategy.[12] As salespeople, are we trying to push ourselves, our companies, and our products to prospects? If so, then the seller can use social media tactics, such as live question-and-answer sessions on the seller's Facebook page, using LinkedIn to gather prospect names, and so forth. As salespeople, are we trying to pull customers toward us and our products? If so, tactics might include the use of seller blogs, wikis, video blogs (called vlogs), microblogs like Twitter, and so forth.

Here are some social networking tips from Mike Krause,[13] a pro on the use of social networking for salespeople, and others:[14]

- Go to the prospect's Web site. Read blogs posted there and register yourself to receive any type of material the prospect might occasionally send out.
- Go to LinkedIn and search for the company and the person you want to call on. Try to get connected to the individual through a connection you already have.
- Once you are connected, review the prospect's LinkedIn page carefully. Look for things you have in common. See what organizations and groups your prospect belongs to or follows. Follow the same procedure for other social networking sites like Facebook, as well as specialized networking sites like CFOZone (www.cfozone.com), and make sure you tailor messages to fit the mission and tone of each specific networking site.
- Follow the prospect (both the company and the individual you will be calling on) on Twitter. Sometimes a prospect won't have a Twitter account showing on the company Web site, so you will need to do a company search on Twitter to find the prospect (search.twitter.com). Also, see whom your prospect is following on Twitter.
- Search for special interest groups that your prospect belongs to on Twitter, and read those tweets.
- If the prospect decides to follow you on Twitter, send her or him a direct message. If the prospect doesn't follow you on Twitter, you can still send a message by commenting on one of his or her tweets using Twitter's @ feature.
- Search for the prospect and the company on other networking sites like YouTube and SlideShare.
- If your company has just launched a new product or service, ask users what they think about it via Twitter. Or ask any question. Twitter is great for getting opinions from people.
- Upload your contacts from your e-mail program (like Microsoft Outlook and Gmail) to LinkedIn and Facebook to search for more connections.
- Use Find Friends in Facebook to find other people whom you might be able to add to your network.
- Look at your friends' lists of friends. Invite them to link to you or ask your friend to initiate this linking.
- Start a group page for your product in Facebook.
- Use Search to find groups and fan pages that might be related to your business.
- Use the search updates feature in LinkedIn and data intelligence tools like InsideView to see if prospects have secured any new business, are developing new products, and so forth.
- Create a blog that includes your opinions, educates prospects, provides news, and encourages reactions and postings from prospects. Carefully establish a personal brand identity for yourself in all social media venues.
- Follow competitors' social media postings to gather competitor intelligence.
- Monitor your social media sites for comments/postings by competitors and unsatisfied customers.
- Use the TweetDeck feature to be alerted whenever a key word (like your company name or your product) has appeared in any tweet. Use other social media monitoring tools, like HootSuite, to pick up when someone needs help or is dissatisfied.

As an example of the effectiveness of using social networking, Madeline's Catering in Rochester, New York, redesigned its Web page to fully integrate with Facebook, LinkedIn, and Twitter.[15] As a result, in only six weeks Web site traffic grew by 41 percent and phone inquiries doubled, increasing sales and profits tremendously. As another example, an employee of SoftBrands was trying to find a way to connect with the software giant SAP. The employee decided to start following the tweets of a local SAP worker, and this resulted in some small talk via tweets about sports. Eventually this moved to a face-to-face meeting with the prospect and a profitable sale.[16] As a final example, IBM has set up Web sites that allow their sales reps to create blogs with feeds tied directly to LinkedIn and Twitter.[17] IBM reps also use Twitter to provide customers information about events and news.

OTHER INTERNET USES

Successful salespeople are using their companies' Web sites, e-mail, listservs, bulletin boards, forums, roundtables, and newsgroups to connect to individuals and companies that may be interested in their products or services.

For example, John Deere, which sells construction and agriculture equipment, uses its Web site to give leads information about products, show them where the nearest dealers are located, and gather their names and addresses if they desire more information. One advantage of Web-based promotions is the number of international leads that can be secured, and John Deere realizes this benefit by making its Web site available in many different languages.

Personal Medicine, a start-up company that is bringing the house call back to medicine, had trouble enlisting both doctors and patients. Its solution was to use LeadShare, a Web tool offered by SlideShare. With LeadShare marketers post interesting and important information online (in the form of PowerPoint slides, PDF documents, and so forth). To review that information, the viewer must supply contact information. That information is then sent to the organization posting the information and forms the basis for sales leads.

Firms are also developing **extranets**—Internet sites that are customized for specific target markets. Extranets are usually used to build relationships with current customers, but some companies are also using these sites to generate leads. For example, Turner, a TimesWarner Company, owns CNN, TNT, Cartoon Network, Adult Swim, truTV, and NBA on TNT. Turner set up an extranet that is accessible only to media buyers. Buyers can access programming information, cable research data, and Turner's salespeople from the site.

ADS AND DIRECT MAIL

Firms have developed sophisticated systems to generate inquiries from leads by using advertising and direct mail. For example, Fiskars, a Finnish scissors manufacturer, used a direct marketing campaign targeted at purchasing managers and directors at high-volume German hardware stores. The company sent a special package to each individual that included a unique form of a letter, with each word carefully cut out letter by letter in a single piece of paper, along with a pair of Fiskars to clip out a redeemable coupon for more information. The result was a 19 percent increase in orders during that month.[18] As another example, health insurer Anthem sent mailers to health benefit consultants and brokers who help companies choose health insurance plans. A group of brochures, all with a food-theme background, were bound in a white tablecloth to gain attention. Nearly a third of recipients visited the Anthem Web site, and 74 percent became leads for salespeople.[19]

SHOWS, FAIRS, AND MERCHANDISE MARKETS

Trade shows and fairs help salespeople discover and qualify leads.

Many companies display or demonstrate their products at trade shows, conventions, fairs, and merchandise markets. Sales representatives, usually stationed at booths, as shown in the following picture, are present to demonstrate products to visitors, many of whom salespeople have not called on before. In some cases a manufacturer lives or dies by how well it does in these special selling situations. MeadWestVaco, a company that manufactures office products such as calendars, depends heavily on the annual national office products association show. Its salespeople report that selling year-round is easier due to the impression the company makes on prospects at the show. And don't forget that one way to prospect is to simply "walk" the show and meet and learn about people who are working at other booths.

Trade shows are short (usually less than a week), temporary exhibitions of products by manufacturers and resellers. In Europe trade shows are called **trade fairs**. Once the show is over, all vendors pack up and leave. The Consumer Electronics Show showcases electronics products each year. The more than 2,500 vendors at this show are all manufacturers looking for dealers for their products; the end users of the products are not admitted. Dealers often make an entire year's worth of purchases at the show, so the show is a make-or-break situation for many manufacturers. The New York National Boat Show differs in that it has a dual audience: Vendors exhibit to end users (the boating public) as well as to resellers.

Even firms that do not use resellers may have salespeople involved in trade shows. At many trade shows all attendees are customers. For example, when the National Association of Legal Career Professionals holds its annual convention, it also invites manufacturers of office equipment and other products to exhibit wares. The trade show is an adjunct of the convention, with the audience composed entirely of end users. Progressive companies, like Thomson Reuters, create elaborate booths, develop contests and interesting takeaways, and do on-site demonstrations at trade shows. Its Camp Thomson, a whimsical summer camp-themed booth at the American Association of Law Libraries annual meeting, was very successful in generating buzz and produced over 4,000 actual demonstrations of its offerings.[20]

Merchandise markets are places where suppliers have sales offices and buyers from resellers visit to purchase merchandise. The Dallas Market Center, for example, hosts more than 50 separate markets for children's wear, western apparel, linens, and other soft goods. The sellers are the manufacturers or distributors, and they sell only to resellers, not to the public. Sellers may lease showroom space permanently or only during market weeks. Sellers who lease space permanently usually bring in buyers during off-market periods or when no markets are being held.

Buyers visit many vendors during markets, selecting the products they will carry for the next season. In some industries, almost all sales to resellers occur during markets.

Instead of mechanically asking, Are you enjoying the show? or Can I help you with something today? sharp salespeople try to discover whether the lead has a need or a want they can meet. The seller then gives the lead helpful information and gathers information that will be used later in further qualifying the lead and preparing for a sales call. Timely follow-up of leads is critical if sales are to follow a show.

WEBINARS AND SEMINARS

Many firms use seminars and **webinars** (online seminars) to generate leads and to provide information to prospective customers.[21] For example, a local pharmaceutical representative for Bristol-Myers Squibb will set up a seminar for 8 to 10 oncologists and invite a nationally known research oncologist to make a presentation. The research specialist usually discusses some new technique or treatment being developed. During or after the presentation, the pharmaceutical representative for Bristol-Myers Squibb might describe how Squibb's drug Taxol helps in the treatment of ovarian and breast cancer.

What are some key things to keep in mind when planning a webinar or seminar? Make sure your seminar appeals to a specialized market and invite good prospects, especially those prospects who might not be willing to see you one-on-one. The subject should be something your attendees have a strong interest in, while your speaker must be considered an authority on the topic. Try to go as high quality as possible (remember, you're building an image) and consider serving food. Finally, you should take an active role before, during, and after the seminar.

LISTS AND DIRECTORIES

Individual sales representatives can develop prospect lists from sources such as public records, telephone directories, chamber of commerce directories, newspapers, trade publications, club membership lists, and professional or trade membership lists. Secondary sources of information from public libraries also can be useful. For example, industrial trade directories are available for all states. It is often useful to know the **standard industrial classification (SIC)** code or the **North America industry classification system (NAICS)** code, which is a uniform classification for all countries in North America, when researching using secondary sources.[22]

Salespeople can purchase a number of prospecting directories and lead-generating publications. You can purchase mailing lists for all gerontologists (specialists in geriatrics), Lions clubs, T-shirt retailers, yacht owners, antique dealers, Catholic high schools, motel supply houses, multimillionaires, pump wholesalers, and thousands of other classifications. These lists can be delivered as printed mailing labels or secured directly from the Web from such sources as www.salesgenie.com.

Salespeople should keep in mind that lists may not be current and may contain inaccurate information regardless of any guarantee of accuracy. In international selling situations, procuring lists can be much more difficult.

DATABASES AND DATA MINING

Sophisticated firms are developing interactive **databases** that contain information about leads, prospects, and customers. For example, Pioneer, one of the country's largest producers of seed corn, has a dynamic database of 600,000 farm operators in the United States and Canada that everyone in the firm can access. The system has resulted in better sales prospecting and more tailored sales presentations.

Companies are using **data mining,** which consists of artificial intelligence and statistical tools, to discover insights hidden in the volumes of data in their databases. For example, Eagle Equipment of Norton, Massachusetts, uses iMarket software to target its sales calls to the best prospects. Using the company's

From the BUYERS SEAT

6.1

I'm an assistant buyer for Macy's. My company does our best to attend trade shows. Through these trade shows, we are actually the ones prospecting suppliers for potential products. If we see a product from a supplier that we feel matches our needs, we will then get in contact with that supplier and salesperson.

In my industry, it is also common for salespeople to prospect and develop leads through cold calling. For a salesperson to make the most efficient use of their time, it is a *must* that they do their homework on my company so that they know at least the basics (the more the better). Here are a few things that salespeople have done in the past that have really set them apart from the competition:

• Knowing what Macy's provides to our end customer before cold calling me by a salesperson being able to tell me how my end customer will perceive their product.

• When a salespeople send samples of their product to our office to be reviewed. If a salesperson really thinks out the product that they are sending us and ties it in to what they have learned about our company, it sends the message that they really are looking to build a relationship and not just make a sale.

There are also those salespeople who just come in, do the minimum they need to do to get their paycheck, and get out. To me, this is very evident. An example of this revolves around pricing. Even if a product that is brought to me is of exceptional quality, we still need to stick to our pricing range and not venture out of that to maintain our organizational goals. Salespeople should come to me knowing something about the structure of our organization before trying to sell us on products that are outside of our price range.

Source: Brooke Downey, Macy's; names changed as requested; used with permission.

database, the software identifies prospects most likely to buy something and then matches that profile against a database of 12 million businesses. Chapter 15 more fully examines the use of data mining and databases.

COLD CALLING

Before learning about other prospecting methods, college students often assume that salespeople spend most of their time making cold calls. In using the **cold canvass method,** or **cold calls** (by call we usually mean a personal visit, not a telemarketing call), a sales representative tries to generate leads for new business by calling on totally unfamiliar organizations. Cold calling can waste a salesperson's time because many companies have neither a need for the product nor the ability to pay for it. This fact stresses the importance of qualifying the lead quickly in a cold call so as not to waste time. Also, today cold calling is considered rude by many purchasing agents and other professionals.

Salespeople often rate making cold calls as the part of the job they like least. Thus, as mentioned earlier, most firms now encourage their salespeople to qualify leads instead of relying on cold calls. In fact, Ameriprise banned cold calling for its salespeople nationwide years ago. This policy forced the reps to use other methods, such as networking and referrals. But sometimes firms requires their salespeople to start making cold calls, especially in downtimes. For example, Ted Sperides, a customer service rep at Bankcard Associates, was required, as were all employees, to start making cold calls on prospects during the recent recession. He found that the key to successful cold calling was to generate attention immediately, which he did by claiming that his firm could help the buyer save money in credit card processing fees.[23] From the Buyer's Seat 6.1 shares some thoughts from one buyer about salespeople who cold call.

Still, some companies use cold calling. And some companies use a selective type of cold calling they refer to as a **blitz:** A large group of salespeople attempts to call on all the prospective businesses in a given geographical territory on a specified day. For example, an office machine firm may target a specific four-block area in Guadalajara, Mexico; bring in all the salespeople from the surrounding areas; and then have them, in one day, call on every business located in that four-block area. The purpose is to generate leads for the local sales representative as well as to build camaraderie and a sense of unity among the salespeople.

SPOTTERS

Some salespeople use **spotters,** also called **bird dogs.** These individuals will, for a fee, provide leads for the salesperson. The sales rep sometimes pays the fee simply for the name of the lead but more often pays only if the lead ends up buying the product or service. Spotters are usually in a position to find out when someone is ready to make a purchase decision. For example, a janitor who works for a janitorial service company and notices that the heating system for a client is antiquated and hears people complaining about it can turn this information over to a heating contractor.

A more recent development is the use of outside paid consultants to locate and qualify leads. Small firms attempting to secure business with large organizations are most likely to use this approach. For example, Synesis Corporation, a small firm specializing in computerized training, used the services of a consultant to identify and develop leads. The result of one lead was a major contract with AT&T.

Use caution, however, when offering a cash payment to a customer for spotting. Your action may be misconstrued by the customer as exploiting the relationship. Also, some customers' firms may prohibit such behavior. Sometimes it is better to send a personal thank-you note or small gift to the customer instead.

TELEMARKETING

Increasingly, firms are relying on telemarketing to perform many functions that field sales representatives used to perform. **Telemarketing** is a systematic and continuous program of communicating with customers and prospects via telephone. Telemarketing is now used to sell everything from 25-cent supplies to $10 million airplanes.

In **outbound telemarketing** telephones are used to generate and then qualify leads. These calls may be initiated directly by the salesperson, by inside sales representatives (inside sales reps were discussed in Chapter 1), or by third-party vendors. **Inbound telemarketing** uses a telephone number (usually a toll-free number) that leads and customers can call for additional information. Again, the call may be answered by several types of people: the salesperson, an inside salesperson, or a customer service representative.[24]

Firms combine outbound and inbound telemarketing to prospect effectively. For example, Motorola's government division, which sells mobile communication systems to such entities as police stations and fire departments, can use outbound telemarketing to generate and then qualify leads for its sales force. Qualified leads are turned over to field sales representatives if the order is large enough to warrant a personal visit to the company. If the prospect needs a smaller system, a separate telemarketing salesperson will handle the account. Motorola also uses inbound telemarketing by providing a toll-free number for people who

Progressive firms use telemarketers to qualify leads before sending a salesperson on a call.

want more information about a product or service Motorola offers. Because of this excellent telemarketing organization, Motorola's field reps have more time to spend with qualified prospects and more time to develop long-term customer relations.

Although the telephone is a wonderful tool that can enhance productivity, it also has some limitations. Customers often find telephone calls an annoying inconvenience, which is why a huge percent use voice mail to screen their calls. When telephoning customers—in fact, at all times—salespeople need to respect the customers' privacy concerns and the do-not-call rules, as discussed in Chapter 2. Attracting and maintaining the customer's attention and interest is harder over the telephone than it is in person, and prospects may even continue to work or read a report or magazine. While it is true that is it much easier for a prospect to say no over the phone than in person, salespeople should often take that "no" to mean exactly what they say—no, rather than continue to try to badger the prospect into complying.

BECOMING AN EXPERT

Salespeople can prospect by becoming recognized experts in their field, resulting in prospects seeking information from them. Admittedly, that won't happen for most salespeople when they first graduate from college, but over time they can develop their expertise and seek avenues to showcase their talent.

Salespeople have many ways to demonstrate their expertise in a particular subject. Some will engage in public speaking on topics related to their expertise. Speeches at industry conventions, at luncheons and dinners hosted by prospects and industry representatives, and on college campuses provide outlets for expertise to be disseminated.

Salespeople can also demonstrate their expertise in writing. This can take many forms, including writing journal articles, publishing articles in trade publications, hosting a blog, posting on other's blogs, and so forth. One study found that technical buyers often read white papers before making decisions.

SALES LETTERS

Prospecting sales letters can be integrated into an overall prospecting plan. For example, Xerox salespeople who handle smaller businesses send prospecting sales letters every day. They follow up three days later with a telephone prospecting call and ask for an appointment for a personal visit. The telephone call begins with a question about the letter.

One way to make sales letters stand out is to include a promotional item with the mailer. Here are some good examples:[25]

- First National Bank of Shreveport, Louisiana, targeted certified public accountants (CPAs) for one mailer. The bank timed the mailers to arrive on April 16, the day after the federal income tax filing deadline. Included in each mailer was a small bottle of wine, a glass, and cheese and crackers—a party kit designed to celebrate the end of tax season. The bank followed up with telephone calls two days later and ultimately gained 21 percent of the CPAs as new customers.

- OfficeMax sent top executives at a large bank a metal suitcase filled with piles of fake money. The box also contained an MP3 player that included videos of how OfficeMax could meet that bank's specific needs.

- Sprint sent top decision makers a personal meeting invitation housed in a specially designed attractive box with a Louisville Slugger bat enclosed. Those who agreed to meetings would receive professional baseball jerseys for their favorite baseball teams.

What would be your reaction if you received the Louisville Slugger bat just described as part of a direct mail piece? Would there be a better way to gain your attention in such a mailing? If so, how could a salesperson learn what that would be?

The salesperson must first consider the objective of any written communication (like a sales letter or e-mail message) and the audience. What action does the salesperson desire from the reader? Why would the reader want to undertake that action? Why would the reader not want to undertake the action? These questions help guide the salesperson in writing the letter.

The opening paragraph must grab the reader's attention, just as a salesperson's approach must get a prospect's attention in a face-to-face call. The opening gives the readers a reason to continue reading, drawing them into the rest of the letter. Another way to gain attention is to have a loyal client whom the prospect respects write the introduction (or even the entire letter) for the salesperson. Here's an example of an opening paragraph:

> Thanks for stopping by the Datasource booth at the VON San Jose IP Communications Show. I hope you enjoyed the show and had some fun shooting hoops with us! Were you there when one highly energetic attendee shot the basketball clear over into the Mac booth and knocked the presenter's iPhone right out of his hand? You won't believe what he did next! I'll fill you in on the details in a moment, but first I'd like to invite you to something I know you're not going to want to miss.

The next paragraph or two, the body of the letter, considers why the reader would and would not want to take the desired action. Benefits of taking the action should be presented clearly, without jargon, and briefly. The best-presented benefits are tailored to the specific individual, especially when the salesperson can refer to a recent conversation with the reader. A reference such as the following example can truly personalize the letter:

> As you said during our visit at the show, you're looking for a software firm that can work with a small business like yours without making you feel like a second-class citizen. At Datasource, we've committed ourselves to working exclusively with small to midsized firms like yours.

If the salesperson and the buyer do not know each other, part of the body of the letter should be used to increase credibility. References to satisfied customers, market research data, and other independent sources can be used to improve credibility:

> You may have heard that last year we won the prestigious Youcon Achievement Award, presented by the Tennessee Small Business Development Center in recognition for outstanding service specifically to small businesses. In fact, the small businesses themselves are the voters for the award. We're proud of that award because it tangibly reflects the commitment we've shown. And we have dedicated ourselves to continue in that tradition.

The final paragraph should seek commitment to the desired course of action. Whatever the action desired, the letter must specifically ask that it take place. The writer should leave no doubt in the prospect's mind about what he or she is supposed to do. The writer should make the action for the prospect easy to accomplish, fully explain why it should be done now, and end with a positive picture. Here's an example:

> So I want to personally invite you to a free lunch seminar at Datasource. You'll hear from our partners about the very latest solutions to your technology challenges. The food promises to be great, and the information will be presented in a casual, small group setting. Please take a moment to reserve your spot at the lunch by visiting our Web site, www.datasource.com, or calling 800-343-8764. You'll be glad you did.

A postscript (or PS) can also be effective. Postscripts stand out because of their location and should be used to make an important selling point. Alternatively, they can be used to emphasize the requested action, such as pointing out a deadline.

While you are writing, remember to check your work carefully for misspelled words and grammar problems. And read it carefully because you often don't see problems in a quick glance, as the following paragraph illustrates:[26]

> i cdnuolt blveiee taht I cluod aulaclty uesdnatnrd waht I was rdanieg. The phaonmneal pweor of the hmuan mnid, aoccdrnig to a rscheearch at Cmabrigde Uinervtisy, it dseno't mtaetr in waht oerdr the ltteres in a wrod are, the olny iproamtnt tihng is taht the frsit and lsat ltteer be in the rghit pclae. The rset can be a taotl mses and you can sitll raed it whotuit a pboerlm. Tihs is bcuseae the huamn mnid deos not raed ervey lteter by istlef, but the wrod as a wlohe.

And of course spell check won't catch everything; the following passed with flying colors:[27]

> I have a spelling checker, it came with my PC. It plainly marks four my revenue mistakes I cannot sea. I've run this poem threw it, I'm sure your pleased too no, its letter perfect in it's weigh, my checker tolled me sew.

OTHER SOURCES OF LEADS

Many salespeople find leads through personal observation, as "Building Partnerships 6.1" describes. For example, by reading trade journals carefully, salespeople can learn the names of the most important leaders (and hence decision makers) in the industry. Sellers also read general business publications (such as the *Wall Street Journal*) and local newspapers.

Nonsales employees within the salesperson's firm can also provide leads. Some companies strongly encourage this practice. For example, Computer Specialists Inc., a computer service firm, pays its nonsales employees a bonus of up to $1,000 for any names of prospective customers they pass along. In one year the program resulted in 75 leads and 9 new accounts.

Government agencies can also supply lead information. The FedBizOpps site, for example, provides information about federal government bid opportunities and can be viewed at www.fbo.gov.

Leads can be found in many other places as well. Some prospect while doing something they enjoy, such as belonging to a cycling club. Salespeople for non-competing but related products can often provide leads, as can members of trade associations. You can find leads while volunteering in your community, doing things like helping build a house for Habitat for Humanity. Good friends can also provide leads. Of course one of the best ways to learn about new business opportunities is to keep up with regional, national, and world trends from sources such as *World Watch* magazine and industry surveys (Manufacturing USA, Service USA, Standard & Poor's Industry Surveys, U.S. Industrial Outlook, and the like).

BUILDING Partnerships

As an independent distributor of building supplies, BlueLinx has more than 10,000 products and 70,000 SKUs of interest to contractors and builders. These include siding and trim, metal products, structural framing products, and molding and millwork, to name just a few. We have a broad array of the most well respected brands in the industry.

In terms of prospecting, we at BlueLinx do our best to come in contact with any possible client that we can. Our motto is "keep your feet on the streets and meet folks face to face." When our salespeople learn about a potential customer, they enter the information into our CRM system. Our system consists of many drop-down boxes, making the information easy to input for our salespeople and taking as little time as possible for them to store valuable information. This not only helps salespeople keep track of what they have done with each of their potential customers but also builds our database with information that others can check to see what their coworkers are doing.

The information in our CRM system is not only valuable to current salespeople while they are in their current positions; once they move on to other positions, this information is extremely valuable to their successors. Nothing is worse than wasting a client's time asking for information that has already be contacted by BlueLinx. With the vast information in our database, new salespeople can see what has previously been done with current clients.

Other ways that prospecting done in our organization is through trade shows and by our salespeople just stopping at a job site that they see while out making their sales calls. When stopping at a job site, it gives our salespeople the opportunity to assess firsthand the types of products we offer that may benefit the company. Also, this enables us to put a face to the name.

Source: Jason Ungar, BlueLinx, names have been changed at the request of the provider, used with permission.

LEAD QUALIFICATION AND MANAGEMENT SYSTEMS

Salespeople need to develop a process for qualifying leads, often called a **lead qualification system.** As mentioned early in this chapter, salespeople must ensure that their leads meet the five basic criteria of a prospect. Let's look more closely at this process.

Many firms view prospecting as a funneling process in which a large number of leads are funneled (or narrowed down) into prospects and some, finally, into customers. Marketing often generates these leads, but it is interesting that most leads thus generated by marketing departments are not followed up by salespeople.

To help salespeople use their time wisely and to increase the number of leads that sellers actually follow up with, some firms engage in **prequalification** of leads before turning them over to the field sales force. Sometimes the prequalification process is as simple as purchasing a prequalified list. At other times a firm will use the resources of telemarketers to prequalify leads. Many lead qualification systems assign points to a prospect, rather than simply designating them as hot or cold, offering the salesperson more insight into the lead's value.

Salespeople can get leads during volunteering activities.

Salespeople must not only qualify leads but also carefully analyze the relative value of each lead. This part of the process is called a **lead management system,** which is discussed more fully in Chapter 15. Part of the decision process often includes a valuation of the prospects' expected customer lifetime value or return on investment, as well as an appraisal of what types of value the selling firm can add to the prospect. Grading prospects and establishing a priority list result in increased sales and the most efficient use of time and energy. There is even an association dedicated to helping companies manage their leads more effectively: the Sales Lead Management Association.[28]

The use of technology makes lead qualification and management more efficient and effective. For example, IBM has tied its lead generation and management system into its CRM system. The results have been better tracking and prioritization of leads and prospects. The scoring system recommended by the Corporate Executive Board rates leads on five traits (organizational basics, operating environment, view of the status quo, receptivity to new or disruptive ideas, and potential for emerging needs) and then, based on the score, offers suggestions on whether to pursue the opportunity.[29]

Any good lead management system, like IBM's, should evaluate the profitability of sales resulting from various lead-generating activities instead of just counting the number of names a particular method yields. Analysis may show that the present system does not produce enough prospects or the right kinds of prospects. Salespeople may, for example, depend entirely on referred names from company advertising or from the service department. If these two sources do not supply enough names to produce the sales volume and profits desired, other prospecting methods should be considered.

Salespeople must learn how to overcome a reluctance to prospect.

OVERCOMING A RELUCTANCE TO PROSPECT

People often stereotype salespeople as bold, adventurous, and somewhat abrasive. But salespeople often struggle with a reluctance to prospect that persists no matter how well they have been trained and how much they believe in the products they sell.

Research shows a number of reasons for reluctance to call, including worrying about worst-case scenarios; spending too much time preparing; being overly concerned with looking successful; being fearful of making group presentations, of appearing too pushy, of losing friends or losing family approval, and of using the phone for prospecting; feeling intimidated by people with prestige or power or feeling guilt at having a career in selling; and having a compulsive need to argue, make excuses, or blame others.

Reluctance to call can and must be overcome to sell successfully. Several activities can help:

- Start by listening to the excuses other salespeople give to justify their call reluctance behavior. Evaluate their validity. You'll usually be surprised to find that most excuses really aren't valid.

- Engage in sales training and role-playing activity to improve your prospecting skills and your ability to handle questions and rejections that arise.

- Make prospecting contacts with a supporting partner or sales manager. Just their presence will often provide additional needed confidence (you won't feel so alone).

- Set specific goals for all your prospecting activity. Put them in your "to do" list. Chapter 15 will provide more direction in this activity.
- Realize the economic value of most prospecting activities. For example, if you keep good records, you may discover that every phone call you make (regardless of whether that particular prospect buys) results in an average of $22 commission in the long run.
- Stop negative self-evaluations from ruling your behavior. Learn to think positively about the future instead of focusing on your past blunders.
- Remember that you are calling on prospects to solve their needs, not just so you can line your pocket with money. You are performing a vital, helpful, important service to your prospects by calling on them. (If this isn't true, maybe you should find another sales job.)
- Control your perceptions of what prospects might say about you, your company, or your products. You don't know what their reactions will be until you meet with the prospects. Leads do buy from salespeople.
- Learn and apply relaxation and stress-reducing techniques.
- Recount your own prospecting successes or those of others.

SELLING YOURSELF

It's time to put the material in this chapter to practical use. Getting your first job out of college can seem like a full-time job in itself. If you find yourself in a job-hunting rut, it may be time to stop simply looking for a job and start actively *prospecting* for one. Many potential employers can be completely overlooked without prospecting because often jobs are not advertised.

As the chapter discussed, leads are not automatically prospects and must be qualified first. This means that not all jobs are going to be good prospects for you. When researching your job leads, ask yourself these important questions: Does the company have a want or need that I can satisfy?, Do I have the skills and experience necessary to bring value to the company?, Is the salary within an acceptable range?, and Does my contact have the authority to make a hiring decision? Answering these questions can help you sort through the job leads out there so that you can make the most of your time and theirs by applying only for jobs that are a good fit.

There are many sources of prospects for a job, including internships, business organizations, job fairs, and networking. College internships and prior jobs would be obvious choices for prospective careers. Current and previous employers can be contacted for leads. Getting involved in business organizations, such as the American Marketing Association and Students in Free Enterprise, can expose you to executives and hiring managers that may be impossible to access otherwise. Attending job fairs can be priceless, allowing face-to-face interaction with hiring managers before the interview. A bonus to job fairs is that there are often employees manning the booths who can give you additional insight into the career you are looking into. Networking through social media (i.e. LinkedIn), your school's alumni group, family and friends, volunteer groups, and other organizations will help get the word out that you are looking for a career. People like helping others and making connections; you've heard the saying, "It's not what you know, but who you know."

As the chapter relates, you can be the perfect candidate for a job, but if you are applying to the wrong companies, you are letting your skills go to waste. Prospecting is important for nearly all salespeople, and, after all, you are *selling yourself*.

Source: Angela Bertero, Liberty Mutual, used with permission.

SUMMARY

Locating prospective customers is the first step in the sales process. New prospects are needed to replace old customers lost for a variety of reasons and to replace contacts lost in existing customers because of plant relocations, turnover, mergers, downsizing, and other factors.

Not all sales leads qualify as good prospects. A qualified prospect has a need that can be satisfied by the salesperson's product, has the ability and authority to buy the product, can be approached by the salesperson, and is eligible to buy.

Many methods can be used to locate prospects. The best source is a satisfied customer. Salespeople can also use the endless-chain method, networking, social media, lists and directories, cold canvassing (including blitzes), spotters, and becoming known as experts via blogs, speeches, and so forth. Companies provide leads to salespeople through promotional activities such as the Internet, inquiries from advertising and direct mail, telemarketing, trade shows, merchandise markets, and webinars/seminars.

Effective prospecting requires a strong plan that hinges on developing a lead qualification and management system and overcoming reluctance to prospect.

KEY TERMS

bird dog   161
blitz   161
buying community   155
center-of-influence method   154
cold call   160
cold canvass method   160
customer referral value   151
databases   159
data mining   159
endless-chain method   152
exclusive sales territories   150
extranet   157
house accounts   150
inbound telemarketing   161
insight selling   150
lead   148
lead management system   166
lead qualification system   165
merchandise market   158
negative referral   152
networking   152

North America industry classification system (NAICS)   159
outbound telemarketing   161
prequalification   165
promoters   151
prospect   148
prospecting   148
qualify the lead   148
referral event   152
referred lead   152
sales funnel   149
selling deeper   152
social media   155
spotter   161
standard industrial classification (SIC)   159
systems integrator   149
telemarketing   161
trade fairs   158
trade show   158
webinars   159

ETHICS PROBLEMS

1. Suppose you're working at a trade show. You walk the floor of the show during one of your breaks, and you strike up a conversation with a sales rep from a competitor. She starts talking about their products and gives details on price breaks she offers to banks. She asks, "What kind of price deals do you give banks?" What would you say?

2. Suppose a spotter not only tells you about a potential prospect but also provides you with confidential memos and e-mails, detailing the people involved and what the issues are. However, all the e-mails and notes are marked with statements that prohibit the information from being shared with anyone outside of the company. What will you do with that confidential information that you're not supposed to have?

QUESTIONS AND PROBLEMS

1. Describe a referral event that could be created, assuming you are a member of a service club in your college. Your target market for new leads consists of students not currently members in any service club.

2. Think of a time when you acted as a negative referral for a product or service or company. Why did you do it? What could the company or salesperson have done to cause you to not be a negative referral?

3. What things would concern you about prospecting? How will you deal with those concerns?

4. Assume you are a landscape contractor, and you specialize in planting quality trees and plants. Whom might you use as paid spotters to generate leads?

5. Reluctance to prospect is a real phenomenon. What can you do now (and avoid doing now), while you're in school, to avoid being reluctant to prospect when you become a salesperson?

6. Assume you sell restaurant supplies, such as cooking equipment, tabletop accessories, tables, and chairs. Locate at least one merchandise mart and one trade show or fair where you might be able to display your products.

7. How would you develop a prospect list under the following situations?
   a. You belong to a Lions Club that needs to recruit new members.
   b. You sell carpet-cleaning services to businesses.

8. "Building Partnerships 6.1" describes how salespeople for BlueLinx look for prospects as they drive in their territory. Would there be any risks to relying exclusively on that technique?

9. "From the Buyer's Seat 6.1" described how some sellers try to get Macy's to buy clothing products that are too expensive. Assume that you are a seller who is selling clothing that is above Macy's price lines. What would you do?

10. If you were a salesperson for the following, how would you develop a prospect list?
   a. A new line of doors that are energy efficient.
   b. A travel agency specializing in vacations to Chile.
   c. A manufacturer of a theft deterrent device for Blue Ray players.

CASE PROBLEMS

case **6.1**

Federated Insurance

A few years back, I was a Federated Insurance salesperson and had a large Redi-Mix Concrete contractor I was quoting. This was the second time I had quoted this account, and I had built a good relationship there. My price was $159,000 for their property and casualty insurance. I knew they paid only $150,000 the year before, but I had uncovered many coverage disadvantages and issues in their current program. I had a really great shot at selling this account. The commission rate on P&C is about 15 percent, so I would make about $23,000 if I made the sale.

The buyer said that I was to stop by on Friday morning and that his current agent was coming later that afternoon with a quote. The insurance expiration day was that Saturday.

I gave my proposal, and it went very well. I gave the buyer a list of 10 things to ask the other agent in which I had coverage advantages. The buyer said he wanted to do business with me, but because his current agent was already coming in that afternoon, he felt like he should see what she had to offer and go through the issues I had pointed out.

I left and set an appointment for first thing Monday morning. On Monday at 8:00, I was there, and the owner said that I had earned the business! I was pumped! He pulled out his checkbook and gave me a check for $15,900 as a down payment. I called my underwriter to tell him the great news, and he said, "Awesome!" He asked, "When is it effective?" I said, "As of last Saturday." He said to have them sign a form saying they had not had any claims since Saturday.

I asked the owner, and he said he didn't have any claims. Then he said, "Oh, I forgot, Joe hit a deer on the way home from a job on Saturday in the company truck. It wasn't bad, though, about $1,200 in damages we are guessing. Joe wasn't hurt or anything."

I was devastated! What were my options? I could call the underwriter and tell him about the claim, knowing that he most likely would tell me to give the check back and that I could not bind an account that already had a claim pending. And I'd lose $23,000 in commission. Or I could tell the owner not to worry about it, knowing that Federated would pay the claim if I pretended I didn't know about the accident and bind the account. Or I could tell the owner that I would pay for the $1,200 claim out of my pocket because I would earn a hefty $23,000 commission check.

Questions

1. What should the salesperson do?
2. How should the salesperson communicate that decision to his customer? To his own company, Federated?

Source: Jim Sodoma, district manager, Federated Insurance; used with permission.

case **6.2**

Chicago Marriott Downtown Magnificent Mile

The Chicago Marriott Downtown Magnificent Mile is a Windy City landmark on Michigan Avenue's Magnificent Mile. Located in the heart of world-class shopping and dining, this hotel is within walking distance of top attractions, including the Navy Pier, Shedd Aquarium, Millennium Park, as well as the landmark Chicago Theater District. The hotel rooms and suites have state-of-the-art flat-screen TVs, deluxe bedding, and ergonomic furnishings. With 66,400 square feet of event space, including 54 meeting rooms, this luxury hotel creates a distinguished venue for business engagements, social gatherings, and elegant wedding receptions. The largest meeting room is the Grand Ballroom with maximum meeting space of 19,193 square feet and a maximum seating capacity of 2,200. The hotel is known for its outstanding service coupled with magnificent style.

Assume that you are a salesperson for the Chicago Marriott Downtown Magnificent Mile. Your goal is to book meetings and conventions from businesses and not-for-profit organizations.

Questions

1. Provide a list of company names and addresses of five actual leads for the Chicago Marriott Downtown Magnificent Mile. You don't have to know whether the leads already have used the hotel. Explain where you got the list of leads.
2. Develop the details of an appropriate referral event for the Chicago Marriott Downtown Magnificent Mile. Provide information about the place of the event as well as what should happen during the event. Be creative. Remember that referral events should be fun for current clients as well as leads.

Source: www.marriott.com/hotels/travel/chidt-chicago-marriott-downtown-magnificent-mile.

ROLE PLAY CASE

As a NetSuite salesperson, how can you help your buyer prospect better? Think about how NetSuite might be able to help your buyer develop a comprehensive prospecting system, from lead generation to making the first appointment. One way that NetSuite can help is to automate direct mail. Using the database that salespeople create, the marketing department can send mail to every contact who meets certain criteria. For example, it can select an industry and send a letter only to prospects in that industry. Similarly, NetSuite provides reporting capabilities. Salespeople can see how effective they are at each method of prospecting and then focus their efforts on the methods that work the best. These are only some ideas—you may want to visit the Web site for more or think about how the concepts in the chapter can help your account.

Using the same account you've been selling to (BancVue, GelTech, HighPoint Solutions), write out some questions you'd like to ask your buyer to determine how he or she prospects now and how NetSuite might help. (*Note:* If you have not done role plays before, you will need to review the information about the various role play customers that can be found at the end of Chapter 3.)

Then role-play with your buyer, trying to determine her or his needs for assistance with prospecting. Once you've identified those needs, give a short presentation about how NetSuite can help. Your professor will pass out buyer sheets.

Note: For background information about these role plays, please see page 26.

To the instructor: Additional information needed to complete the role play is available in the Instructor's Manual.

ADDITIONAL REFERENCES

Allen, Jeff F., and Gary D. McGugan. *NEEDS Selling Solutions*. Bloomington, IN: Trafford Publishing, 2009.

Bachrach, Anne M. "Getting to the Right People." *American Salesman* 57, no. 5 (May 2012), pp. 27–30.

Bednarz, Timothy F., and Monika Pawlak. *Productive Sales Networking: Pinpoint Sales Skill Development Training Series*. Stevens Point, WI: Majorium Business Press, 2011.

Blythe, Jim. "Trade Fairs as Communication: A New Model." *Journal of Business and Industrial Marketing* 25, no. 1 (2010), pp. 57–62.

Brogan, Chris. *Social Media 101: Tactics and Tips to Develop Your Business Online*. Hoboken, NJ: Wiley, 2010.

Brynko, Barbara. "Hoover's Links Up with LinkedIn." *Information Today* 28, no. 2 (February 2011), p. 32.

Caramanico, Dan, Marie Maguire, and Dave Kurlan. *The Optimal Salesperson: Mastering the Mindset of Sales Superstars and Overachievers*. Great Falls, VA: LINX Corp., 2009.

Carter, Brian. *LinkedIn for Business: How Advertisers, Marketers and Salespeople Get Leads, Sales and Profits from LinkedIn*. Indianapolis, Indiana: Que, 2012.

Chase, Landy. "Value, Selling, and the Social Media Sales Revolution." *American Salesman* 56, no. 7 (July 2011), pp. 3–5.

Cole, Tony, and John Graham. "Prospecting—The Only 'A' Priority." *American Salesman* 57, no. 3 (March 2012), pp. 18–27.

Curtis, Joan C., and Barbara Giamanco. *The New Handshake: Sales Meets Social Media*. Westport, CT: Praeger, 2010.

Eggert, Andreas, and Murat Serdaroglu. "Exploring the Impact of Sales Technology on Salesperson Performance: A Task-Based Approach." *Journal of Personal Selling and Sales Management* 31, no. 2 (Spring 2011), pp. 169–85.

Gitomer, Jeffrey H. *Social BOOM!* FT Press, 2011.

Godson, Mark. *Relationship Marketing*. New York City: Oxford University Press, 2009.

Good, Bill. Hot *Prospects: The Proven Prospecting System to Ramp Up Your Sale*. New York City: Scribner, 2011.

Greenberg, Kevin. "Managing Social Customers for Profit." *CRM Magazine* 13, no. 8 (August 2009), p. 1

Handley, Ann. "Uncovering New Territories." *Entrepreneur* 40, no. 4 (April 2012), p. 62.

Jaffe, Joseph. *Flip the Funnel: How to Use Existing Customers to Gain New Ones*. Hoboken, NJ: Wiley, 2010.

Kahle, Dave. "7 Power-Packed Prospecting Pointers." *American Salesman* 57, no. 8 (August 2012), pp. 23–27.

Lager, M. "Looking to SCORE." *CRM Magazine* 13, no. 3 (March 2009), pp. 38–42.

Marshall, Greg W., William C. Moncrief, John M. Rudd, and Nick Lee. 2012. "Revolution in Sales: The Impact of Social Media and Related Technology on the Selling Environment." *Journal of Personal Selling and Sales Management* 32, no. 3 (2012), pp. 349–63.

Meyerson, Mitch. *Success Secrets of Social Media Marketing Superstars*. New York City: Entrepreneur Press, 2010.

Misner, Ivan, David Alexander, and Brian Hilliard. *Networking Like a Pro: Turning Contacts into Connections*. New York City: Entrepreneur Press, 2010.

Mitrega, Maciej, Sebastian Forkmann, Carla Ramos, and Stephan C. Henneberg. Networking Capability in Business Relationships—Concept and Scale Development. *Industrial Marketing Management* 41, no. 5 (July 2012), pp. 739–51.

Peppers & Rogers Group. "Turning Prospects into Profits: Using Lead Management Innovation to Win Customers" (white paper). Retrieved from http://www.peppersandrogers group.com, March 5, 2010.

Schep, Brad. *How to Find a Job on LinkedIn, Facebook, Twitter, MySpace, and Other Social Networks*. New York City: McGraw-Hill, 2009.

Stevens, Ruth P. *Maximizing Lead Generation: The Complete Guide for B2B Marketers*. Indianapolis, Indiana: Que, 2011.

Weinberg, Mike, and S. Anthony Iannarino. *New Sales. Simplified: The Essential Handbook for Prospecting and New Business Development*. New York City: AMACOM, 2012.

Wilson, David James. *Prospecting 101: The Ultimate Guide to Prospect Successfully to Super Grow Your Pipeline or Business*. Seattle, WA: CreateSpace, 2009.

Xu, Jun, and Mohammed Quaddus. *E-Business in the 21st Century: Realities, Challenges and Outlook*. Hackensack, NJ: World Scientific Publishing, 2010.

Knowledge and Skill Requirements

chapter

4

USING COMMUNICATION PRINCIPLES TO BUILD RELATIONSHIPS

SOME QUESTIONS ANSWERED IN THIS CHAPTER ARE

- What are the basic elements in the communication process?
- Why are listening and questioning skills important?
- How can salespeople develop listening skills to collect information about customers?
- How do people communicate without using words?
- What are some things to remember when communicating via technology like phones, e-mail, and social media?
- How does a salesperson adjust for cultural differences?

1

PART

PROFILE

"By asking the right questions, actively listening and mastering the use of technology, each one of us has an opportunity to make our mark on our customer."

Sally Cook, 3M

PROFILE My name is Sally Cook, and I graduated from St. Catherine University in 2011 with a bachelor of science degree in health care sales. One of the very first key takeaways from my first sales course taught by Lynn Schleeter was about effective communication. It is more and more apparent to me how communication with customers has dramatically changed in the last decade.

It used to be imperative to get that face-to-face meeting, but now I rely equally on other technology platforms in order to get myself, my company, and my products in front of my customer. Almost every buyer has a cell phone that can receive e-mails and text messages for shipping information and so on. Plus, with other technology, such as Skype and Facebook, businesses and their owners are constantly on the go. With that being said, how can we, as current and future sales professionals, get our foot in the door? By asking the right questions, actively listening, and mastering the use of technology, each one of us has an opportunity to make our mark on our customer. Companies and corporations alike are looking for that diverse sales talent that can provide these skills.

At St. Catherine's, one of my professor's requirements for his class was to do telesales for the alumni association, which is definitely no easy feat. I found myself calling on a variety of previous St. Kate students whose graduation from the school ranged from 1 year to 50 years. With the small amount of background information given about these possible donors, I had to call on them and figure out how I could help these individuals see the benefit in donating to their alma mater. The first calls didn't go as smoothly as hoped, but as I continued to make calls, I discovered that by tailoring my questioning and listening actively, I was actually having more "luck" in creating the sale.

Not every customer has the same story, and with that not every customer wants to hear the same story. This is the reality of almost every sales call: Your customers want to be treated as individuals. This requires the sales professional to adjust and adapt to each customer's needs and wants. In order to do that, the sales professional needs to be actively listening to each customer to identify what it is that may be important to them. The sales professional would not be calling on said customer if they didn't think that they had a product or service that would benefit the customer. It is up to the sales professional to identify the key points to drive the sale forward, which again all comes back to actively engaging yourself in the conversation.

Visit our Web site at:
www.3m.com

BUILDING RELATIONSHIPS THROUGH TWO-WAY COMMUNICATION

As we will discuss further in Chapter 13, open and honest communication is a key to building trust and developing successful relationships. To develop a good understanding of each other's needs, buyers and sellers must effectively communicate with each other by actively talking and listening.

THE COMMUNICATION PROCESS

Exhibit 4.1 illustrates the **two-way communication** process. The process begins when the sender, either the salesperson or the customer, wants to communicate some thoughts or ideas. Because the receiver cannot read the sender's mind, the sender must translate these ideas into words. The translation of thoughts into words is called **encoding.** Then the receiver must decode the message and try to understand what the sender intended to communicate. **Decoding** involves interpreting the meaning of the received message.

Consider a salesperson who is describing a complex product to a customer. At one point, a perplexed look flits across the customer's face. The salesperson receives this nonverbal message and asks the customer what part of the presentation needs further explanation. This **feedback** from the customer's expression tells the salesperson that the message is not being received. The customer then sends verbal messages to the salesperson in the form of questions concerning the operation and benefits of the product.

COMMUNICATION BREAKDOWNS

Communication breakdowns can be caused by encoding and decoding problems and the environment in which the communications occur. The following sales interaction between a copier salesperson and a prospect illustrates problems that can arise in encoding and decoding messages:

What the salesperson means to say: We have an entire line of Toshiba copiers. But I think the Model 900 is ideally suited for your needs because it provides the basic copying functions at a low price.

What the salesperson actually says (encodes): The Model 900 is our best-selling copier, and it's designed to economically meet the copying needs of small businesses like yours.

Exhibit 4.1
Two-Way Flow of Information

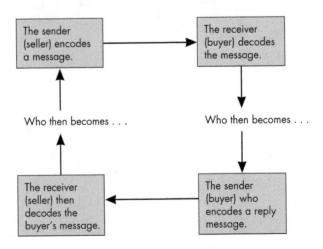

Background noise from traffic can hinder effective communication. The salesperson should attempt to move the discussion to a quieter location so the noise will not distract the customer.

What the customer hears: The Model 900 is a low-priced copier for small businesses.

What the customer thinks (decodes): This company makes cheap copiers with limited features, probably for businesses that don't have much money. But I need a copier with more features. I think I'd better look elsewhere for a better copier.

What the customer actually says: I don't think I'm interested in buying a copier now.

In this situation the salesperson assumed that price was very important to the prospect, and the prospect thought (incorrectly) that the salesperson's company made only low-priced, low-performance copiers.

Communication can also be inhibited by the environment in which the communication process occurs. For example, noises can distract the salesperson and the customer. **Noises** are sounds unrelated to messages being exchanged by the salesperson and the customer, such as ringing telephones or other conversations nearby. To improve communication, the salesperson should attempt to minimize noises in the environment by closing a door to the room or suggesting that the meeting move to a quieter place.

Other environmental issues must be dealt with before effective communication can occur. For example, people communicate most effectively when they are physically comfortable. If the room is too hot or too cold, the salesperson should suggest changing the temperature controls or moving to another room. These types of environmental issues and possible solutions are discussed in Chapters 7 and 8. For now, realize that effective communication can't occur without the proper environment.

Finally, it is important to note that buyers do not always follow this communication model perfectly.[1] Some buyers—and sellers for that matter—have agendas that do not always result in honest, straightforward attempts to reveal truth. Rather, they may at times use communication as a tool to mask their true motives and intentions. You have probably done this yourself—when caught doing something wrong and wishing to avoid detection or punishment, you masked the truth or said things you hoped would be interpreted in ways that were favorable to you.

thinking **it** through

Think of a big disagreement you had with someone recently (perhaps with a boyfriend, girlfriend, professor, or parents). Did any miscommunication occur? Why was the communication poor? Was it due to noise, poor feedback, poor encoding, poor decoding, or what?

SENDING VERBAL MESSAGES EFFECTIVELY

A basic reason that salespeople communicate is to simply provide information to the buyer. Salespeople also often attempt to engage in **persuading,** the process by which the salesperson attempts to convince other people (e.g., buyers) to change their attitudes or behaviors regarding an issue while understanding that the other person is free to accept or reject the idea. This section will explore methods of communicating via verbal communication.

CHOICE OF WORDS

As Quintilion, the famous Roman orator, said, "Choice of words is the origin of eloquence." Salespeople don't have to be eloquent, but most could use some pointers to develop their skills in word choice. Use short words and phrases to demonstrate strength and force (like *accelerated* and *intervened*) or to provide charm and grace (like *crystal clear* and *crisp copies*). Avoid trite words[2] such as *nice* and *good* and phrases that make you sound like an overeager salesperson such as *a great deal, I guarantee you will . . .* , and *No problem!* Also avoid using off-color language, slang, and foul language, even with established customers.

Every salesperson should be able to draw on a set of words to best help present the features of a product or service. The words might form a simile, such as *This battery backup is like a spare tire;* a metaphor, such as *This machine is a real workhorse;* or a phrase drawing on sensory appeal, such as *smooth as silk* or *strong as steel.* To find the best way to use words, it often helps to listen to the way your customer talks.

Be careful about using words that have become so common in business conversations as to be almost meaningless. Words like *core competence, value added, enterprisewide, fault-tolerant,* and *mission-critical* are often cited as examples. Avoid them because they can make you come across as phony.

Words have different meanings in different cultures and even in different subcultures of the United States. In England the hood of a car is called the *bonnet,* and the trunk is called the *boot.* In Boston a milkshake is simply syrup mixed with milk, whereas a frappe is ice cream, syrup, and milk mixed together.

VOICE CHARACTERISTICS

A salesperson's delivery of words affects how the customer will understand and evaluate his or her presentation. Poor voice and speech habits make it difficult for customers to understand a salesperson's message. **Voice characteristics** include rate of speech, loudness, inflection, and articulation.

Customers tend to question the expertise of salespeople who talk much slower or faster than the normal rate of 140 words per minute. Salespeople should vary their rate of speech depending on the nature of the message and the environment in which the communication occurs. Simple messages can be delivered at faster rates, and more difficult concepts should be presented at slower rates.

Loudness should be tailored to the communication situation. To avoid monotony, salespeople should learn to vary the loudness of their speech. Loudness can also be used to emphasize certain parts of the sales presentation, indicating to the customer that these parts are more important.

Inflection is the tone or pitch of speech. At the end of a sentence, the tone should drop, indicating the completion of a thought. When the tone goes up at the end of a sentence, listeners often sense uncertainty in the speaker. Use inflection to reduce monotony. If you speak with enthusiasm, it will help your customer connect emotionally. However, don't forget to be yourself. The buyer can be turned off if you're obviously just trying to copy the successful communication traits of someone else.

Articulation refers to the production of recognizable sounds. Articulation is best when the speaker opens his or her mouth properly; then the movements of the lips and tongue are unimpeded. When the lips are too close together, the enunciation of certain vowels and consonants suffers.

In order for the salesperson to communicate with this buyer, he must use words and stories that are meaningful and interesting to the buyer.

STORIES

While they are entertaining, stories can also make points most effectively. Great stories often include conflicts, trials, and crises and help the listener think through choices and outcomes of those decisions. Of course salespeople cannot assume all customers are familiar with trade jargon, and thus they need to check with their customers continually to determine whether they are interpreting sales messages and stories properly.

Salespeople can paint word pictures to help customers understand the benefits or features of a product. A **word picture** is a graphic or vivid story designed to help the buyer easily visualize a point. To use a word picture effectively, the salesperson needs to paint as accurate and reliable a picture as possible.[3] Exhibit 4.2 provides an example of a word picture that a Toyota Highlander salesperson might use when calling on the owner of a real estate firm.

Effective stories often include an **analogy,** which is when the speaker attempts to draw a parallel between one thing and another. For example, to explain how a new machine controller is always monitoring and is ready to respond instantly, the seller could say this:

> It's kind of like a broadband Internet connection. It's always on. This controller never goes to sleep, never hangs up. This controller is sitting there, 24 hours a day, 7 days a week, 365 days a year, watching for the smallest malfunction and then taking immediate action to resolve the problem.

KEEP OPEN LINES OF COMMUNICATION

Although this might seem obvious, sometimes the obvious needs to be stated: As a salesperson you must always keep the lines of verbal communication with the buyer

Exhibit 4.2

Example of a Word Picture

Situation

A Toyota salesperson is calling on Jill, the owner of a commercial real estate firm. The goal of the word picture is to demonstrate the value of the four-wheel-drive option.

Word Picture

Jill, picture for a moment the following situation. You have this really hot prospect—let's call him Steve—for a remote resort development. You're in your current car, a Cadillac XTS. You've been trying to get Steve up to the property for months, and today is his only free day for several weeks. The property, up in the northern Georgia mountains, is accessible only by an old logging road. The day is bright and sunny, and Steve is in a good mood. When you reach the foot of the mountains, the weather turns cloudy and windy. As you wind up the old, bumpy road, a light rain begins. You've just crossed a small bridge when a downpour starts; the rain is pelting your windshield. Steve looks a little worried. Suddenly your car's tires start spinning. You're stuck in the mud.

Now let's replay the story, assuming that you buy the Toyota Highlander we've been talking about. [Salesperson quickly repeats the first paragraph of this story, substituting "Toyota Highlander" for "Cadillac XTS."] Suddenly your car tires start spinning. You're stuck in the mud. Calmly you reach down and shift into four-wheel drive. The Toyota pulls out easily, and you reach the destination in about five minutes. Although it's raining, the prospect looks at the land and sees great potential. On the way back down the mountain, you discuss how Steve should go about making an offer on the property. Jill, I hope I've made a point. Can you see why the four-wheel-drive option is important for you, even though it does add to the base price of the car?

From the BUYER'S SEAT

4.1

PLEASE LEARN HOW TO COMMUNICATE!

As a senior buyer at Microsoft, I see many different types of salespeople. I receive numerous calls each day from salespeople trying to make appointments with me and there are usually one of two outcomes:

A. The salesperson that has done their research about my company prior to the call and has a very concise and clear message tends to have the best chance of actually getting the appointment that they are shooting for.

B. Often salespeople will say, "I didn't expect you to answer your phone!" The salespeople who have this response are caught completely off guard and stand very little chance of obtaining their desired appointment.

With many means options of communication methods that a salesperson has, I believe that their choice should strongly rely on the message being delivered. When it is a salesperson who is new to me and with who I don't have a relationship, I feel as though a phone call is sufficient. In this phone call, I will usually share my e-mail with the salesperson so that he or she can send me a profile of his or her company. Once a relationship has been established and we have begun doing business together, I tend to prefer to call my salespeople when a problem or issue arises. After this phone call, I will then follow-up with an e-mail that outlines the problem and solution.

I personally feel it is important for salespeople to avoid texting a buyer. However, once you have developed a very strong relationship and have asked the buyer if he or she is okay with an occasional text, then I would say it is deemed acceptable.

The following are examples I have personally experienced that have helped salespeople strengthen their relationship with me:

- Using active listening skills during a conversation with me and then remembering specifics from that conversation in future meetings. This proves to me that they really listen to what the objectives were, have retained this information, and then have acted on it to prepare for the next meeting.

- A salesperson who knows what situations are better to be handled via the telephone as opposed to e-mail. Under certain circumstances, sending an e-mail instead of making a phone call can make the problem worse, so knowing the proper means of communication can definitely help a salesperson build a relationship with me.

The following are two examples of things that I have personally experienced with salespeople that have hindered our relationship:

- I was facing a quality issue, and I felt as though Jerry, my salesperson, had disappeared. We had discussed the problem on the phone, and when I followed up later that day and the next day, I received no response, not even an "I'm working on it; allow me time to get back to you." Instead, each time I called, I was told Jerry was in a meeting.

- When a salesperson does not know how to respectfully use means of communications, it can lead to a poor relationship. For example, a salesperson with whom I had not worked in the past, Tyler, received my e-mail address from one of my coworkers. That was fine with me. However, Tyler sent me nine e-mails within one hour in attempts to set up a meeting!

Source: Maria Longori, personal correspondence, used with permission, names changed on request.

open. That means you must contact buyers often, keep them fully informed, and make sure you are accessible for their contact, as "From the Buyer's Seat 4.1" indicates.

ACTIVE LISTENING

Many people believe effective communication is achieved by talking a lot. Inexperienced salespeople often go into a selling situation thinking they have to out-talk the prospect. They are enthusiastic about their product and company, and

Exhibit 4.3
Levels of Listening

Level	Name	Characteristics
1	Hearing	Tuning in and tuning out. Mainly paying attention to yourself. Not responding to the speaker. Often just pretending to listen.
2	Passive listening	Not making a great effort to understand what the speaker is trying to convey. Not listening to the deeper meaning of what the speaker is saying. More concerned with content of the message than the speaker's feelings. Speaker may think the listener is really listening.
3	Active listening	Actively tries to put self in the speaker's place. Sees things from the speaker's point of view, including feelings. Reading speaker's body language carefully. Avoids all distractions.

they want to tell the prospect all they know. However, salespeople who monopolize conversations cannot find out what customers need. One authority suggests an **80–20 listening rule:** Salespeople should listen 80 percent of the time and talk no more than 20 percent of the time.[4] Studies have shown that salespeople with outstanding communication skills actually support the value creation process.[5]

People can speak at a rate of only 120 to 160 words per minute, but they can listen to more than 800 words per minute. This difference is referred to as the **speaking–listening differential.** Because of this differential, salespeople often become lazy listeners. They do not pay attention and often remember only 50 percent of what is said immediately after they hear it.

Effective listening is not a passive activity. There are three levels of listening, as Exhibit 4.3 illustrates. Salespeople who practice **active listening** project themselves into the mind of the speaker and attempt to feel the way the speaker feels. Firms are spending millions of dollars on speech analytics technology for their call centers so they can discover the customer's emotions during a phone conversation. Salespeople should be able to do that more effectively because they are face-to-face with the customer. If a customer says she needs a small microphone, a Sony salesperson needs to listen carefully to find out what the term *small* means to this particular customer—how small the microphone has to be, why she needs a small microphone, and what she will be willing to sacrifice to get a small microphone. Active listening enables the salesperson to recommend a type of microphone that will meet the customer's specific needs.

Active listeners think while they listen. They think about the conclusions toward which the speaker is building, evaluate the evidence being presented, and sort out important facts from irrelevant ones. Active listening also means the listener attempts to draw out as much information as possible. Gestures can motivate a person to continue talking. Head nodding, eye contact, and an occasional *I see, Tell me more,* or *That's interesting* all demonstrate an interest in and understanding of what is being said. Take a moment to complete the questionnaire in Exhibit 4.4 to rate your active listening skills.

Suggestions for active listening include (1) repeating information, (2) restating or rephrasing information, (3) clarifying information, (4) summarizing the conversation, (5) tolerating silences, and (6) concentrating on the ideas being communicated.

Exhibit 4.4
Test Your Active
Listening Skills

	My performance could be improved substantially			My performance needs no improvement	
During a typical conversation:					
1. I project an impression that I sincerely care about what the person is saying.	1	2	3	4	5
2. I don't interrupt the person.	1	2	3	4	5
3. I don't jump to conclusions.	1	2	3	4	5
4. I ask probing questions.	1	2	3	4	5
5. I ask continuing questions like "Could you tell me more?"	1	2	3	4	5
6. I maintain eye contact with the person.	1	2	3	4	5
7. I nod to show the person that I agree or understand.	1	2	3	4	5
8. I read the person's nonverbal communications.	1	2	3	4	5
9. I wait for the person to finish speaking before evaluating what has been said.	1	2	3	4	5
10. I ask clarifying questions like "I'm not sure I know what you mean."	1	2	3	4	5
11. I restate what the person has stated or asked.	1	2	3	4	5
12. I summarize what the person has said.	1	2	3	4	5
13. I make an effort to understand the person's point of view.	1	2	3	4	5
14. I try to find things I have in common with the person.	1	2	3	4	5

Scoring: 60–70 = Outstanding; 50–59 = Good; 40–49 = Could use some improvement; 30–39 = Could definitely use some improvement; Under 30 = Are you listening?

Source: An adaptation of the ILPS scale, Stephen B. Castleberry, C. David Shepherd, and Rick E. Ridnour, "Effective Interpersonal Listening in the Personal Selling Environment: Conceptualization, Measurement, and Nomological Validity," *Journal of Marketing Theory and Practice*, Winter 1999, pp. 30–38.

REPEATING INFORMATION

During a sales interaction the salesperson should verify the information he or she is collecting from the customer. A useful way to verify information is to repeat, word for word, what has been said. This technique minimizes the chance of misunderstandings:

CUSTOMER: I'll take 20 cases of Nestlé milk chocolate hot cocoa and 12 cases of the rich chocolate.

SALESPERSON: Sure, Mr. Johnson, 20 cases of milk chocolate and 12 cases of rich chocolate.

CUSTOMER: Wait a minute. I got that backward. The rich chocolate is what sells the best here. I want 20 cases of the rich chocolate and 12 cases of the milk chocolate.

SALESPERSON: Fine. Twelve milk chocolate, 20 rich chocolate. Is that right?

CUSTOMER: Yes. That's what I want.

Salespeople need to be careful when using this technique, however. Customers can get irritated with salespeople who echo everything.

RESTATING OR REPHRASING INFORMATION

To verify a customer's intent, salespeople should restate the customer's comment in his or her own words. This step ensures that the salesperson and customer understand each other:

> CUSTOMER: Your service isn't what I had expected it would be.
>
> SALESPERSON: I see, you're a bit dissatisfied with the financial advisor services I've been giving you.
>
> CUSTOMER: Oh, no. As a matter of fact, I've been getting better service than I thought I would.

CLARIFYING INFORMATION

Another way to verify a customer's meaning is to ask questions designed to obtain additional information. These can give a more complete understanding of the customer's concerns:

To be an effective listener, the salesperson demonstrates an interest in what the customer is saying and actively thinks about questions for drawing out more information.

> CUSTOMER: Listen, I've tried everything. I just can't get this drill press to work properly.
>
> SALESPERSON: Just what is it that the drill press doesn't do?
>
> CUSTOMER: Well, the rivets keep jamming inside the machine. Sometimes one rivet is inserted on top of the other.
>
> SALESPERSON: Would you describe for me the way you load the rivets onto the tray?
>
> CUSTOMER: Well, first I push down the release lever and take out the tray. Then I push that little button and put in the rivets. Next, I push the lever again, put the tray in the machine, and push the lever.
>
> SALESPERSON: When you put the tray in, which side is up?
>
> CUSTOMER: Does that make a difference?

This exchange shows how a sequence of questions can clarify a problem and help the salesperson determine its cause.

SUMMARIZING THE CONVERSATION

An important element of active listening is to mentally summarize points that have been made. At critical spots in the sales presentation, the salesperson should present his or her mentally prepared summary. Summarizing provides both salesperson and customer with a quick overview of what has taken place and lets them focus on the issues that have been discussed:

> CUSTOMER: So I told him I wasn't interested.
>
> SALESPERSON: Let me see whether I have this straight. A salesperson called on you today and asked whether you were interested in reducing your costs. He also said he could save you about $125 a month. But when you pursued the matter, you found out the dollar savings in costs were offset by reduced service.
>
> CUSTOMER: That's right.

SALESPERSON: Well, I have your account records right here. Assuming you're interested in getting more for your company's dollar with regard to cell service costs, I think there's a way we can help you—without having to worry about any decrease in the quality of service.

CUSTOMER: Tell me more.

TOLERATING SILENCES

This technique could more appropriately be titled "Bite your tongue." At times during a sales presentation, a customer needs time to think. This need can be triggered by a tough question or an issue the customer wants to avoid. While the customer is thinking, periods of silence occur. Salespeople may be uncomfortable during these silences and feel they need to say something. However, the customer cannot think when the salesperson is talking. The following conversation about setting a second appointment demonstrates the benefits of tolerating silence:

SALESPERSON: What day would you like me to return with the samples and give that demonstration to you and your team?

CUSTOMER: [*obviously thinking*]

SALESPERSON: [*silence*]

CUSTOMER: OK, let's make it on Monday, the 22nd.

CONCENTRATING ON THE IDEAS BEING COMMUNICATED

Frequently what customers say and how they say it can distract salespeople from the ideas the customers are actually trying to communicate. For example, salespeople may react strongly when customers use emotion-laden phrases such as *bad service* or *lousy product*. Rather than getting angry, the salesperson should try to find out what upset the customer so much. Salespeople should listen to the words from the customer's viewpoint instead of reacting from their own viewpoint, as "Building Partnerships 4.1" discusses.

READING NONVERBAL MESSAGES FROM CUSTOMERS

In addition to asking questions and listening, salespeople can learn a lot from their customers' nonverbal behaviors.[6] When two people communicate with each other, spoken words play a surprisingly small part in the communication process. Words are responsible for only 40 percent of the information people acquire in face-to-face communication. Voice characteristics account for 10 percent of the message received, and the remaining 50 percent comes from nonverbal communications.[7] In this section we discuss how salespeople can collect information by observing their customers' **body language**. Later in the chapter we examine how salespeople can use the three forms of **nonverbal communication**—body language, space, and appearance—to convey messages to their customers. Note that experts don't always agree on what nonverbal cues mean. The examples provided in this chapter are those commonly accepted by sales trainers.

Studies have shown that the brain can actually lose it's ability to understand nonverbals if face-to-face contact decreases. One fear of over-use of social media is that people will lose their nonverbal reading skills.[8]

BUILDING Partnerships

4.1

USE COMMUNICATION PRINCIPLES TO BUILD STRONG RELATIONSHIPS

As a salesperson for Sadelco, Inc., a manufacturer of digital signal meters, I am in such an industry that I rarely walk out of a sales call with an order in hand. I must rely on my customer to come to me when he or she has a need for my category of products. Communicating with my clients on a regular basis provides me the opportunity to keep them abreast of the latest product changes, special promotions, and other information that is essential for their company to be successful.

My customers are very busy, and I must have their trust that if they are to take my phone call or accept my invitation to meet. They must realize that when I contact them that I am bringing something useful to them that is necessary for them to do their job effectively. Listening to my customers is the starting point to understanding their needs and motivations. Their needs are the only thing that I should be focused on as I begin to establish a strong business relationship. The more quickly one masters the ability to listen, the faster you will build the level of trust and lead to your greater success as a salesperson.

Examples of important information that my customers appreciate in a very timely manner are the following:

- Informing them of new pricing that will affect products that they are reselling in the marketplace and giving them the option to place an order prior to new pricing taking effect.
- Informing them when one of my products is out of stock and unable to fill their orders as needed. This includes offering viable alternatives of replacement products to fill their orders until the requested products are available.

- Changes in the technical specifications of my products that could have an impact for their customers.
- Suggesting complementary accessories or other products that would work well with products already being purchased.
- Situations with one of my factories that could have an adverse effect on lead times, trying to prevent an unhappy customer on their end.

I feel if I do a great job in communication many of these important matters to enable my customer to make more informed decisions, they are more likely to come to me with their business versus my competition.

Occasionally, I must tell my customers information that they don't want to hear (e.g., that products will not ship in time or that I cannot get them the pricing they need to make a project work). Communicating the bad news in a timely manner will lead to their trusting me more and greatly strengthening the critical trust level that is so vital in sales.

One of the most satisfying parts of my business is when a customer comes to me looking for a solution to a problem or a specific need for a product. It tells me that I have done my job and that my customers trust me to help them solve a problem. I may not profit in the immediate future, but I know I have a good customer and often a good friend who will help me to be successful in my job.

Source: RDM, personal correspondence, used with permission, names changed on request.

BODY ANGLE

Back-and-forth motions indicate a positive outlook, whereas side-to-side movements suggest insecurity and doubt. Body movements directed toward a person indicate positive regard; in contrast, leaning back or away suggests boredom, apprehension, or possibly anger. Changes in position may indicate that a customer wants to end the interview, strongly agrees or disagrees with what has been said, or wants to place an order.

FACE

The face has many small muscles capable of communicating innumerable messages. Customers can use these muscles to indicate interest, expectation, concern,

The customer in the upper panel is giving negative nonverbal signals of arms crossed and no smile. Both buyers and the seller in the lower panel are giving positive, nonverbal signals.

disapproval, or approval. The eyes are the most important area of the face. The pupils of interested or excited people tend to enlarge. Thus, by looking at a customer's eyes, salespeople can often determine when their presentations have made an impression. For this reason many Chinese jade buyers wear dark glasses so they can conceal their interest in specific items and bargain more effectively. Even the rate at which someone blinks can tell a lot about a person. The average blink rate for a relaxed person is 10 to 20 blinks per minute (bmp). During normal conversation, it increases to about 25 bmp. A bmp rate over 50, and particularly over 70, indicates high stress levels.

Eye position can indicate a customer's thought process. Eyes focused straight ahead mean a customer is passively receiving information but devoting little effort to analyzing the meaning and not really concentrating on the presentation. Intense eye contact for more than three seconds generally indicates customer displeasure. Staring indicates coldness, anger, or dislike.

Customers look away from the salesperson while they actively consider information in the sales presentation. When the customer's eyes are positioned to the left or right, the salesperson has succeeded in getting the customer involved in the presentation. A gaze to the right suggests the customer is considering the logic and facts in the presentation, and gazing to the left suggests more intense concentration based on an emotional consideration. Eyes cast down offer the strongest signal of concentration. However, when customers cast their eyes down, they may be thinking, *How can I get my boss to buy this product?* or *How can I get out of this conversation?* When customers look away for an extended period, they probably want to end the meeting.

Skin color and skin tautness are other facial cues. A customer whose face reddens is signaling that something is wrong. That blush can indicate either anger or embarrassment. Tension and anger show in a tightness around the cheeks, jawline, or neck.

ARMS

A key factor in interpreting arm movements is intensity. Customers will use more arm movement when they are conveying an opinion. Broader and more vigorous movement indicates the customer is more emphatic about the point being communicated verbally. Always remember cultural differences. For example, it's rude to cross your arms in Turkey.

HANDS

Hand gestures are very expressive. For example, open and relaxed hands are a positive signal, especially with palms facing up. Self-touching gestures typically indicate tension. Involuntary gestures, such as tightening of a fist, are good indicators of true feelings. The meanings of hand gestures differ from one culture to another. For example, the thumbs-up gesture is considered offensive in the Middle East, rude in Australia, and a sign of OK in France. In Japan the OK sign

The open hands on the left are a positive signal by a salesperson. The intertwined fingers in the middle indicate that the salesperson is expressing his power and authority. On the right the salesperson is playing with his hands, indicating underlying tension. Source: Stephen B. Castleberry, used with permission

made by holding the thumb and forefinger in a circle symbolizes money, but in France it indicates that something is worthless.

LEGS

When customers have uncrossed legs in an open position, they send a message of cooperation, confidence, and friendly interest. Legs crossed away from a salesperson suggest that the sales call is not going well. Note that crossing your feet and showing the bottoms of your shoes are insulting in Japan.

BODY LANGUAGE PATTERNS

Exhibit 4.5 illustrates the patterns of signals that generally indicate the customer is reacting positively or negatively to a salesperson's presentation. However, no single gesture or position defines a specific emotion or attitude. To interpret a customer's feelings, salespeople need to consider the pattern of the signals via a number of channels. For example, many men are comfortable in informal conversations with their arms crossed. It doesn't necessarily mean they're against you or what you're saying.

In business and social situations, buyers often use nonverbal cues to try to be polite. As a result salespeople often have difficulty knowing what a customer is really thinking. For example, smiling is the most common way to conceal a strong emotion. Salespeople need to know whether a customer's smile is real or just a polite mask. The muscles around the eyes reveal whether a smile is real or polite.

Exhibit 4.5
Patterns of Nonverbal
Reactions to Presentation

Positive Signals	Negative Signals
Uncrossed arms and legs	Crossed arms or legs
Leaning forward	Leaning backward or turned away from you
Smiling or otherwise pleasant expression	Furrowed brow, pursed lips, frowning
Nodding	Shaking head
Contemplative posture	Fidgeting, distracted
Eye contact	No eye contact
Animated, excited reaction	Little change in expression, lifeless

When a customer is truly impressed, the muscles around the eyes contract, the skin above the eyes comes down a little, and the eyelids are slightly closed.

Here are some other signals that customers may be hiding their true feelings:

- *Contradictions and verbal mistakes.* People often forget what they said previously. They may leak their true feelings through a slip of the tongue or a lapse in memory.
- *Differences in two parts of a conversation.* In the first part of a conversation, a customer may display some nervousness when asked about the performance of a competitor's product and then respond by outlining the competitor's product's faults. Later in the conversation, the evaluation of the competitor's product may be much more positive.
- *Contradictions between verbal and nonverbal messages.* For example, a facial expression may not match the enthusiasm indicated by verbal comments. Also, a decrease in nonverbal signals may indicate that the customer is making a cautious response.
- *Nonverbal signals.* Voice tone going up at the end of a sentence, hesitation in the voice, small shrugs, increased self-touching, and stiffer body posture suggest that the customer has concerns.

When customers disguise their true feelings, they are often trying to be polite, not deceptive. To uncover the customer's true feelings and build a relationship, the salesperson needs to encourage the customer to be frank by emphasizing that she or he will benefit from an open exchange of information. Here are some comments a salesperson can make to encourage forthright discussion:

- Perhaps there is some reason you cannot share the information with me.
- Are you worried about how I might react to what you are telling me?
- I have a sense that there is really more to the story than what you are telling me. Let's put the cards on the table so we can put this issue to rest.

SENDING MESSAGES WITH NONVERBAL COMMUNICATION

The preceding section described how salespeople can develop a better understanding of their customers by observing their body language. Salespeople can also use their own body language, spacing, and appearance to send messages to their customers. This section explores that aspect of body language.

USING BODY LANGUAGE

During a 30-minute sales call around 800 nonverbal signals are exchanged.[9] Astute salespeople use these signals to communicate more effectively with customers.[10] For example, salespeople should strive to use the positive signals shown in Exhibit 4.5. Cooperative cues indicate to customers that the salesperson sincerely wants to help them satisfy their needs. Obviously salespeople should avoid using negative cues. In fact, salespeople should consider engaging in **mirroring**, which is where one person copies the nonverbals of another. In this case, salespeople should use their nonverbals carefully, hoping that the buyer will mirror their positive and open nonverbals.

Remember this word of warning: The most effective gestures are natural ones, not those you are forcing yourself to perform. A buyer can spot nongenuine nonverbals. Use as much of this information as you can, but don't become so engrossed in following all the rules that you can't be yourself.

Facial Muscles

Nonverbal communication is difficult to manage. Facial reactions are often involuntary, especially during stressful situations. Lips tense, foreheads wrinkle, and eyes glare without salespeople realizing they are disclosing their feelings to a customer. Salespeople will be able to control their facial reactions only with practice.

As with muscles anywhere else in the body, the coordination of facial muscles requires exercise. Actors realize this need and attend facial exercise classes to learn to control their reactions. Salespeople are also performers to some extent and need to learn how to use their faces to communicate emotions.

Nothing creates rapport like a smile.[11] The smile should appear natural and comfortable, not a smirk or an exaggerated, clownlike grin. To achieve the right smile, stand before a mirror or a video camera and put your lips in various smiling positions until you find a position that feels natural and comfortable. Then practice the smile until it becomes almost second nature.

Eye Contact

Appropriate eye contact varies from situation to situation.[12] People should use direct eye contact when talking in front of a group to indicate sincerity, credibility, and trustworthiness. Glancing from face to face rapidly or staring at a wall has the opposite effect. However, staring can overpower customers and make them uncomfortable.

Gestures and Handshaking

Gestures can have a dramatic impact.[13] For example, by exposing the palm of the hand, a salesperson indicates openness and receptivity. Slicing hand movements and pointing a finger are very strong signals and should be used to reinforce only the most important points. In most cases pointing a finger should be avoided. This gesture will remind customers of a parent scolding a child. When salespeople make presentations to a group, they often use too few hand gestures. Gestures should be used to drive home a point. But if a salesperson uses too many gestures, acting like an orchestra conductor, people will begin to watch the hands and miss the words.

The location of your hands during gestures can have a huge impact on the message received.[14] For example, imagine a salesperson standing and giving a presentation to a small group of businesspeople. If she drops her hands down by her sides while presenting and keeps them there, she will come across as passive and lacking enthusiasm. Hand gestures presented at about the height of her navel help the salesperson come across as truthful. Gestures at chest level suggest she has real passion about a topic, while those above the head are interpreted as great passion. Try each of these locations of gestures in front of a mirror while saying "I love you" to see what impact the location of gestures has on the interpretation of the spoken words.

In terms of shaking hands, salespeople should not automatically extend their hands to prospects, particularly if a prospect is seated.[15] Shaking hands should be the prospect's choice. If the prospect offers a hand, the salesperson should respond with a firm but not overpowering handshake while maintaining good eye contact. Chances are that you have experienced both a limpid handshake—a hand with little or no grip—and a bone-crunching grip. Either impression is often lasting and negative. Also, if you tend to have sweaty hands, carry a handkerchief.

Women should shake hands in the same manner men do. They should avoid offering their hand for a social handshake (palm facing down and level with the ground, with fingers drooping and pointing to the ground). Likewise, a man should not force a social handshake from a woman in a business setting.

The salesperson selling in an international context needs to carefully consider cultural norms regarding the appropriateness of handshaking, bowing, and other forms of greeting. For example, the Chinese prefer no more than a slight bow in their greeting, whereas an Arab businessperson may not only shake hands vigorously but also keep holding your hand for several seconds. A hug in Mexico communicates a trusting relationship, but in Germany such a gesture would be offensive because it suggests an inappropriate level of intimacy. Germans tend to pump the hand only once during a handshake. Seventy-four percent of British adults admit they no longer reach out a hand to greet friends or colleagues.[16] Some African cultures snap their fingers after shaking hands, but other Africans would see this act as tasteless. And some Eastern cultures use the left hand for hygienic purposes, so offering a left hand to them would insult them.

Posture and Body Movements

Shuffling one's feet and slumping give an impression of a lack of both self-confidence and self-discipline. On the other hand, an overly erect posture, like that of a military cadet, suggests rigidity. Salespeople should let comfort be their guide when searching for the right posture.

To get an idea of what looks good and feels good, stand in front of a mirror and shift your weight until tension in your back and neck is at a minimum. Then gently pull your shoulders up and back and elevate your head. Practice walking by taking a few steps. Keep the pace deliberate, not halting; deliberate, controlled movements indicate confidence and empathy. Note cultural differences like the fact that Japanese people value the ability to sit quietly and can view a fidgety American as uncontrolled.

This buyer and seller are in the intimate zone.

THE ROLE OF SPACE AND PHYSICAL CONTACT

The physical space between a customer and a salesperson can affect the customer's reaction to a sales presentation. Exhibit 4.6 shows the four distance zones people use when interacting in business and social situations. The **intimate zone** is reserved primarily for a person's closest relationships, the **personal zone** for close friends and those who share special interests, the **social zone** for business transactions and other impersonal relationships, and the **public zone** for speeches, teachers in classrooms, and passersby. The exact sizes of the intimate and personal zones depend on age, gender, culture, and race. For example, the social zone for Latinos is much closer than that for North Americans. Latinos tend to conduct business transactions so close together that North Americans feel uncomfortable.

Customers may react negatively when they believe salespeople are invading their intimate or personal space. To show the negative reaction, customers may assume a defensive posture by moving back or folding their arms. Although approaching too close can generate a negative reaction, standing too far away can create an image of aloofness, conceit, or unsociability.

In general, salespeople should begin customer interactions at the social zone and not move closer until an initial rapport has been established. If the buyer indicates that a friendlier relationship has developed, the salesperson should move closer.

In terms of touching, buyers fall into two touching groups: contact and noncontact. Contact people usually see noncontact people as cold and unfriendly. On the other hand, noncontact people view contact people as overly friendly and obtrusive. People who like to be touched tend to respond to touch with increased

Exhibit 4.6
Distance Zones for Interaction

Intimate zone:
0–2 feet

Social zone:
4–12 feet

Personal zone:
2–4 feet

Public zone:
beyond
12 feet

persuasion and liking for the salesperson. Although some customers may accept a hand on their backs or a touch on their shoulders, salespeople should generally limit touching to a handshake. Touching clearly enters a customer's intimate space and may be considered rude and threatening—an invasion.

APPEARANCE

Physical appearance, specifically dress style, is an aspect of nonverbal communication that affects the customer's evaluation of the salesperson. Two priorities in dressing for business are (1) getting customers to notice you in a positive way and (2) getting customers to trust you. If salespeople overdress, their clothing may distract from their sales presentation. Proper attire and grooming, however, can give salespeople additional poise and confidence. One salesperson for Smith & Nephew, a medical equipment company, says he always dresses like a chameleon. "Dress like your doctor," is his motto. If the doctor is in suit and tie, he wears a suit and tie; if the doctor prefers casual dress, the seller does likewise.

At one time dressing for work was simple: You just reached in the closet and picked from your wardrobe of blue, gray, and pinstripe suits. Today things are not that simple. With casual days and dress-down Fridays, styles and dress codes vary considerably from office to office. Salespeople should learn the norms for dress in their field and follow them closely.

During a given day a salesperson may have to visit his or her company's and customers' offices, each of which may have a different dress code. And sometimes the buyer will have dress codes that even visiting salespeople must follow. For example, Target has dress codes that apply to salespeople who want to make presentations at its company offices.

Vicki West has developed five timeless principles for a salesperson wanting to dress for success.[17] We describe these here.

Principle 1: Consider the Geography

The temperature: Clothing choices are obviously influenced by temperature trends and variations. San Francisco is different from Minneapolis, which differs from Austin, Texas, in humidity, temperature, and weather patterns. These factors dictate the fiber and type of clothing worn. Although linen and cotton are cool, warm-weather fabrics suitable almost the entire year in the southern part of the United States, they would be appropriate only in the late spring and summer in other locales.

The local cultural norms: Some cities are formal, and others are known for their casual culture. The economic and business sectors of a community often play a pivotal role in the local cultural norms for clothing choices. An example of a cultural norm difference within the short distance of 200 miles is that between Dallas and Austin, Texas. Dallas is more formal than Austin in most industry sectors. Dallas is known as a "headquarters" town with large regional and national businesses represented. Austin has a large segment of population employed in education, high technology, and the music industry, all of which typically have a younger, more casual workforce.

Principle 2: Consider Your Customers

Their appearance: Customers wear many different types of clothing, which are often dictated by the demands of their profession. Farmers, bankers, high-technology workers, and educators all dress differently depending on the functional demands of their daily work. A salesperson's appearance is certainly impacted by the customers' industry.

Their expectations for your appearance, however, generally reflect their impression of your industry. Salespeople representing the banking industry would be expected to dress differently from salespeople in the music recording industry.

Principle 3: Consider Your Corporate Culture

Norms for your industry should dictate the general parameters for appearance choices. It is obvious that corporate cultures change from time to time. The trend has been to dress more casually in the hot-weather months, even in conservative industries such as banking and finance. However, the consensus of many industry groups is that it is important to wear professional business attire regularly, with some exceptions based on geography and a salesperson's customer base.

Principle 4: Consider Your Aspirations

Top levels of your organization generally set the tone for an entire organization. If you aspire to reach a high level in the organization, it's important to note what expectations your organization might have for your general appearance.

An old rule is to dress *one level above your position.* Watch your immediate superior, who will decide whom to promote. If you want a promotion to the next level in the organization, dress as if you already have the position; then you will be perceived as a good fit for the job.

Principle 5: Consider Your Own Personal Style

Wait until you have the halo effect before making a personal style statement. The "halo effect" refers to the tendency to generalize one positive aspect of your behavior to all aspects of your behavior. This phenomenon can work to your benefit. No one wants to look like a corporate drone with no individual style, but the first week on the job may not be the best time to make your personal appearance statement. Wait until you have proved your professional skills, no matter what the industry, before wearing clothing that may be deemed inappropriate to your particular industry.

Be reasonable in your wardrobe choices. Being individualist and memorable can be a positive decision, depending on the range of choices that are acceptable to a specific industry group. However, choosing outrageous or completely unsuitable clothing is probably not in the best interests of your personal career development. Like it or not, large jewelry, piercings, tattoos, heavy perfumes and colognes, short skirts, shorts, revealing blouses or shirts, pink or turquoise hair, and so forth are simply considered inappropriate in most sales situations.

COMMUNICATING VIA TECHNOLOGY

In addition to face-to-face interactions, salespeople communicate with customers by using the telephone, fax, e-mail, and voice mail. As shown in Exhibit 4.7, these methods vary in the interactivity of the communications, the ability to use verbal and nonverbal communication channels, and the quantity of information that can be conveyed. **Response time** is the time between sending a message and getting a response to it. Salespeople should use the communication method preferred by the buyer and should not overdo communicating with the buyer to the point of being a nuisance.[18]

TELEPHONE AND VOICE MAIL COMMUNICATIONS

Salespeople need to use the phone correctly and effectively. All of us have used telephones since childhood; many of us have developed bad habits that reduce our effectiveness when talking over the phone.[19] Perfect your phone style by practicing alone before making any calls. Make sure you know what you want to say before placing the call. Many would argue that it is a polite gesture to start by asking, "Is this a good time to talk?" Don't be too rushed to be nice; it is never acceptable to be rude. And don't forget to smile as you talk. Even though the prospect won't see it, he or she will hear it in your enthusiastic tone of voice.

Active listening is as important when conversing over the phone as when conversing in person. Take notes and restate the message or any action you have agreed to undertake. In addition, you will need to encourage two-way communication. If you have ever talked with two-year-olds over the phone, you know that if you ask them a yes-or-no question, they tend to shake their heads yes or no rather than verbalize a response. Similarly, you cannot nod your head to encourage someone to continue talking on the phone. Instead you must encourage conversations with verbal cues such as *Uh-huh, I see,* or *That's interesting.* Finally, just as in face-to-face conversation, you must be able to tolerate silences so customers have an opportunity to ask questions, agree or disagree, or relate a point to their circumstances.

Exhibit 4.7
Comparison of Various Methods of Salesperson Communications*

	Face-to-Face	Telephone	Voice Mail	Fax	E-Mail
Response time	Fast	Fast	Slow	Slow	Slow
Salesperson can use verbal communications	Yes	Yes	Yes	No	No
Salesperson can hear buyer's verbal communications	Yes	Yes	No	No	No
Salesperson can read buyer's nonverbal communications	Yes	No	No	No	No
Quantity of information seller can send	Highest	Average	Lowest	Varies	Varies
Quantity of information buyer can send	Highest	Average	None	None	None

*Ratings can vary greatly given the situation.

It is important to set objectives for your phone call and strategize what you're going to say and why. Here is an example of using the phone to make an appointment:

1. [*State customer's name.*] Hello, Mr. Peterson? (*Pause.*)
2. [*Introduce yourself and show preparation.*] This is Amanda Lowden with Cisco Systems. I was talking to your director of operations, Marvin Schepp, and he suggested I talk with you.
3. [*Politely check time.*] I hope I didn't catch you in the middle of something urgent or pressing? (*Pause.*)
4. [*State purpose and build credibility.*] I'm calling to let you know about our new carrier routing system. I've shown it to several other systems engineers in town, and they found its self-healing and self-defending operating system to be something they wanted to explore further.
5. [*Commitment to action.*] I'd like to meet with you and share some feedback from your business associates. Could you put me on your calendar for 30 minutes next Monday or Tuesday?
6. [*Show appreciation and restate time, or keep door open.*] Thank you, Mr. Peterson. I'll be at your office at 9 a.m. on Tuesday. [*or*] I appreciate your frankness, Mr. Peterson. I'd like to get back to you in a couple of months. Would that be all right?

Use proper techniques and etiquette when leaving voice mail messages:[20]

- If making a cold call to set up an appointment, don't leave a message. Just call back later.
- Leave a clear, concise message that includes a suggested time for a return call (so you can be prepared for that call).
- Speak slowly and distinctly.
- A little casual conversation up front is acceptable, but don't waste the prospect's time.
- Ask for a callback.
- Slowly repeat your name and phone number at the end of your message.

For your own voice mail system, use a fresh greeting on your system each day. Tell callers if a time limit exists for your voice mail, and if possible, offer the option to talk to someone immediately.

E-MAIL COMMUNICATIONS

Developments in technology enable salespeople to improve their communications with customers.

Technology makes the transfer of information fast and easy. But it also holds the salesperson at arm's length and makes it difficult to develop rapport. High tech doesn't replace face-to-face interactions; it merely supplements and enhances personal exchanges. Following are some suggestions for salespeople with regard to e-mail communication:

- Don't be lulled into thinking that immediacy (fast) means the same thing as intimacy (close, friendly relationship) in communication. Buyers generally prefer face-to-face communications over other media types. When asked, most buyers said face-to-face communication builds high trust, reduces confusion and misunderstanding, and is easier to understand. And sometimes snail mail still works the best.

- For the subject line, use important information to avoid having the e-mail deleted unread (for example, don't use "hello" as your subject line). And make it sound easy to deal with (such as "Two Short Questions").

- Make sure the first few lines of the e-mail are important. Many people read only the first few lines before deleting a message. Use a heading and bullets to help the reader follow a longer e-mail message.

- It is hard for buyers to read your nonverbal messages in e-mail because they can't see them (and you can't read theirs). Studies show that many users do not grasp the tone or intent of e-mail, and using smiley faces or other emoticons just makes it more confusing.

- Learn the customer's preferences for e-mail. Adapt the content to the customer's preferred communication style. For example, some firms have instituted "no e-mail Fridays." And never be viewed by your prospect as a spammer!

- Avoid "techno overkill." Written communication (such as letters and printed brochures or catalogs) may be better when the customer wants to study the information at his or her leisure.

- Customers are drowning in information. Don't send long e-mail messages or large attachments unless the buyer is expecting them. If you decide to send a PowerPoint presentation via e-mail, use special software that will help ensure that it gets through the virus and spam filters.

- Use speed to impress customers—especially for damage control. Exceed a customer's expectations, such as responding immediately to urgent calls via e-mail. E-mail sent to you by customers should be answered by the end of the workday.

- Don't deliver bad news via e-mail; rather, use e-mail to arrange a meeting to discuss the issue.

- If you want your e-mail read, at least according to one study, send it on Wednesdays around 11:00 a.m. The worst time to send is (not surprisingly) Saturday and Sunday. See Sales Technology 4.1 for more hints on successful e-mailing.

SOCIAL NETWORKING

Social networking is the use of Web tools that allow users to share content, interact, and develop communities around similar interests. Salespeople are using social networking, like blogs, LinkedIn, Twitter, Pinterest, and Facebook, to communicate with customers and prospects.[21] While many of the suggestions already covered in this chapter apply to these networks, salespeople should consider other issues as well. Some suggestions for networking sites like LinkedIn and Facebook include the following:

- Fill out your profile completely to build trust and establish common bonds. Spend the time and money to get a great head shot photo and include it on your site. Make sure it is appropriate for business purposes. Update your profile regularly to keep it current and interesting. Remember that many members get updates every time someone changes his or her profile, so you're getting more exposure with every adjustment to your profile.

- Create contacts/friends lists such as "Family" and "Work Related" so you can better control the privacy of your profile and information.

- Follow all rules for the networking sites.

- Share articles and links to presentations and other information that might be helpful to prospects. Posting comments from experts will improve your credibility. Studies show that 55 percent of buyers use social media when looking for informatiion.[22]

4.1

E-MAILS: TEN EASY RULES TO FOLLOW

With technology being a prominent piece of today's business world, it is essential that one know the proper way to construct a professional business e-mail. The following is a list of things to consider to help ensure proper e-mail etiquette:

1. Have a meaningful subject line. For a deadline, do not just put "important" or "product 'x.'" Instead use, "Deadline approaching for product 'x.'"

2. Don't beat around the bush; you have a reason for the e-mail, so state it right away in the opening sentence.

3. Use specifics in your opening—avoid using words such as "this" or "that."

4. Use proper capitalization and punctuation—use correct uppercase and lowercase. Maybe write your e-mail first in a word processing document; this will give you the ability to utilize its spelling and grammar-check function.

5. Do not use chat room abbreviations, such as "LOL."

6. Be concise and detailed. The use of bullet points will help organize the information and make it easier and quicker for the recipient to read.

7. Be polite. "Please" and "thank you" can go a long way.

8. Create a signature block that will go on the end of the e-mail with good contact information.

9. Proofread, proofread, and proofread—the small things you may not notice when you are writing the e-mail may translate to carelessness in the eyes of the reader.

10. When receiving an important e-mail, be sure to respond quickly. If more than 24 hours will be needed to provide a response, it is a great idea to send a quick reply explaining your delay.

Failing to follow these simple rules may make it seem as though the recipients were not worth your time, and in turn they may feel as though you should not be worth their time.

Sources: Kitty O. Locker and Stephen Kyo Kaczmarek, *Business Communication: Building Critical Skills*, 5th ed. (New York: McGraw-Hill, 2011); Richard Nordquist, "Ten Tips on How to Write a Professional Email," *About.com Grammar & Composition*, August 30, 2012, http://grammar.about.com/od/developingessays/a/profemails.htm.

- Remember to post updates on your wall about your business. Tell about upcoming events like webinars and conferences where you will be speaking.
- Combine your Facebook/LinkedIn account with other social media sites you participate in, like Twitter and Pinterest.
- Respond quickly to posts and queries.
- Add your Facebook/LinkedIn URL to your e-mail signature so prospects can learn more about you.

Businesses are starting to build relationships and stay connected to their customers and prospects with microblogging tools like Twitter. The 140-or-less character messages are called tweets. Due to the nature of Twitter, some additional considerations apply:[23]

- Build your account and include a picture.
- Use a Twitter search tool to listen for your name, the name of your product, or your company.
- Use a friendly and casual tone in messages. But make sure your tweets reflect the culture of your company.

This American salesperson needs to recognize the differences between communicating in an Arab culture and an American culture.

- Make a link to things you think prospects would find interesting, like articles and Web sites. Tweets should have real value to the receiver.
- Don't create spam with Twitter.
- You can schedule when the tweets will be sent with add-ons like Social Oomph.
- Share interesting things about your community and nonbusiness items to help make yourself real. Remember that you are trying to create a friendly relationship.
- Remember to listen, not just send out tweets. Respond to at least some of the replying tweets. Don't feel guilty if you don't read or respond to all tweets.

Because of the growing use of social networking, Chapters 6 and 7 will discuss ways to use these tools to prospect and learn more about new customers.

ADJUSTING FOR CULTURAL DIFFERENCES

Communication in international selling often takes place in English because English is likely to be the only language salespeople and customers have in common. To communicate effectively with customers whose native language is not English, salespeople need to be careful about the words and expressions they use. People who use English in international selling should observe the following rules:

- Use common English words that a customer would learn during the first two years of studying the language. For example, use *expense* rather than *expenditure* or *stop* instead of *cease*.
- Use words that do not have multiple meanings. For example, *right* has many meanings, whereas *accurate* is more specific. When you use words that have several meanings, recognize that nonnative speakers will usually use the most common meaning to interpret what you are saying.
- Avoid slang expressions peculiar to American culture, such as *slice of life, struck out, wade through the figures,* and *run that by me again.*
- Use rules of grammar more strictly than you would in everyday speech. Make sure you express your thoughts in complete sentences, with a noun and a verb.
- Use action-specific verbs, as in *start the motor,* rather than action-general verbs, as in *get the motor going.*
- Never use vulgar expressions, tell off-color jokes, or make religious references.

Even if you are careful about the words you use, misunderstandings can still arise because terms have different meanings, even among people from different English-speaking countries.[24] For example, in the United States *tabling a proposal* means "delaying a decision," but in England it means "taking immediate action." In England promising to do something by the end of the day means doing it when you have finished what you are working on now, not within 24 hours. In England *bombed* means the negotiations were successful, whereas in the United States this term has the opposite meaning.

ethics

International salespeople need to understand the varying perceptions of time in general and the time it takes for business activities to occur in different countries. For example, in Latin American and Arab countries people are not strict about keeping appointments at the designated times. If you show up for an appointment on time in these cultures, you may have to wait several hours for the meeting to start. Lunch is at 3:00 p.m. in Spain, 12:00 noon in Germany, 1:00 p.m. in England, and 11:00 a.m. in Norway. In Greece no one makes telephone calls between 2:00 p.m. and 5:00 p.m. The British arrive at their desks at 9:30 a.m. but like to do paperwork and have a cup of tea before getting any calls. The French, like the Germans, like to start early in the day, frequently having working breakfasts. Restaurants close at 9:00 p.m. in Norway—just when dinner is starting in Spain. The best time to reach high-level Western European executives is after 7:00 p.m., when daily activities have slowed down and they are continuing to work for a few more hours. However, Germans start going home at 4:00 p.m.

Significant cultural differences dictate the appropriate level of eye contact between individuals. In the United States salespeople look directly into their customers' eyes when speaking or listening to them. Direct eye contact is a sign of interest in what the customer is saying. In other cultures looking someone in the eye may be a sign of disrespect:

- In Japan looking directly at a subordinate indicates that the subordinate has done something wrong. When a subordinate looks directly into the eyes of his or her supervisor, the subordinate is displaying hostility.

- In Muslim countries, eye contact is not supposed to occur between men and women.

- In Korea eye contact is considered rude.

- Brazilians look at people directly even more than Americans do. Americans tend to find this direct eye contact, when held over a long period, to be disconcerting.

SELLING YOURSELF

You've been applying for jobs and recently heard back from HR at one of your top choices. After e-mailing back and forth, you have finally set up a time for the two interviews with two different professionals from the business. The surprising element was that each of these interviews will be via phone.

Communication is vital not only to obtaining a sale but also to obtaining a job. Because the first two rounds of the interview are conducted on the phone, you will not be able to identify nonverbal cues, which makes being actively engaged in the conversation even more important. You can do this by asking clarifying questions and restating key points, which will help to keep the conversation flowing. Again, you want to make sure you have an understanding of who your audience is and what may be important to them. The first round may be a screening with HR, while the second round could be with a potential manager. A good point of reference for job objectives can always be found in the job description. It would also be a good idea to have a notebook and pencil so you can take notes during the interview for reference and also for future interviews you may have. These notes could really help you develop good, key questions.

One of the hardest things to remember, especially when you are used to talking to family and friends on the telephone, is to speak slowly and concisely. You want to make sure that whatever message you are trying to convey is a true reflection of who you are as a professional. This means adapting to your audience and leaving the slang and abbreviations at home.

With all of these tools at your side, the tele-interview will seem less daunting. Your confidence will shine through, and the flow of the conversation will be as if you were at a face-to-face meeting.

Source: Sally Cook, used with permission.

SUMMARY

This chapter discussed the principles of communication and how they can be used to build trust in relationships, improve selling effectiveness, and reduce misunderstandings. The communication process consists of a sender, who encodes information and transmits messages, and a receiver, who decodes the messages. A communication breakdown can occur when the sender does a poor encoding job, when the receiver has difficulty decoding, and when noise and the environment interfere with the transmission of the message.

Effective communication requires a two-way flow of information. At different times in the interaction, both parties will act as sender and receiver. This two-way process enables salespeople to adapt their sales approach to the customer's needs and communication style.

When communicating verbally with customers, salespeople must be careful to use words and expressions their customers will understand. Effective communication is facilitated through the use of word pictures and by appropriate voice characteristics like inflection, articulation, and the proper rate of speech and loudness.

Listening is a valuable communication skill that enables salespeople to adapt to various situations. To listen effectively, salespeople need to actively think about what the customer is saying and how to draw out more information. Some suggestions for actively collecting information from customers are to repeat, restate, clarify, summarize the customer's comments, and demonstrate an interest in what the customer is saying.

About 50 percent of communication is nonverbal. Nonverbal messages sent by customers are conveyed by body language. The five channels of body language communication are body angle, face, arms, hands, and legs. No single channel can be used to determine the feelings or attitudes of customers. Salespeople need to analyze the body language pattern composed of all five channels to determine how a customer feels.

Salespeople can use nonverbal communication to convey information to customers. In addition to knowing how to use the five channels of body language, salespeople need to know the appropriate distances between themselves and their customers for different types of communications and relationships. Salespeople should learn to use their physical appearance and dress to create a favorable impression on customers.

Learning how to communicate effectively with technology is critical in today's marketplace. Not only should salespeople learn how to use the phone and e-mail effectively; they should also master the use of social networking like Facebook and LinkedIn, as well as Twitter and blogs, to connect with their customers and prospects.

Finally, two-way communication increases when salespeople adjust their communication styles to the styles of their customers. In making such adjustments, salespeople need to be sensitive to cultural differences when selling internationally and in diverse subcultures.

KEY TERMS

active listening   101
analogy   99
articulation   98
body language   104
decoding   96
80–20 listening rule   101
encoding   96
feedback   96
inflection   98
intimate zone   110
loudness   98
mirroring   108

noises   97
nonverbal communication   104
personal zone   110
persuading   97
public zone   110
response time   113
social networking   115
social zone   110
speaking–listening differential   101
two-way communication   96
voice characteristics   98
word picture   99

ETHICS PROBLEMS

1. In an effort to improve relationships and open communications, is it OK to enjoy a few beers on the golf course with your clients?

2. Assume you are making a call on a person of the opposite sex in a culture where direct eye contact between the sexes is not supposed to occur. Much to your amazement, the buyer continues to look intently into your eyes. You are in an office alone with the buyer. What should you do?

QUESTIONS AND PROBLEMS

1. As a student in a college classroom, you may encounter many distractions that affect your listening ability.
   a. List three things you have seen professors do that are distracting to you.
   b. What can you do to reduce each of these distractions?

2. Have a friend score you using the listening test (See Exhibit 4.4) found in this chapter.
   a. Compare your friend's score with the one you gave yourself.
   b. What did this exercise teach you about your listening skills?

3. Make a chart with three columns: *Items, What I Want This Item to Communicate to Others,* and *What Others Will Think My Item Is Communicating.* In the first column list the following: *my hairstyle, the clothing I'm wearing today,* and *any jewelry or body accents* (like earrings or tattoos). In the second column describe the message you want to communicate with each item. Have someone else fill in the third column, describing what the items communicate to him or her.

4. Develop a word picture that helps explain to a 60-year-old the merits of buying a smartphone, assuming the person doesn't own a cell phone currently.

5. What do the following body language cues indicate?
   a. Looking at something out the window while you're talking.
   b. Tapping the feet on the floor rhythmically.
   c. Leaning back in a chair with arms folded across the chest.
   d. Sitting on the edge of the seat.

6. Word choice is important. Some words, by themselves, may be perceived negatively. Come up with a better word choice that could be more positive for each of the following words: *cost, down payment, deal, objection, cheaper, appointment, commission.*

7. In "From the Buyer's Seat 4.1" you learned about Jerry, who was always "in a meeting" when the buyer called. Assume you are Jerry and you didn't get any of the buyer's messages until now. How will you communicate to the buyer that you didn't receive her messages?

8. Closely examine 10 e-mail messages you receive. Evaluate them on the basis of the suggestions offered in this chapter for the proper use of e-mail.

9. Assume you sell football tickets for a nearby NFL team and you wish to use Twitter to build relationships with potential season ticket holders. Create two tweets that you would post to accomplish this objective.

CASE PROBLEMS

case **4.1**

Denmark Interiors

Ben Alan, a salesperson for Yellow Book USA, has just entered the elaborate office of Laura C. Curran, owner of Denmark Interiors, an upscale interior decorator in Louisville. Laura is seated behind a vast mahogany desk in a high-backed stylish executive chair working on some paperwork. She doesn't look up as Ben enters the room.

Ben: [walking around Laura's desk and extending his hand] Good morning, Laura! It's sure nice to finally get a chance to meet you. [laughing] Forgive me for saying so, but I'll have to admit this is the nicest office, and you're the prettiest person I've called on this week!

Laura: [not looking up from her paperwork or extending her hand as she finally responds] Please have a seat, Mr. … what was your name?

Ben: [dragging up a seat from the side of the room and placing it on the same side of the desk as Laura, then plopping down in the seat] Ben. Ben Alan. I believe it's one of the hottest days in Louisville this summer! Say, here's a good joke I heard yesterday. A man fainted in the middle of a busy intersection, and traffic quickly piled up in all directions, so a woman rushed to help him. When she knelt down to loosen his collar, a man emerged from the crowd, pushed her aside, and said, "It's all right honey, I've had a course in CPR!" The woman stood up and watched as he took the ill man's pulse and prepared to administer artificial respiration. At this point she tapped him on the shoulder and said, "When you get to the part about calling a doctor, I'm already here." Ha ha ha!

Laura: [not laughing but pushing her paperwork away from her and crossing her arms] What can I do for you, Mr. Alan?

Ben: Well, Laura, I'd like to see your company take out a bigger ad in the Yellow Pages. Can't beat the Yellow Pages for business, now can you?

Laura: [turning in her chair to look out the window while looking at her watch] We provide professional interior decorating to high-end clients, depending mostly on word-of-mouth recommendations for new clients, Mr. Alan.

Ben: [taking out a pad of paper from his shirt pocket and searching his pockets for a pen] Now that's news to me, Laura. I thought you were like all the rest, desperately seeking ugly homes to make them prettier. Ha ha ha!

Laura: [making a steeple with her hands while still looking out the office window] I would guess you would, Mr. Alan. [swiveling in her chair to face Ben] Yes, I would guess you would. [pressing a button on her desk] Ms. Deramus, Mr. Alan has completed his interview with me. Will you kindly escort him out? [eyeing Ben with a triumphant look on her face] Have a good day, Mr. [strongly emphasizing the word Mr.] Alan.

Questions

1. Evaluate the exchange.
2. What would you do differently if you were Ben?

case 4.2

Case IH Agricultural

Joel Winnes is a sales rep for Case IH Agricultural, a global leader in agricultural equipment. Headquartered in the United States, Case IH has a vast network of more than 4,900 dealers and distributors that operates in over 160 countries. Case IH sells tractors, planting and seeding equipment, application and harvesting equipment, skid steers, attachments, and other farming-related equipment.

Joel, who grew up in central Minnesota and who has been selling for Case IH in northern Iowa for the past three years, was just transferred to the Case IH office in Mexico City. Joel has never lived or worked in Mexico before and is thinking about what changes he might need to make as he works with farmers in that country.

Questions

1. Investigate the culture of Mexico in more detail by viewing Web pages and reading articles about how business salespeople can best sell there. Briefly summarize four key findings.
2. What changes should Joel consider making (compared to how he probably sold to clients in Iowa) as he calls on prospects in Mexico? Make any assumptions necessary.

Source: www.pwm.com/pwm/pwm_lang_select.htm.

ROLE PLAY CASE

In this chapter's role play interaction, you are still meeting with the same person you did for Chapter 3. (If you did not do the role play at the end of Chapter 3, you will need to review that information now.) That person is telling you about the business. Feel free to ask questions, but your main objective is to listen and understand all you can about the business environment in which he or she operates. Practice active listening skills; after the role play, identify which listening techniques you used. Further, identify the three most important elements about the person's business that you need to understand. Interpret the buyer's body language. Finally, any time you hear jargon, write the word or phrase down.

Note: For background information about these role plays, see page 26.

To the instructor: Additional information needed to complete the role play is available in the Instructor's Manual.

ADDITIONAL REFERENCES

Brooks, Bill. "The Power of Active Listening." *American Salesman* 55, no. 12 (December 2010), pp. 28–30.

Bowden, Mark. *Winning Body Language: Control the Conversation, Command Attention, and Convey the Right Message without Saying a Word.* New York: McGraw-Hill, 2010.

Curtis, Joan C., and Barbara Giamanco. *The New Handshake: Sales Meets Social Media.* Santa Barbara, CA: Praeger, 2010.

Feigon, Josiane Chriqui, and Jill Konrath. *Smart Selling on the Phone and Online: Inside Sales That Gets Results.* New York: AMACOM, 2009.

Ferrari, Bernard T. *Power Listening: Mastering the Most Critical Business Skill of All*. Penguin Group, New York, 2012.

Ghosh, Rishab Aiyer. "There Are 200 Million People Tweeting: Are You Listening?" *Forbes.com*, October 10, 2011, p. 19.

Goulston, Mark, and Keith Ferrazzi. *Just Listen: Discover the Secret to Getting through to Absolutely Anyone*. New York: AMACOM, 2009.

Graham, John R. "What It Takes to Make the Sale: Making Sense Out of Buyer Behavior in a Wired World." *American Salesman* 54, no. 12 (December 2009), pp. 24–30.

Groves, Eric. *The Constant Contact Guide to E-Mail Marketing*. Hoboken, NJ: Wiley, 2009.

Hartley, Gregory, and Maryann Karinch. *The Body Language Handbook: How to Read Everyone's Hidden Thoughts and Intentions*. Pompton Plains, NJ: Career Press, 2010.

Hayden, C. J. "In Marketing and Sales, It Pays to Listen." *American Salesman* 57, no. 8 (August 2012), pp. 8–10.

Hollenbeck, Candice R., George M. Zinkhan, Warren French, and Ji Hee Song. "Collaborative Networks: A Case Study on the New Role of the Sales Force." *Journal of Personal Selling and Sales Management* 29, no. 2 (Spring 2009), pp. 125–36.

Knapp, Mark L., Judith A. Hall, and Terrence G. Horgan. *Nonverbal Communication in Human Interaction*. New York: Wadsworth Publishing, 2013.

Marker, Scott. *Let's Get It On! Realistic Strategies for Winning the Sales Game*. Ogden, UT: MSA Publishing, 2009.

McPheat, Sean. *Eselling: The Alternative Way to Prospect and Sell for Sales Professionals: How to Use the Internet for Prospecting, Personal Branding, Networking and for Engaging the C-Suite Decision Maker*. Leicester, England: Troubador Publishing, 2011.

Mychals, Brandy. *How to Read a Client from Across the Room: Win More Business with the Proven Character Code System to Decode Verbal and Nonverbal Communication*. McGraw-Hill, 2012.

Nelson, Audrey, and Claire Damken Brown. *The Gender Communication Handbook: Conquering Conversational Collisions between Men and Women*. San Francisco: Pfeiffer, 2012.

Raghavan, Anita. "Watch Your Body Language." *Forbes*, March 2009, p. 92.

Sobel, Andrew. *Power Questions: Build Relationships, Win New Business, and Influence*. Hoboken, NJ: Wiley, 2012.

Solomon, Denise H., and Jennifer Theiss. *Interpersonal Communication: Putting Theory into Practice*. New York: Routledge, 2013.

Wollan, Robert. "Knowing Your Customers in the Digital Age." *CRM Magazine* 16, no. 5 (May 2012), p. 8.

Wolvin, Andrew D. *Listening and Human Communication in the 21st Century*. Hoboken, NJ: Wiley-Blackwell, 2010.

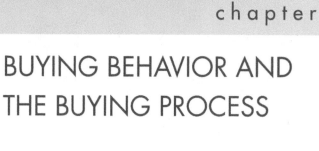

chapter **3**

BUYING BEHAVIOR AND THE BUYING PROCESS

SOME QUESTIONS ANSWERED IN THIS CHAPTER ARE

- What are the different types of customers?
- How do organizations make purchase decisions?
- Which factors do organizations consider when they evaluate products and services?
- Who is involved in the buying decision?
- What should salespeople do in the different types of buying situations?
- Which changes are occurring in organizational buying, and how will these changes affect salespeople?

PROFILE

PROFILE I knew everything about this surgeon. I knew what surgeries he performed, how he performed them, the frequency he performed, even his favorite scrub cap. You could say I had done my homework. So when I began discussing the benefits of my company's product with him in the hallway of the hospital one day, I was a little frustrated when his response was, "That's crap, I don't believe you." I knew this product would work for him and work well. I told him, "You're going to call me in a week when you have a patient and nothing has worked on him, and you're going to want to try our product." Imagine my delight a week later when I did get that call, and sure enough he bought our product.

Understanding your buyer's behavior is the first step to a successful sale. I have discovered four types of buyers. There are the early adopters—those who are eager to try new products and step out of the box to see what's new in the market. These buyers look for new ways to improve their business practices. Then there are the late adopters. These buyers buy products and services early on in the product life cycle but are not quite as eager to jump on the buying train as first adopters. After the late adopters come what you may call "trend followers." When everyone else starts using a product and they see their colleagues buying it, then they too will become buyers. Lastly, there is the group that will never buy. They are not interested, nor will they ever be interested no matter how wonderful your product is. They are set in their ways and have no interest to change.

Knowing what type of buyer you have is not all that difficult. I have found that I can pretty much tell which type I'm dealing with within in the first 20 seconds. Reading your buyers' verbal and non-verbal body language can help you determine what category of buyer you are dealing with and how to approach them. In my industry of selling medical devices, figuring out your buyer type and then getting him or her on your team is critical for success

in the buying process. Unfortunately, getting a "yes, I want to buy" is not enough for a sale.

The buying process is more intricate than that. I not only have to get the support of the surgeon, but the hospital must be on board as well. To make matters more complicated, many times the contracting department must get involved too. Our medical products must be approved at the hospitals we sell to in order for the surgeons to be able to use them. So getting the surgeon's support helps immensely when it comes time to sell to the hospital. If the surgeon will go up to bat for me, the process becomes a whole lot easier. The hospital is more likely to work with the contracting department to approve the product if their own surgeons are the ones backing the product.

Not surprisingly, building a strong relationship with your buyer is critical not only to gain support from everyone in the buying center but also to continuing sales. Most buyers are not one-time buyers. Instead, many customers come back to me with new needs. I constantly work to make my relationships with my buyers more communicative and more supportive. As unfortunate as it may be in the medical field, it's not always about product superiority. Even though I may have the better product, I must constantly compete to maintain strong relationships with my buyers to keep their business. There is always a competitor trying to build a relationship, and more often than not, the sales representative with the better relationship will land the deal.

Understanding the buying process will also lead to success. Every doctor and potential buyer is different, so each buying process differs slightly too. Doing your homework is therefore incredibly important. I research their surgeries, their procedures, what instruments they use, what they like, everything down to the last scalpel on the operating table. After background research, I am ready for the approach. I will only be able to catch some doctors in the hall or in a surgery. Some will want to schedule a meeting. And some will just refuse any contact until a colleague has urged them to take a look at my product. Understanding which approach I will need to use makes a difference. When I do get in front of the buyer, I know I only have the length of time of an elevator pitch to catch their attention and spark interest. Once I do, it is time to meet with them and discuss how the product works and what it can do for them and their patients. Then I ask for their business by inquiring how they would like to try it out or which surgeries they would want to use it in. After they try the product out, the decision is up to them. I have found that buyers weigh what I believe about the product heavily in the buying decision. Buyers can tell from the way I talk, my voice, and my body language that I really believe in our products. This knowledge fuels them to sit down and actually look at the science behind what I am saying. But if I don't illustrate my belief in the product, why would they?

What's most rewarding is the impact I have on people's lives. After coming out of surgery one day, I learned an elderly man was going to have to have surgery on his nose due to devastating skin cancer. The procedure required gruesome steps, including cutting, stitching, and other grisly processes. With this procedure, the normal outcome was ending up looking like Frankenstein. After speaking with the patient and the surgeon in charge, I knew one of my company's products could really make a difference. Our product could actually regrow tissue! The surgeon did decide to use our product as an alternative. When Frankenstein failed to appear after the procedure, everyone was delighted, and I had gained a customer (the surgeon) for life. But what was really rewarding was that the patient would not have to face life with a grotesque, patched-up face.

By understanding the buyer and the buying process, I have made a difference in the lives of many end users. Whether it has been watching a surgeon perform an open-heart surgery with our new product or regrowing a nose, understanding the buyer's behavior and the buying process is a critical step to helping your customer and your customer's customer.

Visit our Web site at:
www.acell.com.

WHY PEOPLE BUY

In general, people buy to satisfy a want or desire, to solve a problem, or to satisfy an impulse. Even in situations where people are buying as part of their jobs, like all people, buyers have personal goals and aspirations. They want to get a raise, be promoted to a high-level position, have their managers recognize their accomplishments, and feel they have done something for their company or demonstrated their skills as a buyer or engineer. These needs can complicate buying decisions that are made on behalf of an employer, not forgetting that there are also the basic needs that the product or service solves.

To complicate matters further, there may needs associated with how the person wants to buy. Think, for a moment, about what you have purchased for yourself via the Internet. You may have many reasons for using the Internet, none of which have anything to do with the product you purchased. But the way you bought met certain needs. As salespeople, we have to be acutely aware of the needs we are solving: the needs that the product solves directly, the individual's needs that are served indirectly, and the needs that are solved by selling the way the buyer wants to buy.

TYPES OF CUSTOMERS

Business is full of a wide variety of customers, including producers, resellers, government agencies, institutions, and consumers. Each of these customer types has different needs and uses a different process to buy products and services. In many situations salespeople will have only one type of customer, but in other territories they may have many different types of customers. Thus salespeople may need to use different approaches when selling to different types of customers.

PRODUCERS

Producers buy products and services to manufacture and sell their products and services to customers. Buyers working for producers are involved in two types of buying situations: buying products that will be included in the products the company is manufacturing or buying products and services to support the manufacturing operation.

OEM Purchasers

Buyers for **original equipment manufacturers (OEMs)** purchase goods (components, subassemblies, raw and processed materials) to use in making their products. For example, when a distributor sells pizza toppings to a restaurant, that it is an OEM purchase. The pizza topping is a processed material used in making the restaurant's product, pizza. Another example of an OEM buyer would be Dell. Dell is an OEM purchaser. It may use Intel processors in its computers, but Dell is the OEM. Sometimes, though, Dell sells computers to other OEM manufacturers. For example, when you use a kiosk at the airport to print your boarding pass, the computer inside it is a Dell, but the kiosk is put together and sold by someone else.

Salespeople selling OEM products need to demonstrate that their products help their customers produce products that will offer superior value. For example, Tim Pavlovich, OEM salesperson for Dell, says that one reason why Dell gets contracts like the kiosk contract is because Dell has a nationwide service team already in place and can fix the computers anywhere in the world.

Most OEM products are bought in large quantities on an annual contract. The purchasing department negotiates the contract with the supplier; however, engineering and production departments play a major role in the purchase decision. Engineers evaluate the products and may prepare specifications for a custom design. The production department works with the supplier to make sure the OEM products are delivered "just in time."

OEM customers are building long-term relationships with a limited number of OEM suppliers. Thus, relationship building with more than one department in a customer firm is particularly important when selling OEM products.

End Users

When producers buy goods and services to support their own production and operations, they are acting as **end users**. End-user buying situations include the purchase of capital equipment; maintenance, repair, and overhaul (MRO) supplies; and services. **Capital equipment** items are major purchases, such as mainframe computers and machine tools that the producer uses for a number of years. **MRO supplies** include paper towels and replacement parts for machinery. **Services** include Internet and telephone connections, employment agencies, consultants, and transportation.

Because capital equipment purchases typically require major financial commitments, capital equipment salespeople need to work with a number of people involved in the purchase decision, including high-level corporate executives. These salespeople need to demonstrate the reliability of their products and their support services because an equipment failure can shut down the producer's operation. Capital equipment buying often focuses on lifetime operating cost rather than the initial purchase price because the equipment is used over a long period. Thus, capital equipment salespeople need to present the financial implications as well as the operating features and benefits of their products.

MRO supplies and services are typically a minor expense and therefore are usually less important to businesses than are many other items. Purchasing agents typically oversee MRO buying decisions. Because they often do not want to spend the time to evaluate all suppliers, they tend to purchase from vendors who have performed well in the past, creating functional relationships.

Although the cost of MRO supplies is typically low, availability can be critical. For example, the failure of a $10 motor in an industrial robot can shut down an entire assembly line. Some professional services, such as accounting, advertising, and consulting, also are important to the company and may be purchased in a manner similar to capital equipment purchases.

RESELLERS

Resellers buy finished products or services with the intention to resell them to businesses and consumers. Hormel sells precooked meats, such as pepperoni for pizza toppings, to resellers—distributors who then sell to restaurants. Other examples of resellers include McKesson Corporation, a wholesaler that buys health care products from manufacturers and resells those products to drugstores; Brazos Valley Equipment, a dealer for John Deere, selling tractors, harvesters, combines, and other agricultural implements to farmers; and Dealer's Electric, selling lighting, conduit, and other electrical components to electricians and contractors. All these are resellers, and they buy for similar reasons.

Resellers consider three elements when making decisions about which products to sell: profit margin, turnover, and effort. Resellers want to maximize their return on investment (ROI), which is a function of **profit margin,** or how much they make on each sale; **turnover,** or how quickly a product will sell; and how much effort it takes to sell the product. Buyers for resellers often simplify their decisions by a focus on either profit margin or turnover, but all resellers are interested in putting together an assortment of products that will yield the greatest overall ROI.

Salespeople work with resellers to help them build their ROI. Not only do salespeople help resellers choose which products to sell, but they also train resellers on how to sell and service products and build point-of-purchase displays and promotions and may also help resellers with developing advertising and marketing campaigns to boost sales. For example, with increasing competition between grocery chains, retailers are asking suppliers to create excitement and generate traffic in stores.

"Retailers' expectations for our products' performance continue to escalate. Price is important but not the only thing retailers are demanding," Eddy Patterson, of Stubb's Legendary Kitchen, said. "We need to look at innovative ways that not only help sell our products and create brand awareness but also ways to contribute to the success of our customers, the retailers who sell our products." For example, Stubb's Bar-B-Q has sold its line of barbecue sauces and marinades in supermarkets and has created a loyal following. In fact, the following is so loyal that they created the "Que Crew," a loyalty marketing program for consumers. The program helps local retailers increase their sales of Stubb's products and helps consumers find new and creative uses for Stubb's products.

Stubb's partners with grocers to cross-promote the full line of Stubb's products with in-store displays, building sales for both Stubb's and the retailer.

Note that the same customer can act as an OEM manufacturer, an end user, and a reseller. For example, Dell Computer makes OEM buying decisions when it purchases microprocessors for its computers, acts as an end user when it buys materials handling equipment for its warehouse, and functions as a reseller when it buys software to resell to its computer customers when they place orders.

GOVERNMENT AGENCIES

The largest customers for goods and services in the United States are federal, state, and local governments, which collectively purchase goods and services valued at more than $1 trillion annually. Including government-owned utilities, federal, state, and local governments purchase the equivalent of 12 percent of the country's entire gross domestic product, making it the largest customer in the world.[1] Government buyers typically develop detailed specifications for a product and then invite qualified suppliers to submit bids. A contract is awarded to the lowest bidder. The government has also developed procedures for small purchases without a bid, streamlining the process and reducing costs.

Effective selling to government agencies requires a thorough knowledge of their unique procurement procedures and rules. Salespeople also need to know about projected needs so they can influence the development of the buying specifications. For example, Harris Corporation worked for six years with the Federal Aviation Administration and finally won a $1.7 billion contract to modernize air traffic communication systems.

Some resources available to salespeople working with the federal and state governments are the following:

- The *Commerce Business Daily* provides notice of new federal sales opportunities each day at www.cbd-net.com. Companies can sign up to be notified of opportunities in specific product categories.
- The National Association of State Purchasing Officials in Washington, D.C., which publishes information for all 50 states, including the availability of vendor guides, registration fees, and how to get on bidder lists (see www.NASPO.org).
- The Small Business Administration offers a Web site (www.sba.gov) that educates small businesses on how to sell to governments and also lists sales opportunities specifically available only to small businesses.
- FedBizOpps.gov, a Web site listing all business opportunities greater than $25,000. At any given time, there are over 40,000 open sales opportunities described on this Web site.

Many international salespeople are selling to government agencies, even though private companies may be the biggest buyers of these products and services in the United States. For example, Alcatel-Lucent, a French company that manufactures telephone equipment, sells not only to private companies such as Verizon and AT&T in the United States but also to the post, telephone, and telegraph (PTT) government agencies in many countries in Europe, Asia, and Africa. In fact, PTTs can represent as much as 40 percent of the government's purchases in countries such as the Netherlands and the Slovak Republic.[2]

Selling to foreign governments is challenging. The percentage of domestic product (countries may require that a certain percentage of the product be manufactured or assembled locally) and exchange rates (the values of local currencies in U.S. dollars) are as important as the characteristics of the product. Different economic and political systems, cultures, and languages also can make international selling difficult.

INSTITUTIONS

Another important customer group consists of public and private institutions such as churches, hospitals, and colleges. Often these institutions have purchasing rules and procedures that are as complex and rigid as those used by government agencies.

Packaged goods manufacturers, such as Stubbs and Hormel, sell to both resellers (supermarkets) and institutional customers (restaurants and hospitals). These customers have different needs and buying processes. In some instances, institutions purchase more like resellers, worrying about the same needs, such as how fast the product will sell or be consumed. In other ways, institutions can be like producers, concerned with how their clients will view their services.

CONSUMERS

Consumers purchase products and services for use by themselves or by their families. A lot of salespeople sell insurance, automobiles, clothing, and real estate to consumers. However, college graduates often take sales jobs that involve selling to business enterprises, government agencies, or institutions. Thus, the examples in this text focus on these selling situations, and this chapter discusses organizational rather than consumer buying behavior.

In the next section we contrast the buying processes of consumers and organizations. Then we describe the buying process that organizations use in more detail, including the steps in the process, who influences the decisions, and how salespeople can influence the decisions.

ORGANIZATIONAL BUYING AND SELLING

Salespeople who sell to consumers and salespeople who call on organizations have very different jobs. Because the organizational buying process typically is more complex than the consumer buying process, selling to organizations often requires more skills and is more challenging than selling to consumers. Relationships, too, can differ because of the size of the organizations involved.

COMPLEXITY OF THE ORGANIZATIONAL BUYING PROCESS

The typical organizational purchase is much larger and more complex than the typical consumer purchase. Organizations use highly trained, knowledgeable purchasing agents to make these decisions. Many other people in organizations are involved in purchase decisions, including engineers, production managers, business analysts, and senior executives.

Organizational buying decisions often involve extensive evaluations and negotiations over time. The average time required to complete a purchase is five months, and during that period salespeople need to make many calls to gather and provide information.

Ashley Anderson, salesperson for "The Ranch" country-western radio station in the Dallas–Fort Worth area, worked for over a year with one account before getting the sale. The account is an eye surgeon promoting his Lasik surgery practice. Ashley worked with his PR agency and him, calling at least twice a month on one or both. "I think three factors finally won him over," says Ashley. "First, over the course of the year, I built a strong relationship with him and he began to trust me. Second, I was able to show him that advertising with us would reach a market no one else was going after. And third, I leveraged a free month of advertising to create an urgency to make a decision." Two years later he still advertises with "The Ranch."

The complexity of organizational purchase decisions means salespeople must be able to work effectively with a wide range of people working for their customer and their company. For example, when selling a new additive to a food processor such as Nabisco, an International Flavors and Fragrances salesperson may interact with advertising, product development, legal, production, quality control, and customer service people at Nabisco. The salesperson needs to know the technical and economic benefits of the additive to Nabisco and the benefits to consumers.

In addition, the salesperson coordinates all areas of his or her own firm to assist in making the sale. The salesperson works with research and development to provide data on consumer taste tests, with production to meet the customer's delivery requirements, and with finance to set the purchasing terms. (Working effectively within the salesperson's organization is discussed in more detail in Chapter 16.)

The complexity of organizational selling is increasing as more customers become global businesses. For example, Deere and Company has a special unit to coordinate worldwide purchases. The unit evaluates potential suppliers across the globe for each of its product lines and manufacturing facilities. Further, the company wants to standardize products made in different plants. A harvester made in Ottumwa, Iowa, should have the same belt as the same model harvester made at Arc-les-Gray, France. Thus, a salesperson selling belts to Deere must work with the special corporate buying unit as well as with the employees at each manufacturing location around the world.[3] There's no doubt that global competitiveness is a key factor increasing the complexity of organizational buying, but global sourcing is also a key factor for achieving a sustainable competitive advantage.[4]

If you want to sell a part such as a belt for a John Deere harvester made in Ottumwa, Iowa, then you must be able to sell and service this plant in Arc-les-Gray, France, too.

DERIVED VERSUS DIRECT DEMAND

Salespeople selling to consumers typically can focus on individual consumer or family needs. Organizational selling often requires salespeople to know about the customer's customers. Sales to OEMs and resellers are based on derived demand rather than direct demand. **Derived demand** means that purchases made by these customers ultimately depend on the demand for their products—either other organizations or consumers. For example, Apple's iPad has not only increased sales for touch screens made by Wintek and computer chips made by Samsung; the demand for the equipment that makes touch screens and computer chips has also been affected.[5]

HOW DO ORGANIZATIONS MAKE BUYING DECISIONS?

To effectively sell to organizations, salespeople need to understand how organizations make buying decisions. This section discusses the steps in the organizational buying process, the different types of buying decisions, and the people involved in making the decisions.

STEPS IN THE BUYING PROCESS

Exhibit 3.1 shows the eight steps in an organizational buying process.

Exhibit 3.1
Steps in the
Organizational
Buying Process

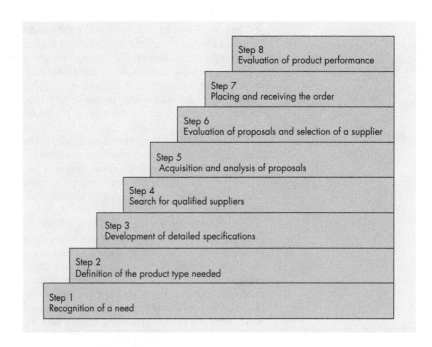

Step 8
Evaluation of product performance

Step 7
Placing and receiving the order

Step 6
Evaluation of proposals and selection of a supplier

Step 5
Acquisition and analysis of proposals

Step 4
Search for qualified suppliers

Step 3
Development of detailed specifications

Step 2
Definition of the product type needed

Step 1
Recognition of a need

Recognizing a Need or a Problem (Step 1)

The buying process starts when someone realizes a problem exists. Employees in the customer's firm or outside salespeople can trigger this recognition. For example, a supermarket cashier might discover that the optical scanner is making mistakes in reading bar code labels. Salespeople often trigger the buying process by demonstrating how their products can improve the efficiency of the customer's operation.

Defining the Type of Product Needed (Step 2)

After identifying a problem, organization members develop a general approach to solving it. For example, a production manager who concludes that the factory is not running efficiently recognizes a problem, but this insight may not lead to a purchase decision. The manager may think the inefficiency is caused by poor supervision or unskilled workers.

However, a production equipment salesperson might work with the manager to analyze the situation and show how efficiency could be improved by purchasing some automated assembly equipment. Thus, the problem solution is defined in terms of purchasing a product or service—the automated assembly equipment needed—and the buying process moves to step 3. If the decision to continue requires senior management participation, research suggests that these executives will approve the manager's request to consider the purchase, then leave it up to the manager to cover the next few steps before stepping back in when a final decision is made.[6]

Developing Product Specifications (Step 3)

In step 3 the specifications for the product needed to solve the problem are prepared. Potential suppliers will use these specifications to develop proposals. The buyers will use them to objectively evaluate the proposals.

Steps 2 and 3 offer great opportunities for salespeople to influence the outcome of the buying process. Using their knowledge of their firm's products and the customer's needs, salespeople can help develop specifications that favor their particular product. For example, a Hyster forklift might have superior performance in terms of a small turning radius. Knowing this advantage and the customer's small, tightly packed warehouse, the Hyster salesperson might influence the customer to specify a very small turning radius for forklifts—a turning radius that only Hyster forklifts can provide. Competing salespeople, who first become aware of this procurement after the specifications are written, will be at a severe disadvantage.

Searching for Qualified Suppliers (Step 4)

After the specifications have been written, the customer looks for potential suppliers. The customer may simply contact previous suppliers or go through an extensive search procedure: do a Web search, read customer reviews online, download case studies and position papers, and call customers found on a list on the potential supplier's Web site.

Acquiring and Analyzing Proposals (Step 5)

In step 5 qualified suppliers are asked to submit proposals. Salespeople work with people in their company to develop their proposal. In many instances, proposals are slide presentations delivered by the salesperson over the Web through Webex, Skype, or some other form of online conference call.

Evaluating Proposals and Selecting a Supplier (Step 6)

Next, the customer evaluates the proposals. After a preferred supplier is selected, further negotiations may occur concerning price, delivery, or specific performance features.

Placing an Order and Receiving the Product (Step 7)

In step 7 an order is placed with the selected supplier. The order goes to the supplier, who acknowledges receipt and commits to a delivery date. After the product is shipped, the buying firm inspects the received goods and then pays the supplier for the product. During this step salespeople need to make sure the paperwork is correct and their firm knows what has to be done to satisfy the customer's requirements. In many instances, the customer may be responsible for placing the order through a secure Web site.

Evaluating Product Performance (Step 8)

In the final step of the purchasing process, the product's performance is evaluated. The evaluation may be a formal or informal assessment made by people involved in the buying process. The supplier is also evaluated on such characteristics as whether the billing was accurate, how quickly service calls were handled, and similar criteria.

Salespeople play an important role in this step. They need to work with the users to make sure the product performs well. In addition, salespeople need to work with purchasing agents to ensure that they are satisfied with the communications and delivery.

This after-sale support ensures that the salesperson's product will get a positive evaluation and that he or she will be considered a qualified supplier in future procurement. This step is critical to establishing successful long-term relationships. (Building relationships through after-sale support is discussed in more detail in Chapter 14.)

CREEPING COMMITMENT

Creeping commitment means a customer becomes increasingly committed to a particular course of action while going through the steps in the buying process. As decisions are made at each step, the range of alternatives narrows; the customer becomes more and more committed to a specific course of action and even to a specific vendor. Thus, it is vital that salespeople be involved in the initial steps so they will have an opportunity to participate in the final steps.

In instances involving purchasing components or materials as part of new product development, buyers are more interested in early involvement by possible vendors than when buying other types of products. Called *early procurement involvement* or *early supplier involvement,* this strategy has potential suppliers participate in the actual design process for a new product. BASF, the giant German chemical company, engages in early vendor involvement to ensure that the proper levels and quality of supply are available.[7] Other companies use supplier involvement to aid in designing a more effective new product.[8] Whatever the reason, each design decision represents a creeping commitment to a final set of decisions that are difficult to undo.

thinking **it** through   What steps did you go through in making the choice to attend this university? How can you relate your decision-making process to the eight steps in the organizational buying process? Did any decisions you made early in the process affect decisions you made later in the process? What roles did your family and friends play in the decision process?

TYPES OF ORGANIZATIONAL BUYING DECISIONS

Many purchase decisions are made without going through all the steps just described. For example, a Frito-Lay salesperson may check the supply of his or her products in a supermarket, write a purchase order to restock the shelves, and present it to the store manager. After recognizing the problem of low stock, the manager simply signs the order (step 6) without going through any of the other steps. However, if the Frito-Lay salesperson wanted the manager to devote more shelf space to Frito-Lay snacks, the manager might go through all eight steps in making and evaluating this decision.

Exhibit 3.2 describes three types of buying decisions—new tasks, modified rebuys, and straight rebuys[9]—along with the strategies salespeople need to use in each situation. In this exhibit the "in" company is the seller that has provided the product or service to the company in the past, and the "out" company is the seller that is not or has not been a supplier to the customer.

NEW TASKS

When a customer purchases a product or service for the first time, a **new-task** situation occurs. Most purchase decisions involving capital equipment or the initial purchase of OEM products are new tasks.

Because the customer has not made the purchase decision recently, the company's knowledge is limited, and it goes through all eight steps of the buying process. In these situations customers face considerable risk. Thus, they typically seek information from salespeople and welcome their knowledge. Two studies found that organizational buyers rate salespeople as a more important information source than the Internet, particularly when the success of the purchase is likely to be difficult to achieve and to evaluate.[10]

Exhibit 3.2
Types of Organizational Buying Decisions

	New Task	Modified Rebuy	Straight Rebuy
Customer Needs			
Information and risk reduction	Information about causes and solutions for a new problem; reduce high risk in making a decision with limited knowledge.	Information and solutions to increase efficiency and/or reduce costs.	Needs are generally satisfied.
Nature of Buying Process			
Number of people involved in process	Many	Few	One
Time to make a decision	Months or years	Month	Day
Key steps in the buying process (Exhibit 3.1)	1, 2, 3, 8	3, 4, 5, 6, 8	5, 6, 7, 8
Key decision makers	Executives and engineers	Production and purchasing managers	Purchasing agent
Selling Strategy			
For in-supplier	Monitor changes in customer needs; respond quickly when problems and new needs arise; provide technical information.	Act immediately when problems arise with customers; make sure all of customer's needs are satisfied.	Reinforce relationship.
For out-supplier	Suggest new approach for solving problems; provide technical advice.	Respond more quickly than present supplier when problem arises; encourage customer to consider an alternative; present information about how new alternative will increase efficiency.	Convince customer of potential benefits from reexamining choice of supplier; secure recognition and approval as an alternative supplier.

From the salesperson's perspective, the initial buying process steps are critical in new-task situations. During these steps the alert salesperson can help the customer define the characteristics of the needed product and develop the purchase specifications. By working with the customer in these initial steps, the salesperson can take advantage of creeping commitment and gain a significant advantage over the competition. The final step, postpurchase evaluation, is also vital. Buyers making a new purchase decision are especially interested in evaluating results and will use this information in making similar purchase decisions in the future.

STRAIGHT REBUYS

In a **straight rebuy** situation, the customer buys the same product from the same source it used when the need arose previously. Because customers have purchased the product or service a number of times, they have considerable knowledge about their requirements and the potential vendors. MRO supplies and services and reorders of OEM components often are straight rebuy situations.

Typically, a straight rebuy is triggered by an internal event, such as a low inventory level. Because needs are easily recognized, specifications have been developed, and potential suppliers have been identified, the latter steps of the buying process assume greater importance.

Some straight rebuys are computerized. For example, many hospitals use an automatic reorder system developed by Baxter, a manufacturer and distributor of medical supplies. When the inventory control system recognizes that levels of supplies such as tape, surgical sponges, or IV kits have dropped to prespecified levels, a purchase order is automatically generated and transmitted electronically to the nearest Baxter distribution center.

When a company is satisfied and has developed a long-term supplier relationship, it continues to order from the same company it has used in the past. Salespeople at in-companies want to maintain the strong relationship; they do not want the customer to consider new suppliers. Thus, these salespeople must make sure that orders are delivered on time and that the products continue to get favorable evaluations.

Salespeople trying to break into a straight rebuy situation—those representing an out-supplier—face a tough sales problem. Often they need to persuade a customer to change suppliers, even though the present supplier is performing satisfactorily. In such situations the salesperson hopes the present supplier will make a significant mistake, causing the customer to reevaluate suppliers. To break into a straight rebuy situation, salespeople need to provide compelling information to motivate the customer to treat the purchase as a modified rebuy.

MODIFIED REBUYS

In a **modified rebuy** situation, the customer has purchased the product or a similar product in the past but is interested in obtaining new information. This situation typically occurs when the in-supplier performs unsatisfactorily, a new product becomes available, or the buying needs change. In such situations sales representatives of the in-suppliers need to convince customers to maintain the relationship and continue their present buying pattern. In-suppliers with strong customer relationships are the first to find out when requirements change. In this case customers give the supplier's salespeople information to help them respond to the new requirements.

Salespeople with out-suppliers want customers to reevaluate the situation and to actively consider switching vendors. The successful sales rep from an out-supplier will need to influence all the people taking part in the buying decision.

WHO MAKES THE BUYING DECISION?

As we discussed previously, a number of people are involved in new-task and modified rebuy decisions. This group of people is called the **buying center,** an informal, cross-department group of people involved in a purchase decision. People in the customer's organization become involved in a buying center because they have formal responsibilities for purchasing or they are important sources of information. In some cases the buying center includes experts who are not full-time employees. For example, consultants usually specify the air-conditioning equipment that will be used in a factory undergoing remodeling. Thus, the buying center defines the set of people who make or influence the purchase decision.[11]

Salespeople need to know the names and responsibilities of all people in the buying center for a purchase decision, and sometimes they need to make sure the right people are participating. For example, one of Bill Dunne's prospects for a customer relationship management software application was certain that the company would buy Bill's offering, a customized version of SugarCRM. Yet when it came time to buy, the CEO, who had not been involved in any prior meetings, stepped in and selected another vendor. Why? There was one key feature about the other vendor's product that he really liked, and while Bill had uncovered the CEO's interest in the feature, he didn't realize it would be a deal killer for him. "The lesson I learned," says Bill, "is to meet with every person who uses the system at least once."

USERS

Users, such as the manufacturing personnel for OEM products and capital equipment, typically do not make the ultimate purchase decision. However, they often have considerable influence in the early and late steps of the buying process—need recognition, product definition, and postpurchase evaluation. Thus users are particularly important in new-task and modified rebuy situations. Salespeople often attempt to convert a straight rebuy to a modified rebuy by demonstrating superior product performance or a new benefit to users.

INITIATORS

Another role in the buying process is that of **initiator,** or the person who starts the buying process. A user can play the role of the initiator, as in "This machine is broken; we need a new one." In fact, often it is users' dissatisfaction with a product used by the organization that initiates the purchase process.[12] In some instances, though, such as in OEM product decisions, the initiator could be an executive making a decision such as introducing a new product, which starts the buying process.

INFLUENCERS

People inside or outside the organization who directly or indirectly provide information during the buying process are **influencers.** These members of the buying center may seek to influence issues regarding product specifications, criteria for evaluating proposals, or information about potential suppliers. For example, the marketing department can influence a purchase decision by indicating that the company's products would sell better if they included a particular supplier's components. Architects can play a critical role in the purchase of construction material by specifying suppliers, even though the ultimate purchase orders will be placed by the contractor responsible for constructing the building. Influence can be technical, such as in product specifications, but can also involve finances and how a decision is made.

Miller and Heiman, two noted sales consultants, assert that there are four types of influencers. One is the **economic influencer,** or person who is concerned about the financial aspects of the decision. Another is the user, which we will discuss later. A third is the **technical influencer,** a person who makes sure the technical requirements (including logistics, terms and conditions, quality measurements, or other specifications) are met. Miller and Heiman state that these people usually have the authority only to say no (meaning the salesperson did not meet the specifications, so the proposal is rejected), so they play a gatekeeping role (discussed more in a moment). The fourth role or type of influencer is the coach. The **coach** is someone in a buying organization who can advise and direct you, the salesperson, in maneuvering through the buying process in an effective fashion, leading to a sale. In addition, this person may advocate for you in private conversations among members of the buying center. As you can imagine, finding a coach is an important factor when decision processes are complex and involve a lot of people.[13]

The buying center for radiology equipment includes (clockwise from lower left) the technicians operating the equipment (users), the radiologists (gatekeepers and influencers), and the hospital administrator (the decision maker).

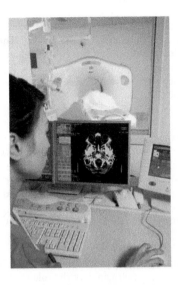

GATEKEEPERS

Gatekeepers control the flow of information and may limit the alternatives considered. For example, the quality control and service departments may determine which potential suppliers are qualified sources.

Purchasing agents often play a gatekeeping role by determining which potential suppliers are to be notified about the purchase situation and are to have access to relevant information. In some companies all contacts must be made through purchasing agents. They arrange meetings with other gatekeepers, influencers, and users. Such gatekeeping activity is not a power play; rather, it ensures that purchases are consolidated under one contract, thus reducing costs and increasing quality. These single contracts are growing in popularity as a way to reduce costs globally.[13] When dealing with such companies, salespeople may not be allowed to contact members of the buying center directly. When purchasing agents restrict access to important information, salespeople are tempted to bypass the purchasing agents and make direct contact. This backdoor selling approach can upset purchasing agents so much that they may disqualify the salesperson's company from the purchase situation. In Chapter 7 we discuss ethical strategies that salespeople can use to deal with this issue.

DECIDERS

In any buying center one or more members of the group, **deciders,** make the final choice. Determining who actually makes the purchase decision for an organization is often difficult. For straight rebuys the purchasing agent usually selects the vendor and places the order. However, for new tasks many people influence the decision, and several people must approve the decision and sign the purchase order.

In general, senior executives get more involved in important purchase decisions that have a greater effect on the performance of the organization. For example, the chief executive officer (CEO) and chief financial officer (CFO) play an important role in purchasing a telephone system because this network has a significant impact on the firm's day-to-day operations.

Exhibit 3.3

Importance of Hospital Buying Center Members in the Buying Process for Intensive Care Monitoring Equipment

Step in Buying Process	Physicians	Nurses	Hospital Administrators	Purchasing Engineers	Agents
Need recognition (step 1)	High	Moderate	Low	Low	Low
Definition of product type (step 2)	High	High	Moderate	Moderate	Low
Analysis of proposal (step 5)	High	Moderate	Moderate	High	Low
Proposal evaluation and supplier selection (step 6)	High	Low	High	Low	Moderate

To sell effectively to organizations, salespeople need to know the people in the buying center and their involvement at different steps of the buying process. Consider the following situation. Salespeople selling expensive intensive care monitoring equipment know that a hospital buying center for the type of equipment they sell typically consists of physicians, nurses, hospital administrators, engineers, and purchasing agents. Through experience, these salespeople also know the relative importance of the buying center members in various stages of the purchasing process (see Exhibit 3.3). With this information the intensive care equipment salespeople know to concentrate on physicians throughout the process, nurses and engineers in the middle of the process, and hospital administrators and purchasing agents at the end of the process.

SUPPLIER EVALUATION AND CHOICE

At various steps in the buying process, members of the buying center evaluate alternative methods for solving a problem (step 2), the qualifications of potential suppliers (step 4), proposals submitted by potential suppliers (step 5), and the performance of products purchased (step 8). Using these evaluations, buyers select potential suppliers and eventually choose a specific vendor.

The needs of both the organization and the individuals making the decisions affect the evaluation and selection of products and suppliers (see Exhibit 3.4). Often these organizational and personal needs are classified into two categories: rational needs and emotional needs. **Rational needs** are directly related to the performance of the product. Thus, the organizational needs discussed in the next section are examples of rational needs. **Emotional needs** are associated with the personal rewards and gratification of the person buying the product. Thus, the personal needs of buying center members often are considered emotional needs.

ORGANIZATIONAL NEEDS AND CRITERIA

Organizations consider a number of factors when they make buying decisions, including economic factors such as price, product quality, and supplier service. In addition, organizations also consider strategic objectives, such as sustainability (choosing vendors and products that are good for the planet) and social diversity.

Economic Criteria

The objective of businesses is to make a profit. Thus, businesses are very concerned about buying products and services at the lowest cost. Organizational buyers are now taking a more sophisticated approach to evaluating the cost of equipment. Rather than simply focusing on the purchase price, they consider

Exhibit 3.4
Factors Influencing
Organizational Buying
Decisions

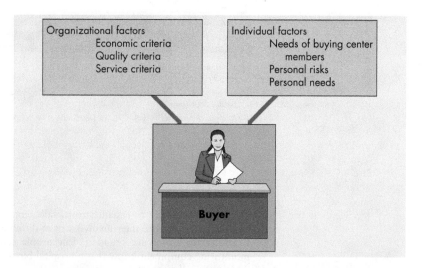

Exhibit 3.5
Life-Cycle Costing

	Product A	Product B
Initial cost	$35,000	$30,000
Life of machine	10 years	10 years
Power consumption per year	150 MWh*	180 MWh*
Power cost at $30/MWh	$45,000	$54,000
Estimated operating and maintenance cost over 10 years	$25,000	$30,000
Life-cycle cost	$105,000	$114,000

Note: A more thorough analysis would calculate the net present value of the cash flow associated with each product's purchase and use.

*MWh = megawatt-hour.

installation costs, the costs of needed accessories, freight charges, estimated maintenance costs, and operating costs, including forecasts of energy costs. Retail buyers also consider other financial factors, such as promotion plans, as described in Building Partnerships 3.1.

Life-cycle costing, also referred to as the total cost of ownership, is a method for determining the cost of equipment or supplies over their useful lives. Using this approach, salespeople can demonstrate that a product with a higher initial cost will have a lower overall cost. An example of life-cycle costing appears in Exhibit 3.5. (Approaches, that salespeople can use to demonstrate the value of their products to customers are discussed in more detail in Chapter 9.)

Quality Criteria

Many firms recognize that the quality and reliability of their products are as important to their customers as price. Firms expect their suppliers to support their efforts to provide quality products. A recent study in Japan indicates that suppliers are evaluated on both the quality of their service and the quality of their products because both impact the quality that the buyer can deliver to its customer.[14] Salespeople often need to describe how their firms will support the customer's quality objectives.

BUILDING Partnerships

3.1

ADAPTING TO BUYERS

Jenna Weber followed up a college internship with Hormel Foods with a sales position with the company. Selling meat products like HORMEL® chili, DINTY MOORE® beef stew, and even SPAM®, she calls on retailers. Each retailer has a corporate buyer that she has to convince to allow Hormel products into the store, but then it is up to each store manager to decide if and how many to carry. As she says, her role is "to give the consumer every opportunity to purchase Hormel products by getting the products on the shelf and supporting the products through promotions."

"I currently work with a regional retail customer that has over 100 stores in the Northeast. I must sell products, promotions, and strategies for each one of my categories. However, the most difficult part of my job is dealing with different buyers. Some categories have the same buyer. For example HORMEL® chili, DINTY MOORE® beef stew, and SPAM® are all purchased by the same grocery buyer. But there are five different buyers overall, and each buyer has a different style. For example, my meat buyer is very relationship oriented and appreciates that I bring him donuts and coffee. We talk about his children, his plans for the weekend, and, of course, the business. He doesn't like long presentations with data-filled pages. He just wants to know, "Will this item sell?" He is easy to deal with, especially on promotions that are run annually (such as hams during the holidays).

Another buyer is the complete opposite. He wants to know every detail of the item, including pages of analytical data that support the success of the product. He takes longer to make a decision and needs data to prove his choice. This can be good and bad. For example, we were running a bacon promotion, and I

argued with my meat buyer that one truckload wasn't enough. It didn't matter to him that I had past history of similar promotions that proved he needed more; he simply refused. Conversely, for a large promotion in grocery, I used multiple analytical tools to prove the volume my grocery buyer needed. By showing him the facts, I successfully sold him three truckloads of displays. As you can see, it's important to understand your buyer's personality and the most effective way to connect with him or her.

The end consumer is also very important in the buying process. While I do not sell to consumers directly, they play a key role in my decision making. When planning a promotion, does it make the most sense to present a deal at two for $4 or one at $1.99? In making that choice, I have to decide which price point seems like the best deal to my end user. For an item that a customer may already buy multiples of, CHI-CHI'S® salsa, for example, two for $4 makes the most sense. However, most people won't purchase more than one 38-ounce DINTY MOORE® beef stew, so that item is better left at a single price point. Along with deciding price, I also have to choose which products are items that should be displayed. Most of Hormel's products are impulse items, but it is up to the retailer if they are worthy of an end cap or aisle display. My job is to ensure that Hormel products are highly visible to our end user, thus encouraging increased sales."

Whether it is the corporate buyer or the end consumer, the purchasing process is very complex. A lot of planning goes into how Jenna approaches each buyer and presents a promotion. Whatever Hormel comes up with for her to offer, it is still up to her to adapt it to the needs and buying style of each of her individual buyers.

To satisfy customer quality needs, salespeople need to know what organizational buyers are looking for. Quality criteria can include such objective measures as the number of defects per thousand products, the amount of time a machine operates before needing service, or the number of items a system can process in a given period of time. Some buyers also utilize subjective measures, such as if a piece of office furniture looks sturdy or if the vendor has great ratings on the Web. Either way, the salesperson has to identify what criteria will be used to determine quality.

Service Criteria

Organizational buyers want more than products that are low cost, that perform reliably, and that are aesthetically pleasing. They also want suppliers that will work with them to solve their problems. One primary reason firms are interested in developing long-term relationships with suppliers is so they can learn about each other's needs and capabilities and use this information to enhance their products' performance. **Value analysis** is an example of a program in which suppliers and customers work together to reduce costs and still provide the required level of performance.[15]

Representatives from the supplier and the purchasing department and technical experts from engineering, production, or quality control usually form a team to undertake the analysis. The team begins by examining the product's function. Then members brainstorm to see whether changes can be made in the design, materials, construction, or production process to reduce the product's costs but keep its performance high. Some questions addressed in this phase are the following:

- Can a part in the product be eliminated?
- If the part is not standard, can a standard (and presumably less expensive) part be used?
- Does the part have greater performance than this application needs?
- Are unnecessary machining or fine finishes specified?

Salespeople can use value analysis to get customers to consider a new product. This approach is particularly useful for the out-supplier in a straight rebuy situation. David Lenling, a sales representative for Hormel, used value analysis to sell pepperoni to a 35-unit group of pizzerias in the Cincinnati area. The owner had been using the same pepperoni and bacon topping for over 15 years and was reluctant to switch. Lenling showed how the Hormel pepperoni product cost $5 per case more but offered 1,200 more slices in a case with the same weight, which equated to an additional $12 of pepperoni, or a $7 per case net savings, enough to make about 35 more pizzas per case. The owner of the chain was unaware of these differences until Lenling actually weighed his current product. Through value analysis, Lenling was able to interrupt a straight rebuy. Further, Lenling's buyer agreed that the Hormel product tasted better and was less greasy, resulting in a better-looking and tastier pizza, which might result in customers coming back more often. Because Hormel products are of high quality and sell at a premium price, Lenling and other sales representatives have to prove that the products are worth the extra money. They use value analysis to help purchasing agents determine how much it costs to use the product rather than how much the product costs. That's why Lenling was able to win that large pizza chain's business.[16]

INDIVIDUAL NEEDS OF BUYING CENTER MEMBERS

In the preceding section we discussed criteria used to determine whether a product satisfies the needs of the organization. However, buying center members are people. Their evaluations and choices are affected by their personal needs as well as the organization's needs.

Types of Needs

Buying center members, like all people, have personal goals and aspirations. They want to get a raise, be promoted to a high-level position, have their managers recognize their accomplishments, and feel they have done something for their company or demonstrated their skills as a buyer or engineer.

Salespeople can influence members of the buying center by developing strategies to satisfy individual needs. For example, demonstrating how a new product will reduce costs and increase the purchasing agents' bonus would satisfy the purchasing agents' financial security needs. Encouraging an engineer to recommend a product employing the latest technology might satisfy the engineer's need for self-esteem and recognition by his or her engineering peers.

Risk Reduction

In many situations, members of the buying center tend to be more concerned about losing benefits they have now than about increasing their benefits. They place a lot of emphasis on avoiding risks that may result in poor decisions, decisions that can adversely affect their personal reputations and rewards as well as their organization's performance. Buyers first assess the potential for risk and then develop a risk reduction strategy.[17] To reduce risk, buying center members may collect additional information, develop a loyalty to present suppliers, or spread the risk by placing orders with several vendors.

Because they know suppliers try to promote their own products, customers tend to question information received from vendors. Customers usually view information from independent sources such as trade publications, colleagues, and outside consultants as more credible than information provided by salespeople and company advertising and sales literature. Therefore, they will search for such information to reduce risk when a purchase is important.

Advertising, the Internet, and sales literature tend to be used more in the early steps of the buying process. Word-of-mouth information from friends and colleagues is important in the proposal evaluation and supplier selection steps. Word-of-mouth information is especially important for risky decisions that will have a significant impact on the organization or the buying center member. "Sales Technology 3.1" illustrates the importance of the Internet for word-of-mouth information.

Another way to reduce uncertainty and risk is to display **vendor loyalty** to suppliers—that is, to continue buying from suppliers that proved satisfactory in the past. Converting buying decisions into

When making a buying decision, this [woman]'s performance is being judged by others in the organization. Thus, she will seek to find ways to reduce her risk, while also reducing risk to the organization.

straight rebuys makes the decisions routine, minimizing the chances of a poor decision. One name for this is **lost for good;** for all the out-suppliers, this account can be considered lost for good because the in-supplier has cemented this relationship for a long time. Organizations tend to develop vendor loyalty for unimportant purchase decisions, though they will often look to vendors who have proved trustworthy when beginning to search in a risky situation. In these situations the potential benefits from new suppliers do not compensate for the costs of evaluating these suppliers.

SALES Technology

3.1

TODAY'S WEB-EMPOWERED CUSTOMER

Customers today have greater power than ever before. In the past, an upset customer might have told 20 friends about a bad experience. But if you've tweeted about a store or restaurant giving you bad service, how many more people have you told?

If you've purchased a night at a hotel at Hotels.com, you're probably like most who read other consumers' reviews of the hotel first. The Web makes product and supplier information readily available to anyone who will look for it. Deitra Pope, for example, was looking for a CRM solution for her company. The first consultant who called on her, though, had such a bad reputation online that she wanted nothing to do with him or his company. She's not alone. One study found that 87 percent of business buyers turn to the Internet for information on important purchases (and, frankly, we're surprised that it wasn't 100 percent).

Recently, a new service was launched called Decide.com, which aggregates and summarizes all of the consumer reviews that it can find on the Web. The company cites

one example of how vendor information on the Web can provide only part of the story. A leading television on Amazon's Web site looks like a great buy, but the broader array of information from Decide.com suggests that you should look for another.

Buyers also use the Web to offer input into new product development. IdeaStorm, for example, is a platform that Dell uses to allow users to post ideas for new products or features (see www.ideastorm.com), and other users can then vote for the ideas. Submissions earn points for good ideas that submitters can then redeem for prizes. A recent review of the site indicated that Dell had implemented over 500 of the ideas submitted.

Buyers are using the Web to engage with each other and with companies. Smart companies participate in these interactions in many ways to grow their business.

Sources: Deitra Pope, personal interview, August 29, 2012; Richard Bush, "The Changing Face of B2B," *Marketing*, January 14, 2009, p. 5; www.decide.com, accessed August 29, 2012; www.ideastorm.com, accessed August 29, 2012.

The consequences of choosing a poor supplier can be reduced by using more than one vendor. Rather than placing all orders for an OEM component with one supplier, for example, a firm might elect to purchase 75 percent of its needs from one supplier and 25 percent from another. Thus, if a problem occurs with one supplier, another will be available to fill the firm's needs. If the product is proprietary—available from only one supplier—the buyer might insist that the supplier develop a second source for the component. Such a strategy is called **"always a share,"** which means the buyer will always allocate only a share to each vendor.

These risk reduction approaches present a major problem for salespeople working for out-suppliers. To break this loyalty barrier, these salespeople need to develop trusting relationships with customers. They can build trust by offering performance guarantees or consistently meeting personal commitments. Another approach is to encourage buyers to place a small trial order so the salesperson's company can demonstrate the product's capabilities. On the other hand, the salesperson for the in-supplier wants to discourage buyers from considering new sources, even on a trial basis.

PROFESSIONAL PURCHASING'S GROWING IMPORTANCE

The purchasing profession is undergoing dramatic changes. Companies have recognized the impact that effective purchasing can make on the bottom line. For example, if a company can save $5,000 on a purchase, $5,000 is added to net income. If sales go up $5,000, of which most is additional costs, only $500 may be added to net income. Most large firms have elevated their directors of purchasing to the level of senior vice president to reflect the increasing importance of this function. For example, Alcoa's profits have recently been so strategically tied to sourcing that the purchasing function is given direct attention by the CEO. Combine recognition of the power of purchasing with technology, and you can see why trends in professional purchasing are changing the business environment. The overall strategy is called supply chain management.

SUPPLY CHAIN MANAGEMENT

Supply chain management (SCM) began as a set of programs undertaken to increase the efficiency of the distribution channel that moves products from the producer's facilities to the end user. More recently, however, SCM has become more than just logistics; it is now a strategy of managing inventory while containing costs. SCM includes logistics systems, such as just-in-time inventory control, as well as supplier evaluation processes, such as supplier relationship management systems.

The **just-in-time (JIT) inventory control** system is an example of a logistics SCM system used by a producer to minimize its inventory by having frequent deliveries, sometimes daily, just in time for assembly into the final product. In theory each product delivered by a supplier must conform to the manufacturer's specifications every time. It must be delivered when needed, not earlier or later, and it must arrive in the exact quantity needed, not more or less. The ultimate goal is to eventually eliminate all inventory except products in production and transit.

To develop the close coordination needed for JIT systems, manufacturers tend to rely on one supplier. The selection criterion is not the lowest cost, but the ability of the supplier to be flexible. As these relationships develop, employees of the supplier have offices at the customer's site and participate in value analysis meetings with the supplier. The salesperson becomes a facilitator, coordinator, and even marriage counselor in developing a selling team that works effectively with the customer's buying center. Resellers are also interested in managing their inventories more efficiently. Retailers and distributors work closely with their suppliers to minimize inventory investments and still satisfy the needs of customers. These JIT inventory systems are referred to as **quick-response system** or **efficient consumer response** (ECR) systems in a consumer product distribution channel. (Partnering relationships involving these systems are discussed in more detail in Chapter 14.)

Automatic replenishment is a form of JIT where the supplier manages inventory levels for the customer. The materials are provided on consignment, meaning the buyer doesn't pay for them until they are actually used. These types of arrangements are used in industrial settings, where the product being consumed is a supply item used in a manufacturing process, as well as in retail settings. Efficient consumer response systems use automatic replenishment technology through **electronic data interchange (EDI)**, or computer systems that share data across companies. Exhibit 3.6 illustrates the communications associated with placing orders and receiving products that are transmitted electronically through EDI. Recent research has indicated that adopting systems involving both EDI and quick response or JIT delivers a number of benefits to the firm, in addition to lower costs. These benefits include greater flexibility in manufacturing, improved stability of supply, and other operating benefits. Though EDI has been around a long time, global sourcing challenges still exist that influence EDI, as you can see in "From the Buyer's Seat 3.1."

Exhibit 3.6
EDI Transactions

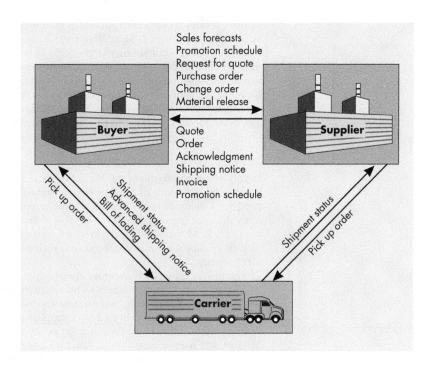

Material requirements planning (MRP) systems are an important element in JIT programs. These systems are used to forecast sales, develop a production schedule, and then order parts and raw materials with delivery dates that minimize the amount of inventory needed, thereby reducing costs. Effective JIT requires that customers inform suppliers well in advance about production schedules and needs.

SUPPLIER RELATIONSHIP MANAGEMENT

Supplier relationship management (SRM) is a strategy by which organizational buyers evaluate the relative importance of suppliers and use that information to determine with whom they want to develop partnerships. The first step is to identify the annual spend, or amount that is spent with each vendor and for what products. One outcome is the ability to consolidate purchases and negotiate better terms. After the relative importance is identified, organizational buyers frequently use a formal method, called vendor analysis, to summarize the benefits and needs satisfied by a supplier. When using this procedure, the buyer rates the supplier and its products on a number of criteria, such as price, quality, performance, and on-time delivery.[18] Note that the ratings of suppliers can be affected by the perceptions and personal needs of the buyers. Then the ratings are weighted by the importance of the characteristics, and an overall score or evaluation of the vendor is developed. Exhibit 3.7 shows a vendor evaluation form used by Chrysler Corporation. The next section describes the multiattribute model, which is useful in analyzing how members of the buying center evaluate and select products. The model also suggests strategies salespeople can use to influence these evaluations.

SRM software is being used by companies like Kingfisher plc, a company with some 1,400 stores across 17 countries and leading European retail brands, such

From the BUYER'S SEAT

3.1

CHALLENGES IN GLOBAL SOURCING

Ten years ago, mention global sourcing to a business executive, and you'd start a conversation about finding low-cost sources in other countries. Now the topic isn't always about the lowest cost; rather, it's about getting global organizations on the same page.

The Web promised to make all of the world easier to access, and you might expect such tools as electronic data interchange (EDI) to be ubiquitous. But while the basic advantages of EDI haven't changed—that is, assured supply and lower operating costs due to automatic ordering and inventory management—global supply chain management systems have added so many layers of complexity that global EDI systems simply don't exist—at least not yet.

Working on a global EDI system for Nestlé, Sean Gardner, cadre director of B2B strategies, explains the challenges. "One size doesn't fit all, not when you have so many markets and so many countries, each with their own computer network systems and their own preferred ways of doing things, some of which work very efficiently and some of which are not so efficient."

Marvin Wagner, global engineering director for John Deere, agrees that global sourcing faces many local challenges. "Local engineers want to use the same local suppliers they've always used. But that means facing significant redundancy to supply chain management systems." When Deere is able to standardize a part the world over, not only do costs go down because of the larger quantity purchased, so do costs associated with managing inventory and even for simple functions, like reordering.

Gardner notes, "Some units might be paying 20 times what they would pay on a global contract, while others may only be paying five times." That may sound like a great saving is possible for everyone, but, as Gardner notes, "Any change that changes how people operate is not easy."

When you process millions of transactions a month, the lure of global sourcing solutions is awfully tempting. But realizing the benefits can take years. Gardner estimates that it may take as long as four years to fully implement an EDI system throughout all of Nestlé. "If you want to compete in an environment where your customers want to work with fewer suppliers, you have to do what they want. And that includes trimming costs all throughout the supply chain," states Gardner. Wagner agrees but also adds, "It's not just about trimming costs throughout the supply chain. We're also interested in making sure we have a healthy supply chain, one that is innovative and profitable for everyone involved. That way, we have suppliers who help us stay competitive."

as Castorama and BUT. The company's Asia sourcing office in Hong Kong buys over 8,000 products from more than 150 suppliers. SRM software enables the company to identify problems, such as a delivery problem with one vendor in particular. Caterpillar, the construction and agriculture equipment manufacturer, instituted SRM software and training for all employees involved in purchasing. The training, created by Accenture, was more than just about the software; it was also about the strategy so the company could maximize its return on the software investment.[19]

SRM isn't always about improving profits. Sustainability, for example, is an important trend in purchasing and means making purchasing decisions that do not damage the environment. Bell Inc., a Sioux Falls, South Dakota, manufacturer of packaging products, worked with the U.S. Postal Service to develop sustainable packaging products. The project required Bell to work with its suppliers, but the important element that allowed the project to flourish was the trust already built by actively managing relationships with suppliers. As Ben Graham, vice president for sales and supply chain, notes, "The project required us to work with a

Exhibit 3.7
Sample Vendor Analysis
Form

	5 Excellent	4 Good	3 Satisfactory	2 Fair	1 Poor	0 N/A
Supplier Name: _____ Type of Product: _____						
Shipping Location: _____ Annual Sales Dollars: _____						
Quality (45%)						
Defect rates	__	__	__	__	__	__
Quality of sample	__	__	__	__	__	__
Conformance with quality program	__	__	__	__	__	__
Responsiveness to quality problems	__	__	__	__	__	__
Overall quality	__	__	__	__	__	__
Delivery (25%)						
Avoidance of late shipments	__	__	__	__	__	__
Ability to expand production capacity	__	__	__	__	__	__
Performance in sample delivery	__	__	__	__	__	__
Response to changes in order size	__	__	__	__	__	__
Overall delivery	__	__	__	__	__	__
Price (20%)						
Price competitiveness	__	__	__	__	__	__
Payment terms	__	__	__	__	__	__
Absorption of costs	__	__	__	__	__	__
Submission of cost savings plans	__	__	__	__	__	__
Overall price	__	__	__	__	__	__
Technology (10%)						
State-of-the-art components	__	__	__	__	__	__
Sharing research & development capability	__	__	__	__	__	__
Ability and willingness to help with design	__	__	__	__	__	__
Responsiveness to engineering problems	__	__	__	__	__	__
Overall technology	__	__	__	__	__	__

Buyer: _____ Date: _____

Comments: _____

Source: Chrysler Corporation.

third-party accrediting agency that went back to our supply chain to understand the impact of the components of our packaging on the waste stream. It's a huge process, and it's not easy to go back to a supplier asking it to share its recipes. That takes confidentiality, trust, and understanding." Key for suppliers, Graham says, is to recognize the direction Bell's business is taking, the company's goals in the marketplace, and how they as suppliers fit in that strategy. "Once they understand that and see the opportunity they get very excited," he says. "Suppliers take part in our success."[20]

thinking **it** through

Review the stages in the decision-making process described earlier in the chapter. Do you go through those stages when making an important purchase? How does the Internet affect the way you buy products and services? What effect does it have on each stage of the process?

MULTIATTRIBUTE MODEL OF PRODUCT EVALUATION AND CHOICE

The multiattribute model is a useful approach for understanding the factors individual members of a buying center consider in evaluating products and making choices. The multiattribute model is one approach that companies can take to making purchases and is most often used in complex decisions involving several vendors.[21] Many business decisions are straight rebuys, but the original vendor selection decision may have involved a multiattribute approach. The vendor analysis form used by Chrysler (see Exhibit 3.7) illustrates the use of this model in selecting vendors. The model also provides a framework for developing sales strategies.

The multiattribute model is based on the idea that people view a product as a collection of characteristics or attributes. Buyers evaluate a product by considering how each characteristic satisfies the firm's needs and perhaps their individual needs. The following example examines a firm's decision to buy laptop computers for its sales force. The computers will be used by salespeople to track information about customers and provide call reports to sales managers. At the end of each day, salespeople will call headquarters and upload their call reports.

PERFORMANCE EVALUATION OF CHARACTERISTICS

Assume the company narrows its choice to three hypothetical brands: Apex, Bell, and Deltos. Exhibit 3.8 shows information the company has collected about each brand. Note that the information goes beyond the physical characteristics of the product to include services provided by the potential suppliers.

Each buying center member (or the group as a whole in a meeting) might process this objective information and evaluate the laptop computers on each characteristic. These evaluations appear in Exhibit 3.9 as ratings on a 10-point scale, with 10 being the highest rating and 1 the lowest.

How do members of the buying center use these evaluations to select a laptop computer? The final decision depends on the relationship between the

Exhibit 3.8
Information about Laptop Computers

Characteristic/Brand	Apex	Bell	Deltos
Reliability rating	Very good	Very good	Excellent
Weight (pounds)	3.0	4.5	7.5
Display size (inches)	15.0	13	10.1
Display visibility	Good	Very good	Excellent
Speed (clock rate in gigahertz)	2.4	3.0	2.4
RAM (memory in gigabytes)	2	2	4
Number of U.S. service centers	140	60	20

Exhibit 3.9
Performance Evaluation
of Laptop Computers

Characteristic/Brand Rating	Apex	Bell	Deltos
Reliability	5	5	8
Weight	8	5	2
Display size	8	6	4
Display visibility	2	4	6
Speed	4	8	4
RAM	3	3	8
Service availability	7	5	3

performance evaluations and the company's needs. The buying center members must consider the degree to which they are willing to sacrifice poor performance on one attribute for superior performance on another. The members of the buying center must make some trade-offs.

No single product will perform best on all characteristics. For example, Apex excels on size, weight, and availability of convenient service; Bell has superior speed; and Deltos provides the best reliability and internal memory.

IMPORTANCE WEIGHTS

In making an overall evaluation, buying center members need to consider the importance of each characteristic. These importance weights may differ from member to member. Consider two members of the buying center: the national sales manager and the director of management information systems (MIS). The national sales manager is particularly concerned about motivating his sales-people to use the laptop computers. He believes the laptops must be small and lightweight and have good screen visibility. On the other hand, the MIS director foresees using the laptop computers to transmit orders and customer inventory information to corporation headquarters. She believes expanded memory and processing speed will be critical for these future applications.

Exhibit 3.10 shows the importance these two buying center members place on each characteristic using a 10-point scale, with 10 representing very important and 1 representing very unimportant. In this illustration the national sales manager and the MIS director differ in the importance they place on characteristics; however, both have the same evaluations of the brands' performance on the characteristics. In some cases people may differ on both importance weights and performance ratings.

OVERALL EVALUATION

A person's overall evaluation of a product can be quantified by multiplying the sum of the performance ratings by the importance weights. Thus, the sales manager's overall evaluation of Apex would be as follows:

$$4 \times 5 = 20$$
$$6 \times 8 = 48$$
$$7 \times 8 = 56$$
$$1 \times 4 = 4$$
$$1 \times 3 = 3$$
$$8 \times 2 = 16$$
$$3 \times 7 = \underline{21}$$
$$168$$

Exhibit 3.10
Information Used
to Form an Overall
Evaluation

	Importance Weights		Brand Ratings		
Characteristic	Sales Manager	MIS Director	Apex	Bell	Deltos
Reliability	4	4	5	5	8
Weight	6	2	8	5	2
Display size	7	3	8	6	4
Display visibility	8	5	2	4	6
Speed	1	7	4	8	4
RAM	1	6	3	3	8
Service availability	3	3	7	5	3
Overall evaluation					
Sales manager's			168	150	141
MIS director's			137	157	163

Exhibit 3.11
Value Offered by Each
Brand

	Overall Evaluation (Benefits Points)	Assigned Value	
		Computer Cost	Benefit/Cost
Sales manager			
Apex	167	$1,600	$0.10
Bell	152	1,800	0.08
Deltos	143	1,800	0.08
MIS director			
Apex	130	$1,600	0.08
Bell	169	1,800	0.09
Deltos	177	1,800	0.10

Using the national sales manager's and MIS director's importance weights, the overall evaluations, or scores, for the three laptop computer brands appear at the bottom of Exhibit 3.10. The scores indicate the benefit levels the brands provide as seen by these two buying center members.

VALUE OFFERED

The cost of the computers also needs to be considered in making the purchase decision. One approach for incorporating cost calculates the value—the benefits divided by the cost—for each laptop. The prices for the computers and their values are shown in Exhibit 3.11. The sales manager believes Apex provides more value. He would probably buy this brand if he were the only person involved in the buying decision. On the other hand, the MIS director believes that Bell and Deltos offer the best value.

SUPPLIER SELECTION

In this situation the sales manager might be the key decision maker, and the MIS director might be a gatekeeper. Rather than using the MIS director's overall evaluation, the buying center might simply ask her to serve as a gatekeeper and determine whether these computers meet her minimum acceptable performance standards on speed and memory. All three laptops pass the minimum levels she established of a 2-gigahertz clock rate and a 3-gigabyte internal memory. Thus, the company would rely on the sales manager's evaluation and purchase Apex laptops for the sales force.

Even if a buying center or individual members do not go through the calculations described here, the multiattribute model is a good representation of their product evaluations and can be used to predict product choices. Purchase decisions are often made as though a formal multiattribute model were used.

thinking **it** through

If you were selling the Bell computer to the national sales manager and MIS director depicted in the text and in Exhibits 3.10 and 3.11, how would you try to get them to believe that your computer provides more value than Apex or Deltos does? What numbers would you try to change?

IMPLICATIONS FOR SALESPEOPLE

How can salespeople use the multiattribute model to influence their customers' purchase decisions? First, the model describes the information customers use in making their evaluations and purchase decisions. Thus, salespeople need to know the following information to develop a sales strategy:

1. The suppliers or brands the customer is considering
2. The product characteristics being used in the evaluation
3. The customer's rating of each product's performance on each dimension
4. The weights the customer attaches to each dimension

With this knowledge salespeople can use several strategies to influence purchase decisions. First, salespeople must be sure their product is among the brands being considered. Then they can try to change the customer's perception of their product's value. Some approaches for changing perceived value follow:

1. Increase the performance rating for your product.
2. Decrease the rating for a competitive product.
3. Increase or decrease an importance weight.
4. Add a new dimension.
5. Decrease the price of your product.

Assume you are selling the Bell computer and you want to influence the sales manager so he believes your computer provides more value than the Apex computer. Approach 1 involves altering the sales manager's belief about your product's performance. To raise his evaluation, you would try to have the sales manager perceive your computer as small and lightweight. You might show him how easy it is to carry—how well it satisfies his need for portability. The objective of this demonstration is to increase your rating on weight from 5 to 7 and your rating on size from 6 to 8.

You should focus on these two characteristics because they are the most important to the sales manager. A small change in a performance evaluation on these characteristics will have a large impact on the overall evaluation. You would not want to spend much time influencing his performance evaluations of speed or memory because these characteristics are not important to him. Of course your objectives when selling to the MIS director would be different because she places more importance on speed and memory.

This example illustrates a key principle in selling. In general, salespeople should focus primarily on product characteristics that are important to the customer—characteristics that satisfy the customer's needs. Salespeople should not focus on the areas of superior performance (such as speed in this example) that are not important to the customer.

Approach 2 involves decreasing the performance rating of Apex. This strategy can be dangerous. Customers prefer dealing with salespeople who say good things about their products, not bad things about competitive products.

In approach 3 you try to change the sales manager's importance weights. You want to increase the importance he places on a characteristic on which your product excels, such as speed, or decrease the importance of a characteristic on which your product performs poorly, such as display visibility. For example, you might try to convince the sales manager that a fast computer will decrease the time salespeople need to spend developing and transmitting reports.

Approach 4 encourages the sales manager to consider a new characteristic, one on which your product has superior performance. For example, suppose the sales manager and MIS director have not considered the availability of software. To add a new dimension, you might demonstrate a program specially developed for sales call reports and usable only with your computer.

Approach 5 is the simplest to implement: Simply drop your price. Typically firms use this strategy as a last resort because cutting prices decreases profits.

These strategies illustrate how salespeople can adapt their selling approach to the needs of their customers. Using the multiattribute model, salespeople decide how to alter the content of their presentation—the benefits to be discussed—based on customer beliefs and needs. (Chapter 4 describes adaptive selling in more detail and illustrates it in terms of the form of the presentation—the communication style the salesperson uses.)

SELLING YOURSELF

When you are selling your ideas or selling yourself in a job search, recognize that there is a buying center. Although a sales manager may make the final decision on whether you are hired, chances are that you'll interview with at least four people before the job offer will come. Who is the gatekeeper, who is the decider, and who are influencers? Similarly, once you have the job and you have an idea for a new program or product, you will have to sell that idea to management. That decision will likely include someone from finance, someone from operations, and so on, creating a buying center. Each member of the center will take on different roles and may be present for only part of the decision. Each member may also have different criteria.

Further, you need to understand the process by which the decision is made. In a job search, the decision to hire someone has been made before anyone talks to you. At that point your concern is making it from the large pool of college students they've interviewed at six different campuses to the group they bring into the office, to the final selection of new employees. Similarly, management approval of your idea is likely to follow a process not unlike that of any organizational purchase. Keep in mind that your idea is competing against other ideas from other people, just as your candidacy for a sales job is compared to other college students from your school and others. Therefore, take some time to understand who is involved in the decision, what criteria they will use, and what process they will use to reach a decision.

SUMMARY

Salespeople sell to many different types of customers, including consumers, business enterprises, government agencies, and institutions. This text focuses on selling to organizations rather than to consumers. Selling to organizations differs from selling to consumers because organizations are more concentrated, demand is derived, and the buying process is more complex.

The organizational buying process consists of eight steps, beginning with the recognition of a need and ending with the evaluation of the product's performance. Each step involves several decisions. As organizations progress through these steps, decisions made at previous steps affect subsequent steps, leading to a creeping commitment. Thus, salespeople need to be involved in the buying process as early as possible.

The length of the buying process and the role of various participants depend on the customer's past experiences. When customers have had considerable experience in buying a product, the decision becomes routine—a straight rebuy. Few people are involved, and the process is short. However, when customers have little experience in buying a product—a new task—many people are involved, and the process can be lengthy.

The people involved in the buying process are referred to as the buying center. The buying center is composed of people who are initiators, users, influencers, gatekeepers, and deciders. Salespeople need to understand the roles buying center members play to effectively influence their decisions.

Individuals in the buying center are concerned about satisfying the economic, quality, and service needs of their organization. In addition, these people have personal needs they want to satisfy.

Organizations face an increasingly dynamic and competitive environment. Purchasing is becoming a strategic weapon with the development of supply chain management and supplier relationship management strategies.

The Internet is playing a much more important role in business-to-business transactions than it plays in the widely publicized business-to-consumer e-businesses. Business-to-business applications of the Internet are designed to support salespeople's ability to build relationships with major customers.

KEY TERMS

always a share 78
annual spend 80
automatic replenishment 79
buying center 70
capital equipment 61
coach 71
creeping commitment 68
deciders 72
derived demand 65
economic influencer 71
efficient consumer response 79
electronic data interchange (EDI) 79
emotional needs 73
end users 61
gatekeepers 72
influencers 71

initiators 71
just-in-time (JIT) inventory control 79
life-cycle costing 74
lost for good 77
material requirements planning 80
modified rebuy 70
MRO supplies 61
new-task 68
original equipment manufacturer (OEM) 61
producers 61
profit margin 62
quick-response system 79
rational needs 73
resellers 62
services 61
straight rebuy 69

supplier relationship management (SRM) 80
supply chain management (SCM) 79
technical influencer 71
turnover 62

users 71
value analysis 76
vendor analysis 80
vendor loyalty 77

ETHICS PROBLEMS

1. You know that both American Airlines and Delta Airlines have goals for purchasing from women- and minority-owned businesses. You have a product that is innovative and patented, and it will save airlines like American and Delta over 30 percent in fuel costs. But your business does not qualify as woman or minority owned because you are a white male, so you are thinking of bringing a partner into the business—your sister. Is this appropriate? Or would it be better to license the product to an already certified minority-owned business?

2. You are talking about this class to someone who isn't familiar with business. When you mention you are studying how people make buying decisions and that this information will help you become a better salesperson, your friend says you are just trying to learn how to manipulate people more effectively. How do you respond?

QUESTIONS AND PROBLEMS

1. Assume that the federal government is going to make reducing obesity a major priority. The process it has adopted includes reducing sugar content in children's cereals, making vegetables more palatable, and reducing fat in the overall diet. Identify three product categories (not including vegetables) for which derived demand would influence manufacturers and producers of consumer packaged goods (foods sold to be cooked or heated and eaten at home). Include at least one product affected positively and one product affected negatively.

2. Read "Building Partnerships 3.1." Jenna Weber, salesperson for Hormel®, described two buyers. One was friendly and easy to get along with, while the other was tough, hard to get an appointment with, and impatient during the meeting and demanded proof of almost everything she said. Are these the only two types of personalities she might run into? What could she have done better with the bacon promotion?

3. Assume you work for a division of 3M that makes medical monitoring systems. How would the purchasing decision process differ in the following situations? Which situation is a new task? A modified rebuy? A straight rebuy?

How likely is the buyer to get other people in the organization involved? Which types of people are likely to get involved in each decision? Which situation is likely to produce the slowest decision?

a. The organization is purchasing a custom-designed machine to be used in the manufacturing of metal racks that house multiple monitoring systems.

b. An organization reorders plastic shields that it uses in making medical monitoring equipment from a regular supplier, a supplier that it has bought from in the past.

c. The organization is designing a new line of medical monitoring equipment and wants an improved and updated microprocessor. It is considering its past suppliers as well as some suppliers that it has not bought from before.

4. Review each purchase in question 3. What information would you need to conduct a value analysis for each? Note: You will need some different and some similar information in each situation.

5. A chain of restaurants wants to purchase a new order entry computer system tied into an accounting system that manages food inventory and automatically replenishes food items. Which criteria for evaluating supplier proposals might be used by (a) the purchasing agent, (b) the information systems department, (c) a store manager, and (d) the head of the legal department? How would this purchase differ from a purchase of the same products by a company that resells store fixtures and equipment to small restaurants?

6. Dub Oliver runs the maintenance department at the paper mill, and he buys lots of hardware to fix equipment. Right now, he orders most of it through a Web site at NCH. If you work for Home Depot, how would you try to make a sale to Oliver? Assume you have a Web site he can order through, too.

7. When is vendor loyalty important? Find at least one example in the chapter (there are several) where vendor loyalty would prove to be important and discuss why it was important in that particular instance. What can buyers do to improve vendor loyalty? When might vendor loyalty be inefficient or wasteful?

8. Create a matrix of types of needs and types of customers. Which customer types share the same types of needs or express needs in the same way? Which ones differ? Why? Relate your chart to the multiattribute matrix. How would your chart help you prepare to sell?

9. Mitchell's Metal Shop is considering the purchase of a new press, a machine that bends sheet metal. The cost is $10,000, which is about 25 percent of the firm's profit for the quarter. Ford Motor Company is also considering buying new presses—30 of them. Discuss how risk is different for Frank Mitchell, owner of Mitchell's Metal Shop, and Ford.

10. How would your multiattribute matrix for a new car differ from that of your parents? How is it that you might have some of the same desires (such as high gas mileage) yet consider completely different cars?

CASE PROBLEMS

case 3.1

Going Out through the Back Door

Travis Bruns is a sales representative for Crown Lift Services in Houston, Texas. In his own words, he describes an ethics issue with a buyer.

Last year I was in a real cutthroat bidding war for a $300,000-plus sales opportunity. Over the course of two months the competitive field had been narrowed down to two organizations, mine and the incumbent organization. The customer had set up a set of strict guidelines for the bidding process. One of those was that they had designated a "point of contact" (POC) that was to be the liaison through which all bids and proposals were to channel through to the VP. My organization and I had truly put our best foot forward on pricing and proposed service after the sale, and although the negotiations had been rough, we were able to sell the value of our solution, retain a fair amount of profit, and were told we had the deal: a true win–win. On the final day that the bid was open, I received a call from the point of contact asking me to lower my price. I was confused. I inquired about the previous discussions that had taken place in which we had mutually agreed that the price of our proposal was fair and good. I could hear some level of discomfort if not embarrassment in the POC's voice, so I came right out and asked him, "I get the sense that you are not comfortable with what is happening here either. What happened?"

He replied, "Well, Travis, [your competitor] called one of the other managers in the office and was able to find out the pricing in your proposal. He then went around me and called the VP directly and offered a much lower price. The VP then called me and asked me to get you to lower your price or the other company will get the business."

I was dumbfounded. I asked the customer, "If I cannot lower my price, are you telling me this deal is over for me?"

"I think so," he replied.

Source: Travis Bruns. Used with permission.

Questions

1. What would you do? Do you lower your price or walk away? Why? Write out specifically what you would say next.
2. Do buyers have to follow the same ethics principles as sellers? For example, sellers have to fully disclose all information. Do buyers? Why or why not? What ethical principle violation occurred here?

case **3.2**

Heritage Health

Frank Briles, account executive and his boss, Kylie Martinez, were talking over one of his accounts, Parker Pet Products. Frank was describing his initial meeting with Shirley Parker, CEO of the family pet food manufacturer.

"She said that Mark Davis, the company's HR director, asked her if he could look into getting health care for the company. She said he was having trouble finding new employees because there were so few benefits. But she also said that the CFO was against adding more costs," Frank reported.

"Do you think she was serious about the costs?" asked Shirley.

"I think so." Frank's face showed his lack of confidence in knowing the answer. "What I do know is that they have no budget set aside for it."

"How will they determine a budget? And what will their process be in making a decision?"

Frank looked at his computer for notes he had taken on the meeting. "Well, we're lucky in the sense that they've not really set up a process. So we can help them determine what's important, assuming I can get to the right people fast enough. As for budget, that will be decided by Shirley and the CFO."

Kylie gave Frank a sharp look. "Right people? What do you mean?"

"They're setting up a committee," said Frank. "I've asked to have an opportunity to meet with them and just talk through options and process. I know that there will be two employee representatives, one from each plant, along with the HR guy, the CFO, Shirley, and the two plant managers. What I don't know is how they will make the decision or what they want."

Questions

1. What is the likely makeup of the buying center? Who plays or has played which roles?
2. What type of purchase situation is this? What are the implications for Frank?
3. How can Frank use the multiattribute matrix to guide his sales plan?

ROLE PLAY CASE

During much of the rest of the semester, you will be calling on one of three accounts. The accounts are listed here with some information. Information that you gain on each call can be used in subsequent calls as you practice the skills and apply the concepts introduced in each chapter.

BancVue: BancVue works with community banks to enable these smaller banks provide big-bank products and services. They are a marketing agency that has built its own brands for products and services that community banks can then sell as their own.

GelTech: Originally just a manufacturer of firefighting systems, this company began by selling fire suppression products to fire departments and to commercial property owners and builders. Now international, the company also manufactures other chemical products that serve the agriculture market (including forestry and golf course maintenance) and the fishing industry.

HighPoint Solutions: HighPoint Solutions is a business services company. They are a midsize company that can provide complete outsourced human resource solutions or software and support. With offices in 30 major cities, they do everything from managing the hiring/separation processes and payroll to administering benefit packages and more.

Today, you have an appointment with a sales manager whom you met at a workshop sponsored by the American Marketing Association. You were presenting a case study of how one of your clients improved sales productivity through your CRM software. Start the sales call from the beginning as if you were entering the sales manager's office. Reintroduce yourself and your company, thank the person for the appointment, and then tell the buyer you'd like to ask some questions. Your questions should be about the buying process and who is involved. Afterward, see if you can chart the buying center and the company's organizational structure.

ADDITIONAL REFERENCES

Andersson, Svante, and Per Servais. "Combining Industrial Buyer and Seller Strategies for International Supply and Marketing Management." *European Business Review* 22 (2010), pp. 64–82.

Autry, Chad W., and Susan L. Golicic. "Evaluating Buyer-Supplier Relationship-Performance Spirals: A Longitudinal Study." *Journal of Operations Management* 28 (March 2010), pp. 87–104.

Briggs, Ellen, and Douglas Grisaffe. "Service Performance-Loyalty Intentions Link in a Business to Business Context: The Role of Relational Exchange Outcomes and Customer Characteristics." *Journal of Service Research* 13 (2010), pp. 37–52.

Brown, B., Alex Zablah, and Danny Bellenger. "When Do B2B Brands Influence the Decision Making of Organizational Buyers? An Examination of the Relationship between Purchase Risk and Brand Sensitivity." *International Journal of Research Marketing* 28, no. 3 (2011), pp. 194–204.

Geigenmüller, Anja, and Harriette Bettis-Outland. "Brand Equity in B2B Services and Consequences for the Trade Show Industry." *Journal of Business and Industrial Marketing* 27, no. 6 (2012), pp. 428–35.

Kotabe, Masaaki, Michael J. Mol, and Janet Y. Murray. "Outsourcing, Performance, and the Role of E-Commerce: A Dynamic Perspective." *Industrial Marketing Management* 37, no. 1 (2008), pp. 37–49.

Leach, Mark. "Examining Exchange Relationships among High-Tech Firms in the Evolving Global Economy." *Journal of Business and Industrial Marketing* 24 (2009), pp. 78–94.

Lindgreen, Adam, Balazs Revesz, and Mark Glynn. "Purchasing Orientation." *Journal of Business and Industrial Marketing* 24 (2009), pp. 148–72.

Lucero, Carrete. "A Relationship Model between Key Problems of International Purchasing and the Post-Purchase Behavior of Industrial Firms." *Journal of Business and Industrial Marketing* 23 (2008), pp. 332–47.

Makkonen, Hannu, Rami Olkkonen, and Aino Halinen. "Organizational Buying as Muddling Through: A Practice Theory Approach." *Journal of Business Research* 65, no. 6 (June 2012), pp. 773–81.

Miocevic, Dario, and Biljana Crnjak-Karanovic. "The Mediating Role of Key Supplier Relationship Management Practices on Supply Chain Orientation: The Organizational Buying Effectiveness Link." *Industrial Marketing Management* 41, no. 1 (2012), pp. 115–25.

Pels, Jaqueline, Kristian Moller, and Michael Saren. "Do We Really Understand Business Marketing?" Getting beyond the RM and BM Matrimony." *Journal of Business and Industrial Marketing* 24 (2009), pp. 322–49.

Rutherford, Brian N., Nwamaka Anaza, and Adrienne Hall Phillips. "Predictors of Buyer-Seller Firm Conflict." *Journal of Marketing Theory and Practice* 20 (Spring 2012), pp. 161–71.

Saini, Amit. "Purchasing Ethics and Inter-Organizational Buyer-Supplier Relationship Determinants: A Conceptual Framework." *Journal of Business Ethics* 95, no. 3 (2010), pp. 439–55.

Sashi, C. M. "Buyer Behavior in Business Markets: A Review and Integrative Model." *Journal of Global Issues* 3 (Summer 2009), pp. 129–38.

Skarmeas, Dionysis, Constantine S. Katsikeas, Stavroula Pyropoulou, and Esmail Salehi-Sangari. "Market and Supplier Characteristics Driving Distributor Relationship Quality in International Marketing Channels of Industrial Products." *Industrial Marketing Management* 27, no. 1 (2008), pp. 23–29.

Spekman, Robert, and R. Thomas. "Organizational Buying Behavior: Where We Have Been and Where We Need to Go." Darden Business School Working Paper No. 1993207, Georgetown McDonough School of Business Research Paper No. 2012-05, 2011. Retrieved from http://papers.ssrn.com/sol3/papers.cfm?abstract_id= 1993207, September 27, 2012.

Svahn, Senja, and Mika Westerlund. "Purchasing Strategies in Supply Relationships." *Journal of Business and Industrial Marketing* 24 (2009), pp. 173–89.

Van Der Rhee, Brian, R. Verma, and G. Plaschka. "Understanding Trade-Offs in the Supplier Selection Process: The Role of Flexibility, Delivery, and Value-Added Services/ Support." *International Journal of Production Economics* 120, no. 1 (2009), pp. 30–31.

The Partnership Process

chapter **7**

PLANNING THE SALES CALL

SOME QUESTIONS ANSWERED IN THIS CHAPTER ARE

- Why should salespeople plan their sales calls?
- What precall information is needed about the individual prospect and the prospect's organization?
- How can this information be obtained?
- What is involved in setting call objectives?
- Should more than one objective be set for each call?
- How can appointments be made effectively and efficiently?

2

PART

PROFILE

PROFILE

My name is Brett Georgulis, and I graduated from Texas State University–San Marcos in 2011 with a bachelor's degree in marketing and a master's degree in business administration. My experience in "Professional Selling," taught by Mrs. Vicki West, has impacted my life more than any other course. "Professional Selling" provided an in-your-face perspective of how to prepare yourself for nearly any business situation, no matter what field you entered. Throughout the course work were real-world scenarios that reinforced textbook and lecture material, including role play sales calls, mock sales presentations, and interactive interview preparation. The knowledge and experienced I gained from the professional selling class has benefited me during my first year as a sales rep for 3M's Electrical Markets Division.

With a broad and diverse end-user and distributor client base encompassing an endless array of needs, sales call preplanning is an absolute must for me to be successful. There are several things to consider when planning for a sales call. Possibly the most important part of my planning is to know my audience and understand their needs. Gathering information about personality, attitude, relationships, past decisions, and current business environment, among other information, helps me tailor my sales approach and know what to say in any given situation. But just as important, this information helps me know what not to say. As the information about my customer is gathered, I am able to get a clearer view of what his or her needs are.

Just as important as understanding you audience and their needs is understanding what you want to accomplish while making the call. Using the information collected, I create call objectives to help me organize what goals I want to accomplish. Creating these call objectives keeps me on track and uses the time I have with the customer in the most efficient and effective way possible. These objectives must be specific, measurable, and attainable. Do they have to be extravagant? No. For example, if I am meeting a job site superintendent for the first time, my primary goal may be to simply introduce myself, gain an understanding of the project, and secure a second call. On a large construction project, it may be the seventh or eighth call, when a number of factors align, that the customer has all the information they need to be comfortable in their purchasing decision.

Because of the nature of my job with 3M, I could be making a pitch in an office setting, on a construction site to a job foreman, or at a trade show in a distributor warehouse. In each situation, planning the sales call helps me to be as prepared as possible in any given situation.

Visit our Web site at:
www.mmm.com/electrical

Exhibit 7.1
A Flow Diagram of the Planning Process

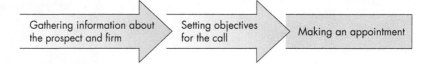

Gathering information about the prospect and firm → Setting objectives for the call → Making an appointment

WHY PLAN THE SALES CALL?

Successful salespeople know that advance planning of the sales call is essential to achieve in selling. The salesperson should remember that the buyer's time is valuable. Without planning the sales call, a salesperson may cover material in which the buyer has no interest, try to obtain an order even though that is an unrealistic expectation for this sales call, or strike off into areas that veer from what the buyer needs to hear. The results are wasted time and an annoyed prospect. However, by having a clear plan for the call, the salesperson more likely will not only obtain commitment but also win the buyer's respect and confidence.

Salespeople should also remember the value of their own time. Proper planning helps them meet their call objectives efficiently and effectively. They then have more time to make additional calls, conduct research on customers, fill out company reports, and complete other necessary tasks. The result is better territory management. (See Chapter 15 for more discussion of time and territory management.)

Of course planning must fit into the salesperson's goals for the account. Some accounts have greater strategic importance and thus require more planning. (See Chapter 13 for a discussion of the types of relationships that a seller can have with a buyer and Chapter 15 about classifying accounts and prospects.) Accounts with which a firm is partnering obviously need the most planning, whereas smaller accounts may warrant less planning. Also, salespeople must not make planning an end in itself and a way to avoid actually making calls. Exhibit 7.1 shows how the concepts in this chapter are related.

OBTAINING PRECALL INFORMATION

Often the difference between making and not making a sale depends on the amount of homework the salesperson does before making a call. The more information the salesperson has about the prospect, the higher the probability of meeting the prospect's needs and developing a long-term relationship. However, the salesperson must be aware of the costs involved in collecting information. At some point, the time and effort put into collecting information become greater than the benefits obtained. And of course, for some cold calls, there will be little if any precall information collected.

Clearly a salesperson who has been calling regularly on a prospect or customer may not need to collect a lot of additional information; records and notes from prior calls may be adequate to prepare for the sales call. The same holds true for a new salesperson if the previous one kept good records. But beware! In this fast-paced world, things are changing every day. Consider the following dialogue:

SALESPERSON [*walking up to the receptionist of one of his best customers*]: Hello, Jim. I'm here

Gathering information from individuals in the prospect's firm before making a call on the prospect is often a wise investment of time.

to see Toby. I have some information I promised to share with her about our new manufacturing process. She was pretty excited about seeing it!

RECEPTIONIST [*looking tired*]: Sorry, Jeff. Toby was transferred last week to our Toronto plant. Haven't you heard about our latest reorganization? Just went into effect two weeks ago. I'm still trying to figure it out. It seems that all our engineering people are moving to the Toronto site.

The key: Don't assume that your knowledge about the account is automatically up to date.

Of course, before you make an initial call on an important prospect, you will often expend considerable effort in collecting precall information about both the individual prospect and the prospect's company. Don't expect this information gathering to be quick, easy, or cheap.

It is important to learn and maintain current knowledge about both the prospect as an individual and his or her firm. The sections that follow examine these areas more closely. Of course the salesperson should keep in mind privacy concerns, as related in Chapter 2.

THE PROSPECT/CUSTOMER AS AN INDIVIDUAL

Salespeople should attempt to learn the following types of information about a prospect or a customer:

Personal (Some of This Information Can Be Confidential)

- Name (including pronunciation).
- Family status.
- Education.
- Aspirations.
- Interests (such as hobbies) and disinterests.
- Social style (driver or another category—see Chapter 5).

Attitudes

- Toward salespeople.
- Toward your company.
- Toward your product.

Relationships

- Formal reporting relationships.
- Important reference groups and group norms.
- Bonds that the prospect has already formed with other salespeople.

Evaluation of Products/Services

- Product attributes that are important.
- Product evaluation process (see Chapter 3 for details).

THE PROSPECT'S/CUSTOMER'S ORGANIZATION

Information about the prospect's or customer's company obviously helps the salesperson understand the customer's environment. This type of information lets the salesperson identify problem areas more quickly and respond accordingly.

For example, in a modified rebuy situation, it would not be necessary to educate the prospect about general features common to the product class as a whole. Using the prospect's valuable time by covering material he or she already knows is minimized. Information like the following about the prospect's organization would be helpful:

Demographics

- Type of organization (manufacturing, wholesaling, retailing).
- Size; number of locations.
- Products and services offered.
- Financial position and its future.
- Overall culture of the organization (risk averse, highest ethical standards, forward thinking).

Prospect's Customers

- Types (consumers, retailers, wholesalers).
- Benefits they seek from the prospect's products and services.

Prospect's Competitors

- Who they are.
- How they differ in their business approaches.
- Prospect's strategic position in the industry (dominant, strong, weak).

Historical Buying Patterns

- Amount purchased in the product category.
- Sole supplier or multiple suppliers. Why?
- Reason for buying from present suppliers.
- Level of satisfaction with suppliers.
- Reasons for any dissatisfaction with suppliers or products currently purchased.

Current Buying Situation

- Type of buying process (new task, straight rebuy, or modified rebuy—see Chapter 3).
- Strengths and weaknesses of potential competitors.

People Involved in the Purchase Decision

- How they fit into the formal and informal organizational structure.
- Their roles in this decision (gatekeeper, influencer, or the like).
- Who is most influential.
- Any **influential adversaries** (carry great influence but are opposed to us)?
- Current problems the organization faces.
- Stage in the buying cycle.

Policies and Procedures

- About salespeople.
- About sales visits.
- About purchasing and contracts.

thinking **it** through

It's your first week on the job as a new salesperson. Your sales manager tells you to collect a lot of information about the prospects you call on, including their preferred political party and their children's names. What would be your reaction to her request? If you didn't want to ask these personal questions, how would you approach the situation with your manager?

SOURCES OF INFORMATION

Gathering all the information listed in the preceding sections for every prospect and organization is initially impossible. The goal is to gather what is both possible and profitable. Remember, your time is valuable! Also, you don't want to fall into the trap sometimes referred to as **analysis paralysis,** which can occur if you prefer to spend practically all your time analyzing situations and finding information instead of making sales calls. Salespeople must strike a proper balance between time spent in acquiring information and time spent making calls. The Marine Corps teaches what it calls the 70 percent solution: If you've got 70 percent of the information, have done 70 percent of the analysis, and feel 70 percent confident, then act!

It is important to gather useful information—not just piles of trivial facts about a prospect, as "From the Buyer's Seat 7.1" illustrates. In addition, salespeople need to check the quality of any data gathered rather than assuming they are good. Salespeople must also be concerned about information overload, which can be detrimental to their jobs.

RESOURCES WITHIN YOUR COMPANY

One of the best sources of information can be the records in your own company, especially if your firm has developed a sophisticated CRM database, as described in Chapter 6.[1] The most useful databases include (in addition to standard demographic information) information about any direct inquiries made by the prospect (from direct mail inquiries, telemarketing, online requests, social media contact, or the like), a sales history for the firm, whether anyone from your company has called on the prospect, and the results of any sales meetings.

Firms are devising many ways to keep the field sales force well informed. Some are using **sales portals:** online databases that include many sources of information in one place. This information can include items like account data, competitor intelligence, and news about the company, the industry, and the economy. All the salesperson has to do is use a single log-on to access all this information. For example, Delta Airlines salespeople can log into their company's portal and quickly and easily access key insights about their business customers.

Even if your firm doesn't have such a database, you should try to gather information about your prospect. For example, wouldn't it be nice to find out before, as opposed to during, a sales call that the prospect used to be a big customer of your firm but quit for some reason?

From the BUYER'S SEAT

7.1

PLAN BEFORE SELLING ME

I'm a buyer for ACME Tools. For me personally, I receive many sales calls each and every day, and at the end of the week it is not uncommon for a majority of them to blend together in my mind. Those that stand out typically have put time and effort into the plans of their sales call. I find that the amount of time salespeople dedicate in preparation of a sales call is a good indicator as to how they will handle my account if we give them our business.

Knowing background information about my company is a great way to stand out against competitors, but knowing who they are calling on is also going to help give them the upper hand. For salespeople to find information about me as a buyer, I would recommend they look at our Web site and my social media sites, whether that be LinkedIn to find my professional past or Facebook to see some things that interest me other than work. Also, salespeople can visit some of our brick-and-mortar locations

and ask around to figure out things that may be beneficial when calling on me.

It is very easy to tell when a salesperson has been on our Web site, researched our Facebook page, and know who exactly our target demographic is. As a buyer, it can be very frustrating when a salesperson comes to me pitching a product that is nowhere near our target demographic. For example, all too often during a phone call from a prospective salesperson, I will give her a brief history of the company and ask her to send me some samples of the products or services that the company can provide us with. When the samples arrive, I see that they in no way match the needs of our organization. So, please, salesperson, do your homework before calling on me!

Source: James Nickerson, ACME Tools; all names and titles have been changed on request; used with permission.

For important sales, you may well be working with a sales team that interacts with a prospect (a topic more fully addressed in Chapter 16). This team, sometimes called a **selling center,** consists of all the people in the selling organization who participate in a selling opportunity. Members of the team may be able to provide or help you secure needed information.

THE INTERNET

A first place to look for information would be the prospect company's own Web page. It is amazing what you can find on company Web pages.

Don't forget to use social media like LinkedIn and Facebook to learn more about prospects, as described in Chapter 6. And there are many business information providers online, like InsideView, Pipl.com, and ZoomInfo, that salespeople can use to extract information about companies and people from million of published sources. Some of this information is free, and some requires payment for more exact information.

SECRETARIES AND RECEPTIONISTS

Secretaries and receptionists in the prospect's firm usually are a rich source of information. Be courteous, however, because secretaries and receptionists are accustomed to having salespeople pry for all sorts of free information. Prioritize your questions and provide justification for asking them. Above all, treat secretaries and receptionists with genuine respect. Dawn Hedges, a Zimmer salesperson who sells surgical joint replacements, has built tremendous relationships with the receptionists she calls on. For example, she knows one receptionist who doesn't let Dawn's competitors in to see the doctors. And the receptionist collects any brochures left with her by competitors and then calls Dawn and gives her the information.[2]

NONCOMPETING SALESPEOPLE

Another source for precall information is noncompeting salespeople. In fact, one of the best sources of information is the prospect's own salespeople because they empathize with your situation.

TRADITIONAL SECONDARY SOURCES

Traditional secondary data sources can also be helpful. Firms such as Standard & Poor's, Hoover's, and Moody's publish a number of informative documents in print and online that are available in many public libraries. These sources can help answer questions about brand names, key contacts, historical information, the current situation and outlook for the firm and the industry, location of plants and distribution centers, market shares, and so on.

THE PROSPECT

Much information can be gleaned directly from the prospect. However, don't expect prospects to sit down and answer any and all questions you might have, especially for topics where the information is fairly easy to get (like what products the prospect makes or sells). Prospects don't have time to fill you in on all the details of their business. If you don't know the basics, many prospects will justifiably refuse to deal with you.

It is also worth mentioning that just as you are gathering information about the prospect prior to a meeting, the prospect often does collect information about you. Even before the sale your prospect can request price quotes via e-mail. He or she can also view your Web page as well as your competitors' Web pages. And the prospect can easily chat with colleagues and read about you on newsgroups, blogs, and social media sites to learn about you and your firm. Any salesperson who doesn't understand these realities won't be prepared for the kinds of questions a prospect might ask or for comments a prospect might make.

OTHER SOURCES

Many other sources can provide information. Some information may have been gleaned at a trade show the prospect attended. Much information will be in the lists and directories from which the prospect's name came. For example, a center of influence will often be able to provide information to a Merrill Lynch financial advisor about his friends. Your current customers can often provide information about new clients. Occasionally a prospect will be important enough to warrant hiring an outside consultant to collect information, especially if you are gathering precall information for international selling. Although some information about foreign companies is available, much will not be obtainable. Salespeople in the United States are often amazed at the lack of information about foreign companies. Two good sources are the U.S. government's export portal and the U.S. Commercial Service market research library.

SETTING CALL OBJECTIVES

The most important step in planning is to set objectives for the call. Merely stating the objective "I want to make a sale" or "to tell her about my product" will not suffice. The customer's decision-making process (see Chapter 3) involves many steps, and salespeople need to undertake many activities as they guide customers through the process.

Yet, as Neil Rackham, an internationally respected sales researcher, notes, "It's astonishing how rarely salespeople set themselves call objectives of any kind—let alone effective ones. Although most books on selling emphasize the importance of clear call objectives, it's rare to see these exhortations turned into practice."[3] Why? Probably because many salespeople want to start doing something instead of "wasting time" planning. But without a plan, they actually increase their chances of wasting time.

As a first step in setting objectives, the salesperson should review what has been learned from precall information gathering. Any call objectives should be based on the results of this review. Also, the seller must keep in mind the relationship the firm wishes to have with the prospect. Not all prospects will or should become strategic partners with the seller's firm. Call objectives should not be created in a vacuum. They should be developed while taking into account the firm's goals, the sales team's goals, and the salesperson's goals. Regardless of the type of goal you are referring to, the old adage is true: If you don't know where you're going, you may wind up somewhere else.

In their well-received sales training books about strategic selling, Miller and Heiman stress the importance of sales call planning being related to the firm's strategic goals for the account.[4] This important topic is covered in Chapter 15. For now, realize that call objectives are based on strategic decisions about the account.

CRITERIA FOR EFFECTIVE OBJECTIVES

All objectives should be specific, realistic, and measurable. A call objective that meets only one or two of these criteria will be an ineffective guide for the salesperson. We now examine each criterion in more detail.

An objective must be specific to be effective. It should state precisely what the salesperson hopes to accomplish, what the objective targets are, and any other details (suggested order quantity, suggested dates for future meetings, length of time needed for a follow-up survey, or the like). Specific objectives help the salesperson avoid "shooting from the hip" during the presentation and perhaps moving the prospect along too rapidly or too slowly.

Objectives must also be realistic. Inexperienced salespeople often have unrealistic expectations about the prospect's or customer's response in the sales call. For example, if Kia Motors currently uses Sony radios in all of its models, a Philips salesperson who expects Kia to change over to Philips radios in the first few sales calls has an unrealistic objective. It is important for sellers to plan objectives for a call that can be accomplished within the time allocated for that sales call. That doesn't mean the objectives should be easy. In reality, challenging but reachable goals tend to lead to better performance.

For objectives to be realistic, the salesperson needs to consider factors such as cultural influences. For example, some firms have an extremely conservative corporate culture. Creating change in such a culture is time consuming and often frustrating for the seller. The national culture is important in selling to international prospects. When selling to Arab or Japanese businesses, salespeople should plan to spend at least several meetings getting to know the other party. Developing relationships with Chinese businesspeople requires a great deal of entertaining. Selling in Russia is often slowed because of bureaucracy and incredible amounts of red tape. As these examples illustrate, culture is an important consideration in attempts to set realistic call objectives.

Finally, call objectives must be measurable so salespeople can objectively evaluate each sales call at its conclusion and determine whether the objectives were met. This suggests they should be written down. If a salesperson's stated objective is to get acquainted with the prospect or to establish rapport, how can the salesperson assess whether this goal was achieved? How can someone measure "getting acquainted"? To what extent would the salesperson have to be acquainted with the prospect to know that he or she achieved the sales call objective? A more measurable sales call objective (as well as a more specific and realistic one) is something like the following: to get acquainted with the prospect by learning which clubs or organizations she or he belongs to, which sports the prospect follows, what his or her professional background is, and how long the prospect has held the current position. With this revised call objective, a salesperson can easily determine whether the objective was reached.

A simple way to help ensure that objectives are measurable is to set objectives that require a buyer's response. For example, achievement of the following objective is easy to measure: to make a follow-up appointment with the buyer.

Successful salespeople in almost every industry have learned the importance of setting proper call objectives. Pharmaceutical salespeople for Novartis set clear objectives for each sales call they make to a physician. Then they lay out a series of objectives for subsequent calls so they know exactly what they hope to accomplish over the next several visits. One industrial products sales manager recommends that her salespeople keep their call objectives in view while they are on the sales call, helping them focus on the true goals of the sales call. Both these examples share a common theme: The salesperson needs to set specific, realistic, measurable call objectives. Exhibit 7.2 lists examples of call objectives that meet these criteria.

Some trainers use the acronym SMART to help salespeople remember how to set proper call objections. SMART suggests that call objectives should be specific, measurable, and achievable but realistic and time based.

SETTING MORE THAN ONE CALL OBJECTIVE

Salespeople have learned the importance of setting multiple objectives for a sales call. Not only do they set a **primary call objective** (the actual goal they hope to achieve) before each sales call; they also set a **minimum call objective** (the

Exhibit 7.2
Examples of Call Objectives

Objectives Related to the Process Leading Up to the Sale

- To have the prospect agree to come to the Atlanta branch office sometime during the next two weeks for a hands-on demonstration of the copier.
- To set up another appointment for one week from now, when the buyer will allow me to do a complete survey of her printing needs.
- To inform the doctor of the revolutionary anticlotting mechanism that has been incorporated into our new drug and have her agree to read the pamphlet I will leave.
- To have the buyer agree to pass my information along to the buying committee with his endorsement of my proposal.
- To have the prospect agree to call several references that I will provide to develop further confidence and trust in my office-cleaning business.
- To have the prospect agree on the first point (of our four-point program) and schedule another meeting in two days to discuss the second point.
- To have the prospect initiate the necessary paperwork to allow us to be considered as a future vendor.

Objectives Related to Consummating the Sale

- To have the prospect sign an order for 100 pairs of Levi's jeans.
- To schedule a co-op newspaper advertising program to be implemented in the next month.
- To have the prospect agree to use our brand of computer paper for a trial period of one month.
- To have the retailer agree to allow us space for an end-of-aisle display for the summer promotion of Raid insect repellent.

Even a salesperson who fails to achieve the primary call objective will be encouraged to at least achieve the minimum call objective.

minimum they hope to achieve) because they realize the call may not go exactly as planned (the prospect may be called away or the salesperson may not have all the necessary facts).[5] On the other hand, the call may go better than the salesperson originally thought it would. Thus, although rarely achieved, an **optimistic call objective** (the most optimistic outcome the salesperson thinks could occur) is also set. The optimistic call objective will probably relate to what the salesperson hopes to accomplish for the account over the long term (that is, the account objectives—see Chapter 15).

The primary call objective, for example, of a Nestlé rep might be to secure an order from a grocer for 10 cases of Nestlé Morsels for an upcoming coupon promotion. That is what the seller realistically hopes to accomplish in the call. A minimum call objective could be to sell at least 5 cases of Morsels, whereas an optimistic call objective would be to sell 20 cases, set up an end-of-aisle display, and secure a retail promotional price of $5.68.

Multiple call objectives have many benefits. First, they help take away the salesperson's fear of failure because most salespeople can achieve at least their stated minimum objective. Second, multiple objectives tend to be self-correcting. Salespeople who always reach their optimum objective realize they are probably setting their sights too low. On the other hand, if they rarely meet even their minimum objective, they probably are setting their goals too high.

It is possible to have more than one primary call objective for a single call. For example, several primary objectives a salesperson might hope to accomplish in a single meeting are to sell one unit, be introduced to one other member of the buying center, and have the prospect agree to send along a packet of information to an executive. In this example, if the salesperson genuinely hopes and expects to achieve all three objectives in the next meeting, they will all be considered primary call objectives. To aid in planning the call, some trainers suggest that the salesperson further prioritize these primary objectives into two groups: The most important primary objective is called the primary call objective, whereas the remaining ones become **secondary call objectives.** So, in this example, if selling the product is the most important thing to accomplish in the next meeting, the objectives will be as follows:

Primary call objective	Sell one unit.
Secondary call objectives	Be introduced to one other member of the buying center.
	Have the prospect agree to send along a packet of information to an executive.

SETTING OBJECTIVES FOR SEVERAL CALLS

By developing a series of specific objectives for future calls, the salesperson can develop a comprehensive strategy for the prospect or customer. This approach is especially important in a partnering relationship. To illustrate the use of multiple call objectives, Exhibit 7.3 gives a set of call objectives for visits over a period of time. The left side of the exhibit contains the long-term plan and each call objective that the Samsung salesperson developed for Johnson Electronics. Note the logical strategy for introducing the new product, the F104 DVD player. The right side of Exhibit 7.3 shows the actual call results.

The salesperson was not always 100 percent successful in achieving the call objectives. Thus, several subsequent objectives needed to be modified. For example, because the meeting on October 10 resulted in the buyer dropping F92 DVD

Exhibit 7.3

Multiple Call Objectives of a Samsung Salesperson Selling to Johnson Electronics

Overall Plan Developed on Oct. 1		Actual Call Results	
Expected Date of the Call	Call Objective	Date of Call	Call Results
Oct. 10	Secure normal repeat orders on F88 and F92. Increase normal repeat order of F100 DVD player from three to five units. Provide product information for new DVD product F104.	Oct. 10	Obtained normal order of F88. Steve decided to drop F92 (refused to give a good reason). Purchased only four F100 players. Seemed responsive to F104 but needs a point-of-purchase (POP) display.
Oct. 17	Erect a front-counter POP display for F104 and secure a trial order of two units.	Oct. 18	Steve was out. His assistant didn't like the POP (thought it was too large). Refused to use POP. Did order one F104. Told me about several complaints with F100.
Nov. 10	Secure normal repeat orders for F88, F92, and F100. Schedule one co-op newspaper ad for the next 30 days featuring F104. Secure an order for F104s.	Nov. 8	Obtained normal orders. Steve agreed to co-op ad but bought only five F104s. Thinks the margins are too low.
Nov. 17	Secure normal repeat orders of F88, F92, and F100. Secure an order for F104s.	Nov. 18	Obtained normal order on F88, but Steve refused to reorder F100. Claimed the competitor product (Sony) is selling much better. Obtained an order of 15 units of F104.

players, the call objectives on November 10 and November 17 need to reflect that Johnson Electronics no longer carries the F92 DVD players. The seller may also want to add a call objective for October 17: to discuss more about the situation with the F92 (because of the outcome of the October 10 meeting) and perhaps try to reintroduce it. This example illustrates the importance of keeping good records, making any necessary adjustments in the long-term call objectives, and then preparing for the next sales call. One sales vice president for a large sales force has some specific advice about setting multiple call objectives:

> The primary objective of the first session is to have another chance to visit. What this allows you to do is have your standards relatively low because you are trying to build a long-term relationship. You should be very sensitive to an opportunity to establish a second visit. What you want to do is identify aspects of the business conversation that require follow-up and make note of them. . . . The key is not the first visit . . . it is the second, the third, the twenty-second visit.[6]

Some industries typically have a long interval between when a prospect is first visited and when an actual sale is consummated. If so, this factor needs to be considered when setting up multiple call objectives and may imply that others get involved in the selling cycle. For example, the typical sale of a Kodak Image Sensor scanner (an image sensor for automated inspection applications in industrial plants) could take several years to close. After having its field sales force demonstrate the image-sensing scanner, the company can use inside sales reps (see Chapter 1 for a description of inside salespeople) to keep the prospects updated in a fashion that is consistent with the prospects' buying time frames. Kodak may also send out newsletters several times a year to prospects. It is important for salespeople to consider the company's other promotional efforts when developing multiple call objectives for a prospect.

When setting multiple call objectives, the salesperson should obviously consider whom to call on in upcoming meetings. Although it seems obvious that the decision maker (who is often a middle manager for many products and services) should be included in those calls, visiting briefly with senior-level managers may also make sense. But what information would you share with the CEO, for example? As discussed in Chapter 1, the answer is the **customer value proposition:** a written statement (usually one or two sentences) that clearly states how purchasing your product or service can help solve the customer's perceived business issue ("BI"). Further, the CVP focuses on what an individual manager needs to address and resolve to be able to better contribute to overall company objectives. The customer value proposition will be more fully discussed in Chapter 9 and will include numerous examples. Frequently the problem needing assistance involves a significant impediment to the firm's revenues and profits. Four common "BI's" include the following:[7]

- Increase revenue, market share, and shareholder value
- Increase efficiency and productivity
- Manage costs
- Control quality and reliability

Appointments increase the chances of seeing the right person and having uninterrupted time with the prospect.

Often a very important consideration is the success of the individual who is your contact within the customer's firm. And there needs to be a struggle (distinct emotion) associated with it.

BUYERS ARE SETTING GOALS ALSO

Salespeople must understand that buyers may also be setting objectives for the salesperson's sales call. These objectives are based on perceptions of how the salesperson's product or service can add value, as described in Chapters 1 and 3. Salespeople's job is to discover what customers value and then find ways to improve customer value relative to their own products or services.

What are some things that buyers look for to increase value? Purchasing managers continually point to the following areas: on-time delivery, products that are exactly to specifications, competitive pricing, proper packaging/paperwork, technical support/service, quality of sales calls, level of technological innovation, and good emergency response. Thus, sellers can expect that buyers may set goals for sales calls in these areas.

MAKING AN APPOINTMENT

After gathering precall information and setting objectives, the salesperson's next step is generally to make an appointment. Many sales managers insist that their salespeople make appointments before calling on prospects or customers. Appointments dignify the salesperson and help get the sales process off to a good start by putting the salesperson and the prospect on the same level—equal participants in a legitimate needs solution process. Appointments also increase the chances of seeing the right person and having uninterrupted time with the prospect.

Experienced sales representatives use different contact methods for different customers. It's also important to point out that attitude (and the salesperson's mood) can have a tremendous impact on success in making appointments. This section describes how to see the right person at the right time and the right place, how to interact with gatekeepers, and how to gain an appointment.

THE RIGHT PERSON

Some experts emphasize the importance of going right to the top and making the first call on the highest-level decision maker. After carefully studying more than 35,000 sales calls, Neil Rackham offers a radically different view.[8] His research suggests that a salesperson should initially try to call on the **focus of receptivity**—the person who will listen receptively and give the seller needed valuable information. Note that this person may not be the decision maker or the one who understands all of the firm's problems. In fact, this person might not even be in the buying center. (See Chapter 3 for details about various people who serve as buying center members.) But this person will talk to the salesperson and provide information.

The focus of receptivity, according to the research, will then lead the salesperson to the **focus of dissatisfaction:** the person who is most likely to perceive problems and dissatisfactions. Finally, the focus of dissatisfaction leads to the **focus of power:** the person who can approve, prevent, and/or influence action. Getting to the focus of power too quickly can lead to disaster because the seller has not yet built a relationship and does not really know the buyer's needs. In summary, Rackham notes, "There's a superstition in selling that the sooner you can get to the decision maker the better. Effective selling, so it's said, is going straight to the focus of power. That's a questionable belief."[9]

Recent research has indicated that a salesperson should work with specific types of individuals because they are better at generating consensus in the buying firm.[10] These include "go-getters," those who are always on the lookout for good ideas; "teachers," those who love to share insights and ideas with others in the firm; and "skeptics," those who tend to be cautious and generally slow down the adoption of new processes. These three groups, collectively called "mobilizers," will question, be skeptical, yet help the firm move in the right direction when convinced.

Often someone needs to introduce you to the decision maker, especially in some cultures. For example, to do business with companies in Mideast countries, it is often necessary to have introductions by trusted individuals. Former senators, ambassadors, and even celebrities provide this role.

Frequently in industrial selling situations, as Chapter 3 described, no single person has the sole authority to buy a product because it is a team buying decision. For example, a forklift sales representative for Clarke may have to see the safety engineer, the methods engineer, the materials-handling engineer, and the general superintendent before selling the product to a manufacturing company. In this case the salesperson should usually try to arrange a meeting with the entire group as well as with each individual.

THE RIGHT TIME

There is little agreement on the subject of the best time for a sales interview; obviously the most opportune time to call will vary by customer and type of selling. The salesperson who calls on wholesale grocers, for example, may find from experience that the best times to call are from 9 a.m. to 11 a.m. and from 1:30 p.m.

MAKE SURE YOU ACTUALLY MEET WHERE YOU CLAIMED TO MEET

When my brother was a doctor, he once told me about a pharmaceutical representative who worked for a large drug company that had provided their sales representatives with GMC Yukons, complete with the OnStar navigation system. What the reps didn't know was that the company was using OnStar to keep track of vehicle locations during work hours. Several salespeople were terminated when the vehicle OnStar report did not sync with the rep's call reports. Other reps felt betrayed by this and began plotting ways to beat the system, such as parking the vehicles at a hospital and having someone else pick them up in a noncompany car or taking the vehicle to a dealership for servicing so as to justify not using it.

I later asked a pharmaceutical sales rep friend how likely she thought this was. She told me it wouldn't surprise her at all, pointing out that "Big Pharma is equal to Big Brother, and as companies consolidate, they are all becoming Big Pharma." She thought it was more likely among companies that provide reps with drug samples

than those that don't or if a company was looking to fire someone; they could see if the car even left the driveway that week. She explained that a lot of firms that use samples also typically provide reps with iPads or other handheld devices and require doctor signatures and time/date stamps to verify when and where the reps are. She added that a friend of hers works for a company that checks company gas cards to ensure that sales reps are getting gas within assigned territories as a way of verifying that the vehicle is not driven outside of its designated area.

She even shared that once when she worked for a "Big Pharma" company and was picking up her new company vehicle, she "called ahead to the dealership and told them that if there was a GPS tracking device in the car, I'd pay whatever it took to disable it."

Source: John E. Cicala, assistant professor, Texas A&M University, Kingsville, personal correspondence, used with permission.

---

to 3:30 p.m. A hospital rep, on the other hand, may discover that the most productive calls on surgeons are made between 8:30 a.m. and 10 a.m. and after 4 p.m. Car washes are busiest in the winter months, with spring being the second-busiest time of year. For most types of selling, the best hours of the day are from approximately 9 a.m. to 11:30 a.m. and from 1:30 p.m. to 4 p.m. For companies that call on Web-generated leads, the best days are Wednesdays and Thursdays between 4 p.m. and 6 p.m. and as soon as possible after the lead is generated.[11]

THE RIGHT PLACE

Meetings can occur just about anywhere, including by video on the Internet. The sales call should take place in an environment conducive to doing business. Such is not always the case, however. For example, some salespeople still take customers to topless bars. In addition to distractions, topless bars present a number of problems for the salesperson who uses them to achieve sales. For example, is it ethical to gain business by using such tactics? Also, once a buyer has purchased on the basis of this entertainment, chances are the seller will have to keep it up or lose the customer. Salespeople should also understand that their companies do care about where they meet a client and are tracking that information for a number of purposes, as "Building Partnerships 7.1" illustrates.

"Sales Technology 7.1" provides the experience of one company that used online Webcasting to its advantage.

Videoconferencing—meetings in which people are not physically present in one location but are connected via voice and video—is growing in usage. In a variant on videoconferencing, called **Webcasting** or **virtual sales calls,** the meeting

USING WEBEX TO SELL EDUCATIONAL PRODUCTS

CEV Multimedia creates educational tools (e.g., DVDs, PowerPoint presentations, lesson plans, activities, and assessments) for students from junior high school through college. The company needed a way to showcase its more than 1,800 titles to teachers and principals, and with a geographically disbursed sales force, this was quite a challenge.

The solution is to demonstrate their products using WebEx. Through online video sales calls, salespeople are able to demonstrate videos, graphics, and all other elements of their titles. CEV Multimedia also uses WebEx to provide customer support and train teachers if they are having trouble with the materials.

The result has been that salespeople have reached more customers and increased the volume of prospects greatly. WebEx has also allowed CEV to reach out to a wider range of schools, including smaller, sometimes remote school districts. The technology has reduced travel expenses and avoided the need to hire additional salespeople. Finally, the technology has made it easier for salespeople to collaborate between themselves, resulting in efficiencies and a greater sense of community.

Sources: http://www.cevmultimedia.com and http://www.webex.com/includes/documents/case-studies/cev-multimedia.pdf.

---

is broadcast over the Internet.[12] For example, due to downsizing, emWare, Inc., has only eight salespeople. According to Michael Nelson, CEO of emWare, the use of virtual sales calls is now necessary and is actually quite successful. Salespeople should learn how to plan for such meetings. One key is to carefully plan all technical elements of the presentation and to rehearse them as much as possible. (Chapter 9 provides more insight into practicing and avoiding problems.)

Videoconferencing makes it easy for a U.S. salesperson to make a presentation in Germany.

CULTIVATING RELATIONSHIPS WITH SUBORDINATES

Busy executives usually have one or more subordinates who plan and schedule interviews for them. These **screens** (or **barriers,** as salespeople sometimes call them) often make seeing the boss difficult. These screens can also take on the role of gatekeepers for the buying center (Chapter 3 discusses gatekeepers).

Sales strategists have identified several ways to interact with a screen:

• The salesperson can work "through the screen." The seller has to convince the gatekeeper that a meeting with the boss is in the boss's best interests.

• The salesperson can go "over the screen." While talking to the screen, the seller drops names of people higher up in the organization. The screen may allow the seller in to see the boss right away for fear of getting into trouble.

• The salesperson can go "under the screen" by trying to make contact with the prospect before or after the screen gets to work (or while the screen is taking a coffee break). This is a strategy that can easily backfire. For example, Oracle learned, the hard way, the impact of having pushy, aggressive salespeople who constantly bypassed screens and formal committees. The result was great customer dissatisfaction.

Salespeople should work to achieve friendly relationships with the prospect's subordinates.

TELEPHONING FOR APPOINTMENTS

The telephone is most often used to make an initial appointment. Salespeople can save many hours by phoning, or having others phone for them, to make appointments. Chapter 4 provided many insights on how to use the phone effectively and suggested a way to gain an appointment with a prospect.

The goal of the telephone call is to make an appointment, not to sell the product or service. Exhibit 7.4 shows appropriate responses to common objections that Xerox copier salespeople encounter when making appointments. Salespeople need to anticipate objections and decide exactly how to respond, as Chapter 10 will more fully discuss.

ADDITIONAL PLANNING

A successful salesperson thinks ahead to the meeting that will occur and plans accordingly. For example, salespeople should plan how they intend to make a good first impression and build credibility during the call. It is also important to plan how to further uncover the customer's needs and strengthen the presentation. Salespeople should anticipate the questions and concerns the prospect may raise and plan to answer them helpfully. These issues are discussed in detail in the next several chapters. For now, be aware that these activities should be planned before the meeting begins.

Exhibit 7.4
Responses to Objections concerning Appointments

Objection from a Secretary	Response
I'm sorry, but Mr. Wilkes is busy now.	What I have to say will take only a few minutes. Should I call back in a half hour, or would you suggest I set up an appointment?
We already have a copier.	That's fine. I want to talk to Mr. Wilkes about our new paper flow system design for companies like yours.
I take care of all the copying.	That's fine, but I'm here to present what Xerox has to offer for a complete paper flow system that integrates data transmission, report generation, and copiers. I'd like to speak to Mr. Wilkes about this total service.

Objection from the Prospect	Response
Can't you mail the information to me?	Yes, I could. But everyone's situation is different, Mr. Wilkes, and our systems are individually tailored to meet the needs of each customer. Now . . . [benefit statement and repeat request for appointment].
Well, what is it you want to talk about?	It's difficult to explain the system over the telephone. In 15 minutes, I can demonstrate the savings you get from the system.
You'd just be wasting your time. I'm not interested.	The general objection is hiding a specific objection. The salesperson needs to probe for the specific objection: Do you say that because you don't copy many documents?
We had a Xerox copier once and didn't like it.	Probe for the specific reason of dissatisfaction and have a reply, but don't go too far. The objective is to get an appointment, not sell a copier.

Source: Courtesy of Xerox Corporation. Used by permission.

Before making the sales call, it is important to practice. How long should a rep spend practicing? Longer than many would think. As Mark Twain wrote, "It usually takes more than three weeks to prepare a good impromptu speech." Some have even suggested that for very important presentatons, the seller spend 30 minutes preparing and practicing for each minute of presentation time. While often broken, the rule does indicate the importance of planning and practicing the presentation. Of course the time spent in practicing would depend on how much time the seller has and on the goals of the presentation.

One other thing that salespeople do is **seeding**—that is, sending the customer important and useful information. For example, a rep can constantly search newspapers, blogs, and social media postings for material that may be useful for a prospect. This material is sent to the prospect with a note saying something like, "Jim, I thought you would find this article useful!" The material does not include the selling firm's catalogs, brochures, pricing, and so on. Rather, it is good, useful information that will help the prospect's business. The result? The buyer views the seller as someone trying to be truly helpful and as someone who really understands the buyer's business.

SELLING YOURSELF

The information learned about planning the sales call can be applied to more than just business settings. Using the same approach in your personal life can pay dividends, regardless if the decision you are making is large or small. For example, when purchasing a new car, you should use the same concepts about planning before you visit a dealership. Most people probably do this without thinking. You start by obtaining precall information about the dealerships you will visit and about the type of vehicle that you want to purchase. Using the Internet, friends, and other sources, you gather all the relevant information for your call. Then some call objectives are set. The first visit might entail only getting a feel for which dealerships have the best deals, where the best financing options are, and so on. Setting the appointment follows. Maybe you think just before or just after lunch might be the best time to get the best deal. Regardless, it is easy to see how this information can be translated to everyday life.

As graduation approaches and the job hunt begins, it would be smart to apply this strategy to the interviewing process. When looking at potential employers, it makes sense to collect information about the company to understand if it is a leader in the marketplace, what kind of reputation the company has, and whether there are opportunities for advancement. That information will help to determine if the company is a proper fit. Setting call objectives is a must so that you know what you want to accomplish from the interview. You probably want to understand more about the job position, what they expect from potential candidates, what benefits the company provides, and so on. I'm assuming that most of you will be setting a primary goal of moving to the next step in the interview process or securing the position. Precall planning could make the difference between success and failure in today's job market. Putting the effort in up front, much like in sales, will help you achieve your goals.

A job in sales may not be for everyone, but everyone is going to be selling regardless of professional focus. Selling your ideas to your boss/coworker and selling yourself for a promotion are two situations where knowing how to sell can be valuable. My advice is to gain a thorough understanding of all the steps in the sales process, from precall planning to asking for the business. The better you understand the process, the easier it will be for you to apply it in any situation.

Source: Brett Georgulis; used with permission.

SUMMARY

This chapter stressed the importance of planning the sales call. Developing a clear plan saves time for both salespeople and customers. In addition, it helps salespeople increase their confidence and reduce their stress.

As part of the planning process, salespeople need to gather as much information about the prospect as possible before the first call. They need information about both the individual prospect and the prospect's organization. Sources of this information include lists and directories, secretaries and receptionists, noncompeting salespeople, and direct inquiries made by the prospect.

To be effective, a call objective should be specific, realistic, and measurable. In situations requiring several calls, the salesperson should develop a plan with call objectives for each future call. Also, many salespeople benefit from setting multiple levels of objectives—primary, minimum, and optimum—for each call.

As a general rule, salespeople should make appointments before calling on customers. This approach enables the salesperson to talk to the right person at the customer's site.

A number of methods can be used to make appointments. Perhaps the most effective is the straightforward telephone approach.

KEY TERMS

analysis paralysis   177
barriers   187
customer value proposition   184
focus of dissatisfaction   185
focus of power   185
focus of receptivity   185
influential adversaries   176
minimum call objective   181
optimistic call objective   182

primary call objective   181
sales portals   177
screens   187
secondary call objectives   182
seeding   189
selling center   178
videoconferencing   186
virtual sales call   186
Webcasting   186

ETHICS PROBLEMS

1. Suppose that during your information-gathering phase you identify a hostile influential adversary named Larry. You know that Larry will do everything possible to see your competitor get the business. In talking about this with your sales manager, she suggests that you find some way to covertly strip Larry of his credibility and thus cause him to be a nonissue. Would you follow your manager's advice? What kinds of things would you be willing to do? What would you be uncomfortable doing?

2. During precall planning, you learn that an important prospect enjoys being treated by salespeople to visit strip clubs, of which there are several in your town. Your firm doesn't have any policy about whether you can visit one of these clubs with a client. You've never visited one with a client before. How will these facts affect your planning for your upcoming sales visit to this prospect? What will you do?

QUESTIONS AND PROBLEMS

1. Think about a teacher you have had in college. Assume that a salesperson wanted to sell that teacher an important product or service. Who

would be a good focus of receptivity for this salesperson? Do you think the focus of receptivity would cooperate with the salesperson?

2. In "Sales Technology 7.1" you learned how one firm uses WebEx to give presentations. Can you think of any negative aspects of using such technology for giving sales presentations to prospects?

3. This chapter listed a number of information items that a salesperson should find out about a prospect/customer as an individual. Assume you are going to sell your best friend a new iPod. See how much information you can supply from the list in the text.

4. Evaluate the following objectives for a sales call:
   a. Show and demonstrate the entire line of 10 squash racquets.
   b. Find out more about competitors' offerings under consideration.
   c. Make the buyer believe what I say.
   d. Determine which service the prospect is currently using for furniture cleaning and how much it costs.
   e. Have the buyer agree to hold our next meeting at a quieter location.
   f. Get an order for 15 carpet cleanings.
   g. Make the buyer not worry about the fact that our newspaper has been in business only two years.

5. Think for a moment about trying to secure a job. Assume you are going to have your second job interview next week with Fastenol for a sales position. The interview will take place over the phone with the senior recruiter. You've already had one informational interview on campus. Most candidates go through a set of four interviews. List your primary objective, minimum objective, and optimistic objective for your second interview.

6. In "Building Partnerships 7.1" you learned that some firms use technology to keep tabs on their salespeople, like where they have driven their company cars and when they

have given out samples. What would you say if a manager asked you why you used the company car to visit a mall in the middle of the day? Assume that you stopped at the mall to get your hair cut.

7. Evaluate the following approach for getting an appointment: Ms. Stevens, I've not got any calls on my calendar for next Thursday. Would it be OK if I stopped by for a few minutes, say, sometime between 1:00 and 4:00?

8. Although there is no firm rule, list what you think to be the best time of day to call on the following individuals:
   a. A college bookstore manager (to sell water bottles).
   b. A manager at an automotive glass replacement company (to sell a new tool to remove broken glass shards).
   c. An apartment complex manager (to sell a new lawn watering system).
   d. A heating contractor (to sell a new model of heating system).

9. Review the list of prospects in Question 8 and identify the following:
   a. The worst time of day to call on each individual.
   b. The worst time of year to call on each individual.

10. Suppose you have graduated and you belong to the alumni association of your school. Your association plans to raffle off a number of donated items to raise funds for a new multimedia center at your school. To be a success, the event will need many donated raffle prizes.
   a. Which sources will you use to identify potential sponsors?
   b. What information do you need to qualify them properly?

CASE PROBLEMS

case **7.1**

Presidential Aviation (Part A)

Presidential Aviation has provided charter flights to a wide array of customers, including business travelers worldwide. Thanks to the Presidential online booking system, business travelers can secure reliable quotes and book both domestic and international flights. Presidential has a sizable fleet of aircraft, including jets (light, midsize, and large jets) and turboprops.

The company is known for its ability to cater to passengers' every desire, including gourmet meals, special beverages, entertainment while in the air, and other luxury accommodations. Presidential also staffs a full-service VIP jet concierge program, similar to what major airlines offer.

Santiago Diego is a salesperson for Presidential Aviation. He is currently planning an important first visit to Juan Espinosa, a procurement officer at

Regent Seven Seas Cruises. Company officials travel across the country a great deal in their work. Santiago would like to tell Juan how Presidential can provide outstanding benefits to the Regent Seven Seas Cruises. Some of the special features for business travelers include the following:

- Privacy—you have the entire aircraft to yourself and can travel with passengers you know and enjoy.
- Comfort—including extra-roomy leather seats, in-flight movies, fully stocked bar, and gourmet meals that you choose.
- Ease—no time-consuming check-in process. You drive right up to the plane, and your luggage goes from your car into the plane.
- Point-to-point travel—there are no set schedules, so you fly when you want. Presidential uses 10 times more airports than commercial airlines, so you can fly from less congested airports closer to where you live.

Questions

1. What kind of information should Santiago gather about Juan before their meeting?

2. What kind of information should Santiago gather about Regent Seven Seas Cruises before his meeting?

3. Which sources can Santiago use to gather that needed information?

Sources: http://www.rssc.com and http://www.presidential-aviation.com.

case 7.2

Underground Construction Magazine

Underground Construction magazine is a publication with special appeal for any contractor, municipal manager, or engineering professional involved in the construction, rehabilitation, and remediation of underground pipeline systems. The magazine covers the entire underground utilities infrastructure market, including water/wastewater, oil, gas, telephone, cable, and power. Each issue of the magazine includes latest news, changes in technology, and significant innovations that can be used by industry professionals in managing their underground construction projects.

Andres Orrino is a salesperson for *Underground Construction*, and his territory includes all of states each of the Mississippi River in the United States. In a few weeks, Andres will be calling on Takeuchi, a company that makes track loaders. Track loaders are used in underground construction projects for a variety of tasks. Takeuchi has never advertised in *Underground Construction* magazine. Andres is not sure if anyone from his magazine has ever even called on Takeuchi.

Questions

1. Assume that you are Andres Orrino. List your call objectives for your first call with the marketing director for Takeuchi. Develop a three-call follow-up schedule and list the objectives for each call.

2. What kind of information would you like to have before your first meeting? How could you obtain that information?

Sources: http://www.undergroundconstructionmagazine.com and http://www.takeuchi-us.com.

ROLE PLAY CASE

This role play continues with the same customer firm you have been selling to: BancVue, GelTech, or HighPoint Solutions. (If you have not done role plays before, you will need to review the information about the various role play customers that can be found at the end of Chapter 3.)

Your buyer has agreed to allow you to meet with the rest of the buying center. Now it is time to plan the sales call. Write out your sales call objectives. In case you need assistance, here is some additional information from your previous calls, and feel free to ask your buyer for additional information. In addition to your call objectives, outline an agenda, or what you plan to do step-by-step.

BancVue: You are planning for a sales call with the VP of sales and marketing. You know that the company is growing about 15 percent per year. There are 45 salespeople, managed by four regional sales managers.

GelTech: Your sales call will be with the same person plus some of the agents who have contact management software that they bought. The ultimate decision will be made by Mr. McLane, but he is likely to buy whatever this group recommends.

HighPoint Solutions: You are going to meet with the two VPs of sales. Recall that one manages a sales force of 59 salespeople and sells to distributors, while the other has institutions and government agencies as accounts, with 18 salespeople.

Once you've written your objectives, review them with your group. Make sure they meet the criteria for objectives as specified in the chapter.

Note: For background information about these role plays, please see page 26.

To the instructor: Additional information needed to complete the role play is available in the Instructor's Manual.

ADDITIONAL REFERENCES

Adams, Susan. "The New Rules of Business Etiquette." *Forbes.* Retrieved from http://www.forbes.com/sites/susanadams/2011/10/05/the-new-rules-of-business-etiquette, October 15, 2012.

Bachrach, Anne M. "Getting to the Right People." *American Salesman* 57, no. 5 (May 2012), pp. 27–30.

Barnes, Cindy, Helen Blake, and David Pinder. *Creating and Delivering Your Value Proposition: Managing Customer Experience for Profit.* Philadelphia, PA: Kogan Page, 2009.

Boulton, C. "Web Conferencing Fills Void in Tight Times." *eWeek* 26, no. 1 (January 5, 2009), pp. 14–16.

Chang, Man-Ling, Cheng-Feng Cheng, and Wann-Yih Wu. "How Buyer-Seller Relationship Quality Influences Adaptation and Innovation by Foreign MNCs' Subsidiaries." *Industrial Marketing Management* 41, no. 7 (October 2012), pp. 1047–57.

Ivens, Björn Sven, Catherine Pardo, Robert Salle, and Bernard Cova. "Relationship Keyness: The Underlying Concept for Different Forms of Key Relationship Management." *Industrial Marketing Management* 38, no. 5 (July 2009), pp. 513–19.

Kahle, Dave. "Creating a Powerful Sales Plan." *American Salesman* 56, no. 11 (November 2011), pp. 3–7.

Lewin, Jeffrey E., and Jeffrey K. Sager. "An Investigation of the Influence of Coping Resources in Salespersons' Emotional Exhaustion." *Industrial Marketing Management* 38, no. 7 (October 2009), pp. 798–805.

Macdivitt, Harry, and Mike Wilkinson. *Value-Based Pricing: Drive Sales and Boost Your Bottom Line by Creating, Communicating and Capturing Customer Value.* New York: McGraw-Hill, 2011.

Mayo, M., and M. Mallin. "The Impact of Sales Failure on Attributions Made by 'Resource-Challenged' and 'Resource-Secure' Salespeople." *Journal of Marketing Theory and Practice* 18, no. 3 (2010), pp. 233–47.

Shelton, Robert. "Integrating Product and Service Innovation: Industry Leaders Complement Their Product Offerings with Service Innovations to Boost Overall Customer Value." *Research-Technology Management* 52, no. 3 (2009), pp. 38–44.

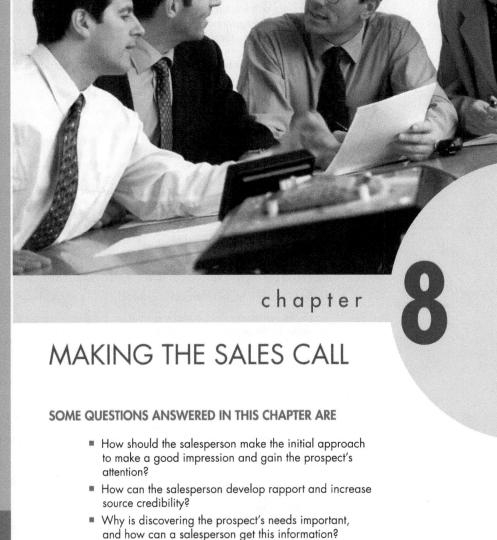

The Partnership Process

PART 2

chapter 8

MAKING THE SALES CALL

SOME QUESTIONS ANSWERED IN THIS CHAPTER ARE

- How should the salesperson make the initial approach to make a good impression and gain the prospect's attention?

- How can the salesperson develop rapport and increase source credibility?

- Why is discovering the prospect's needs important, and how can a salesperson get this information?

- How can the salesperson most effectively relate the product or service features to the prospect's needs?

- Why is it important for the salesperson to make adjustments during the call?

- How does the salesperson recognize that adjustments are needed?

- How can a salesperson effectively sell to groups?

PROFILE

PROFILE My name is David Maebane. I graduated with a BS in marketing and a certificate in professional selling from Northern Illinois University, where I had the privilege of studying principles of selling from professors Ridnour, Weilbaker, and Vollmert. On graduation, I took a position as a district manager for PepsiCo-Frito Lay.

I lead a territory of 11 salespeople who drive sales and increase market share in a very competitive consumer foods industry. My primary focus is to grow territory and reduce costs. The responsibility of my sales team is to create profit and customized solutions for buyers and decision makers in the grocery retail industry. It is very important that we create effective sales calls and deliver value-added strategies to increase our customer's profits. Having a prepared and fact-based call is the most strategic way to grow a win–win relationship in my industry and across other functions in business.

When making a sales call, I do my homework on that company, identifying opportunities and strengths as well as what value proposition my company can offer in order to give them a competitive advantage in their industry. It's important that I am professional and prepared for each sales call because I am representing not only myself but also PepsiCo-FritoLay. I want to be genuinely myself, showing that I will build a long-term relationship based on values and good business ethics.

When addressing competition in a sales call, I always want to be professional and never voice negative opinions about the other company. Price sometimes can be a very sensitive topic in a sales call. I try to remain consistent and confident and know what my company specifies on price. I make sure that I do not compromise on my personal ethics or those of my company by promising things that I cannot deliver. During each sales call, I always check for understanding and ask questions to make sure the person I'm selling to is following along and is not confused. As I ask for feedback and follow through on everything after the sale, only then am I providing true relationship selling and not just a one-time business transaction.

Visit our Web site at:
www.pepsico.com/brands/frito_lay-brands.html

Exhibit 8.1
Essential Elements of the
Sales Call

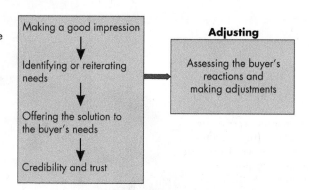

At this point in the sales process, we assume that an appointment has been made, sufficient information about the prospect and his or her organization has been gathered, and the salesperson has developed strong objectives for the call. In this chapter we discuss how to make the actual sales call. The content of a sales call depends on the specific situation the salesperson encounters as well as the extent of the relationship the salesperson has already established with the other party.[1] Exhibit 8.1 provides an organizing framework for our discussion. We start by considering how to make a good impression and begin to develop a long-term relationship. We then examine the initial needs assessment phase of a relationship and how to relate solutions to those needs. Finally, we discuss the relationship between adaptability and successful sales calls. Recent research echoes past research in showing that knowledge, adaptability, and trust are critical for successful sales to occur.[2]

There are, of course, many conceptualizations of the selling process. For example, one trainer finds value in describing the selling process as the **Four A's** (*a*cknowledge, *a*cquire, *a*dvise, and *a*ssure).[3] First the seller acknowledges the buyer by greeting/welcoming/honoring and building trust. Next the seller acquires information via needs analysis and a summary of that analysis outlining the agreement between buyer and seller about the current situation and the desired solution. Advising comes next, during which the seller narrows the possible choices to specific options, sells benefits of those options (not just features), watches for buying signals, and asks for the order. Finally, the seller assures the buyer after the sale by enhancing satisfaction with the buying decision and giving proper follow-up and referrals.

MAKING A GOOD IMPRESSION

When salespeople arrive late, make a poor entrance, fail to gain the buyer's interest, or lack rapport-building skills, it is difficult for them to secure commitment and build partnerships.[4] This section discusses how salespeople can manage the buyer's impression of them, a process termed **impression management**. Most of the information presented here assumes that the salesperson is making a first call on a prospect. However, impression management continues throughout calls.

One of the most important ways to ensure a good first impression is to be well prepared (as we discussed in Chapter 7). Some salespeople prepare a checklist of things to take to the presentation so they won't forget anything.

WAITING FOR THE PROSPECT

Being on time for a scheduled sales call is critical to avoid giving the buyer a negative impression. With cell phones, there is no good reason for not calling if you're

Salespeople should use waiting time effectively.

going to be a few minutes late to the appointment.

Every salesperson must expect to spend a certain portion of each working day waiting for sales interviews. Successful salespeople make the best possible use of this time by working on reports, studying new product information, checking e-mail and text messages, planning and preparing for their next calls, and obtaining additional information about the prospect. (Chapter 15 covers time management more fully.)

Some trainers suggest that salespeople not wait for any prospect, under normal circumstances, more than 15 minutes after the appointment time. Why? To demonstrate that the seller's time is also important. Exceptions are necessary, of course, depending on the importance of the customer, the reason the customer is running late, and the distance the salesperson has traveled. In all cases salespeople should keep the sales call in perspective, realizing that their time is also valuable. Chapter 15 discusses just how valuable that time really is.

When the salesperson arrives, the receptionist may merely say, "I'll tell Ms. Schimpf that you are here." After the receptionist has spoken with Ms. Schimpf, the salesperson should ask approximately how long the wait will be. If the wait will be excessive or the salesperson has another appointment, it may be advisable to explain this tactfully and to ask for another appointment. Usually the secretary either will try to get the salesperson in to see the prospect more quickly or will arrange for a later appointment.

FIRST IMPRESSIONS

In the first meeting between a salesperson and a prospect or customer, the first two or three minutes can be very important. Making a favorable first impression usually results in a prospect who is willing to listen. A negative first impression, on the other hand, sets up a barrier that may never be hurdled.

Salespeople may make a poor impression without realizing it. They may know their customer's needs and their own product but overlook seemingly insignificant things that can create negative impressions. As Chapter 5 related, how you dress can affect the message you send to the buyer. Also, studies have shown that the physical attractiveness and gender of salespeople can influence purchase intentions of buyers. And don't forget that according to generation gap experts, it is often quite difficult for a Generation X (born 1965–1978) salesperson to relate to a baby-boom (born 1946–1964) buyer and even harder to relate to a traditionalist (born 1922–1946) buyer.

So what should a seller do to create a good first impression? You should be well groomed and enter confidently (but not arrogantly) by using erect posture, lengthy stride, and a lively pace, and among the first words out of your mouth should be something like, "Thanks for seeing me." And don't forget to smile. Watch what happens when you look at someone and smile. In 99 out of 100 cases, you will receive a smile in return.

But here's a caveat to the counsel just offered: Observe the prospect's state and modify your behavior as needed. When customers are in a bad mood, the last thing they want is a happy, bouncy salesperson. In fact, in such a situation, the prospect might be inattentive or even refuse to meet with such a salesperson. Adapt and even ask if this is not a good time to meet if you perceive that the buyer is very stressed. Also, be aware that many buyers are repulsed by a salesperson who enters the room with exaggerated and false enthusiasm that her product is for sure going to solve all of the buyer's problems. It's better to be humble than to be cocky.[5]

It is also important to remember prospects' names and how to pronounce them (www.hearnames.com provides verbal pronunciation of many hard-to-say names). There are many ways to try to remember someone's name—such as giving your full attention when you hear it and then repeating the name immediately, associating it with someone else you know with the same name, associating it with the person's most prominent feature or trait, using it during the conversation, and writing it down phonetically.

Some experts argue that the customer's name should be used in the opening statement. Dale Carnegie, a master at developing relationships, said a person's name is "the sweetest and most important sound" to that person. Using a person's name often indicates respect and a recognition of the person's unique qualities. Others disagree with this logic, claiming that using the person's name, especially more than once in any short time, sounds phony and insincere. A compromise is to use the prospect's name in the opening and then to use it occasionally during the rest of the call.

thinking it through

You walk into a prospect's office confidently. Even though you've never met her before, you aren't nervous. You've done your homework and have strong objectives for this meeting. After you introduce yourself to the prospect and sit down, you suddenly remember that you left your iPad in your car. And in that iPad is your entire presentation! Your car is several blocks away. What should you do? What would you say to the prospect?

SELECTING A SEAT

When selecting a seat, it is a good idea to look around and start to identify the prospect's social style and status (see Chapter 5). For example, in the United States important decision makers usually have large, well-appointed, private offices. But this isn't always true. In Kuwait a high-ranking businessperson may have a small office and lots of interruptions. Don't take that environment to mean he or she is a low-ranking employee or is not interested. Walmart buyers interview salespeople in rough conditions to help instill the idea that they want the lowest prices they can get.

Asking permission to sit down is usually unnecessary. The salesperson should read the prospect's nonverbal cues to determine the right time to be seated. And note that many calls will not involve sitting down at all, such as talking to a store manager in a grocery store aisle, conversing with a supervisor in a warehouse, or asking questions of a surgeon in a post-op ward.

GETTING THE CUSTOMER'S ATTENTION

Recall from Chapter 5 that there are several types of sales presentations, including standard memorized, outlined, and customized. In this chapter we assume that the salesperson has chosen a customized presentation.

Getting the customer's attention is not a new concept. It is also the goal of many other activities you are familiar with, such as advertising, making new friends, writing an English composition, giving a speech, or writing a letter to a friend. Also, gaining the prospect's attention can be started before the sales call via social media tools (like sending surveys and polls via LinkedIn to generate interest in your idea).[6]

Time is valuable to prospects, and prospects concentrate their attention on the first few minutes with a salesperson to determine whether they will benefit from the interaction. The prospect is making a decision: Do I want to give this salesperson 15 minutes of my time? Thirty minutes of my time? None of my time? This decision is made even while the salesperson is walking in the door and selecting a seat. Some claim that salespeople have less than six minutes to establish credibility with a client. The first few words the salesperson says often set the tone of the entire sales call. The **halo effect** (how and what you do in one thing changes a person's perceptions of other things you do) seems to operate in many sales calls. If the salesperson is perceived by the prospect as effective at the beginning of the call, he will be perceived as effective during the rest of the call and vice versa. There are many ways to open a presentation. An **opening** is a method designed to get the prospect's attention and interest quickly and to make a smooth transition into the next part of the presentation (which is usually to more fully discover the prospect's needs). Because each prospect and sales situation is unique, salespeople should be adaptable and be able to use any or a combination of openings. Again, keep in mind that openings are generally less important with partnering customers whom the salesperson has already met. Exhibit 8.2 provides details about a number of possible openings. But remember, many prospects won't like what they deem to be "canned" approaches and will react negatively.

Exhibit 8.2
Openings That Salespeople Can Use to Gain Attention

Opening Method	Example	Things to Consider
Introduction opening (simply introduce yourself).	Ms. Hallgren, thank you for seeing me today. My name is Daniel Mundt, and I'm with ServiceMaster.	Simple but may not generate interest.
Referral opening (tell about someone who referred you to the buyer).	Mr. Schaumberg, I appreciate your seeing me today. I'm here at the suggestion of Ms. Fleming of Acumen Ornamental Iron Works. She thought you would be interested in our line of wrought iron products and railings.	Always get permission. Don't stretch the truth.
Benefit opening (start by telling some benefit of the product).	Mr. Penney, I would like to tell you about a color copier that can reduce your copying costs by 15 percent.	Gets down to business right away.
Product opening (actually demonstrate a product feature and benefit as soon as you walk up to the prospect).	[Carrying an iPad into an office] Ms. Hemming, you spend a lot of time on the road as an investigative lawyer. Let me show you how this little handheld item can transform your car (or any place you go) into an efficient, effective office.	Uses visual and not just verbal opening; can create excitement.
Compliment opening (start by complimenting the buyer or the buyer's firm).	I was calling on one of your customers, Jackson Street Books, last week, and the owner couldn't say enough good things about your service. It sure says a lot about your operation to have a customer just start praising you out of the blue.	Must be sincere, not just flattery. **ethics**
Question opening (start the conversation with a question).	Ms. Borgelt, what is your reaction to the brochure I sent you about our new telemarketing service?	Starts two-way communication.

DEVELOPING RAPPORT

Rapport in selling is a close, harmonious relationship founded on mutual trust. You build rapport when the prospect perceives you to be like him or her in some way. Ultimately the goal of every salesperson should be to establish rapport with each customer. Often salespeople can accomplish this with some friendly conversation early in the call. Part of this process involves identifying the prospect's social style and making necessary adjustments (see Chapter 5).

The talk about current news, hobbies, mutual friends, and the like that usually breaks the ice for the actual presentation is often referred to as **small talk.** One of the top traits of successful salespeople is the ability to be sociable. Examples include the following:[7]

> I understand you went to Nebraska? I graduated from there with a BBA in 2007.
>
> Did you see the Houston Rockets game on TV last night?
>
> I read in the paper that you won the bass fishing tournament last weekend. I bet that was pretty exciting!
>
> So did you have trouble getting home from work last week with that snowstorm?
>
> Your receptionist was very helpful when I set this appointment. I never would have found this building if she hadn't told me where to park.
>
> You don't happen to remember Marla Jones, do you? She said she went to college with you and said to say hi.

Sharing letters from satisfied customers helps a salesperson establish credibility.

Customers are more receptive to salespeople with whom they can identify—that is, with whom they have something in common. Thus, salespeople will be more effective with customers with whom they establish such links as mutual friends, common hobbies, or attendance at the same schools. Successful salespeople engage in small talk more effectively by first performing **office scanning:** looking around the prospect's environment for relevant topics to talk about. "Sales Technology 8.1" describes how several salespeople use social networking sites to learn about appropriate topics of conversation.

Be careful, however, when engaging in small talk because it can be to your detriment.[8] One salesperson told of a client who asked her opinion about the economic outlook. The seller said she thought it was going down. The buyer had a different opinion, and it took months to repair the relationship. It is generally best to avoid controversial topics like politics and religion. Don't talk about your personal problems in an effort to get sympathy. Don't complain about others (boss, wife) or gossip about your competitors. Also, especially for first calls on prospects, you want to avoid using trite phrases like "How are you doing today?" because they don't sound sincere.

USING INFORMATION FOUND IN SOCIAL MEDIA IN A SALES CALL

Everyone always says that you need to make a great first impression; and it is true. With all of the social media sites out there today, it is very easy to gain valuable information that will assist you in making a great first impression on your prospective client. Finding something in common with your potential buyer can help you develop a common ground with them and possibly give you the upper hand against competition.

For example, imagine you are working for an appliance company and are preparing for a sales call to the senior buyer of major appliances at Best Buy. When you go to LinkedIn, you can search for that exact person and get an extensive background on what he or she has done and where he or she is coming from. If you can find a similarity in interest, this can be a great way to break the ice and get the meeting off to a great start.

Being current on company initiatives can greatly increase your ability to present information that will be valuable to your client. With many businesses being involved in social media these days, you can find a lot of very current information. For example, on April 23, 2012, Best Buy tweeted, "No matter where you bought it, we'll recycle it!" This tweet linked with the recycling page on Best Buy's Web site. Knowing that Best Buy is making a big effort to become more "green" by offering a recycling service to their customers, you can now take this into account during your presentation by making sure that you stress the way your organization is making efforts to produce the product that you are attempting to sell them in a "green" way. For example, if you are selling them a large home appliance and if your product beats current offerings at Best Buy in energy usage, this may help you win their business over competitors.

Social media offer endless information; you just need to put in the time and effort to find it. By doing your research about a potential company and buyer, you are not being "creepy" as some may think of it; rather, you are being proactive, and many buyers will be impressed with the fact that you have put forth the extra effort to get to know them and their company before you ever even meet them.

Of course salespeople should consider cultural and personality differences and adapt the extent of their nonbusiness conversation accordingly. For example, an AT&T rep would probably spend considerably less time in friendly conversation with a New York City office manager than with, say, a manager in a rural Texas town. Businesspeople in Africa place such high value on establishing friendships that the norm calls for a great deal of friendly conversation before getting down to business. Chinese customers want a lot of rapport building before they get down to business. Amiables and expressives tend to enjoy such conversations, whereas drivers and analyticals may be less receptive to spending much time in nonbusiness conversation. Studies show that salespeople who adapt and mirror their prospects are more successful in gaining desired results.[9] Also, there could be less need for small talk if the salesperson uses a question or product opening when getting the customer's attention.

At this point in the sales call, after gaining the prospect's attention and establishing some rapport, a salesperson will often share his or her goals or agenda for the meeting with the prospect. This step can help build further rapport and trust. For example:

> Just so you know, my goal today is simply to verify what your needs might be and then, as I promised in the phone call, to share with you the results of the lab test we conducted last fall.

WHEN THINGS GO WRONG

Making and maintaining a good impression is important. How nice it would be if the beginning of every call went as smoothly as we have described here. Actually, things do go wrong sometimes. The best line of defense when something goes wrong is to maintain the proper perspective and a sense of humor. It's not the first thing you have done wrong and won't be your last.

For example, assume that a seller accidently scratched a prospect's desk with her portfolio. The worst response by this salesperson would be to faint, scream, or totally lose control. A better response would include a sincere apology for the scratch and an offer to pay for any repairs.

What if you say something that is truly embarrassing? According to Mark Twain, "Man is the only animal that blushes, or needs to." For example, one salesperson calling on an older buyer motioned to a picture of a very young lady on the buyer's desk. "Is that your daughter?" the seller asked, smiling. "That's my wife," the buyer replied, frowning. In another sales call, the salesperson saw a picture on the prospect's desk and said, "Oh wow! What a great picture! How'd you ever get a picture of yourself with John Madden, the football guy!" The buyer replied angrily, "That's not John Madden, that's my wife!"[10] Obviously both sellers made major blunders. The first thing you should do in such a situation is to apologize sincerely. Then change the subject or move on in your presentation. Try to relax and put the incident behind you. And learn this lesson: Think before you speak!

Of course you can get into trouble without even saying a word. As Chapter 4 indicated, you must be careful when using gestures in other cultures because they often take on different meanings.

IDENTIFYING THE PROSPECT'S NEEDS: THE POWER OF ASKING QUESTIONS

Once the salesperson has entered and captured the buyer's attention, it is time to identify the buyer's needs. Remember that this might have occurred in the preapproach and might involve more than one buyer and more than one sales call. To begin this process, a salesperson might use transition sentences like the following (assuming a product approach was used to gain attention):

> Well, I'm glad you find this little model interesting. And I want to tell you all about it. But first I need to ask you a few questions to make sure I understand what your specific needs are. Is that okay?

If the buyer gives permission, the salesperson begins to ask questions about the buyer's needs. Don't be surprised if the buyer is reluctant to provide confidential information. There are many people out there trying to steal valuable company information. The seller has to establish credibility and trust.

Occasionally a salesperson makes the mistake of starting with product information rather than with a discussion of the prospect's needs. The experienced salesperson, however, attempts to uncover the prospect's needs and problems at the start of the relationship. In reality, discovering needs is still a part of qualifying the prospect.

Research continually demonstrates the importance of needs discovery. An analysis by Huthwaite, Inc., of more than 35,000 sales calls in 23 countries over a 12-year period revealed that the distinguishing feature of successful salespeople was their ability to discover the prospect's needs.[11] Discovering needs was more important than opening the call strategically, handling objections, or using closing techniques effectively.

Exhibit 8.3
Discovering the Root Cause of the Need

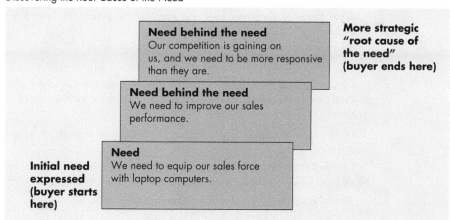

Need behind the need
Our competition is gaining on us, and we need to be more responsive than they are.

More strategic "root cause of the need" (buyer ends here)

Need behind the need
We need to improve our sales performance.

Need
We need to equip our sales force with laptop computers.

Initial need expressed (buyer starts here)

There is an underlying reason for every customer need, and the salesperson must continue probing until he or she uncovers the root problem or need. This process could be called "discovering the root cause of the need" and is graphically illustrated in Exhibit 8.3.

This salesperson is discovering the prospect's needs before describing the services he offers.

As you discover needs, keep in mind that this process can be uncomfortable for the prospect. The prospect may resent your suggesting that there could be a problem or a better way to do things. When faced with direct evidence that things could be better, the prospect may express fear (fear of losing her job if things are not corrected or of things changing and the situation getting worse than it is now). Also, remember that the time needed to discuss needs varies greatly depending on the type of industry, the nature of the product, how well the salesperson and buyer know each other, and so forth. We will come back to this issue after we examine methods of identifying needs.

Chapter 4 covered most of the important communication principles regarding how to effectively ask questions of the prospect and be a better listener. Remember to speak naturally while asking questions. You don't want to sound like a computer asking a set of rote questions. Nor do you want to appear to be following a strict word-for-word outline that you learned in your sales training classes.

We now briefly describe two of the most widely used systems of needs identification taught to salespeople today.

ASKING OPEN AND CLOSED QUESTIONS

In the first method of needs discovery, salespeople are taught to distinguish between open and closed questions and then encouraged to utilize more open questions. Many highly respected sales training organizations, such as Wilson Learning and Achieve Global, use this type of approach. **Open questions** require the prospect to go beyond a simple yes-or-no response. They encourage the prospect to open up and share a great deal of useful information. For example:

What kinds of problems have the new federal guidelines caused for your division?

What projects are crucial for your company right now?

What are your decision-making criteria for choosing the successful vendor?

Closed questions require the prospect to simply answer yes or no or to offer a short, fill-in-the-blank type of response. Examples include the following questions:

Have you ever experienced computer downtime as a result of an electrical storm?

Do you have a favored vendor?

Did you make the decision that resulted in your current vendor?

Who else will be involved in the decision-making process?

In most cases salespeople need to ask both open and closed questions. Open questions help paint the broad strokes of the situation, whereas closed questions help zero in on specific problems and attitudes. Some trainers believe simple, closed questions are best at first. Prospects become accustomed to talking and start to open up. After a few closed questions, the salesperson moves to a series of open questions. At some point he or she may revert back to closed questions.

Angie Main, a radio advertising salesperson, likes to ask her prospects the following two open questions to discover their needs:

What misconceptions do people have about your business?

If you could tell people one thing about your business, what would you want to tell them?[12]

Notice how these questions focus on the needs of the prospect rather than the solution (how her radio station can meet those needs).

Exhibit 8.4 contains an illustrative dialogue of a bank selling a commercial checking account to a business. In this sales presentation the salesperson's questions follow a logical flow. Note that follow-up probes are often necessary to clarify the prospect's responses. At the conclusion of asking open and closed questions, the salesperson should have a good feel for the needs and wants of the prospect.

One final suggestion is to summarize the prospect's needs:

So let me see if I have this right. You write about 35 checks a month, you keep about a $5,000 balance, and you are looking for a checking account that pays interest on your unused balance and has overdraft protection. ... Is that correct?

Summarizing helps solidify the needs in the prospect's mind and ensures that the prospect has no other hidden needs or wants.

SPIN® TECHNIQUE

The SPIN method of discovering needs was developed by Huthwaite, an international research and training organization, after analyzing thousands of actual sales calls.[13] The results indicated that successful salespeople go through a logical needs identification sequence, which Huthwaite labeled **SPIN:** *s*ituation questions, *p*roblem questions, *i*mplication questions, and *n*eed payoff questions. SPIN works for salespeople involved in a **major sale:** one that involves a long selling cycle, a large

Exhibit 8.4
Using Open and Closed Questions to Discover Needs

Salesperson's Probe	Prospect's Response
Have you ever done business with our bank before? [closed]	No, our firm has always used First of America Bank.
I assume, then, that your checking account is currently with First of America? [closed]	Yes.
If you could design an ideal checking account for your business, what would it look like? [open]	Well, it would pay interest on all idle money, have no service charges, and supply a good statement.
When you say "good statement," what exactly do you mean? [open]	It should come to us once a month, be easy to follow, and help us reconcile our books quickly.
Uh-huh. Anything else in an ideal checking account? [open]	No, I guess that's about it.
What things, if any, about your checking account have dissatisfied you in the past? [open]	Having to pay so much for our checks! Also, sometimes when we have a question, the bank can't answer it quickly because the computers are down. That's frustrating!
Sure! Anything else dissatisfy you? [open]	Well, I really don't like the layout of the monthly statement we get now. It doesn't list checks in order; it has them listed by the date they cleared the bank.
Is there anything else that I need to know before I begin telling you about our account? [open]	No, I think that just about covers it all.

customer commitment, an ongoing relationship, and large risks for the prospect if a bad decision is made. Major sales can occur anywhere but often involve large or national accounts. For example, both SC Johnson and Bridgestone have used SPIN for their major accounts but may use other techniques for smaller accounts.

SPIN actually helps the prospect identify unrecognized problem areas. Often, when a salesperson simply asks an open question, such as, "What problems are you having?" the prospect replies, "None!" The prospect isn't lying; he or she may not realize that a problem exists. SPIN excels at helping prospects test their current opinions or perceptions of the situation. Also, SPIN questions may be asked over the course of several sales calls, especially for large or important buyers. An abbreviated needs identification dialogue appears in Exhibit 8.5; it demonstrates all components of SPIN for a salesperson selling cell phone services.

Situation Questions

Early in the sales call, salespeople ask **situation questions,** which are general data-gathering questions about background and current facts. The goal of these questions is to better understand the prospect's current situation. Because these questions are broad, successful salespeople learn to limit them; prospects quickly become bored or impatient if they hear too many of them. Inexperienced and unsuccessful salespeople tend to ask too many situation questions. In fact, many situation-type questions should be answered through precall information gathering and planning. If a salesperson asks too many situation questions, the prospect will think the salesperson is unprepared. Here are some examples of situation questions:

What's your position? How long have you been here?

How many people do you employ? Is the number growing or shrinking?

What kind of handling equipment are you using at present? How long have you had it?

Exhibit 8.5
Using the SPIN
Technique to Sell Cell
Phone Internet Access

Salesperson: Do your engineers use cell phones in their work? [situation question]

Prospect: Yes, we supply each field engineer with a cell phone.

Salesperson: Do you have many problems with cell calls being lost while an engineer is talking? [problem question]

Prospect: Not really. Most of our engineers work in the city, and there are plenty of towers here to take care of calls.

Salesperson: Sure. Have you ever had engineers who need to access the Internet for details about a client's situation while on-site? Or a need to access files from your central server? [problem question]

Prospect: Well, now that you mention it, that is starting to be a problem. Most engineers like to carry paper copies of the documents they will need, but there are times when a document is back at the office.

Salesperson: What happens if an engineer doesn't have the document she needs while at a client's location? [implication question]

Prospect: That happened just last week to Carlee. She was at a client and thought she had all the paperwork. Turns out there was a spreadsheet she needed but didn't have. She had to drive back to the office to get it. Our client got pretty upset because their staff had to just stand around and wait for Carlee to get back.

Salesperson: If I can show you a way to make sure your engineers have access to all of their important files as well as complete Internet access while at the clients' locations and do so for no more than 10 percent above what you're paying for cell service now, would you be interested? [need payoff question]

Prospect: Sure. The more I think about it, the more I realize that we need to give our engineers the tools that our competitors are using. I'd hate to lose business because we're too cheap to invest in the right tools.

Problem Questions

When salespeople ask about specific difficulties, problems, or dissatisfactions the prospect has, they are asking **problem questions.** The goal is to discover a problem. Here are some examples of problem questions:

Is your current machine difficult to repair?

Do your operators ever complain that the noise level is too high?

Do you get fast turnaround when you outsource your work?

Is the cost of maintaining your own server becoming an issue?

If a seller can't discover a problem using problem questions, then she might need to ask additional situation questions first to uncover more issues that might lead to better problem questions.

Implication Questions

Questions that logically follow one or more problem questions and are designed to help the prospect recognize the true ramifications of the problem are **implication questions.** Implication questions cannot be asked until some problem area has been identified (through problem questions). The goal of implication questions is for the prospect to see that the identified problem has some serious ramifications and implications that make the problem worthy of being resolved. These questions attempt to motivate the prospect to search for a solution to the problem.

Implication questions relate back to some similar issues that were described in the multiattribute model in Chapter 3. In the multiattribute model, customers weigh various attributes differently in terms of importance. In the same way, some problems that are identified by problem questions have more weight (are more serious in the eyes of the buyer) than others. The goal of the salesperson is to identify problems that have high importance to the buyer.

Examples of implication questions include these:

What happens if you ship your customer a product that doesn't meet specs?

What does having to pay overtime do to your price, as compared to your competitors'?

Does the slowness of your present system create any bottlenecks in other parts of the process?

What happens if you miss a deadline?

Could that situation have repercussions for your job security?

Do you think competitors will notice what is going on and attempt to gain market share at your expense due to the problem?

If the buyer answers these questions in a way that indicates she doesn't see serious implications of the problem identified, the seller would have to go back and ask additional implication questions, problem questions, and maybe even situation questions. The seller doesn't move ahead to need payoff questions until the prospect sees that there are serious ramifications if he does not solve the problem.

Need Payoff Questions

When salespeople ask questions about the usefulness of solving a problem, they are asking **need payoff questions.** In contrast to implication questions, which are problem centered, need payoff questions are solution centered:

If I can show you a way to eliminate paying overtime for your operators and therefore reduce your cost, would you be interested?

Would you like to see a reduction in the number of products that don't meet quality specifications?

Would an increase in the speed of your present system by 5 percent resolve the bottlenecks you currently experience?

If the prospect responds negatively to a need payoff question, the salesperson has not identified a problem serious enough for the prospect to take action. In that case, the salesperson should probe further by asking additional problem questions, implication questions, and then a new need payoff question.

Conclusions about SPIN

One critical advantage of SPIN is that it encourages the prospect to define the need. During the questioning phase the salesperson is focusing on problems and isn't focusing on her product. As a result, the prospect views the salesperson more as a consultant trying to help than as someone trying to push a product. "Building Partnerships 8.1" describes the importance of being a consultant and discovering needs before talking about solutions.

SPIN selling has been taught to thousands of salespeople. Many salespeople quickly master the technique, whereas others have more difficulty. The best advice is to practice each component and to plan implication and need payoff questions before each sales call. SPIN works well for buyers that have a real problem (like inventory piling up). It is perhaps more difficult to use when the seller is only discussing an opportunity (no real problems, but "my solution could help you make more money").

BUILDING Partnerships

8.1

MY POORLY CONDUCTED MEETING

I had a meeting recently that I conducted somewhat poorly in my opinion. I wanted to share some mistakes I made in order to help everyone learn from them. First, I think it's best to understand my interpretation of some background research on the psychology of making major decisions.

In buying situations or in other situations involving a decision or changing mind, Huthwaite (a research firm that focuses primarily on sales technique) found that decision makers goes through four phases: recognition of needs, evaluation of options, resolution of concerns, and implementation. In the first phase, people are realizing that the status quo has problems. Then they graduate from the first phase to the second phase once they realize both that they have problems and that they want to change those problems and take action. In the second stage, decision makers are deciding which actions to take. The third phase involves resolving any worries about side effects their decisions may cause, and the fourth involves implementing solutions the decision makers choose. Most decision makers bounce around from one phase to the next, sometimes moving forward, sometimes backward, but it's always important for anyone coaching a person through a decision to empathize with what phase the decision maker is in.

I believe my meeting yesterday went poorly because I spent 90 percent of the meeting talking about what our company does with little regard to what my customers were feeling. I think a lot of sales reps love to talk about their companies, and there is a time and place for this. However, there is also a great deal of hard research verifying that the "recognition of needs" phase is not that time. In fact, sales reps who do talk about themselves or their solutions within that phase are proven to be considerably less likely to win the decision maker's agreement.

The "recognition of needs" phase should be reserved for talking about decision makers' problems and helping decision makers come to their own realization that those problems need to change. *Our job as salespeople during the first part of the buying process is not to discuss our solutions but rather to uncover and grow problems that can best be solved by our solutions.*

What I did in my recent meeting was skip that phase altogether and move to a discussion about solutions. It doesn't make sense to do this because the buyer probably doesn't care about solutions for problems he or she doesn't want to solve. For example, with the advancement of medical science, there are some amazing cosmetic dental treatments. My insurance might get me a $10,000 treatment for a very low deductible, so I'd get great value on a technologically advanced service. I can get an incredible service and a great value, but because I think my teeth look fine, I'm going to be pretty irritated with the dentist who tries to me sell a procedure I don't want.

We're all subjected to this behavior from time to time by unlearned sales reps, but then we carry on one-sided conversations with our own clients without first taking the time to understand them and to let them grow a need for our products. It's hard to fight this personal demon. It takes patience, empathy, and self-control—three tools that aren't much fun to use. It might take many meetings to fully exhaust the scope of a decision maker's problems and to build a genuine mutual desire to fix them. Waiting will conflict with our desire to close business right away and also conflict with pressures that we might face from others inside and outside our organizations.

Perhaps in the future, I'll do a better job of remembering that, as sales reps, we're the final defense against actions that might not be best for our companies and our customers. This means controlling our own desire to skip forward to a later phase of the sale. First focusing on the customer and later creating a dialogue about my company at the appropriate time is the right move for everyone involved. It will have the highest probably of winning business and the highest probability of finding a solution that will best help our customers.

Source: Karl Anderson, Powertex Group, personal correspondence, used with permission.

REITERATING NEEDS YOU IDENTIFIED BEFORE THE MEETING

The salesperson may fully identify the needs of the prospect before making the sales call. In that case reiterating the needs early in the sales call is advisable so that both parties agree about the problem they are trying to solve. For example:

> Mr. Reed, based on our several phone conversations, it appears that you are looking for an advertising campaign that will position your product for the rapidly growing senior citizen market, at a cost under $100,000, using humor and a well-known older personality, and delivered in less than one month. Is that an accurate summary of your needs? Has anything changed since we talked last? Is there anything else I need to know at this point?

Likewise, in multiple-call situations, going through a complete needs identification at every call is unnecessary. But it is still best to briefly reiterate the needs identified to that point:

> In my last call we pretty much agreed that your number one concern is customer satisfaction with your inventory system. Is that correct? Has anything changed since we met last time, or is there anything else I need to know?

ADDITIONAL CONSIDERATIONS

How many questions can a salesperson ask to discover needs? It depends on the situation. Generally, as the buyer's risk of making the wrong decision goes up, so does the amount of time the salesperson can spend asking the prospect questions.

Occasionally the prospect will refuse to answer important questions because the information is confidential or proprietary. The salesperson can do little except emphasize the reason for asking the questions. Ultimately the prospect needs to trust the salesperson enough to divulge sensitive data. Chapters 13 and 14 discuss trust-building strategies.

At times buyers do not answer questions because they honestly don't know the answers. The salesperson should then ask whether the prospect can get the information. If the prospect cannot do so, the salesperson can often ask the buyer's permission to probe further within the prospect's firm.

On the other hand, some buyers will not only answer questions but also appear to want to talk indefinitely. In general, the advice is to let them talk, particularly in many cultures. For example, people in French-speaking countries tend to love rhetoric, the act and art of speaking; attempts to cut them off will only frustrate and anger them.

ethics

thinking it through

> Prospects often provide sensitive and confidential information when they reveal facts about their situations and needs. Assume that a prospect at Allied reveals to you her firm's long-term strategy for taking business away from her number one competitor, Baker's. You are close friends with the buyer at Baker's, which is one of your biggest customers. Will you share the confidential information with the Baker's buyer?

DEVELOPING A STRATEGY FOR THE PRESENTATION

Based on the needs identified, the salesperson should develop a strategy for how best to meet those needs. This process includes sorting through the various options available to the seller to see what is best for this prospect. To do so, the salesperson usually must sort out the needs of the buyer and prioritize them. Decisions have to be made about the exact product or service to recommend, the optimal payment terms to present for consideration, service levels to suggest, product or service features to stress during the presentation, and so on. Chapter 7 also talks about developing a strategy.

Products have many, many features, and one product may possess a large number of features that are unique and exciting when compared to competitive offerings. Rather than overload the customer with all the great features, successful salespeople discuss only those that specifically address the needs of the prospect. Talking about lots of features of little interest to the customer is a waste of time and is sometimes called **feature dumping.**

OFFERING VALUE: THE SOLUTION TO THE BUYER'S NEEDS

After developing a strategy for the presentation based on a customer's needs, it is time to relate product or service features that are meaningful to the buyer, assess the buyer's reaction to what is being said, resolve objections (covered in Chapter 10), and obtain commitment (the topic of Chapter 11). As one best-selling author stated, "Ditch the canned 1-2-3, sometimes pushy, usually insensitive, and almost always repetitive sales strategies glamorized in the past. ... We must be willing to learn, adapt, and listen to our customers."[14]

The salesperson usually begins offering the solution with a transition sentence, something like the following: "Now that I know what your needs are, I would like to talk to you about how our product can meet those needs." The seller's job is then to translate product features into benefits for solving the buyer's needs. To do this effectively, the salesperson must know the metrics of the prospect's decision; that is, on what criteria and in what way is the prospect evaluating possible solutions? This will be discussed more in Chapter 9 and in other chapters.

RELATING FEATURES TO BENEFITS

A **feature** is a quality or characteristic of the product or service. Every product has many features designed to help potential customers. A **benefit** is the way in which a specific feature will help a particular buyer and is tied directly to the buying motives of the prospect.[15] A benefit helps the prospect more fully answer the question "What's in it for me?" Exhibit 8.6 shows a list of features and sample benefits for a product. The way in which a salesperson shows how a product addresses the buyer's specific needs is sometimes called the **customer benefit proposition.** This concept will be described more fully in Chapter 9.

The salesperson usually includes a word or a phrase to make a smooth transition from features to benefits:

> This china is fired at 2,600°F, and what that means to you is that it will last longer. Because it is so sturdy, you will be able to hand this china down to your children as an heirloom, which was one of your biggest concerns.

> Our service hotline is open 24 hours a day, which means that even your third-shift operators can call if they have any questions. That should be a real help to you because you said your third-shift supervisor was inexperienced in dealing with problems.

Some trainers suggest going beyond mentioning features and benefits. One variation, **FAB,** has salespeople discussing *features*, *advantages* (why that feature would be important to anyone), and *benefits*. For example:

> This car has antilock brakes [*feature*], which help the car stop quickly [*advantage*], which provides the safety you said you were looking for [*benefit*].

Exhibit 8.6
An Example of Features and Benefits

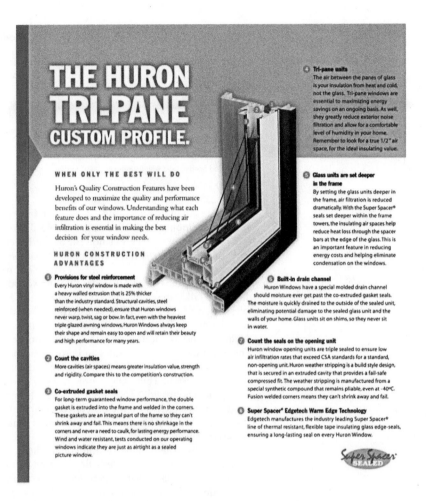

In another variation, **FEBA** (*features*, *evidence*, *benefits*, *agreement*), salespeople mention the feature, provide evidence that the feature actually exists, explain the benefit (why that feature is important to the buyer), and then ask whether the buyer agrees with the value of the feature and benefit. For example:

> This car has the highest-quality antilock brakes on the market today [*feature*] as proved by this test by the federal government [*evidence*]. They will provide the safety you said you were looking for [*benefit*]; don't you agree [*agreement*]?

Buyers are not interested in facts about the product or the seller's company unless those facts help solve their wants or needs. The salesperson's job is to supply the facts and then point out what those features mean to the buyer in terms of benefits and value creation. Neil Rackham, noted sales training leader, emphasizes this theme:

> The world has changed and so has selling. Today, the primary sales job is to create value—to add problem solving and creativity, so that the customer buys the advice and expertise of the salesperson as much as they buy the product . . . [in a survey] product pitches were the number one complaint from customers, with comments such as "It's quicker, more convenient, and more objective to go to the Internet than to listen to a product pitch."[16]

Exhibit 8.7
The Problem/Solution
Model

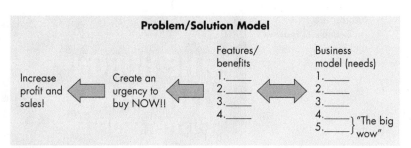

Source: Carl Sooder, used with permission.

Exhibit 8.7 illustrates how one trainer incorporates these concepts into a problem/solution model. The customer's needs are called "business model." The salesperson knows some, but not all, of the buyer's needs before the sales call, represented by the first three lines under "Business model." However, by actively listening (see Chapter 4), the seller learns more needs during the presentation, represented by lines 4 and 5 under "Business model." Using all identified needs, the seller talks about the relevant features and benefits. While doing this, the salesperson offers proof of these assertions, based on the customer's social style (see Chapter 5). The salesperson also engages in activities to help the buyer realize the importance of meeting his or her needs sooner, providing reasons to buy now. The end result is increased sales and profits for the seller.

Buyers typically consider two or more competitive products when making a purchase decision. Thus, salespeople need to know more than just the benefits their products provide. They need to know how the benefits of their products are superior or inferior to the benefits of competitive products. Of course, as you explain the benefits of your service, you must make sure the prospect is looking for those benefits.

Sometimes, when selling certain commodities, it is important to sell the features and benefits of the seller's firm instead of the product. For example, Ray Hanson of Fastenal sells fasteners such as bolts and nuts. He states, "In the fastener industry I have found that a generic product, such as a nut or bolt, doesn't have too many features and benefits. We talk to our potential customers about the features our company has and how these features could benefit them as our customers."[17]

When selling to resellers, salespeople have two sets of benefits to discuss with the prospect: what the features of the product will do for the reseller and what the product features will do for the ultimate consumer of the product. Covering both sets of features and benefits is important. Exhibit 8.8 illustrates the two sets of features.

ASSESSING REACTIONS

While making a presentation, salespeople need to continually assess the reactions of their prospects. The prospect needs to agree that the benefits described would actually help his or her company. By listening to what buyers say and observing their body language (see Chapter 4 to review how to be a better listener), salespeople can determine whether prospects are interested in the product. If buyers react favorably to the presentation and seem to grasp the benefits of the proposed solution, the salesperson will have less need to make alterations or adjustments. But if a prospect does not develop enthusiasm for the product, the salesperson will need to make some changes in the presentation.

Exhibit 8.8

Features and Benefits of Yummy Earth Organic Gummy Bears, as Presented to a Grocery Store

Features	Benefits
Important to the Final Consumer	
Organic.	You want organic products, and this product is certified organic.
Only 90 calories per serving.	You can enjoy a treat without worrying about its effect on your weight.
100 percent of daily need for Vitamin C in every serving.	You are getting needed nutrition from a snack.
Important to the Grocery Store	
Test marketed for two years.	Because of this research, you are assured of a successful product and effective promotion; thus, your risk is greatly reduced.
$500,000 will be spent for consumer advertising in the next 18 months.	Your customers will come to your store looking for the product.
40-cent coupon with front positioning in the national Sunday insert section.	Your customers will want to take advantage of the coupon and will be looking for the product in your store.

Nonverbal cues help salespeople know when to make adjustments. Can you interpret the cues provided by members of this buying team (the three on the right side)?

Using Nonverbal Cues

An important aspect of making adjustments is interpreting a prospect's reactions to the sales presentation. By observing the prospect's five channels of nonverbal communication, salespeople can determine how to proceed with their presentations. Chapter 4 provides more detailed information about nonverbal cues.

Verbal Probing

As salespeople move through a presentation, they must take the pulse of the situation. This process, often called a **trial close,** is more fully described in Chapter 11. For example, the salesperson should say something like the following:

How does this sound to you?

Can you see how these features help solve the problem you have?

Have I clearly explained our program to you?

Do you have any questions?

The use of such probing questions helps achieve several things. First, it allows the salesperson to stop talking and encourages two-way conversation. Without such probing, a salesperson can turn into a rambling talker while the buyer becomes a passive listener. Second, probing lets the salesperson see whether the buyer is listening and understanding what is being said. Third, the probe may show that the prospect is uninterested in what the salesperson is talking about. This response allows the salesperson to redirect the conversation to areas of interest to the buyer. This kind of adjustment is necessary in almost every presentation and underscores the fact that the salesperson should not simply memorize a canned presentation that unfolds in a particular sequence.

Salespeople must listen. Often we hear only what we want to hear. This behavior is called **selective perception,** and everyone is guilty of it at times. For example, read the following sentence:[18]

> Finished files are the result of years of scientific study combined with the experience of years.

Now go back and quickly count the number of *f*'s in that sentence. Most nonnative English speakers see all six *f*'s, whereas native English speakers see only three (they don't count the *f*'s in *of* because it is not considered an important word). The point is that once salespeople stop actively listening, they miss many things the buyer is trying to communicate.

Making Adjustments

Salespeople can alter their presentations in many ways to obtain a favorable reaction. For example, a salesperson may discover during a sales presentation that the prospect simply does not believe the seller has the appropriate product knowledge. Rather than continue with the presentation, the salesperson should redirect her or his efforts toward establishing credibility in the eyes of the prospect.

Other adjustments might require collecting additional information about the prospect, developing a new sales strategy, or altering the style of presentation. For example, a salesperson may believe a prospect is interested in buying an economical, low-cost motor. While presenting the benefits of the lowest-cost motor, the salesperson discovers the prospect is interested in the motor's operating costs. At this point the salesperson should ask some questions to find out whether the prospect would be interested in paying a higher price for a more efficient motor with lower operating costs. On the basis of the prospect's response, the salesperson can adopt a new sales strategy, one that emphasizes operating efficiency rather than the motor's initial price. In this way the sales presentation is shifted from features and benefits based on a low initial cost to features and benefits related to low operating costs.

BUILDING CREDIBILITY DURING THE CALL

To develop a close and harmonious relationship, the salesperson must be perceived as having **credibility**—that is, he or she must be believable and reliable. A salesperson can take many actions during a sales call to develop such a perception.[19] From the Buyer's Seat 8.1 provides examples of when sellers did and did not achieve that goal.

To establish credibility early in the sales call, the salesperson should clearly delineate the time she or he thinks the call will take and then stop when the time is up. How many times has a salesperson said, "This will take only 5 minutes!" and 30 minutes later you still can't get rid of him? No doubt you would have perceived the salesperson as more credible if, after 5 minutes, he or she stated, "Well, I promised to take no more than 5 minutes, and I see our time is up. How would you like to proceed from here?" One successful salesperson likes to ask for half an hour and take only 25 minutes.[20]

Another way to establish credibility is to offer concrete evidence to back up verbal statements. If a salesperson states, "It is estimated that more than 80 percent of the households in America will own tablet computers by 2018," he or she should be prepared to offer proof of this assertion—for instance, hand the prospect a

From the BUYER'S SEAT

8.1

PLEASE REMEMBER WHAT I'VE ALREADY TOLD YOU

I'm a buyer at Home Depot. For the products I buy, many of the sales presentations are actually done in the offices of the companies that are attempting to sell me their products. Before most of my planned meetings with salespeople, I do my best to send them literature to show them what we have been doing as an organization and where we are looking to go in the future. In this information there are also things regarding the different trends that we see going on. There are two ways a salesperson can use this information: They can either use it to their advantage or completely disregard it. Let me share a few examples.

A few weeks back, I went in to visit a salesperson, and when I walked in, I could tell that they were not prepared. They were flying around the office trying to grab different products to show me, like they had forgotten I was coming. When I referred to the information that I sent them, they looked at me like I was speaking a foreign language. I asked them if they had received the information,

and they said yes, but they were not able to take a look at it. To me this really made it seem as though my business was unimportant to them.

Now here's a different example. I had a planned meeting with a salesperson and had sent them the exact same information with the exact same amount of time for them to prepare for the meeting. When I walked in to their office, they were standing and waiting for me with various products lined up for me to look at. When I mentioned something in the information that I had sent them, they said, "Yeah hold on, let me grab that." They had printed off the information that I had sent them and had notes all over the pages. This proved to me that our business meant a lot to them and that they were really going to give it their all to gain our business and work not only with us but also for us and our customers to provide quality products.

Source: Antonio Alfonso, Home Depot; all names changed for anonymity; used with permission.

---

letter or an article from a credible source. Ways to establish credibility are discussed in greater detail in Chapter 9.

Some trainers suggest adding a **credibility statement** early in the sales call that includes features of yourself and your company.[21] The purpose of the statement is to help the buyer realize you are capable of meeting her needs. The statement can be strengthened by proving its assertions with such items as testimonials and test results (more about these in the next chapter). Here's an example of a credibility statement:

> Hank, I don't know how much you may know about Apple Valley Savings and Loan. We were founded by a Swedish immigrant back in 1932 whose stated goal was to offer the best service in the Midwest. We've now grown into the third-largest savings bank in the upper Midwest with assets exceeding $23 billion and are the only savings bank in the Midwest earning the coveted Pinnacle Award for Excellent eight years in a row. We have over 32 branches in the five-state region. I've been with the bank for the last 14 years and have spent the last 6 years working closely with higher education institutions like yours. In terms of investments, we have focused a great deal of effort on higher education. For example, we recently provided a $2.3 million loan to West Valania State University to expand its ice hockey rink.

ethics

Of course, one way to establish credibility is to avoid making statements that do not have the ring of truth to them. For example, some suggest you should avoid using a phrase like "We're the best" or "We're number one." As one skeptical buyer noted, "Just how many number ones are there in the world, anyway?" Salespeople should also remember that, in addition to damaging credibility, truth-stretching comments can come back to haunt them in the form of legal liability (see Chapter 2 for a review of legal issues).

Many salespeople have found that the most effective way to establish credibility is to make a **balanced presentation** that shows all sides of the situation—that is, to be totally honest. Thus, a salesperson might mention some things about the product that make it less than perfect or may speak positively about some exclusive feature of a competitor's product. Will this approach defeat the seller's chances of a sale? No. In fact, it may increase the chances of building long-term commitment and rapport. Salespeople can keep customers happy and dedicated by helping them form correct, realistic expectations about a product or service.

Salespeople can build credibility by recognizing cultural differences, not only in foreign markets but also in North America. How? By demonstrating sensitivity to the needs and wants of specific subcultures and avoiding biased or racist language. See Chapter 4 for more information about cultural differences.

In selling complex products, sales representatives often must demonstrate product expertise at the beginning of the sales process—for example, by telling the customer, without bragging, about their special training or education. They can also strengthen credibility with well-conceived, insightful questions or comments.

When selling complicated technical products and services, Todd Graf notes, "You have to keep it simple. Teach as you go. Make transitions slow and smooth and always ask if they understand (half the time they don't). This is key because they may have to go back and explain some of your features to the decision maker who isn't present in this meeting."[22]

Being willing to say, "I'm sorry, I was wrong on that," or "I don't know the answer to that, but I'll get it to you," will also go a long way toward establishing credibility. A seller should never use a word if he or she doesn't know the exact definition. Some buyers may even test the salesperson. Here's an example from a real salesperson who was calling on a doctor:[23]

> SALESPERSON: Because product X acts as an agonist at the kappa receptor, miosis will occur.
>
> DOCTOR: What does *miosis* mean?
>
> SALESPERSON: It means the stage of disease during which intensity of signs and symptoms diminishes.
>
> DOCTOR: No! *Miosis* means contraction of the pupils.

At this point the doctor walked out of the room, and the seller thought she had lost all credibility. Actually, he had just gone out and grabbed a dictionary. The first definition was the contraction of the pupils, and the second was the seller's definition. The salesperson's definition, not the doctor's, fit the use of the term for this medication. The doctor then shook the seller's hand and thanked her for teaching him a new definition of the word. The salesperson's credibility certainly increased.

SELLING TO GROUPS

Selling to groups can be both rewarding and frustrating. On the plus side, if you make an effective presentation, every member of the prospect group becomes your ally. On the down side, groups behave like groups, with group standards and norms and issues of status and group leadership.

When selling to groups, the salesperson must gather information about the needs and concerns of each individual who will attend. Salespeople should discover (for each prospect group member) member status within the group, authority, perceptions about the urgency of the problem, receptivity to ideas, knowledge

Selling to groups requires special skills in monitoring several individuals at once, as well as being able to respond to customers with occasionally conflicting needs.

of the subject matter, attitude toward the salesperson, major areas of interest and concern, key benefits sought, likely resistance, and ways to handle this resistance. Chapter 3 discusses many things that salespeople should consider about buying centers.

It is important to develop not only objectives for the meeting but also objectives for what the seller hopes to accomplish with each prospect present at the meeting. Planning may include the development of special visual aids for specific individuals present. The seller must expect many more objections and interruptions in a group setting compared to selling to an individual.

An informal atmosphere in which group members are encouraged to speak freely and the salesperson feels free to join the group's discussion usually works best in these situations. Thus an informal location (such as a corner of a large room as opposed to a formal conference room) is preferred. Formal presentation methods, such as speeches, that separate buyers and sellers into them-versus-us sides should be avoided. If the group members decide that the meeting is over, the salesperson should not try to hold them.

Of course most things you have learned about selling to individuals apply equally to groups. You should learn the names of group members and use them when appropriate. You should listen carefully and observe all nonverbal cues. When one member of the buying team is talking, it is especially important to observe the cues being transmitted by the other members of the buying team to see whether they are, in effect, agreeing or disagreeing with the speaker.

There are several types of group selling situations. If the group meeting is actually a negotiation session, many more things must be considered. As a result, we devote an entire chapter (Chapter 12) to the topic of formal negotiations. Also, sometimes a salesperson makes a call on a prospect as part of a selling team from his firm (for example, the team might consist of his sales manager, someone from technical support, someone from customer support, and a sales executive from the firm). These situations require coordination and teamwork. Because of the importance of the various selling team scenarios, the issue of selling teams is more fully discussed in Chapter 16.

SELLING YOURSELF

It's a fact. You're going to be selling yourself while trying to get that first job right out of college. Don't forget to use everything you've read in this chapter as you do so. Otherwise you'll look and sound like the thousands of other students who merely *hope* that the company will hire them without really keying in on what the hiring company is looking for.

Always attempt to build rapport with an interviewer. Find something you have in common with her, based on information you learned from her LinkedIn profile, from your professor, or even from the staff in the career services center at your school. Someone is bound to know something about the person. Use that information to break the ice and build a sense of "liking" between the two of you. You'll be surprised how much that simple act calms you down as you realize you really do have some things in common.

Make sure you discover interviewers' needs. What exactly are they looking for in a job candidate? If you've not already discovered it, and the information is not available on their Web site, then go ahead and ask. The interviewers won't think you're weird; they'll think you are sharp. Once you find out what those needs are, sell yourself by explicitly showing how your "features" meet their needs. For example, your résumé might state the following:

> Reading with Champions Volunteer, Birchwood Elementary School: read to elementary school students two times a week to help them gain a love for books.

You're interviewing for a sales job, not a job to read books to small children. So it's your job to convert that feature into a benefit to the interviewers with something like the following:

> You said you were looking for someone with a hard work ethic and also for someone with an ability to interact with lots of different kinds of clients. Well, my volunteer work demonstrates my work ethic because I did this activity for six months, all while I was also taking 18 credits at school. I never missed a reading at that school, either! Also, the children I interacted with at that school were not like me at all. Most came from poor backgrounds and broken families. Many had never had a book read to them before. Anyway, what all of this means to you is that I am able to interact with people who are very different from me. In fact I enjoy it. I'm sure I'll be able to adapt to the many different types of customers you say you have at your firm. Did that example help you see that I am a hard worker and that I can interact with different types of people?

Finally, establish credibility by bringing your portfolio with you to the interview. The portfolio should include copies of papers you wrote, videos of presentations you gave, and any other evidence that will demonstrate that you have the skills they are looking for.

Source: David Maebane, used with permission.

SUMMARY

Salespeople need to make every possible effort to create a good impression during a sales call. The first few minutes with the prospect are important, and care should be taken to make an effective entrance by giving a good first impression, expressing confidence while standing and shaking hands, and selecting an appropriate seat.

The salesperson can use any of several methods to gain the prospect's attention. Salespeople should adopt the opening that is most effective for the prospect's personality style. Also critical is the development of rapport with the prospect, which can often be enhanced by engaging in friendly conversation.

Before beginning any discussion of product information, the salesperson can establish the prospect's needs by using open and closed questions. The SPIN technique is very effective for discovering needs in a major sale. In subsequent calls the salesperson should reiterate the prospect's needs.

When moving into a discussion of the proposed solution or alternatives, the salesperson translates features into benefits for the buyer. The salesperson also makes any necessary adjustments in the presentation based on feedback provided by the buyer's nonverbal cues and by verbal probing.

A close, harmonious relationship will enhance the whole selling process. The salesperson can build credibility by adhering to stated appointment lengths, backing up statements with proof, offering a balanced presentation, and establishing his or her credentials.

When selling to groups, the salesperson must gather information about the needs and concerns of each individual who will attend. The seller should also uncover the ego involvement and issue involvement of each group member. It is important to develop objectives not only for the meeting but also for what the seller hopes to accomplish with each prospect present at the meeting.

Now that you know how to start the sale, discover needs, relate features to specific benefits for the buyer, and build credibility, it is time to look more closely at how to communicate your ideas more effectively. That's the topic of the next chapter.

KEY TERMS

ETHICS PROBLEMS

1. You're an account executive for Wells Fargo Financial in Minnesota. You had an initial appointment with a customer, June, to find out what her goals were financially. The meeting went just as a typical first meeting should go, and there was a beneficial product you could create for her. However, her husband could not meet with you. After weeks of work and preparation, you have a loan that makes sense. The loan meets the goals June wanted, so you have a second appointment with her to go over exact terms, again without her husband. You asked when her husband could come in and sign the loan documents, and she discloses to you that her husband is not aware of the $35,000 of credit card debts the loan is going to pay off. Both the husband and the wife must be present at the time of the loan. Legally you can call the husband and tell him about the loan application. What should you do?

Source: Erik Abrahamson, Wells Fargo Financial; used with permission.

2. You're calling on an important prospect in the sportswear industry, and she starts asking you how other sportswear retailers are handling a specific problem. You know that this is important competitive information and that you should not provide details about a competitor. Instead you decide to give the prospect the information without specifics (like the name of the sportswear retailer you're talking about). Is that OK?

QUESTIONS AND PROBLEMS

1. Think for a moment about trying to secure a sales job. Assume you are going to have an interview with a district manager of a consumer products firm next week for a sales position. What can you do to develop rapport and build credibility with her?

2. "I don't need to discover my prospect's needs. I sell frozen pizzas to grocery stores and convenience stores. I know what their needs are: a high profit margin and fast turnover of products!" Comment.

3. Develop the FEBA for one of the features shown in Exhibit 8.8.

4. Assume that you are selling swimming pool maintenance services to a small hotel. Develop a series of open and closed questions to discover the prospect's needs.

5. Assume that you represent your school's placement service. You are calling on a large business nearby that never hires graduates from your college. Generate a list of SPIN questions, making any additional assumptions necessary.

6. Prepare a list of features and benefits that could be used in a presentation to other students at your college. The objective of the presentation is to encourage them to declare the same major you are taking.

7. "Sales Technology 8.1" told about the use of social networking to gain information and

hence do a better job of gaining the prospect's attention. Look at the profiles of two of your friends or contacts on LinkedIn, Facebook, or some other social networking site. Using strictly the information you find there, what are some ways you could gain that person's attention in a sales call, assuming you didn't actually know them before the call?

8. In "Building Partnerships 8.1" you read about a salesperson who admitted that he performed poorly in a sales meeting. Even though he knew what to do, he didn't do it. Why do you think that happened?

9. In which situations should a salesperson use a prospect's first name? When should a more formal salutation be used?

10. You're selling a new line of candy to a grocery store (choose some brand of candy). Write a list of features and benefits for the grocery store, as well as a list of features and benefits for the store's customers (the shoppers who come in and buy candy).

11. In "From the Buyer's Seat 8.1" you heard a buyer describe one good and one poor salesperson. What can a company do to ensure that salespeople act more like the good salesperson profiled?

CASE PROBLEMS

case **8.1**

Presidential Aviation
(Part B)

Presidential Aviation has provided charter flights to a wide array of customers, including business travelers worldwide. The company is known for its ability to cater to passengers' every desire, including gourmet meals, special beverages, entertainment while in the air, and other luxury accommodations. Santiago Diego is a salesperson for Presidential Aviation. Today he will be making his first visit to Juan Espinosa, a procurement officer at Regent Seven Seas Cruises.

For more details about Presidential Aviation and Regent Seven Seas Cruises, see Case 7.1 in Chapter 7.

Questions

1. Develop a set of open and closed questions to fully discover Juan Espinosa's needs.

2. Develop a set of SPIN questions to discover Juan Espinosa's needs.

Sources: http://www.rssc.com and http://www.presidential-aviation.com.

case **8.2**

Citrix Systems

Jamie Skrbis of Citrix Systems had an important appointment with a senior buyer and her assistant at a pharmaceutical company. It had taken Jamie three months to get the appointment, and she was excited about the chance to finally demonstrate her company's new cloud networking system. As Jamie was leaving her office, her sales manager learned where Jamie was going and asked to come along. Jamie had no option but to say, "Sure." However, she was worried because his manager often took control of meetings and sometimes wasn't a good listener.

When the sales team got there, the buyer, Tracey, stated that she could participate for only about 30 minutes but that her assistant, Sally, would be staying for the remainder of the time. Before Jamie could begin talking, Kyle, her sales manager, began taking the buyers through his sales binder that had a presentation in it. It began with the history of the company.

Tracey politely interrupted and explained that she was already familiar with Citrix Systems, but there were certain things that she was interested in learning about their services. Tracey asked the sales team if they could produce two items for her.

Again, before Jamie could answer, Kyle jumped in with, "Yes, we could, and I'm going to get there in a minute." Tracey patiently waited as he continued to take her through the company history. By now, almost 10 minutes had passed.

Next, Kyle talked about the work that Citrix Systems had done for other companies. This is something that many buyers are usually interested in. However, Tracey interrupted again and said that they were really looking for a vendor for a couple of specific projects and that she wanted to see what they could do for those specific situations. Kyle replied, "Hang on, Tracey. I'm almost there! I promise to get there soon."

After Kyle finished showing the work Citrix Systems did for other companies, he began to explain the benefits of working with his company because of reputation, pricing, service, and so on. Tracey asked again about the two projects, and instead of answering her questions, Kyle continued to follow his canned presentation. Tracey was becoming noticeably upset and agitated, although Sally seemed quite interested.

Questions

1. You are Jamie. What will you do now?
2. How can you avoid a situation like this in future calls with your manager?

Source: Tracey Brill; used with permission.

ROLE PLAY CASE

Today we are going to start over again, "from the top" as they say in the theater. Start from the beginning of the sales call, from when you knock on the door through the needs identification stage, ending just before your presentation. All that you have learned in previous role plays about the account continues to hold true. If you've been selling to Banc/Vue, you'll continue to do so, but you are now meeting with a different member of the buying center. The same is true for GelTech and HighPoint Solutions. New buyer sheets will be passed out. You can have the same person play the new role or someone else in class. (*Note:* If you have not done role plays before, you will need to review the information about the various role play customers that can be found at the end of Chapter 3.)

If your class is divided into groups of three, the person who is watching should create a check sheet. Write *S, P, I,* and *N* down the left side of the paper. As the salesperson asks a question, check whether it is a situation, problem, implication, or needs payoff question. Also note if and how he or she identified or verified the decision process. *Don't forget:* At the start of the sales call, identify the type of opening used (introduction, benefit, product, curiosity, or some other form).

> *Banc/Vue:* You will meet with the VP of sales and marketing. This is an appointment that was set up by the regional sales manager you called on earlier. You've never talked to this person before.

> *GelTech:* Mr. McLane has asked to see you. You weren't expecting this from your earlier sales calls, but you welcome the opportunity to meet the decision maker. His secretary called and made the appointment.

> *HighPoint Solutions:* You are meeting with one of the VPs of sales. The other VP was fired, but you don't know why. The meeting was set up by the regional sales manager you called on earlier, who also told you about the firing, but she didn't know what had happened.

Note: For background information about these role plays, please see page 26.

To the instructor: Additional information needed to complete the role play is available in the Instructor's Manual.

ADDITIONAL REFERENCES

Ahearne, Michael, Scott B. MacKenzie, Philip M. Podsakoff, John E. Mathieu, and Son K. Lam. "The Role of Consensus in Sales Team Performance." *Journal of Marketing Research* 47, no. 3 (2010), pp. 458–69.

Badrinarayanan, Vishag, Sreedhar Madhavaram, and Elad Granot. "Global Virtual Sales Teams (GVSTs): A Conceptual Framework of the Influence of Intellectual and Social Capital on Effectiveness." *Journal of Personal Selling and Sales Management* 31, no. 3 (Summer 2011), pp. 311–24.

Bednarz, Timothy F. Bednarz. *Consultative Sales Strategies.* Steven's Point, WI: Majorium Business Press, 2011.

Blocker, Christopher P., Joseph P. Cannon, Nikolaos G. Panagopoulos, and Jeffrey K. Sager. "The Role of the Sales Force in Value Creation and Appropriation: New Directions for Research." *Journal of Personal Selling and Sales Management* 32, no. 1 (2012), pp. 15–28.

Burn, Brian. *The Maverick Selling Method: Simplifying the Complex Sale.* Bloomington, IN: Xlibris Corporation, 2009.

Cassell, Jeremy, and Tom Bird. *Brilliant Selling: What the Best Salespeople Know, Do, and Say.* Upper Saddle River, New Jersey: FT Press, 2009.

Chan, Elaine, and Jaideep Sengupta. "Insincere Flattery Actually Works: A Dual Attitudes Perspective." *Journal of Marketing Research* 47, no. 1 (February 2010), pp. 122–33.

Cole, Tony. "7 Steps to Start the Sale." *American Salesman* 56, no. 11 (November 2011), pp. 8–11.

Freedman, David H. "On the Road with a Supersalesman." *Inc* 32, no. 3 (April 2010), pp. 84–91.

Graham, John R. "A Sales Strategy That Works!" *American Salesman* 55, no. 6 (June 2010), pp. 17–21.

Griffin, Jill G., and Susan M. Broniarczyk. "The Slippery Slope: The Impact of Feature Alignability on Search and Satisfaction." *Journal of Marketing Research* 47, no. 2 (April 2010), pp. 323–34.

Jakob, Rehme, and Svensson Peter. "Credibility-Driven Entrepreneurship: A Study of the First Sale." *International Journal of Entrepreneurship and Innovation* 12, no. 1 (February 2011), pp. 5–15.

Johnson, Mark S., Eugene Sivadas, and Vishal Kashyap. "Response Bias in the Measurement of Salesperson Orientations: The Role of Impression Management." *Industrial Marketing Management* 38, no. 8 (November 2009), pp. 1014–24.

Kahle, Dave. "The Three Biggest Mistakes in Sales Presentations." *American Salesman* 56, no. 8 (August 2011), pp. 3–6.

Keh, Hean Tat, and Yi Xie. "Corporate Reputation and Customer Behavioral Intentions: The Roles of Trust, Identification, and Commitment." *Industrial Marketing Management* 38, no. 7 (October 2009), pp. 732–42.

Lager, Marshall. "The Psychology of the Sale: There's a Lot Going on inside the Customer's Head, Whether You Put It There or Not. What Are Salespeople Up Against?" *CRM Magazine* 13, no. 5 (2009), pp. 34–37.

Lovas, Michael, and Pam Holloway. *Axis of Influence: How Credibility and Likeability Intersect to Drive Success.* New York City: Morgan James Publishing, 2009.

Malcolm, Jack. *Strategic Sales Presentations*. Seatlle Washington Editions, 2012.

Malone, Tim. "Improve through Consultative Selling." *JCK* 181, no. 4 (April 2010), p. 49.

Pullins, Ellen Bolman, Michael L. Mallin, Richard E. Buehrer, and Deirdre E. Jones. "How Salespeople Deal with Intergenerational Relationship Selling." *Journal of Business and Industrial Marketing* 26, no. 6 (2011), pp. 443–55.

Read, Nicholas A. C., and Stephen J. Bistritz. *Selling to the C-Suite: What Every Executive Wants You to Know about Successfully Selling to the Top*. New York City: McGraw-Hill, 2009.

Sundtoft Hald, Kim, Carlos Cordón, and Thomas E. Vollmann. "Towards an Understanding of Attraction in Buyer–Supplier Relationships." *Industrial Marketing Management* 38, no. 8 (November 2009), pp. 960–70.

The Partnership Process

chapter **9**

STRENGTHENING THE PRESENTATION

SOME QUESTIONS ANSWERED IN THIS CHAPTER ARE

- How can salespeople use verbal tools to strengthen a presentation?
- Why do salespeople need to augment their oral communication through tools such as visual aids, samples, testimonials, and demonstrations?
- What methods are available to strengthen a presentation?
- How can salespeople use visual aids and technology most effectively?
- What are the ingredients of a good demonstration?
- Is there a way to quantify the salesperson's solution to a buyer's problem?
- How can salespeople reduce presentation jitters?

2 PART

PROFILE

PROFILE I was not "sold" on a career in sales until taking "Fundamentals of Selling" with Professor John Kratz at the University of Minnesota–Duluth. He sold the concept of being able to control your work schedule and, ultimately, your performance. Nowhere is that more evident than in a sales presentation.

In my current role as an account executive with the NCR Corporation, I manage NCR's relationship with retailers based in the upper Midwest as we develop collaborative technology solutions consisting of software, services, and hardware. Due to the potential complexity of the both the technology and the retailer's existing environment, finding ways to convey the benefits of the end solution is one the most pivotal elements in determining the success of the sales process. There are five ways I focus on strengthening a presentation:

Know Your Audience—Conservative or laid back? Old or young? Male or female? Concept driven or fact driven? Interactive or stoic? These are just some of the elements that must be considered in crafting the structure and messaging of your sales presentation. For example, if you are calling on a group of people 50 years old or older, premeeting rapport-building conversation should not focus around the Justin Bieber concert coming to town.

Audience Participation—The most common mistake I see is salespeople who talk far more than their prospect or customer. Remember, nearly all people like to talk and share their opinions. This uncovers additional information for the salesperson and keeps the audience engaged in the dialogue. Also, collaboration through the customer's or prospect's participation creates a sense of ownership on their side that can allow for dramatic advancement of the sales process.

Feature/Function/Benefit—Far too many salespeople get down in the weeds, focused on bits and bites. If you are selling to the most desirable level (the C-Suite), you must explain your product or service in a way that communicates what something is, what it does, and what the end result or positive outcome is.

Tell Them What You Will Tell Them, Tell Them, and Tell Them What You Told Them—Remember, although you may know every minute detail of the concepts you are describing, some of the people you will be presenting to will be hearing it for the first time. While it may seem simplistic, repeating the key points of your message and confirming their understanding will increase the chances of their retention and the ability to move forward.

Customization—If I have learned anything in terms of successful sales presentations, it is the power of customization. It is far too easy to take a standard PowerPoint deck from your company's marketing department and show it "as is" to your customer. However, what are the odds that this is dead-on to what your customer wants to take away from your discussion? You must operate with this concept in mind because the time you are spending is *all* about them. With proper research and planning prior to the meeting, you can find ways to demonstrate that you have learned about their company and listened to what they have told you. There is no greater way to earn respect and credibility.

In summary, strengthening the presentation boils down to one question: Are you willing to invest the time and energy *before* the meeting to ensure success? In the words of renowned sales trainer Jeffrey Gitomer, "Most salespeople are not willing to do the hard work it takes to make selling *easy*!"

Visit our Web site at:
www.ncr.com

CHARACTERISTICS OF A STRONG PRESENTATION

Communication tools such as visual aids, samples, testimonials, demonstrations, and the use of humor are important ingredients in most sales calls. Use of such tools focuses the buyer's attention, improves the buyer's understanding, helps the buyer remember what the salesperson said, offers concrete proof of the salesperson's statements, and creates a sense of value.

KEEPS THE BUYER'S ATTENTION

How many times has your mind wandered during classroom lectures while the instructor earnestly discussed some topic? What happened? The instructor lost your attention. In contrast, your attention probably remains more focused in a class when the instructor uses visuals and humor effectively, brings in guest speakers, and finds ways to get you actively involved in the discussion.

The same is true of buyer–seller interactions. Unless you can get the buyer actively involved in the communication process and doing more than just passively hearing you talk, the buyer's attention will probably turn to other topics. "Building Partnerships 9.1" illustrates how important it is to make sure you are giving the prospect the exact information that she wants if you want to keep her attention.

The buyer's personality can also affect his or her attention span. For example, one would expect an amiable to listen more attentively to a long presentation than, say, a driver would. Thus an effective salesperson should consider the social style of the prospect and adapt the use of communication aids accordingly (see Chapter 5 for more about personality styles).

IMPROVES THE BUYER'S UNDERSTANDING

Many buyers have difficulty forming clear images from the written or spoken word. An old Chinese proverb says, "Tell me—I'll forget. Show me—I may remember. But involve me, and I'll understand." Appeals should be made to as many of the senses (hearing, sight, touch, taste, and smell) as possible. Studies show that appealing to more than one sense with **multiple-sense appeals** increases understanding dramatically, as Exhibit 9.1 illustrates. For example, in selling Ben & Jerry's ice cream novelties to a grocery store manager, the salesperson may describe the product's merits (an appeal to the sense of hearing) or show the product and invite the merchant to taste it (appeals to sight, touch, and taste). Appeals to the grocer's fifth sense, smell, are also possible. On the other hand, salespeople who sell machinery are limited to appeals that will affect the buyers' senses of hearing, sight, and touch.

HELPS THE BUYER REMEMBER WHAT WAS SAID

On average, people immediately forget 50 percent of what they hear; after 48 hours they have forgotten 75 percent of the message. This is unfortunate because securing an order often requires multiple visits, and in many situations the prospect must relay to other people information learned in a sales call. In these circumstances it becomes more critical for the seller to help the buyer remember what was said.

Even selling situations involving one call or one decision maker will be more profitable if the buyer remembers what was said. Vividly communicated features create such a strong impression that the buyer remembers the seller's claims and is more likely to tell others about them.

Lasting impressions can be created in many ways. One salesperson swallows some industrial cleanser to show that it is nontoxic; another kicks the protective

BUILDING Partnerships

9.1

KNOW YOUR AUDIENCE

You have to keep the prospect's attention throughout your presentation. To do that, you really need to "know your audience" and sell to their specific needs. I sell gas monitors and transmitters to industrial firms. These monitors detect the exact level of all sorts of gases present in the building, including O_2, CO, H_2S, NH_3, NO, NO_2, methane, propane, butane, and hydrogen.

If I am giving a sales presentation to an engineer who will be using my product to get her day-to-day tasks completed, she is going to care very little about the cost. The key things they want to know about are reliability and accuracy. So, in this type of scenario, I go more in depth on how my products can make the engineer's job easier

and more efficient as opposed to doing the same job with the competitor's product.

On the other hand, if I am giving a presentation about the exact same product to the plant manager, I am going to highlight how it will save the plant money in the long run and possibly the short run as well if we are able to beat prices of similar competitor products. Going into a call knowing who you are presenting to and their specific needs will not only keep their attention but also make it easier to build the relationship and prove to the client that you really care about helping them out.

Source: Industrial Scientific Company; all names changed for anonymity; used with permission.

Exhibit 9.1
How We Learn and Remember

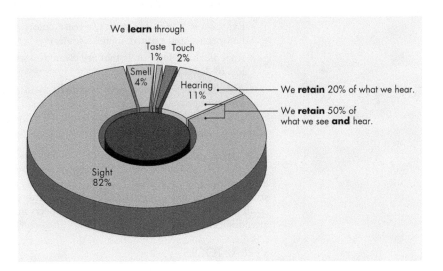

glass in the control panel of a piece of machinery to show that it is virtually unbreakable in even the roughest conditions. Whatever the method used, the prospect is more likely to remember a sales feature if it is presented skillfully in a well-timed demonstration.

OFFERS PROOF OF THE SALESPERSON'S ASSERTIONS

Let's face it: Most people won't believe everything a salesperson tells them. Many of the communication tools we discuss in this chapter provide solid proof to back up a salesperson's claims. For example, a salesperson can easily claim that a liquid is nontoxic, but the claim is much more convincing if the salesperson drinks some of the liquid in front of the prospect.

CREATES A SENSE OF VALUE

The manner in which a product is handled suggests value. Careful handling communicates value, whereas careless handling implies that the product has little value. For example, a delicate piece of china will be perceived as more valuable if the salesperson uses appropriate props, words, and care in handling it.

HOW TO STRENGTHEN THE PRESENTATION

Salespeople should ask themselves the following questions: How can I use my imagination and creativity to make a vivid impression on my prospect or customer? How can I make my presentation a little different and a little stronger? With this frame of mind, salespeople will always try to do a better and more effective job of meeting their customers' needs. In this section we explore the many tools available to strengthen a presentation.

Before we describe the various methods, it is important to reiterate a point made in the preceding chapter. A seller should not grab a method because it sounds trendy or because it worked in a previous sales call or because it is highly entertaining. Rather, a seller should strategically select methods and media that will helpfully address the needs of the buyer. This process includes responding to the buyer's unique style (see Chapter 5 to review social styles):

- Expressives like to see strong, intense colors and lots of photos, cartoons, fancy fonts, and positive images (smiles).
- Analyticals prefer visuals that are clean and simple, a list of references, and lots of details.
- Amiables prefer visuals with people in them and a relatively slow-moving presentation.
- Drivers want crisp, professional visuals with bold lettering to highlight important points.

Strategizing also includes considering such elements as how many people will attend the presentation, which stage of the buying process they are in, what information they need, what type of situation this is (new task, modified rebuy, straight rebuy), and so on (see Chapter 3 for more buying factors to consider). In all cases, it is important to get your prospects involved and keep the focus of attention centered on them.

VERBAL TOOLS
Word Pictures and Stories

The power of the spoken word can be phenomenal. To communicate effectively, the salesperson needs to remember all the hints and tools found in Chapter 4. The latest neuroscience tells us that there are basically three paths to the subconscious mind (habits, beliefs, and emotions), and stories are ways to tap into all of those paths.[1] Word pictures and stories of all types can be effective.[2] Here are some points to keep in mind when using stories:

- It is best to use stories from your own life. If you borrow one, don't act as if it is your personal story.
- Make sure you have a reason for telling the story.

- Consider using a prop, like a glove or a suitcase or something that helps tell the story and will help the prospect remember the story.
- Use the "hook" of the story to tie back directly into your presentation.
- Be accurate and vivid with the words you choose. Learn to paint a clear picture.
- Pace the story, watching your audience for cues. Use silence, loudness, softness, and pauses.
- Choose stories that fit your own style. Don't try to be someone you're not.
- Remember, stories can be short—even a few sentences.

Humor

Another way a salesperson can help keep the buyer's attention is through the use of humor. The wonderful effects of laughter will put everyone more at ease, including the salesperson. Use humorous stories from your own experience, borrowed humor, or humor adapted from another source. Here are some things to keep in mind:

- Don't oversell the joke (Here's one that'll really break you up!).
- Don't apologize before telling a joke (I wasn't ever good at telling a joke, but here goes).
- Identify any facts that are absolutely necessary for the punch line of the story to make sense (Jerry Joyner, my next-door neighbor who was always sticking his nose in other people's business, . . .).
- Use humor from your own life. Most have already heard jokes circulating in e-mail or on the Web.
- Enjoy yourself by smiling and animating your voice and nonverbals.
- Practice telling the joke different ways to see which exact wording works best.
- Make sure your punch line is clear.

Beware of overdoing humor or using off-the-wall or offensive humor. Both can backfire, as one presenter found out when he used the following opening line about an overweight attendee: "Pull up two chairs and have a seat." The presenter knew right away that it was a big mistake. Always be cautious about using insider jokes, especially if you're still considered an outsider.

thinking it through   What humor have you seen backfire? How can you be sure the humor you are using isn't going to offend someone?

Also, understand that what is funny to one person or group may not be funny to others. For example, a foreigner from Egypt may not appreciate someone from America making fun of Egyptian culture—but someone from Egypt can tell that same joke and get plenty of laughs.

VISUAL TOOLS

A salesperson can use various visually oriented tools to strengthen a presentation. This section explores the content and use of those tools, followed by a discussion of the various media available to display the results.

Salespeople should use humor to get and keep the customer's attention.

Graphics and Charts

Graphics and charts help illustrate relationships and clearly communicate large amounts of information. Charts may show, for example, advertising schedules, a breakdown of typical customer profiles, details of product manufacture, profit margins at various pricing points, or the investment nature of purchasing a product.

Here are hints for developing charts and related visuals:

- Know the single point a visual should make, and then ensure that it accomplishes that point.
- Charts should be customized by including the name of the prospect's company in one corner or by some other form of personalization.
- Use current, accurate information.
- Don't place too much information on a visual; on text visuals, don't use more than five or six words per line or more than five lines or bullets per visual. Don't use complete sentences; the speaker should verbally provide the missing details.
- Use bullets (dots or symbols before each line) to differentiate issues and to emphasize key points.
- Don't overload the buyer with numbers. Use no more than five or six columns, and drop all unnecessary zeros.
- Clearly label each visual with a title. Label all columns and rows.
- Recognize the emotional impact of colors, and choose appropriate ones. An abundance of green connected to a humorous graph might be offensive in Islamic countries because green is a religious color. In Brazil and Mexico, purple indicates death. In America, blue indicates confidence and safety, black connotes a strong sense of power, and white indicates sophistication and formality.[3]
- If possible, use graphics (like diagrams, pie charts, and bar charts) instead of tables. Tables are often needed if actual raw numbers are important; graphics are better for displaying trends and relationships.
- Use high-quality drawings and photographs instead of clip art if possible.
- Use consistent art styles, layouts, and scales for your collection of charts and figures. Consistency makes it easier for the buyer to follow along.
- For PowerPoint slides, use 28-point type for the titles and 24-point type for the text, using Arial or Helvetica. And use transition effects and sound clips sparingly.
- Check your visuals closely for typographical errors, misspelled words, and other errors.
- Know and obey copyright laws. You can't just grab images off the Web and use them.

Models, Samples, and Gifts

Visual selling aids such as models, samples, and gifts may be a good answer to the problem of getting and keeping buyer interest. For example, Mul-T-Lock salespeople carry along a miniature working model of the company's electronic door locks when calling on prison security systems buyers. The model allows the salesperson to show how the various components work together to form a fail-safe security network.

Other salespeople use cross-sectional models to communicate with the buyer. For example, salespeople for Motion Industries use a cutaway model of a power transmission friction reduction product. This model helps the buyer, usually an industrial engineer, to clearly see how the product is constructed, resulting in greater confidence that the product will perform as described.

Depending on the service or product, samples and gifts can make excellent sales aids and help maintain the prospect's interest after the call. Loctite displayed the superior holding power of its glue by suspending a man by his shoes at a trade show, held in place by the Loctite adhesive.[4] In a Johnson's Wax sales campaign, salespeople called on buyers of major chains to describe the promotion. Salespeople walked into each buyer's office with a solid oak briefcase containing cans of aerosol Pledge, the product to be highlighted during the promotion. During the call the sales representative demonstrated the Pledge furniture polish on the oak briefcase. At the conclusion of the visit, the rep gave the buyer not only the cans of Pledge but also the briefcase. Of course gift giving must be done with care and not violate the rules of the buyer's company.

Catalogs and Brochures

Catalogs and brochures can help salespeople communicate information to buyers effectively. The salesperson can use them during a presentation and then leave them with the buyer as a reminder of the issues covered. Brochures often summarize key points and contain answers to the usual questions buyers pose.

Firms often spend a great deal of money to develop visually attractive brochures for salespeople. Exhibit 9.2 shows an example of a brochure used by salespeople. Creatively designed brochures usually unfold in a way that enables the salesperson to create and maintain great interest while showing them.

Exhibit 9.2
A Brochure with Great Visual Appeal

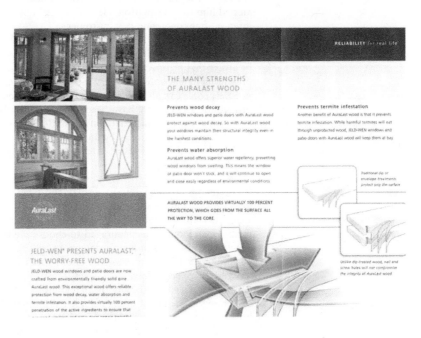

Photos, Illustrations, Ads, and Maps

Photos are easy to prepare, are inexpensive, and permit a realistic portrayal of a product and its benefits. Photographs of people may be particularly effective. For example, leisure made possible through savings can be communicated via photographs of retired people at a ranch, a mountain resort, or the seashore. Illustrations drawn, painted, or prepared in other ways also help dramatize needs or benefits. Copies of recent or upcoming ads may contribute visual appeal. Detailed maps can be easily developed, for example, to show how a magazine's circulation matches the needs of potential advertisers.

Testimonials and Test Results

Testimonials are statements written by satisfied users of a product or service. For example, company representatives who sell air travel for major airlines have found case histories helpful in communicating sales points. Air Canada recounts actual experiences of business firms, showing the variety of problems that air travel can solve.

The effectiveness of a testimonial hinges on the skill with which it is used and a careful matching of satisfied user and prospect. In some situations the testimony of a rival or a competitor of the prospective buyer would end all chance of closing the sale; in other cases this type of testimony may be a strong factor in obtaining commitment. As much as possible, the person who writes the testimonial should be above reproach, well respected by his or her peers, and perhaps a center of influence (see Chapter 6). For example, when selling to certified public accountants (CPAs), a good source for a testimonial would be the president of the state's CPA association.

Before using a testimonial, the salesperson needs to check with the person who wrote it and frequently reaffirm that he or she is still a happy, satisfied customer. One salesperson for Unisys routinely handed all prospects a testimonial from a satisfied customer of a new software package. But unknown to the salesperson, the "satisfied customer" became an unsatisfied one and actually returned the software. The salesperson kept handing out the letter until one of his prospects alerted him to the situation. He will never know how many other prospects lost interest after contacting that customer.

Salespeople should not hand out a testimonial to every prospect. Such letters should be used only if they help to address the buyer's needs or concerns. Also, be aware that prospects probably discount testimonials, thinking that the seller is presenting letters only from very satisfied customers.

Salespeople can also use test results to strengthen the presentation. Tests on the product or service may have been conducted by the seller's firm or some third-party organization (such as Consumer Reports or Underwriters Laboratories). Generally, tests conducted by independent, recognized authorities have more credibility for the prospect than tests done by the seller.

Using Media to Display Visuals

Many media are available to display the types of items just mentioned. New media and improvements to existing media are being introduced almost every week (like 3D interactive viewing, the use of Flash for presentations, and so forth). Salespeople are encouraged to choose media that are appropriate for the exact situation and not merely choose a tool because it is new or exciting. "Sales Technology 9.1" describes the use of one tool that salespeople incorporate.

Most salespeople have developed a **portfolio,** which is a collection of visual aids, often placed in a binder or on a computer. Salespeople do not intend to use everything in the portfolio in a single call; rather, the portfolio should contain a broad spectrum of visual aids the salesperson can find quickly should the need arise. When showing visuals in your portfolio, make sure the portfolio is turned

SALES Technology

9.1

IPADS—WAYS TO INCREASE SALES POTENTIAL?

Many companies have turned to the use of iPads to help their sales force excel, including such firms as IBM, General Mills, Sears, and ADT. According to a vice president of sales at ADT, there are four main ways in which, by using an iPad, sellers' jobs are becoming easier and more efficient:

- iPad gives salespeople the ability to show prospects firsthand how their "ADT Pulse mobile app" works. This app enables users to control things in their buildings, such as heating and cooling as well as lights and video cameras.

- ADT iPads are equipped with a customer relationship management (CRM) app. This app helps to increase the overall productivity of ADT's sales force by allowing them to view their appointments as well as their locations and also retrieve valuable information regarding their customers that has previously been obtained by ADT.

- The camera on the iPad gives the sales representative the chance to take pictures of the potential devices that the customer may want to link with the Pulse mobile app. These pictures are then sent to the ADT office and paired with notes from the salesperson about the particular business that they are selling to.

- The iPad's capability to show the prospect current crime rates in the area helps the salesperson drive home the point that the ADP security system will truly be beneficial to them.

With the use of iPads, ADT's sales force has been able to decrease the time that it takes to make each sales call. This decrease in time per call increases the maximum number of sales calls each representative can make during a given workday. With the implementation of iPads, ADT salespeople in Texas have been able to double their total revenue.

Going forward, ADT plans to have their entire sales force of 4,000 representatives equipped with iPads. Also, they plan on adding two more apps for the iPads; one will give salespeople the chance to obtain a signed contract on their iPad, and the second will be an easy-to-use price configurator.

Source: Eric Lai, "IPads Have Helped Some of This Company's Salespeople DOUBLE Their Sales," *Forbes Magazine*, March 19, 2012, http://www.forbes.com/sites/sap/2012/03/19/ipads-have-helped-some-of-this-companys-salespeople-double-their-sales/2, October 23, 2012.

so the buyer can see it easily. The portfolio should not be placed, like a wall, between you and the buyer. Remember to look at the buyer, not at your visual; maintaining eye contact is always important.

Video is another tool salespeople can use. Salespeople use video to help buyers see how quality is manufactured into a product (showing the production process at the manufacturing plant), how others use a product or service (showing a group of seniors enjoying the golf course at a retirement resort), promotional support offered with the product (showing an upcoming TV commercial for a product), and even testimonials from satisfied users. When using video, make sure the video is fast paced and relatively short. Don't show more than four minutes of a video at one time.

Salespeople have adopted laptops, iPads, and other portable devices for use in sales calls. For example, Merck pharmaceutical salespeople carry laptops with a database of technical information, as well as complete copies of articles from medical journals. Progressive firms, like Aetna, are investing in **digital collateral management systems** (also called **sales asset management systems**) to archive, catalog, and retrieve digital media and text. **Collateral** is a collection of documents that are designed to generate sales, such as brochures, sales flyers and fact sheets, and short success stories. Digital collateral management systems simplify the collection and make it possible for salespeople to easily secure and adapt these selling tools for specific situations. For example, salespeople using the SAVO digital collateral management system (www.savogroup.com) can easily call up photos, videos, audio files, PowerPoint templates, Web pages, legal documents, streaming media, and just about anything else that has been digitally entered into the system.

Some salespeople use PowerPoint to give presentations. However, it is critical that salespeople not merely progress from one slide to the next. Presentations should use visuals that encourage two-way conversation rather than an endless group of slides.

thinking **it** through   You turn the lights down for a PowerPoint computer slide presentation. A few minutes later, you start to panic when your eye catches an unusual jerking movement made by the buyer—she's falling asleep! What do you do now?

Computers not only offer excellent visuals and graphics but also allow the salesperson to perform what-if analyses. For example, when a grocery buyer asked a Procter & Gamble rep what would happen if a new product were sold for $3.69 instead of the $3.75 suggested retail price, the salesperson was able to easily change this number in the spreadsheet program. Instantly all charts and graphs were corrected to illustrate the new pricing point, and comparisons with the competitor's product were generated.

When using computers, be prepared. Have backup batteries, adapters, and copies of any DVDs. Really get to know your hardware and software so you can recover if the system crashes. And make sure both you and your customer can comfortably view the output.

Images can also be displayed using other media. **Document cameras,** also called **visual presenters,** are capable of displaying any three-dimensional object without the use of a transparency. **Electronic whiteboards,** commonly referred

Examples of sales collateral for an industrial product.

Salespeople use electronic tools to display important information.

to as SMART boards or digital easels, are used by salespeople, especially when working with customers who prefer to brainstorm an issue or problem. These are great at encouraging a group to interact with a presentation rather than merely watching it.

PRODUCT DEMONSTRATIONS

One of the most effective methods of appealing to a buyer's senses is through product demonstrations or performance tests.[5] Customers and prospects have a natural desire to prove a product's claims for themselves. For example, orthopedic surgeons are like carpenters for human bodies: They repair damage and build new skeletons. They don't want a salesperson merely to tell them about new products; these surgeons want to touch them, feel them, and use them to see if they are good. When selling hip replacements to such doctors, sales reps demonstrate their products right in the surgery room. Because there is a definite sterile field, sales reps have to stand outside that field and use a green laser pointer to show where the surgeon should place the appliance.

One enterprising sales representative was having trouble convincing the buyer for a national retailer that the salesperson's company could provide service at all the retailer's scattered outlets. On the next trip to the buyer, the sales representative brought along a bag of darts and a map marked with the chain's hundreds of stores and service locations. The buyer was invited to throw darts at the map and then find the nearest stores. The test pointed out that the nearest location for service was always within 50 miles. This "service demonstration" helped win the representative's company a multimillion-dollar order.

Another salesperson was selling feeding tubes to a hospital. A nurse took the salesperson to a patient's bed and stated, "Here, you do it. You said it was easier to insert. Let me see you insert it."[6]

An executive briefing center.

Some products can be sold most successfully by getting the prospect into the showroom for a hands-on product demonstration. Showrooms can be quite elaborate and effective. For example, Kohler operates a marketing showroom in Kohler, Wisconsin. Prospects (architects and designers) from across the world can view and try all of Kohler's kitchen and bath fixtures. **Executive briefing centers**, which are rooms set aside to highlight a company's products and capabilities, are the ultimate presentation room.

Here are a number of helpful hints for developing and engaging in effective demonstrations:

- Be prepared. Practice your demonstration until you become an expert. Plan for everything that could possibly go wrong.
- Secure a proper place for the demonstration, one free of distractions for both you and the buyer. If the demonstration

is at the buyer's office, make sure you have everything you need (power supply, lighting, and so on). Remember, it can even be an online presentation as Chapters 7 and 8 described.

- Check the equipment again to make sure it is in good working order prior to beginning the presentation. Have necessary backup parts and supplies (like paper or bulbs).
- Get the prospect involved in a meaningful way. In a group situation, plan which group members need to participate.
- Always relate product features to the buyer's unique needs.
- Make the demonstration an integral part of the overall presentation, not a separate, unrelated activity.
- Keep the demonstration simple, concise, and clear. Long, complicated demonstrations add to the possibility that the buyer will miss the point. Limit technical jargon to technically advanced buyers who you know will understand technical terms.
- Plan what you will do during any dead time—that is, time in which the machine is processing on its own. You can use these intervals to ask the buyer questions and have the buyer ask you questions.
- Find out whether the prospect has already seen a competitor's product demonstration. If so, strategically include a demonstration of features the buyer liked about the competitor's product. Also, plan to show how your product can meet the prospect's desires and do what the competitor's product will not do.
- Find out whether any buyers present at your demonstration have used your product before. Having them assist in the demonstration may be advantageous if they view your product favorably.
- Probe during and after the demonstration. Make sure buyers understand the features and see how the product can help them. Also, probe to see whether buyers are interested in securing the product.

Remember Murphy's law: What can go wrong will go wrong! If a demonstration "blows up" for any reason, your best strategy usually is to appeal to fate with a humorous tone of voice: "Wow, have you ever seen anything get so messed up? Maybe I should run for Congress!" Don't let technical glitches embarrass or frustrate you. Life is not perfect, and sometimes things just don't work out the way you plan them. If it will help, remember that prospects also are not perfect, and sometimes they mess things up as well. Maintaining a cool and level head will probably impress the prospect with your ability to deal with a difficult situation. It may even increase your chances of a sale because you are demonstrating your ability to handle stress (something that often occurs during the after-sale servicing of an account).

HANDOUTS

Handouts are written documents provided to help buyers remember what was said. A well-prepared set of handouts can be one of the best ways to increase buyer retention of information, especially over longer periods. A common practice is to make a printed copy of the presentation visuals and give that to the buyers at the conclusion of the presentation.

Others would argue that your use of handouts should be more strategically focused. Thus, handouts are not a last-minute thought but rather are a tool that

Getting the buyer actively involved during the call is important.

needs to be carefully planned while you are preparing your presentation. For example, you could draw a line on a piece of planning paper and on the left side list the things you will do and say during the presentation while on the right side listing the items that should go into the handout. In that way the two will work together and be complementary.

What things can go into a handout? Complex charts and diagrams can be included. Because you want to keep your presentation visuals relatively simple (see the preceding hints), your handouts can supply more complete, detailed information. You may also want to include some company reports or literature. However, to avoid making the buyer wade through a lot of nonrelevant information, include only important sections. Other items to include are Web addresses with a description of each site, case studies, magazine articles, and a copy of your presentation visuals themselves (with room to take notes if you're going to give the buyer your handout during the presentation). Whatever you choose, here are some tips:

- Avoid talking while the handout is being passed out.
- Consider highlighting important sections of the handout.
- Don't forget the goal of your meeting. That should drive all your decisions about what to include in your handouts.
- Make sure the handouts look professional. Use graphics instead of text whenever possible.
- Don't cram too much information on a page. White space is fine. Try not to fill more than two-thirds of any page with information.
- Don't drown your prospect in information. Include only helpful information in your handouts.
- Handouts are even more important for foreign buyers, especially those who are nonnative English speakers. You might even consider giving them a copy of your handouts before your meeting so they can become more comfortable and familiar with concepts and phrases. Including a glossary, with definitions, will also be appreciated by foreign buyers.

WRITTEN PROPOSALS

In some industries written proposals are an important part of the selling process. Some proposals are simple adaptations of brochures developed by a corporate marketing department. But in industries that sell customized products or require competitive bidding (as many state and local governments do), a written proposal may be necessary for the buyer to organize and compare various offerings.

The RFP Process

A document issued by a prospective buyer asking for a proposal may be called a **request for proposal (RFP),** request for quote (RFQ), or request for bid (RFB). For brevity's sake, we will refer to all of these as RFPs.

The RFP should contain the customer's specifications for the desired product, including delivery schedules. RFPs are used when the customer has a firm idea of the product needed. From the salesperson's perspective, being a part of the specifying process makes sense. Using the needs identification process, the salesperson can help the customer identify needs and specify product characteristics.

Writing Proposals

Proposals include an **executive summary**—a one- or two-page summary that provides the total cost minus the total savings, a brief description of the problem to be solved, and a brief description of the proposed solution. The summary should satisfy the concerns of an executive who is too busy or unwilling to read the entire proposal. The executive summary also piques the interest of all readers by allowing a quick glance at the benefits of the purchase.

The proposal also includes a description of the current situation in relation to the proposed solution and a budget (which details costs). Some firms have even developed computer programs to automatically generate sales proposals in response to a set of questions the salesperson answers about a particular customer.[7] This is especially helpful because sometimes buyers use RFPs to keep their current suppliers in check. In such a case, a seller might want to minimize the amount of time spent responding to an RFP. (A familiar saying in sales is "You can't cash an RFP.")

When writing proposals, remember to use your most polished writing skills. Skip buzzwords, focusing on actual results that the prospect can gain from going with your proposal.

Presenting the Proposal

Prospects use proposals in many different ways. Proposals can be used to convince the home office that the local office needs the product, or proposals may be used to compare the product and terms of sale with those of competitors. As we mentioned earlier, the intended use will influence the design of the proposal; it will also influence how the salesperson presents the proposal.

When the proposal is going to be sent to the home office, it is wise to secure the support of the local decision maker. Although that person is not the ultimate decision maker, the decision may rest on how much effort that person puts into getting the proposal accepted. Buying centers often use proposals to compare competitive offerings, and the salesperson is asked to present the proposal to the buying committee.

There are several options if you are going to give an oral presentation of your proposal. First, you can give the buyers a copy of the complete proposal before your presentation. During the meeting you would spend about 5 to 10 minutes summarizing the proposal and then ask for questions. Second, if you choose to give the written proposal to the buyers during the oral presentation, you may want to distribute the proposal a section at a time to avoid having them read ahead instead of listening to your oral presentation.

VALUE ANALYSIS: QUANTIFYING THE SOLUTION

To recap what we've described throughout this book, salespeople are selling value. As mentioned in Chapter 3, one of the trends in buying is more sophisticated analyses by buyers. This section explores methods available to help the buyer conduct these types of analyses.

Quantifying a solution is more important in some situations than in others. Some products or services (like replacement parts or repairs) pose little risk for the prospect. These products are so necessary for the continuation of the prospect's business that little quantifying of the solution is usually needed. Other products pose moderate risk (such as expanding the production capacity of a plant for an existing successful product) or high risk (like programs designed to reduce costs or increase sales; these present higher risk because it is hard to calculate the exact magnitude of the potential savings or sales). For moderate-risk and high-risk situations, quantifying the solution becomes increasingly important. Finally, certain products pose super-high risk (brand-new products or services, which are riskier because no one can calculate costs or revenues with certainty). Attempts at quantifying the solution are imperative in super-high-risk situations. In summary, the higher the risk to the prospect, the more attention the salesperson should pay to quantifying the solution.

Salespeople can strengthen a presentation by showing the prospect that the cost of the proposal is offset by added value; this process is often called **quantifying the solution** or **value analysis**. Some of the most common ways to quantify a solution are value propositions, cost–benefit analysis, return on investment, payback period, net present value, and opportunity cost. For retail buyers, the seller usually must prove turnover and profit margins. The key is to offer information that will help buyers evaluate your offering based on their metrics. Thus, if a buyer is evaluating proposals on the basis of ROI, that's the metric you should focus on in your presentation.

Customer Value Proposition

A **customer value proposition**, also called a *value proposition,* is the way in which your product will meet the prospect's needs and how that is different from the offerings of competitors, especially the next-best alternative.[8] Honeywell sales reps create basic value propositions for each market segment and then further refine them for each individual customer. The value bundle contained in a solid customer value proposition includes the features and benefits (financial and emotional) tailored to the prospect, the proof that those benefits actually exist, and the value of the seller and the seller's firm as the solutions provider. Simply having a superior product or delivering on your promises is no longer sufficient. Rather, what distinguishes you is how you make your customers feel while using your product. The experience is what bonds your customers to you.

As you write your customer value proposition, remember that what it contains is tailored to the individual prospect, so it needs to address three key issues: What is important to this specific prospect (which requires we understand the customer's business model)? How does our solution create value for this specific prospect? And how can we demonstrate our capability (which means we have to communicate the value to the customer)?[9]

Here are some weak examples of customer value proposition statements, none of which tell how the prospect is really going to benefit or how the seller can demonstrate that she is able to accomplish the goals for the account:

- It's the most technologically advanced system on the market today.
- We reduce training time more than any of our competitors.
- Our service was rated number one by an independent service lab.

Now here are examples of good customer value proposition statements, which include the elements discussed:[10]

- According to your CFO, dispatching multiple service vans to a customer site has been costing an estimated $20,000 a year in extra fuel costs. When you add that to the cost of unproductive personnel time and missed revenue, the loss is $850,000 per year. When you implement our Call Tracker system you will be able to reduce repeat customer service calls by 20 percent, resulting in a monthly savings of $250,000. This will require an investment of $2 million, which will be returned in only eight months. We implemented a similar solution at Acme Transfer, which began achieving a monthly savings of $500,000 within 90 days of installation. And I have personally overseen 15 such installations and will be there to ensure that all parties are fully trained in use of the new system.

- In this era of heightened airport security concerns, Advanced Engineering, a leading manufacturer of state-of-the-art explosives detective devices, offers a unique solution. The complete "Senso-37 Detection System" for major airports like yours requires a $200,000 investment, fully installed. Our superior system has been shown to save lives, lower human security guard costs, and decrease passenger processing time. My analysis reveals that Orlando International Airport will decrease its general security guard expenses at the major passenger screening area by $80,000 per year for the next four years, giving you a payback in just 2.5 years and also giving you and your passengers peace of mind that ALL passengers are being screened with state-of-the-art technology. When you install the system you also get an added advantage: my commitment and supervision, as one of the top salespeople in my company, that your system will be installed at Orlando International Airport on time and as promised and that your security staff will be trained efficiently and effectively.

Customer value propositions should contain four main parts:

- One or more key features of the product/service complete with external proof
- The benefits, both economical and emotional
- Positioning your company as the prospect's long-term partner
- Offering yourself as the personal problem solver

How do you create a customer value proposition?[11] Having solid, clear information is critical, as "From the Buyer's Seat 9.1" illustrates. Try brainstorming with your sales team and look for statements that truly tell your customers how your solution is going to solve their problems. Every time you write one down, keep asking, "So what difference does that make?" For example, if you write "saves time," ask, "So what does it matter if it saves time?" By doing so, you will eventually be able to reach the core value that your customer will achieve by adopting your product. Another helpful way to create a customer value proposition is by talking to your customers. They know what value you can bring to a prospect because they have experienced it firsthand and are usually willing to offer suggestions.

Cost–Benefit Analysis

Perhaps the simplest method of quantifying a solution is to list the costs to the buyer and the savings the buyer can expect from the investment, often called a **simple cost–benefit analysis.** For this analysis to be realistic and meaningful, information needed to calculate savings must be supplied by the buyer. Exhibit 9.3 shows how one salesperson used a chart to compare the costs and benefits of purchasing a two-way radio system.

In many situations the salesperson does a **comparative cost–benefit analysis** by comparing the present situation's costs with the value of the proposed solution or the seller's product with a competitor's product. For example, a company with

From the **BUYER'S SEAT**

I LOVE TO SEE SELLER'S PLAN!

I'm comanager at an Independent Grocers Alliance (IGA) grocery store located in Iowa. IGA was founded in 1926 to bring together independent grocers across the nation to help ensure that the local grocery store remained strong in the face of growing chain competition. My store is actually one of six that are owned by a single owner. Many of the new products that we carry in our six stores must first be presented during one of our store meetings. During these meetings, managers from all locations are present, along with the owners of the organization and a few other individuals. After salespeople pitch their products to us during our meetings, the floor opens for questions from anyone who may have an objection or question.

There are some simple ways that salespeople can prepare for their sales presentation not only to strengthen their overall presentation but also to increase the chances that our stores will begin to carry their products and/or product lines. First, they should visit as many stores as possible to get a better feel as to the types of people they will be attempting to sell to and to get a better sense of the overall culture of the store (what we currently carry, our current prices, how our current products are packaged, and so on). Second, we are not going to consider bringing a product into our stores that we have never tried ourselves, so sellers should provide enough samples for everyone who wishes to try the product a chance to try it.

I'll never forget the impression made by one particular salesperson from Pepsi. As I was finishing up all of the nightly tasks before closing, she walked into my store carrying a clipboard, a notebook, and a pen in hand. I asked her if there was anything that I could help her with, and she responded, "Well, to be honest, I am going to be presenting a new soft drink line at your managers meeting tomorrow, and I just wanted to see how my current competition is looking in your stores. If you have a little bit of time, I'd love to run a few things by you and see if we're on the same page." We talked for a while, and by the end of our conversation she had taken over two pages of notes on things that we had talked about, from what I feel was missing in our current offerings as well as their strengths.

The next day when she was making her sales pitch, she took into account all the things that we had talked about and tailored her presentation toward the areas that we had discovered were the most weaknesses and how her product was going to help us in those areas. Everything that she had learned about our stores in that short time period was put into her sales presentation and ultimately helped her strengthen his presentation and tailor it to our needs. Needless to say, she got the business!

Source: Herberto Aguila, IGA; all names have been changed for anonymity; used with permission.

---

a premium-priced product may justify the higher price on the basis of offsetting costs in other areas. If productivity is enhanced, the increased productivity has economic value.

Return on Investment

The **return on investment (ROI)** is simply the net profits (or savings) expected from a given investment, expressed as a percentage of the investment:

$$ROI = \text{Net profits (or savings)} \div \text{Investment}$$

Thus, if a new product costs $4,000 but saves the firm $5,000, the ROI is 125 percent ($5,000 ÷ $4,000 = 1.25). Many firms set a minimum ROI for any new products, services, or cost-saving programs. Salespeople need to discover the firm's minimum ROI or ROI expectations and then show that the proposal's ROI meets or exceeds those requirements. For an ROI analysis to be accurate, it is

Exhibit 9.3
Cost–Benefit Analysis
for a Mobile Radio

Monthly Cost		
Monthly equipment payment (five-year lease/purchase)*		$1,555.18
Monthly service agreement		339.00
Monthly broadcast fee		+ 533.60
Total monthly cost for entire fleet		$2,427.78
Monthly Savings		
Cost savings (per truck) by eliminating backtracking, unnecessary trips (based on $.36/mile × 20 miles × 22 days/month)		$158.40
Labor cost savings (per driver) by eliminating wasted time in backtracking, etc. ($8.00/hour × 25 minutes/day × 22 days/month)		+ 73.33
Total cost savings per vehicle		231.73
Times number of vehicles		× 32
Total monthly cost savings for entire fleet		$7,415.36

	Years 1–5	**Year 6+**
Monthly savings	$7,415.36	$7,415.36
Less: monthly cost	− 2,427.78	− 872.85
Monthly benefit	4,987.58	6,542.51
Times months per year	× 12	× 12
Annual benefit	$59,850.96	$78,510.12

*Payment reflects ongoing cost of service agreement and broadcast fees.

important for the seller to collect meaningful data about costs and savings that the buyer can expect.

Payback Period

The **payback period** is the length of time it takes for the investment cash outflow to be returned in the form of cash inflows or savings. To calculate the payback period, you simply add up estimated future cash inflows and divide them into the investment cost. If expressed in years, the formula is as follows:

$$\text{Payback period} = \text{Investment} \div \text{Savings (or profits) per year}$$

For large capital outlays, the prospect usually needs to see the return on investment, payback period, and/or net present value.

Of course the payback period could be expressed in days, weeks, months, or any other period.

As an example, suppose a new machine costs $865,000 but will save the firm $120,000 per year in labor costs. The payback period is 7.2 years ($865,000 ÷ $120,000 per year = 7.2 years).

Thus, for the buyer, the payback period indicates how quickly the investment money will come back to him or her and can be a good measure of personal risk. When a buyer makes a decision, his or her neck is "on the line," so to speak, until the investment money is at least recovered. Hence, it's not surprising that buyers like to see short payback periods.

We have kept the discussion simple to help you understand the concept. In reality the calculation of the payback period would take into account many other factors, such as investment tax credits and depreciation.

Net Present Value

As you may have learned in finance courses, money left idle loses value over time (a dollar today is worth more than a dollar next week) because of inflation and the firm's cost of capital. Thus, firms calculate the value of future cash inflows in today's dollars (this process is called *discounting the cash flows*). One tool to assess the validity of an opportunity is to calculate the **net present value (NPV)**, which is simply the net value today of future cash inflows (discounted back to their present value today at the firm's cost of capital) minus the investment. The actual method of calculating NPV is beyond the scope of this book, but many computer programs and calculators can calculate NPV quickly and easily:

$$\text{Net present value} = \text{Future cash inflows discounted into today's} \\ \text{dollars} - \text{Investment}$$

As an example of the preceding formula, let's assume that a $50 million investment will provide annual cash inflows over the next five years of $15 million per year. The cash inflows are discounted (at the firm's cost of capital), and the result is that they are actually worth $59 million in today's dollars. The NPV is thus $9 million ($59 million − $50 million).

As with ROI and payback period, many firms set a minimum NPV. In no case should the NPV be less than $0. Again, we have kept this discussion simple to help you understand the basic concept.

Opportunity Cost

The **opportunity cost** is the return a buyer would have earned from a different use of the same investment capital. Thus, a buyer could spend $100 million to buy any of the following: a new computer system, a new production machine, or a controlling interest in another firm.

Successful salespeople identify other realistic investment opportunities and then help the prospect compare the returns of the various options. These comparisons can be made by using any of the techniques we have already discussed (cost–benefit analysis, ROI, payback period, NPV). For example, a salesperson might help the buyer determine the following information about the options identified:

	NPV	Payback Period
Buying a new telecommunications system	$1.6 million	3.6 years
Upgrading the current telecommunications system	0.4 million	4.0 years

Salespeople should never forget that prospects have a multitude of ways to invest their money.

Selling Value to Resellers

When resellers purchase a product for resale, they are primarily concerned with whether their customers will buy the product and how much they will make on each sale. For example, when an Xbox salesperson meets with Walmart to sell video games, he is armed with data showing how much profit is made every time Walmart sells a game and how fast the games sell. The Walmart buyer uses this information to compare the performance of Xbox video games with objectives and with other products sold in the same category, such as Sony's PlayStation.

PROFIT MARGIN Profit margin is the net profit the reseller makes, expressed as a percentage of sales. It is calculated, and thus influenced, by many factors. For example, if Linz Jewelers bought 100 rings for $1,000 each ($100,000), spent $45,000 in expenses (for advertising, salesperson commission, store rent, and other items), and sold them all at an average price of $3,000 ($300,000 in revenue), the profit would be $155,000, with a profit margin of 52 percent ($155,000 ÷ $300,000 = .52).

INVENTORY TURNOVER Inventory turnover is typically calculated by dividing the annual sales by the average retail price of the inventory on hand. Thus it measures how fast a product sells relative to how much inventory has to be carried—how efficiently a reseller manages its inventory. The reseller would like to have in the store only the amount needed for that day's sales because inventory represents an investment. Thus, large retailers such as Cub Foods receive daily delivery of some products. If the reseller is able to reduce its inventory level, it can invest this savings in stores or warehouses or in the stock market.

For example, if Linz Jewelers usually kept eight rings in stock, inventory turnover would be calculated by dividing total sales in units (100 rings) by average inventory (8 rings). Thus inventory turnover would be 100 ÷ 8, or 12.5 times. The answer represents the number of times that Linz sold the average inventory level. Another way to calculate this is to divide total sales ($300,000 in the Linz example) by the average price of inventory (8 units at $3,000, or $24,000). The answer is the same: 12.5 times.

A reseller does not necessarily want to increase inventory turnover by reducing the amount of inventory carried. Several negative consequences can result. For example, sales may fall because stockouts occur more frequently and products are not available when customers want to buy them. Expenses can increase because the reseller has to order more frequently. Finally, the cost of goods sold may increase because the reseller pays higher shipping charges and does not get as big a quantity discount.

Sellers provide resellers with information to prove that inventory turnover can be improved by buying from them. They describe their **efficient consumer response (ECR)**, **quick response (QR)**, **automatic replenishment (AR)**, and just-in-time (JIT) inventory management systems designed to reduce the reseller's average inventory and transportation expenses but still make sure products are available when end users want them. Chapter 3 described the use of these information systems in depth.

As an example, the September 11, 2001, tragedy created an outpouring of patriotic feelings among Americans. Within 24 hours there was a shortage of American flags, and there is only one major American flag manufacturer. The company had 80,000 flags in inventory on September 11. By the close of business September 12, both Target and Walmart had completely sold out of flags—over 150,000 each. When the stores opened September 13, Walmart had 80,000 more flags, whereas Target had none. How? Walmart's QR system was updated every five minutes, whereas Target didn't update its inventory system until the stores were closed in the evening. Walmart had an order placed with expedited shipping before the stores closed and before Target knew it was out of flags! Similar situations occurred in other product categories, such as flashlights, batteries, battery-powered radios, bottled water, guns, ammunition, and other products that frightened Americans wanted. As you can see, EDI and ECR systems can give resellers significant competitive advantage.

Electronic data interchange (EDI) is a computer-to-computer transmission of data from a reseller, such as Walmart, to vendors (such as American Flag Company) and back. Resellers and vendors that have ECR or QR relationships use EDI to transmit purchase orders and shipping information.

RETURN ON SPACE A key investment that resellers make is in space—retail store space and warehouse space. A measure that retailers use to assess the return on their space investment is sales per square foot or sales per shelf foot. In a grocery store or a department store, shelf or display space is a finite asset that is used to capacity. Products therefore must be evaluated on how well they use the space allocated to them. For example, if a retailer generates $200 per square foot in sales with Tommy Hilfiger merchandise and only $150 selling Ralph Lauren merchandise, it may increase the space allocated to Tommy Hilfiger and reduce the space allocated to Ralph Lauren.

DEALING WITH THE JITTERS

Let's face it. For many people giving a presentation is a frightening experience. Even seasoned salespeople can get the jitters when the presentation is for a very important client or when the prospect has been rude in an earlier meeting. It all comes down to fear: the fear of being embarrassed or failing, the fear of exposing our lack of knowledge in some area, or the fear of losing our train of thought. The reasons don't even have to be valid. If you have the jitters, you need to help resolve them.

Here are some tips from the experts on how to reduce presentation jitters:

- Know your audience well.
- Know what you're talking about. Keep up to date.
- Prepare professional, helpful visuals. These not only help your audience understand the presentation, but also can help you remember important points.
- Be yourself. Don't try to present like someone else.
- Get a good night's sleep.
- For presentations to groups, feed off the energy and enthusiasm of several friendly, happy-looking people in your audience. (Note: That's what professors often do!)
- Recognize the effect of fear on your body and reduce the accompanying stress manifestations by stretching, taking deep breaths to relax breathing, and so on.
- Visualize your audience as your friends—people who are interested and eager to hear what you have to say.

- Psych yourself up for the presentation. Think of the successes you have had in your life (previous presentations that went well or other things you have done well).
- Realize that everyone gets nervous before a presentation at times. It is natural. In fact, it can help you keep from being cocky.
- *Practice, practice, practice!* And finally, practice.

SELLING YOURSELF

To be successful in selling, customizing the material and method of communication is vital to your success. These points may seem high level, but they act as the foundation of any sales motion. Remember, selling is present in nearly all areas of your life, and preparation can dramatically increase your probability of success. Consider this scenario.

As the school year approaches an end, you are hopeful to land a high-paying internship in an area of business that interests you. You find the marketing research internship of your dreams, but it requests a recommendation from your college or university.

"Marketing Research" was a class in which you excelled, and your goal is to convince John, a professor of marketing at your university, to sponsor you for the opportunity. From your past experiences, John is clearly analytic by nature. As you learned in Chapter 5 on social styles, analytics have several tendencies you can use to best position your request.

Knowing John's background as a market researcher tends to drive his focus to quantitative figures over opinions or concept based information, what would be the best way to sell this professor on recommending you for the internship?

As the chapter suggests, analytics "prefer visuals that are clean and simple, a list of references, and lots of details." Therefore, your request is likely to be accepted if it focuses on specifics and detailed information with proper citing. Be sure to leave no stone unturned in terms of how you describe why would be successful in the role. An analytic will appreciate the detail because this allows for a development of comfort associated with his pending recommendation. While it may feel overdrawn, keep in mind that an analytic tends to review and appreciate full information before making a decision.

While an expressive or amiable professor may be more receptive to a referral from a high-achieving peer student or even another professor, John is more likely to connect with a printed transcript or validated certifications that demonstrate achievement. Be sure to provide information with sources to ensure his comfort with the information presented and, thus, your request.

When creating a value proposition for this professor, what is worth focusing on? Because John appreciates facts, detail, and proper sourcing, he needs to see facts about how your experience will lead to success in the internship. While your personality may be perfect for the internship, this opinion should not lead the sales motion with John. Stay focused on the importance of conscious consideration of who you are selling to because it may be the most vital element but an unnoticed factor in a sales motion.

In summary, strengthening the presentation revolves around first knowing your audience and then creating materials and communication strategies that are most likely to be positively accepted. Good selling!

Source: Mike Buckland; used with permission.

SUMMARY

Strengthening communication with the buyer is important. It helps focus the buyer's attention, improves the buyer's understanding, helps the buyer remember what was said, and can create a sense of value.

Many methods of strengthening communication are available. These include such items as word pictures, stories, humor, charts, models, samples, gifts, catalogs, brochures, photos, ads, maps, illustrations, testimonials, and test results. Media available include portfolios, video, computers, and visual projectors.

A backbone of many sales presentations is the product demonstration. It allows the buyer to get hands-on experience with the product, something most other communication methods do not offer. Handouts and written proposals can also strengthen presentations.

It is often important to quantify a solution so the buyer can evaluate its costs in relation to the benefits he or she can derive from the proposal. Some of the more common methods of quantifying a solution include simple cost–benefit analysis, comparative cost–benefit analysis, return on investment, payback period, net present value, and calculation of opportunity cost, turnover, and profit margins. Salespeople should be prepared to present a clear customer value proposition that offers real value to the customer.

All communication tools require skill and practice to be used effectively. Outstanding salespeople follow a number of guidelines to improve their use of visuals, demonstrate their products more effectively, and reduce their nervousness.

KEY TERMS

automatic replenishment (AR)   244
collateral   233
comparative cost–benefit analysis   240
customer value proposition   239
digital collateral management   233
document cameras   234
efficient consumer response (ECR)   244
electronic data interchange (EDI)   245
electronic whiteboard   234
executive briefing center   235
executive summary   238
handouts   236
inventory turnover   244
multiple-sense appeals   226

net present value (NPV)   243
opportunity cost   243
payback period   242
portfolio   232
profit margin   244
quantifying the solution   238
quick response (QR)   244
request for proposal (RFP)   237
return on investment (ROI)   241
sales asset management system   233
simple cost–benefit analysis   240
testimonials   232
value analysis   239
visual presenters   234

ETHICS PROBLEMS

1. Men tend to respond more to jokes involving sexual innuendo than women do. Assume this statement is true for a male buyer you are going to call on next Tuesday. You learn that he loves jokes with a sexual bent. Is there any reason you

should avoid using a joke with a sexual theme when calling on him?

2. Is encouraging buyers to order a large quantity so they can get a better quantity discount always a good idea? Why or why not?

QUESTIONS AND PROBLEMS

1. Assume you plan a demonstration to prove some of the claims you have made for a new riding lawnmower. How would the demonstration differ for each of these three individuals: a person who is very concerned about the environment, an economy-minded person, and a safety-minded person?

2. How could you demonstrate the following products?
   a. A new Wilson basketball to a high school coach.
   b. The strength of a fiberglass stepladder to an industrial construction contractor.
   c. A line of stay-sharp cutlery to a chef at a five-star restaurant.

3. Which communication tools would you use to provide solid proof to address the following concerns expressed by prospects?
   a. I don't think that type of carpet would sell well in a store like ours.
   b. No one eats popcorn anymore, so I don't need your Nostalgia old-fashioned popcorn cart.
   c. That Tonka steel dump truck won't hold up under rough play with three-year-old boys.
   d. You look too old to know what the younger customers who shop in my store are looking for.

4. This chapter generally accepts the use of PowerPoint presentations as a positive, useful tool for salespeople. Are there any times when the use of PowerPoint could actually be detrimental to communication effectiveness? Explain.

5. Which communication tools would you use to communicate the following facts?
   a. We have been in business for over 10 years.
   b. This driver is going to help you get more distance with the golf ball.

   c. These bedsheets will not pill or wear out even after 100 washings.
   d. This scale is accurate to plus or minus .00015 ounces.
   e. This camera produces extra-high-quality resolution.

6. Assume that you are selling a complete line of canoes and kayaks to a large outfitter to replace all of their current units. The total costs will be $125,000. You expect that repairs will drop by $25,000 a year over the next 10 years. At the outfitter's cost of capital, the discounted cash inflows have a value today of $215,000. Use this information to calculate the following:
   a. Return on investment.
   b. Payback period.
   c. Net present value.

7. Assume that ACME Tools buys 100 portable generators for $425 each and then spends $1,000 in expenses for advertising, salesperson commission, and store rent. The generators sell for $695 each. ACME keeps 100 generators in stock at all times. Average annual sales are 500 generators. Calculate the following:
   a. Profit margin
   b. Inventory turnover

8. Are there any retail situations for which return on space is not a big deal? How about situations where return on space is extremely important?

9. In "Building Partnerships 9.1" you read how the salesperson varied his presentation depending on the customer's job title. Using the various methods described in this chapter, exactly how would you suggest strengthening the presentation to an engineer as described in "Building Partnerships 9.1?"

CASE PROBLEMS

case **9.1**

Zadro Inc. (Part A)

There are many harmful germs found in the home, in public places, and in hotels while traveling. The Programmable UV Sanitizing Wand, made by Zadro, can effectively kill up to 99.99 percent of germs and viruses in just 10 seconds. It can also kill dust mites in mattresses, pillows, and carpets. Since the wand is portable, it can travel with you wherever you travel, removing harmful substances regardless of where you are. The user simply waves the scanner within a quarter inch of the surface for 10 seconds to kill the substances.

The scanner is 1½ inches high × 20 inches wide × 1¾ inches deep and runs on three C batteries. An optional AC adapter is sold separately. The scanner includes an electronic child lock to prevent misuse. A stand is provided and is used to go over keyboards, butcher blocks, and so on for hands-free operation. The programmable unit can be set for 10-, 20-, 40-, and 60-second times as well as two to five minutes, depending on the surface area that needs to be scanned. The unit is not designed to be used on humans or animals. The scanner, which is laboratory certified and tested, retails for $99, and all units come with a 90-day limited warranty. Resellers are offered the units for $60, with a quantity discount price of $50 for all units over 100 in a single order.

Questions

1. Describe how you would use the communication tools described in this chapter to sell the Programmable UV Sanitizing Wand to Target. Target would then resell to its consumers. Make any assumptions necessary.

2. Develop a short (five-minute) slide show that you can use to introduce the product to potential buyers at a retailer trade show.

Source: http://www.zadroinc.com/health-solutions-nano-technology-c-43_44.html; discount information is for illustration purposes only.

case **9.2**

Miller Lite

On December 5, 1933, the U.S. Congress passed a bill that would repeal the Eighteenth Amendment and thus would end prohibition in this country. The implementation of prohibition had been linked to many negative social issues, such as organized crime, bootlegging, and racketeering. Some historians have commented that the alcohol industry accepted stronger regulation of alcohol in the decades after repeal as a way to reduce the chance that Prohibition would return.

Today, the American beer industry is the most heavily regulated industry in the country, even more than the tobacco industry, and Minnesota is a leader when it comes to heavy regulation and high taxes. For example, here are the beer laws in Minnesota:

1. All retailers must be offered the same price at all times.

2. Beer distributors cannot pay for any cooperative advertising.

3. Beer distributors cannot give any product for free.

4. Beer distributors have a maximum of $300 per brand, per year, to promote the brand within the account (using things like neon lights and point-of-sale items), but this can't be in the form of price cuts for an individual retailer.

I was the sales representative for a beer distributor in Minnesota. My territory volume was trending down, and I was told by my manager that I needed to secure incremental activity to promote Miller Lite. My largest customer, Bill, at Save-a-Lot Liquor, gave me an opportunity for an additional holiday ad in his weekly flyer. I knew this ad would yield a 200 percent lift in sales for the week and in turn would pay a nice commission to me.

To secure the ad, Bill was asking me to lower the price of my product by 50 cents per case to cover the cost of the ad. Bill also stated that if I decided not to participate, my competition had already committed to the ad. I believed that my competition had lowered the price in the past, and there had never been any repercussions from the authorities. What should I do? I had totally lost the interest of Bill, who would turn elsewhere to buy the bulk of his beer!

I had several options. I could write a personal check for the amount of the ad, but that would have repercussions down the road, and I was sure I'd be asked to do so again and again. I could try to see if Bill really did have the competitor's agreement to cut the price, but that could backfire on me and make the customer think I didn't trust his word. I could give all the other liquor stores in my territory the same 50-cent discount, but that would cut into our profit margins.

Questions

1. What should the salesperson do at this point?

2. What will be the repercussions of your answer to question 1?

Source: Amir Permeh, Bernick's Beverages & Vending, personal correspondence; used with permission; names of buyer changed to protect confidentiality.

ROLE PLAY CASE

Today you will present to the same person whose needs you identified in Chapter 8. (If you have not done role plays before, you will need to review the information about the various role play customers that can be found at the end of Chapter 3. If you did not do the role play at the end of Chapter 8, choose one of the three companies to sell to.) If you sold to BancVue, you'll do so again; the same goes for GelTech and HighPoint Solutions. Begin by summarizing the buyer's needs and gaining agreement that these are all the needs. Then make your presentation.

As a buyer, do not offer any objections today. Just listen, add your thoughts on how the product might help if asked, and agree. Ask questions if something seems vague or confusing. Further, ask for proof. For example, if the salesperson says everyone loves it, ask to see a testimonial letter or something of that sort.

When you are the odd person out and observing, look for the following:

- Did the seller tie the features to the buyer's needs? Or did the seller present features that were not needed?
- Did the seller try to gain agreement that the buyer recognized and valued the benefit?
- Did the seller use visual aids as proof sources effectively?
- Did the seller use specific language versus general or ambiguous language (for example, "It's the best")?

Note: For background information about these role plays, please see page 26.

To the instructor: Additional information needed to complete the role play is available in the Instructor's Manual.

ADDITIONAL REFERENCES

Boe, John. "Harness the Power of Your Customers' Testimonials." *American Salesman* 56, no. 10 (October 2011), pp. 3–5.

Bradford, Kevin D., and Barton A. Weitz. "Salespersons' Management of Conflict in Buyer–Seller Relationships." *Journal of Personal Selling and Sales Management* 29, no. 1 (Winter 2008–2009), pp. 25–42.

Frey, Robert S. *Successful Proposal Strategies for Small Businesses: Using Knowledge Management to Win Government, Private-Sector, and International Contracts.* 6th ed. Norwood, MA: Artech House, 2013.

Gallo, Carmine. *The Presentation Secrets of Steve Jobs.* New York: McGraw-Hill, 2012.

Handley, Ann. "Uncovering New Territories." *Entrepreneur* 40, no. 4 (April 2012), p. 62.

Isson, Jean-Paul, and Jesse Harriott. *Win with Advanced Business Analytics: Creating Business Value from Your Data.* Hoboken, NJ: Wiley and SAS Business Series, 2012.

Jalkala, Anne, and Risto T. Salminen. "Communicating Customer References on Industrial Companies' Web Sites." *Industrial Marketing Management* 38, no. 7 (October 2009), pp. 825–37.

Lazkani, Nancy. "Harness the Power of Demonstration and Persuasion." *Response* 20, no. 8 (May 2012), p. 2.

Leonard, Devin. "The Last Pitchman." *Bloomberg Businessweek*, no. 4183 (June 14, 2010), pp. 4–5.

London, Jonathan, and Martin Lucas. *Using Technology to Sell: Tactics to Ratchet Up Results*. New York City: Apress, 2012.

McGaulley, Michael. *Sales Presentations and Demonstrations*. New York: Champlain House Media, 2010.

Sant, Tom. *Persuasive Business Proposals: Writing to Win More Customers, Clients, and Contracts*. New York: AMACOM, 2012.

Theriault, Michel. *Win More Business—Write Better Proposals*. Guelph, Ontario: WoodStone Press, 2010.

Urbaniak, Anthony. "The Demonstration." *American Salesman* 56, no. 1 (January 2011), pp. 3–5.

Williams, Robin. *The Non-Designer's Presentation Book*. San Francisco, CA: Peachpit Press, 2009.

The Partnership Process

PART 2

chapter 10

RESPONDING TO OBJECTIONS

SOME QUESTIONS ANSWERED IN THIS CHAPTER ARE

- How should salespeople sell value and build relationships when responding to objections?
- When do buyers object?
- What objections can be expected?
- Which methods are effective when responding to objections?
- How do you deal with tough customers?

PROFILE

PROFILE My name is Renee Miles. I received my bachelor's and master's degrees from Texas State University–San Marcos. I had the privilege of being taught professional selling by Mrs. Vicki West. I currently work as a medical device sales representative for Johnson & Johnson and have been with them for the last seven and a half years.

When I started out in sales, I did a lot of cold calling and knocking on doors. I heard objections and would get nervous and instantly think that this person does not want to be sold to. What I have since come to learn is this: People hate to be sold to, but they love to buy! So my job is to make them love to buy from me and my company. How do you do that? By becoming an amazing listener and embracing objections.

Selling is a career about educating and building value. People don't know what they don't know—until they know it! How do prospects tell you what they don't know? They *object*! For example:

DOCTOR: "Renee, I'm happy with what I've been doing."

ME: "That is wonderful! Tell me about what you like about your process. Is there anything that can be improved? Doctor, after everything we've discussed, I would recommend stocking our lenses for improved efficiency. I have several offices that have found stocking lenses to be helpful with regard to increasing profitability, customer satisfaction, and saving staff time."

DOCTOR: "Renee, I don't want to pay that up-front cost."

ME: "Doctor, let's take a look at what your costs are right now and put pen to paper, as there are several ways to alleviate that up-front cost. But ultimately, I think you might be pleasantly surprised at what this will do for your practice profitability."

Objections are the key to "unlocking the door" to the prospect's business. I always have a pen and notepad—lean forward, listen to what the person is saying, ask good open-ended questions, and keep a pleasant demeanor.

As I present a solution, an objection (or two or three) will always come up. I write them down on the upper right corner of my notebook. I then ask if there is anything else they have a concern or question about that I can address. This gives the prospect an opportunity to see that you are there as a consultant—to address their concerns—not there just for your own agenda. Finally, it is important to confidently educate the person on why you are right!

There are usually the same four or five objections (give or take a few) that I hear the most often, so I need to know how to address each and also know how to roll in additional benefits. Forestalling is critical, and it allows me to proactively address objections that I have consistently heard.

Sales would be really boring and very difficult without objections! If you didn't hear an objection, it would make it hard to know what points to sell to. You know how to sell to the person because he or she tells you—if you take the time to listen.

One of my managers once told me, "Renee, objections are inevitable, but it is how you handle them that counts. The best salespeople are the ones you can look at from across the room and never know if they are talking business or just carrying on a conversation. They keep the same pleasant demeanor whether they are handling an objection, talking about their kids, dealing with a rude customer, or closing the biggest sale of their career!"

Take the time to listen, be engaging, and don't take objections personally, as objections are your key to uncovering the prospect's real need. If you can uncover it, they will love you and love to buy from you!

Visit our Web site at:
www.jnj.com

THE GOAL IS TO BUILD RELATIONSHIPS AND SELL VALUE

An **objection** is a concern or a question raised by the buyer. Salespeople should do everything they can to encourage buyers to voice concerns or questions. The worst type of objection is the one the buyer refuses to disclose because a hidden objection cannot be dealt with. Many sales have been lost because salespeople didn't find out the objections or didn't helpfully respond to them.

Salespeople should keep in mind that the goal with regard to objections is the same as with every other part of the sales call: to sell real value to the buyer. Having a positive attitude about objections is paramount in this regard. Proper attitude is shown by answering sincerely, refraining from arguing or contradicting, and welcoming—even inviting—objections. Objections should be expected and never taken personally.

Simply pretending to be empathetic is useless; buyers can easily see through such pretense. Also, once the buyer gets the idea that the salesperson is talking for effect, regaining that buyer's confidence and respect will be almost impossible. Empathy shows as much in the tone of voice and facial expressions as in the actual words spoken.

The greatest evidence of sincerity comes from the salesperson's actions. One successful advertising agency owner states, "I have always tried to sit on the same side of the table as my clients, to see problems through their eyes." Buyers want valid objections to be treated seriously; they want their ideas to be respected, not belittled. They look for empathetic understanding of their problems. Real objections are logical to the prospect regardless of how irrational they may appear to the salesperson. Salespeople must assume the attitude of helper, counselor, and advisor and act accordingly. To do so, they must treat the prospect as a friend, not a foe. In fact, buyers will feel more comfortable about raising objections and will be much more honest the more they trust the salesperson, the better the rapport, and the stronger the partnering relationship.

The reality is that salespeople run into more rejection in a day than most people have to absorb in weeks or months. Because of the emotional strain, many see selling as a tough way to make a living. However, salespeople must remember that objections present sales opportunities. People who object have at least some level of interest in what the salesperson is saying. Further, objections provide feedback about what is really on the prospect's mind. Only when this openness exists can a true partnering relationship form. This attitude shows in remarks such as the following:

I can see just what you mean. I'd probably feel the same way.

That's a great question!

If I were purchasing this product, I'd want an answer to that same question.

WHEN DO BUYERS RAISE OBJECTIONS?

Salespeople can expect to hear objections at any time during the buyer–seller relationship (see Chapter 3 for a review of the buying process). Objections are raised when the salesperson attempts to secure an appointment, during the approach, during the presentation, when the salesperson attempts to obtain commitment, and during the after-sale follow-up. Objections can also be made during formal negotiation sessions (see Chapter 12).

SETTING UP AN INITIAL APPOINTMENT

Prospects may object to setting the appointment times or dates that salespeople request to introduce the product. This type of objection happens especially when products, services, or concepts are unfamiliar to the buyer. For example, a commercial benefits salesperson for CLS Partners might hear the buyer make the following statement when asked to meet and learn more about a cafeteria-style benefits package: "No, I don't need to see you. I've not heard many good things about the use of cafeteria-style packages for dental products. Most employees just get confused!"

THE PRESENTATION

Buyers can offer objections during the beginning of the presentation (see Chapter 8). They may not like or believe the salesperson's attention-getting opening statement. They may not wish to engage in small talk or may not agree with statements made by the seller attempting to build rapport. Buyers may object to the salesperson's stated goals for the meeting.

Objections often come up to points made in the presentation. For example, a computer disaster recovery salesperson for Rackspace Hosting might hear this objection: "We've never lost a lot of computer data files before! Why should I pay so much money for a service I may never use?"

Such objections usually show the prospect's interest in the topic; thus, they can actually be desirable. Compared to a prospect who just says, "No thanks," and never raises his or her concerns, selling is easier when buyers voice their concerns because the salesperson knows where the buyers stand and that they are paying attention.

ATTEMPTING TO OBTAIN COMMITMENT

Objections may be voiced when the salesperson attempts to obtain commitment. For example, an AK Steel salesperson who has just asked the buyer's permission to talk to the buyer's chief engineer may hear this objection: "No, I don't want you talking to our engineers. My job is to keep vendors from bugging our employees."

Skill in uncovering and responding to objections is very important at this stage of the sales call. Also, knowing the objections that are likely to occur helps the salesperson prepare supporting documentation (letters of reference, copies of studies, and so on).

Salespeople who hear many objections at this point in the sales call probably need to further develop their skills. An excessive number of objections while obtaining commitment may indicate a poor job of needs identification and the omission of significant selling points in the presentation. It may also reveal ineffective probing during the presentation to see whether the buyer understands or has any questions about what is being discussed.

AFTER THE SALE

Even buyers who have agreed to purchase the product or service can still raise objections. During the installation, for example, the buyer may raise concerns about the time it is taking to install the equipment, the quality of the product or service, the customer service department's lack of friendliness, or the credit department's refusal to grant the terms the salesperson promised. To develop long-term relationships and partnerships with buyers, salespeople must carefully respond to these objections. After-sale service is more fully discussed in Chapter 14.

COMMON OBJECTIONS

Prospects raise many types of objections. Although listing every objection is impossible, this section attempts to outline the most common buyer objections.[1]

It should be noted that some buyers like to raise objections just to watch salespeople squirm uncomfortably. (Fortunately, most buyers aren't like that!) Seasoned buyers, especially, sometimes like to make life difficult for sellers—particularly for young, nervous sellers. For example, Peggy, a manufacturer's salesperson for Walker Muffler, used to call on a large auto parts store in an attempt to have the store carry her line of mufflers. Jackie, the store's buyer, gave Peggy a tough time on her first two calls. At the end of her second call, Peggy was so frustrated with the way she was being treated that she decided never to call there again. However, as she was walking out of the store, she ran into a Goodyear rep who also called on Jackie to sell belts and hoses. Because the two salespeople were on somewhat friendly terms, Peggy admitted her frustrations to the Goodyear rep. He replied, "Oh, that's just the way Jackie operates. On the third call he is always a nice guy. Just wait and see." Sure enough, Peggy's next call on Jackie was not only pleasant but also productive! Buyers like Jackie usually just want to see the sales rep work hard for the order.

The following sections examine the five major types of objections (objections related to needs, product, source, price, and time), which are summarized in Exhibit 10.1, as well as several other objections that salespeople sometimes hear.

OBJECTIONS RELATED TO NEEDS

I Do Not Need the Product or Service

A prospect may validly state that the company has no need for what the salesperson is selling. A manufacturer that operates on a small scale, for example, may have no use for expensive machinery designed to handle large volumes of work. Similarly, a salesperson who is selling an accounts receivable collection service will find that a retailer that sells for cash does not require a collection service.

Salespeople may encounter such objections as "My business is different" or "I have no use for your service." These objections, when made by an accurately qualified buyer, show that the buyer is not convinced that a need exists. This problem could have been prevented with better implication and need payoff questions (see Chapter 8).

If the salesperson cannot establish a need in the buyer's mind, that buyer can logically be expected to object. In **pioneer selling**—selling a new and different product, service, or idea—the salesperson has more difficulty establishing a need in the buyer's mind. For example, salespeople for Alken-Murray often hear "I don't think we need it" when the buyer is asked to carry a line of biodegradable citrus degreasers.

I've Never Done It That Way Before

Most human beings are creatures of habit. Once they develop a routine or establish a custom, they tend to resist change. Fear of a new product's failure may be the basis for not wanting to try anything new or different. For example, Target Corporation's buyers are evaluated annually on the products they choose to buy, including such metrics as sales results, gross margins, and guest experience surveys.

Habits and customs also help to insulate the prospect from social risks to some degree. For example, suppose you are selling a new

Exhibit 10.1
Five Major Types of Objections

Objections Related to Needs
I do not need the product or service.
I've never done it that way before.

Objections Related to the Product
I don't like the product or service features.
I don't understand.
I need more information.

Objections Related to the Source
I don't like your company.
I don't like you.

Objections Related to the Price
I have no money.
The value does not exceed the cost.

Objections Related to Time
I'm just not interested today.
I need time to think about it.

line of marine engines to Newton, a newly promoted assistant buyer. If Jane, the previous assistant buyer and now the senior buyer, bought your competitor's product, Newton would appear to take less risk by continuing to buy from your competitor. If Newton buys from you, Jane may think, "I've been doing business with the other firm for 15 years. Now, Newton, you come in here and tell me I've been doing it wrong all these years? I'm not sure you're going to be a good assistant buyer."

OBJECTIONS RELATED TO THE PRODUCT

I Don't Like the Product or Service Features

Often the product or service has features that do not satisfy the buyer. At other times the prospect will request features currently not available. Customers may say things like these: It doesn't taste good to me! I was looking for a lighter shade of red. It took a month for us to receive our last order.

This buyer doesn't understand what the seller is saying.

I Don't Understand

Sometimes objections arise because customers do not understand the salesperson's presentation. Because these objections may never be verbalized, the seller must carefully observe the buyer's nonverbal cues. (See Chapter 4 for a discussion of nonverbal communication.) Misunderstandings frequently occur with customers who are unfamiliar with technical terms, unaware of the unique capabilities of a product, or uncertain about benefits arising from services provided with the product, such as warranties. Unfortunately buyers often will not admit that they do not understand something.

I Need More Information

Some buyers offer objections in an attempt to get more information. They may have already decided that they want the product or service but wish to fortify themselves with logical reasons they can use to justify the purchase to others. Also, the salesperson may not have provided enough credible proof about a particular benefit.

Conflict may also exist in the buyer's mind. One conflict could be a struggle taking place between the dictates of emotion and reason. Or the buyer may be concerned about the risk, and the seller hasn't sufficiently sold value. The buyer may be trying to decide between two competitive products or between buying and not buying. Whatever the struggle, buyers who object to get more information are usually interested, and the possibility of obtaining commitment is good.

OBJECTIONS RELATED TO THE SOURCE

I Don't Like Your Company

Most buyers, especially industrial buyers, are interested in the sales representative's company because the buyer is put at risk if the seller's firm is not financially sound, cannot continually produce the product, and so forth. These buyers need to be satisfied with the selling company's financial standing, personnel, and business policies. Buyers may ask questions such as these: How do I know you'll be in business next year? Your company isn't very well known, is it? Why does your company have a bad image in the industry?

Of course buyers who don't want to be rude may not actually voice these concerns. But unvoiced questions about the sales rep's company may affect their decisions and the long-term partnerships the sales rep is trying to establish.

I Don't Like You

Sometimes a salesperson's personality clashes with a prospect's. Effective salespeople know they must do everything possible to adjust their manner to please the prospect. At times, however, doing business with some people appears impossible.

Prospects may object to a presentation or an appointment because they have taken a dislike to the salesperson or because they feel they cannot trust the salesperson. Candid prospects may say, "You seem too young to be selling these. You've never worked in my industry, so how can you be trained to know what I need?" More commonly, the prospect shields the real reason and says, "We don't need any."

In some situations, the buyer may honestly have difficulty dealing with a particular salesperson. If the concern is real (not just an excuse), the seller's firm sometimes institutes a **turnover** (**TO**), which simply means the account is given to a different salesperson. Unfortunately, TOs occasionally occur because the buyer has gender, racial, or other prejudices or because the salesperson is failing to practice adaptive selling behaviors.

ethics

thinking it through

Assume that you have worked as a salesperson for an industrial chemical firm for six months. You have attended a two-week basic selling skills course but have not yet attended any product knowledge training classes. You are making a sales call with your sales manager. The buyer says, "Gee, you look too young to be selling chemicals. Do you have a chemistry degree?" Before you get a chance to respond, your manager says, "Oh, he [*meaning you*] has already completed our one-month intensive product knowledge course. I guarantee he knows it all!" What would you say or do? What would you do if the buyer later asked you a technical question?

OBJECTIONS RELATED TO THE PRICE

I Have No Money

Companies that lack the resources to buy the product may have been misclassified as prospects. As indicated in Chapter 6, the ability to pay is an important factor in lead qualification. An incomplete or poor job of qualifying may cause this objection to arise.

When leads say they cannot afford a product, they may have a valid objection. If so, the salesperson should not waste time; new prospects should be contacted.

The Value Does Not Exceed the Cost

Buyers usually object until they are sure that the value of the product or service being acquired more than offsets the sacrifice. Exhibit 10.2 illustrates this concept. The question of value received often underlies customers' objections.

Whatever the price of a product or service, somebody will object that it is too high or out of line with the competition. Here are some other common price objections: I can beat your price on these items. We can't make a reasonable profit if we have to pay that much for the merchandise. I'm going to wait for prices to come down.

A more complete discussion of dealing with price objections appears later in this chapter. Implicit in many price objections is the notion of product or service

Exhibit 10.2
Value: The Relationship between Costs and Benefits

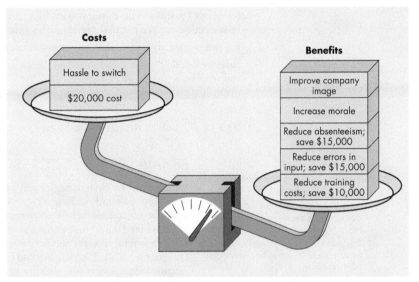

Note: If costs outweigh benefits, the decision will be not to buy. If benefits outweigh costs, the decision will be to buy.

quality. Thus, the buyer who states that your price is too high may actually be thinking, "The quality is too low for such a high price."

OBJECTIONS RELATED TO TIME

I'm Just Not Interested Today

Some prospects voice objections simply to dismiss the salesperson. The prospect may not have enough time to devote to the interview, may not be interested in the particular product or service, may not be in the mood to listen, or may have decided because of some unhappy experiences not to face further unpleasant interviews.

These objections occur when salespeople are cold calling (see Chapter 6) or trying to make an appointment. Particularly aggressive, rude, impolite, or pesky salespeople can expect prospects to use numerous excuses to keep from listening to a presentation.

I Need Time to Think about It

Buyers often object to making a decision "now."[2] Many, in fact, believe that postponing an action is an effective way to say no. Salespeople can expect to hear objections such as the following, especially from analyticals and amiables (see Chapter 5): I haven't made up my mind. I'd like to talk it over with my partner. Just leave me your literature; I'll study it and then let you know what we decide.

OTHER OBJECTIONS

Listing every possible objection that could occur under any situation would be impossible. However, following are a number of additional objections that salespeople often hear:

We have no room for your line.

There is no demand for your product.

Sorry, but I just don't do business with people of [your gender or your race or your ethnicity or your sexual preference or your religion and so forth].

I've heard from my friends that your insurance company isn't the best one to use.

Sure, we can do business. But I need a little kickback to make it worth my time and trouble.

I believe we might be able to do business if you are willing to start seeing me socially.

It's a lot of hassle in paperwork and time to switch suppliers.

Exhibit 10.3

Responding to Objections: Behaviors of Successful Salespeople

> They anticipate objections and prepare helpful responses.
>
> They address known problems before the prospect does; that is, they forestall known concerns.
>
> They relax and listen and never interrupt the buyer.
>
> They make sure that the objection is not just an excuse.
>
> They always tell the truth.

BEHAVIORS OF SUCCESSFUL SALESPEOPLE

With regard to objections, successful salespeople anticipate objections and forestall known concerns, listen without interrupting, evaluate objections before answering, and always tell the truth (see Exhibit 10.3).[3] Responding to objections in a helpful manner requires careful thought and preparation. Some trainers suggest that salespeople use the **LAARC Method** to respond to objections: Listen, Acknowledge, Assess (the validity of the objection), Respond, and Confirm (that the objection has been answered).[4]

ANTICIPATE OBJECTIONS

Salespeople must know that at some time, objections will be made to almost everything concerning their products, their companies, or themselves. Common sense dictates that they prepare helpful, honest answers to objections that are certain to be raised, as "From the Buyer's Seat 10.1" describes.

Many companies draw up lists of common objections and helpful answers and encourage salespeople to become familiar with these lists. Most firms also videotape practice role plays to help salespeople become more proficient in anticipating objections and responding effectively in each situation. Successful sales representatives may keep a notebook and record new objections they encounter.

FORESTALL KNOWN CONCERNS

Good salespeople, after a period of experience and training, know that certain features of their products or services are vulnerable, are likely to be misunderstood, or are materially different from competitors' products. The salesperson may have products with limited features, may have to quote a price that seems high, may be unable to offer cash discounts, may have no service representatives in the immediate area, or may represent a new company in the field.

In these situations, salespeople often forestall the objection. To **forestall** is to prevent by doing something ahead of time. In selling, this means salespeople raise objections before buyers have a chance to raise them. For example, one salesperson forestalled a concern about the different "feel" of a split computer keyboard (the ones that are split down the middle to relieve stress and strain on the hands and wrists):

> I know you'll find the feel to be different from your old keyboard. You're going to like that, though, because your hands won't get as tired. In almost every split keyboard I've sold, typists have taken only one day to get accustomed to the new feel, and then they swear that they would never go back to their old-fashioned keyboards again!

From the BUYER'S SEAT

10.1

THAT TASTES PRETTY AWFUL!

Being part of a buying team for Cub Food Stores, I've heard lots of presentations and offered plenty of objections. Due to the fact that how much someone likes a food product is based solely on their personal preferences, you can have some people who absolutely love the product, while others think it is the worst possible thing in the world, sometimes saying they would never even feed it to their dog.

If I were a salesperson, the first thing I would do is to know as many possible objections as people might have to my food product. Some of the most common objections that salespeople face when pitching a product to us are the following:

- Too spicy.
- It doesn't seem to have as much flavor as some of the comparable products that we already carry.
- Too salty.
- We are trying to get healthier options in our stores due to the growing health-conscious trend in our society.

- We have a strict profit margin that we stick to with all products, and yours isn't good enough.

Offering samples to all those involved in the buying process is a great way for salespeople to allow everyone to get their own opinion and discuss it amongst themselves. However, salespeople can actually create objections if they are unable to prep their samples effectively. If a product is supposed to be served hot and crispy and salespeople arrive with them premade in something to keep them warm, a lot of times they tend to become soggy and ultimately undesirable. Instead of having a salesperson say, "I'm sorry! The product is actually supposed to be hot and crispy, not soggy and barely warm, but this is the best I can do!" the salesperson can simply get in contact with us beforehand and find out that we have all of the appliances needed to prep the product in our office on arrival.

Source: Kathleen Griffin, Cub Foods; all names changes to protect anonymity; used with permission.

A salesperson might bring up a potential price concern by saying, "You know, other buyers have been concerned that this product is expensive. Well, let me show you how little it will really cost you to get the best."

Some salespeople do such a good job of forestalling that buyers change their minds without ever going on record as objecting to the feature and then having to reverse themselves.[5] Buyers are more willing to change their thinking when they do not feel constrained to defend a position they have already stated. Although not all objections can be preempted, the major ones can be spotted and forestalled during the presentation. Forestalling can be even more important in written proposals (see Chapter 9) because immediate feedback between buyer and seller is not possible. Such forestalled objections can be addressed throughout the proposal. For example, on the page describing delivery terms, the seller could insert a paragraph that begins this way: "You may be wondering how we can promise an eight-day delivery even though we have such a small production capacity. Actually, we are able to . . . because. . . ." Another option for forestalling objections in written proposals is to have a separate page or section titled something like "Concerns You May Have with This Proposal." The section could then list the potential concerns and provide responses to them.

This person is listening carefully.

RELAX AND LISTEN—DO NOT INTERRUPT

When responding to an objection, listen first and then answer the objection. Allow the prospect to state a position completely. A wise man said, "He that answereth a matter before he heareth it, it is folly and shame unto him."[6]

Do not interrupt with an answer, even if the objection to be stated is already apparent to you. Listen as though you have never heard that objection before.

Unfortunately too many salespeople conduct conversations somewhat like the following:

SALESPERSON: Mr. Clark, from a survey of your operations, I'm convinced you're now spending more money repairing your own motors than you would by having us do the job for you—and really do it right!

CUSTOMER: We're probably doing it fine right now. Now, I'm sure your repair service is good, but you don't have to be exactly an electrical genius to be able to...

SALESPERSON: Hang on! It isn't a matter of anyone being a genius. It's a matter of having a heavy investment in special motor repair equipment and supplies like vacuum impregnating tanks and lathes for banding armatures, boring bearings, and turning new shafts.

CUSTOMER: Yeah I know all that, but you missed my point. See, what I'm driving at...

SALESPERSON: I know what you're driving at, but you're wrong! You forget that even if your own workers are smart cookies, they just can't do high-quality work without a lot of special equipment.

CUSTOMER: But you still don't get my point! The maintenance workers that we now have doing motor repair work...

SALESPERSON: Could more profitably spend their time on plant trouble-shooting! Right?

CUSTOMER: That isn't what I was going to say! I was trying to say that between their troubleshooting jobs, instead of just sitting around and shooting the bull...

SALESPERSON: Now wait a minute, Mr. Clark. If you think that a good motor rewinding job can be done in someone's spare time, you're wrong!

Obviously attitudes and interruptions like these are likely to bring the interview to a quick end.

Salespeople should plan to relax as buyers offer objections. It's even OK to plan on using humor in your answers to objections. For example, if the buyer objects to the standard payments and asks how low your company could go, you could respond as follows: "Well, if I could get the bank to send you money each month, would you buy it?"

After laughing, the seller could talk about the various payment options. Using humor, as in this example, may help defuse the nervousness that both buyer and seller are feeling during this part of the process. For more insight into the use of humor, see Chapter 4.

What if the buyer asks a question for which you've already covered the material? Don't say, "I've already covered that!" Instead let the buyer finish asking the question and then answer the question with enthusiasm.

EVALUATE OBJECTIONS

To truly sell value and establish a relationship, the seller must evaluate objections before answering.[7] Objections may be classified as unsatisfied needs (that is, real objections) or excuses. **Excuses** are concerns expressed by the buyer that mask the buyer's true objections. Thus, the comment "I can't afford it now" would simply be an excuse if the buyer honestly could afford it now but did not want to buy for some other reason.

A buyer seldom says, "I don't have any reason. I just don't want to buy." More commonly the buyer gives a reason that appears at first to be a real objection but is really an excuse: "I don't have the money" or "I can't use your product." The tone of voice or the nature of the reason may provide evidence that the prospect is not offering a sincere objection.

Salespeople need to develop skill in evaluating objections. No exact formula has been devised to separate excuses from real objections. Sometimes it is best to follow up with a question:

BUYER: I just wish your company sold the full range of insurance products, you know, things like variable annuities.

SELLER: If we did offer variable annuities, would you be interested in having all of your insurance needs met by me?

If the buyer says yes, you know the concern is real. If the buyer says no, you know the buyer is just offering the objection about annuities as an excuse.

Circumstances can also provide a clue to whether an objection is a valid concern. In cold calling, when the prospect says, "I'm sorry, I don't have any money," the salesperson may conclude that the prospect does not want to hear the presentation. However, the same reason offered after a complete presentation has been made and data on the prospect have been gathered through observation and questioning may be valid. Salespeople must rely on observation, questioning, knowledge about why people buy (see Chapter 3), and experience to determine the validity of reasons offered for objections.

ALWAYS TELL THE TRUTH

In dealing with prospects and customers, truthfulness is an absolute necessity for dignity, confidence, and relationship development. Recall that our purpose is not to manipulate but to persuade so that the buyer can make the most effective decision. Lying and deception are not part of a successful long-term relationship. Over time it will be hard to remember which lie you told to which customer. Salespeople should avoid even white lies and half-truths when they answer objections.

ethics

Salespeople who tell lies, even small ones, need to recognize they have a problem and then find ways to change. One way to avoid lies is to spend more time gaining knowledge about their products and the products of their competitors. Sellers who do so aren't as tempted to lie to cover up the fact that they don't know some information requested by the prospect. Sellers also should commit to tell the truth, even if competitors don't follow suit. It is simply the right thing to do.

EFFECTIVE RESPONSE METHODS

Any discussion of specific methods for responding to objections needs to emphasize that no perfect method exists for answering all objections completely. Some prospects, no matter what you do, will never believe their objections have been adequately addressed.

In some instances, spending a lot of time trying to convince the prospect may not be wise. For example, when an industrial recycling salesperson contacts a prospect who says, "I don't believe in recycling," the salesperson may better spend available time calling on some of the vast number of people who do.

This section describes seven common methods for responding to objections. As Exhibit 10.4 indicates, the first two, direct denial and indirect denial, are used only when the prospect makes an untrue statement. The next five methods— compensation, referral, revisiting, acknowledgment, and postponement—are useful when the buyer raises a valid point or offers an opinion.

Before using the methods described in this section, salespeople almost always need to probe to help the prospect clarify concerns and to make sure they understand the objection. This method is often called the **probing method.** If the prospect says, "Your service is not too good," the salesperson can probe by saying, "I'm not sure I understand," or by asking a question. For example, the seller could ask one or more of the following: Not too good? What do you mean by not too good? Exactly what service are you referring to? Is service very important to you? Can you explain what you mean?

While this probing is usually verbal, it can also include nonverbal probing. For example, Professor Donoho at Northern Arizona University teaches a method called the **friendly silent questioning stare (FSQS)** to encourage buyers to elaborate or explain more fully what their concerns are.

Many serious blunders have occurred because a salesperson did not understand a question, answered the wrong question, or failed to answer an objection fully. For example, a sales training manager was listening to a representative for a consulting firm talk about her services. At one point in the conversation,

Exhibit 10.4
Common Methods for Responding to Objections

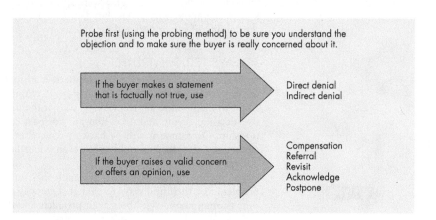

the manager asked, "Has anyone in the electrical products industry ever used this training package before?" The consultant answered, "Sure, we have sold this package to several firms. Why, just last week I received a nice letter from Colgate that had nothing but good things to say...." The manager did not buy the training package; he figured that if the consultant did not even know how to listen, the sales training package she was selling could not be very good either. (Chapter 4 provides many helpful suggestions regarding the art of questioning and probing.)

A salesperson who doesn't know the answer to the buyer's objection might say, "I don't know the answer to that question. But I'll find out and get the answer to you." The seller should paraphrase the buyer's question, write it down (this step helps jog the seller's memory as well as demonstrate to the buyer that the seller really intends to follow up), gather the information, and follow up quickly and exactly as promised. If you call the customer with the information and he or she is not available, leave the information on voice mail and then call later to verify that the prospect got the information. And don't forget that it is your responsibility to know most facts, so be prepared the next time for similar and additional questions and concerns. You can be sure your competitor is going to try to have complete answers ready.

thinking **it** through

How can the use of technology (such as databases, computers, and communication technology) help prevent a seller from having to answer, "I don't know the answer to that question. But I'll find out and call you with the information as soon as I can get it"?

DIRECT DENIAL

At times salespeople face objections based on incomplete or inaccurate information of the buyer. They should respond by providing information or correcting facts. When using **direct denial,** the salesperson makes a relatively strong statement to indicate the error the prospect has made. For example:

> BUYER: I am not interested in hearing about your guidance systems. Your firm was one of the companies recently indicted for fraud, conspiracy, and price fixing by a federal grand jury. I don't want to do business with such a firm.

> SALESPERSON: I'm not sure where you heard that, but it simply is not true. Our firm has never been involved in such activity, and our record is clean. If you would care to tell me the source of your information, I'm sure we can clear this up. Maybe you're confusing us with another firm.

No one likes to be told that he or she is wrong, so direct denial must be used with caution. It is appropriate only when the objection is blatantly inaccurate and potentially devastating to the presentation. The salesperson must also possess facts to back up such a denial. Direct denial should never be used if the prospect is merely stating an opinion or if the objection is true. For example, direct denial would be inappropriate to this objection: "I don't like the feel of simulated leather products." Direct denial should be avoided even for a false statement if the objection is of little importance to the buyer. An indirect denial would be more appropriate in that case.

INDIRECT DENIAL

In the **indirect denial method,** the salesperson denies the objection but attempts to soften the response. The salesperson takes the edge off the response by agreeing with the prospect that the objection is an important one. Prospects expect salespeople to disagree; instead, a salesperson who recognizes the sincerity of the objection will carefully respect the prospect's view. This approach avoids a direct contradiction and confrontation. To begin an answer, a salesperson would do well to agree with the prospect, but only to the extent that the agreement does not weaken the validity of the salesperson's later denial. For example:

> BUYER: Your machines break down more often than those of most of your major competitors.
>
> SALESPERSON: I can see why you might feel that way. Just 10 years ago that statement would have been right on target. However, things have changed with our new quality assurance program. In fact, just last year Syncos Ratings, a well-respected independent evaluator of quality in our industry, rated us as number one for fewest breakdowns.

The important features of indirect denial are that salespeople recognize the position of the customer who makes the objection and then continue by introducing substantial evidence. The beginning statement should always be true and assure the prospect that the question is a good one. Examples of such statements follow:

With the market the way it is today, I can certainly see why you're concerned about that.

I'll bet 90 percent of the people I call on voice the same concern.

That's really an excellent question, and it allows me to clear up a misconception that perhaps I've given you.

Indirect denial should never be used if the prospect has raised a valid point or is merely expressing an opinion. It can be used for all personality types and is especially effective for amiables and analyticals because they like less assertive salespeople.

COMPENSATION METHOD

Every product has some advantages and some disadvantages compared to competing products. Also, an absolutely perfect product or service has never been developed; the firm always has to make cost–benefit decisions about what features to include.

Buyers note these trade-offs and often object because the salesperson's product is less than perfect. The wise salesperson will admit that such objections are valid and then proceed to show any compensating advantages. This approach is called the **compensation method** of responding to objections. Here is an example:

> PROSPECT: This machine has only four filling nozzles. Your competitor's has six nozzles.
>
> SALESPERSON: You're absolutely right. It has only four nozzles, but it costs $4,000 less than the competitor's models, and you said you needed a model that is priced in the lower range. Also, our nozzles are designed for easy maintenance. You have to remove only four screws to get to the filter screens. Most other models have at least 10 screws.

PREPARE FOR OBJECTIONS USING THE INTERNET

Objections can be very hard to overcome during a sales presentation if they are not prepared for. Sitting down and thinking about what objections a buyer may have about your product or service can lead to many possible objections, but there is a strong chance that you will have a bias toward your product and may miss certain things that may come up from a different point of view. With that being said, potential objections need to come from third parties as well.

For example, you are attempting to sell a new line of televisions to Target Corporation for them to sell in their stores. While they are not currently carrying your product, they do carry a wide variety of televisions. By searching their current products, you can now find a product that is comparable to the one that you are going to be presenting to their buyers. Once you find that comparable line, by simply clicking on the product, you will be able to find reviews that customers have posted. Some reviews will be positive and might very well help you discover points that the buyer will bring up in the sales call. If you know some of the specific product strengths that Target's current products have in the

eye of the consumer, you can take these and emphasize the fact that your product will do the same thing for their customers.

You can also read reviews to learn what consumers dislike about the current products carried by the prospect. This information can help you determine the features you will discuss when objections arise (by indicating that your product also provides features that the current products do not).

Technology is growing at such a rapid pace that new, updated information is constantly available to anyone who has access to the Internet. By putting in the time and effort to do some background research on current product offerings of a company, you will find where their offerings are lacking and your product can help them but also where their products are excelling and know how to present your product in a way that will help you overcome the objection of "my current products have these features that my customers really like." This information can aid you in using the compensation method of responding to objections.

The compensation method is an explicit use of the multiattribute model discussed in Chapter 3. A low score on one attribute can be compensated for by a high score on another attribute. In fact, the compensation method is often referred to as the **superior benefit method** because the benefit of one attribute overcomes a concern about a less important attribute. The method can be effective for many objections and concerns. It seems most appropriate for analyticals, who are accustomed to conducting trade-off analyses. However, it is useful for all other personality types as well. "Sales Technology 10.1" describes how to use the Internet to help gather information that will be useful with this method.

Of course the buyer may not value the compensating advantages. The buyer may really need the features at issue (perhaps the machine must have six nozzles to work with another piece of the prospect's equipment). In such cases salespeople can recommend a different product (from their own line, if available, or from a competitor) or search for other prospects.

Another time that the compensation method may be used is when the prospect says, "I'm just going to think about it. I'll be in touch with you later." The seller can show how acting today more than compensates for the "pain" of making a decision today. These reasons usually include explaining the hidden costs of delaying the decision (it will go off sale, you will be saving money over your current system each month that you have our proposed system, our product may be out of stock when you need it, summer is a particularly good time to install a new system, or the like).

REFERRAL METHOD

A buyer may question the credibility and knowledge of a salesperson. In this situation the salesperson can use the referral method to help resolve those concerns.

When buyers' objections reflect their own attitudes or opinions, the salesperson can show how others held similar views before trying the product or service. In this method, called the **referral method** or the **feel–felt–found method**, the salesperson goes on to relate that others actually found their initial opinions to be unfounded after they tried the product:

PROSPECT: I don't think my customers will want to buy a DVD player with all these fancy features.

SALESPERSON: I can certainly see how you feel. Bob Scott, down the road in Houston, felt the same way when I first proposed that he sell these. However, after he agreed to display them next to his current DVD line, he found that his customers were very interested. In fact, he called me four days later to order more.

Those who teach this as the feel–felt–found method highlight the importance of the proper sequence, as well as the person or people identified in each stage. The sequence should be as follows: I can see how *you* feel . . . *others* felt the same way . . . yet *they* found. . . . Inexperienced salespeople often mix up the order or the parties identified (for example, by saying ". . . yet you will find").

Proof of the salesperson's assertion in the form of a testimonial letter strengthens the method; in fact, some trainers refer to this approach as the **third-party-testimony method.** If a letter is not available, the salesperson might be able to supply the name and phone number of the third party. The salesperson should always secure the third party's permission first, however. (See Chapter 9 for suggestions about testimonials and references.)

Although the referral method can be used for all personality types, it seems most appropriate for expressives and amiables. Both types tend to care about what other people think and are doing.

REVISIT METHOD

When using the **revisit method** (also called the **boomerang method**) of responding to objections, the salesperson turns the objection into a reason for buying the product or service. This method can be used in many situations (when making an appointment, during the presentation, when attempting to secure commitment, and in postsale situations):

BUYER: I don't think these would sell in my gun shop. They're really drab looking.

SALESPERSON: It's interesting that you mention that. In fact, their drab color is probably their best selling point and the reason you should carry them. You see, when a hunter is in the field, the last thing she wants to do is attract attention to herself. Thanks to the finish we use on this gear . . .

The revisit method requires care. It can appear very pushy and "salesy." This method does have useful applications, however. Often the product or service is actually designed to save the buyer substantial amounts of time or money. If the buyer objects to spending either the time to listen or the money, the revisit method may be a powerful tool to help the buyer see the benefit of investing these resources.

This method works with most personality types. Drivers may require the revisit method more often than other buyers because drivers tend to erect time constraints and other barriers and are less willing to listen to just any salesperson's presentation.

ACKNOWLEDGE METHOD

At times the buyer voices opinions or concerns more to vent frustration than anything else. When this occurs, the best strategy may be to use the **acknowledge method**, also called the **pass-up method**. Simply let the buyer talk, acknowledge that you heard the concern, pause, and then move on to another topic.

> BUYER: Hey, you use Beyoncé in your commercials, don't you? Sure you do. Now I want to tell you that I don't like what she stands for! Kids today need a role model they can look up to. What happened to the kind of role models we used to have?
>
> SALESPERSON: I certainly understand your concern. I remember my dad talking about some of his role models and the respect he had for them. [*Pause*] What were we talking about? Oh, yes, I was telling you about the coupon drop we are planning.

In this example the salesperson used the acknowledge method because the buyer apparently was just blowing off steam. A buyer who really wanted some response from the salesperson would have used the salesperson's pause to ask a direct question (Can't you change your commercials?) or make a statement (I refuse to do business with companies that use stars like Beyoncé in their commercials!).

In reality a salesperson often can do little about some prospects' opinions. What are the chances that this salesperson's firm will pull a $5 million ad campaign because one buyer objects? It is doubtful that a firm would take such action unless the buyer had tremendous power in the relationship.

Sometimes the salesperson can use the acknowledge method by simply agreeing with the prospect and then moving on, which suggests to the buyer that the concern really should not be much of an issue. For example:

> BUYER: You want $25 for this little plastic bottle?!
>
> SELLER: Uh-huh. That's what they cost...[*Pause*] Now do you see the switch on this side? It's used if you ever need to...

The acknowledge method should not be used if the objection raised is factually false. Also, it should not be used if the salesperson, through probing, could help clarify the buyer's thinking on the topic. Experience is the key to making such a determination. In general, though, the acknowledge method should be used sparingly.

POSTPONE METHOD

In the early part of a sales interview, the prospect may raise objections that the salesperson would prefer to answer later in the presentation, after discovering the prospect's needs. Using the **postpone method,** the salesperson would ask permission to answer the question at a later time:

> BUYER [*very early in the call*]: How much does the brass engraving equipment cost?
>
> SALESPERSON: If you don't mind, I would prefer to answer that question in a few minutes. I really can't tell you how much it will cost until I learn more about your engraving needs and know what kinds of features you are looking for.

The prospect will seldom refuse the request if the sales representative appears to be acting in good faith. The sales representative then proceeds with the presentation until the point at which the objection can best be answered.

Some objections are best answered when they occur; others can be responded to most effectively by delaying the answer. Experience should guide the sales representative. The salesperson should take care not to treat an objection lightly or let it appear that he or she does not want to answer the question. Another danger in postponing is that the buyer will be unable to focus on what the salesperson is saying until the concern is addressed. On the other hand, the salesperson is responsible for helping the buyer to critically evaluate the solution offered, and often the buyer can process information effectively only after learning preliminary facts.

Salespeople make the most use of the postponement method when a price objection occurs early in the presentation. However, this method can be used for almost any type of objection or question. For example, postponing discussions about guarantees, delivery schedules, implementation time frames, and certain unique product features until later in the presentation is often preferable.

What if the buyer is convinced that he or she needs the answer right now? Then the salesperson should answer the objection now. Salespeople usually have more to lose by demanding that the buyer wait for information than by simply providing the answer when the buyer strongly requests it. For example:

> PROSPECT: What are the delivery schedules for this new product?
>
> SALESPERSON: I would really prefer to discuss that after we talk about our unique production process and extensive quality control measures.
>
> PROSPECT: No, I want to know now!
>
> SALESPERSON: Well, keep in mind that my later discussion about the production process will shed new light on the topic. We anticipate a four- to five-month delivery time after the contract reaches our corporate headquarters.

USING THE METHODS

The seven methods just discussed appear in sales training courses across all industries and geographic boundaries. To help you more easily distinguish the differences among the various methods, Exhibit 10.5 provides an example of the use of each method for the objection, "Your product's quality is too low."

Salespeople often combine methods when answering an objection. For example, a price objection may initially be postponed and then be discussed later using

Exhibit 10.5
Responding to
Objections: Using
Each Method

> ### Objection: Your product's quality is too low.
>
> **Responses***
>
> **Direct denial:** That simply is not true. Our product has been rated as the highest in the industry for the last three years.
>
> **Indirect denial:** I can certainly see why you would be concerned about quality. Actually, though, our product quality has been rated as the highest in the industry for the last three years.
>
> **Compensation:** I agree that our quality is not as high as that of some of our competitors. However, it was designed that way for consumers who are looking for a lower-priced alternative, perhaps just to use in a weekend cottage. So you see, our somewhat lower quality is actually offset by our much lower price.
>
> **Referral:** I can certainly understand how you feel. Mortimer Jiggs felt the same way before he bought the product. But after using it, he found that the quality was actually equal to that of other products.
>
> **Revisit:** The fact that the quality is lower than in other products is probably the very reason you should buy it. You said that some of your customers are looking for a low-priced product to buy for their grandchildren. This product fills that need.
>
> **Acknowledge:** I understand your concern. You know, one of the things I always look for is how a product's quality stacks up against its cost. [Pause] Now, we were talking about . . .
>
> **Postpone:** That's an interesting point. Before discussing it fully, I would like to cover just two things that I think will help you better understand the product from a different perspective. OK?
>
> *These are not necessarily good answers to the stated objection. Also, the choice of method would depend on whether the objection is factual. Thus, the replies given here are designed simply to differentiate the various methods.

the compensation method. At other times several methods can be used in one answer. Here is an example:

BUYER: I don't think this product will last as long as some of the other, more expensive competitive products.

SALESPERSON: That's probably the very reason you should buy it [*revisit method*]. It may not last quite as long, but it is less than half the cost of competitive products [*compensation method*]. I can certainly understand your concern, though. You know, Mark Hancock felt the way you do. He was concerned about the product's life. But after he used our product for one year, he found that its life expectancy didn't create any problems for his production staff [*referral method*].

Sometimes the buyer will ask multiple questions at once—for example, "How much did you spend on R&D last year, what percentage of your revenue does that represent, and what is your R&D model going forward?" What is a seller to do? Remembering the questions so they don't get lost, the salesperson answers them one by one.

CONFIRMING THAT THE OBJECTION HAS BEEN ANSWERED

Before moving on with the presentation, the salesperson needs to make sure that the buyer agrees that all objections have been completely answered. Without

Make sure the buyer agrees before moving on.

this commitment, the salesperson does not know whether the buyer understands the answer or whether the buyer's concerns have been fully addressed. To achieve this commitment, the salesperson can use one or more of the following types of phrases: Did I answer your question? Does that make sense? Do you see why that issue is not as important as you originally thought? Did that resolve your concern?

OBJECTIONS WHEN SELLING TO A GROUP OF BUYERS

Selling to a group of buyers (see Chapter 8) requires some extra care. If one person offers an objection, the seller should try to get a sense of whether other buyers share the concern. At times it may make sense to throw the issue back to the group. For example, if a buyer says that the people in his or her department won't attend the type of training sessions being proposed, the seller might respond as follows: Does anyone else have that same problem in their department? You all know your organizational climate better than I do. Have any of you found a way to deal with that issue that you would like to share with us? Any response from the seller should usually be directed to all buyers, not just the one who asked the question. After responding, the seller needs to make sure that all buyers are satisfied with the answer before moving on.

THE PRICE OBJECTION

Price is the perhaps the most frequently mentioned obstacle to obtaining commitment, as "Building Partnerships 10.1" describes. In fact, about 20 percent of buyers are thought to buy purely on the basis of price (which means that a full 80 percent buy for reasons other than price). As a result, all salespeople need to prepare for price objections. This section relates the concepts covered in this chapter to this common objection.

Price is still an issue even between partnering firms. One leading firm in its industry has estimated that only 3 percent of its orders are sold at list price; the rest are price discounted.[8]

Unfortunately the first response of many salespeople to a price objection is to lower the price. Inexperienced salespeople, desiring to gain business, often quote the lowest possible price as quickly as possible. They forget that for a mutually beneficial long-term relationship to exist, their firm must make a fair profit. Also, by cutting prices the firm has to sell more to maintain profit margins, as Exhibit 10.6 clearly illustrates.

When faced with a price objection, salespeople should ensure that they have up-to-date information, establish the value of the product, and use communication tools effectively.

USE UP-TO-DATE INFORMATION

Successful salespeople make sure they have the most current pricing information available to them. They know not only their prices but competitors' prices as well. Firms are helping salespeople in this regard. For example, many firms have developed intranet sites for their salespeople. If a salesperson finds that the company's price points are a little higher than the competition, the salesperson can use the intranet site to look for some sales or trade-in program that she or he can leverage to get the deal. It is important for sellers to have correct pricing facts.

ESTABLISH THE VALUE

The product's value must be established before the salesperson spends time discussing price. The value expected determines the price a prospect is willing to pay. Unless

BUILDING Partnerships

10.1

OBJECTIONS CAN HELP YOU ASSESS YOUR SKILLS

The way we see it, objections tend to arise primarily when you have failed to adequately cover something in your presentation. If any of our salespeople are giving a sales presentation and at the end the buyer is still concerned with the fact that our product pricing may be higher than that of our competitors, this is a red flag that we have gone wrong somewhere in the presentation.

In such a large and developed industry as ours, pricing does not tend to vary too widely, and if we are much more expensive than our competitors, our salespeople need to reassess the situation and the product being offered. Many times, when there is a large disparity in price between the products we are attempting to sell and those which the competitor is selling to solve the same problem, either we are selling the wrong product or the competitor is. With that being said, prices between our products and comparable products that our competitors offer do not vary too widely, and therefore the price factor should have been completely eliminated in the decision-making process for our client throughout the sales presentation. We offer very high quality products that provide value to our clients. When the cost

objection arises at the end, it is crucial that our salespeople take a step back and try to figure out where they went wrong in demonstrating and communicating the value that the products and services we offer have.

Another objection that tends to be a tough one to overcome is that of "I am not sure how I feel about doing business with your company; I worked with so and so a few years back and had a terrible experience." In this situation, it is essential that salespeople emphasize that they are not the same person and that it would be an honor to correct the wrongdoings that they have had to deal with in the past and that we really are an outstanding company to do business with. At this point, the sales call regresses more toward that relationship-building stage as opposed to "get the sale and close the deal."

I'll end with one of my favorite quotes: "Everyone has a reason that they do not want to buy from you—as a salesperson, it is your job to give them the reasons that they need to buy from you."

Source: Kim Guay, AT&T; names changed to protect anonymity; used with permission.

the salesperson can build value to exceed the price asked, a sale will not occur.[9] As a rule, value cannot be established during the early stages of the presentation.

Price objections are best handled with a two-step approach. First, the salesperson should try to look at the objection from the customer's viewpoint, asking questions to clarify the customer's perspective: "Too high in what respect, Mr. Jones? Could you tell me how much we are out of line? We are usually quite competitive on this model, so I am surprised you find our price high.... Are the other quotes you have for the same size engine?"

After learning more about the customer's perspective, the next step is to sell value and quality rather than price (see Chapter 9 for a full discussion of the customer value proposition). Most customers prefer to buy less expensive products if they believe they will receive the same benefits. However, many customers will pay more for higher quality when the quality benefits and features are pointed out to them. Many high-quality products appear similar to lower-quality products; thus, salespeople need to emphasize the features that justify a difference.

For example, a salesperson who sells industrial fasteners and supplies may hear this objection: "That bolt costs $750! I could buy it elsewhere for $75." The salesperson should reply, "Yes, but that bolt is inside your most important piece of production equipment. Let's say you buy that $75 bolt. How much employee

Exhibit 10.6
Look before You Cut
Prices! You Must Sell
More to Break Even

Cut Price	Present Gross Profit					
	5.0%	10.0%	15.0%	20.0%	25.0%	30.0%
1%	25.0	11.1	7.1	5.3	4.2	3.4
2	66.6	25.0	15.4	11.1	8.7	7.1
3	150.0	42.8	25.0	17.6	13.6	11.1
4	400.0	66.6	36.4	25.0	19.0	15.4
5	—	100.0	50.0	33.3	25.0	20.0
6	—	150.0	66.7	42.9	31.6	25.0
7	—	233.3	87.5	53.8	38.9	30.4
8	—	400.0	114.3	66.7	47.1	36.4
9	—	1,000.0	150.0	81.8	56.3	42.9
10	—	—	200.0	100.0	66.7	50.0
11	—	—	275.0	122.2	78.6	57.9
12	—	—	400.0	150.0	92.3	66.7
13	—	—	650.0	185.7	108.3	76.5
14	—	—	1,400.0	233.3	127.3	87.5
15	—	—	—	300.0	150.0	100.0
16	—	—	—	400.0	177.8	114.3
17	—	—	—	566.7	212.5	130.8
18	—	—	—	900.0	257.1	150.0
19	—	—	—	1,900.0	316.7	172.7
20	—	—	—	—	400.0	200.0
21	—	—	—	—	525.0	233.3
22	—	—	—	—	733.3	275.0
23	—	—	—	—	1,115.0	328.6
24	—	—	—	—	2,400.0	400.0
25	—	—	—	—	—	500.0

A business truism says that you can cut, cut, cut until you cut yourself out of business. This can certainly apply to cutting prices in an effort to increase profits. The two don't necessarily go together. For example, select the gross profit being earned at present from those shown at the top of the chart. Follow the left column down until you line up with the proposed price cut. The intersected figure represents the percentage of increase in unit sales required to earn the same gross profit realized before the price cut. Obviously it helps to know this figure so you don't end up with a lot of work for nothing.

See for yourself: Assume that your present gross margin is 25 percent and that you cut your selling price 10 percent. Locate the 25 percent column under Present Gross Profit. Now follow the column down until you line up with the 10 percent cut in selling price in column 1. You will need to sell 66.7 percent more units to earn the same margin dollars as at the previous price.

time and production downtime would it take to disassemble the machine again and replace that one bolt?" The salesperson can then engage in a complete cost–benefit analysis (see Chapter 9) to solidify the point.

A supplier of integrated circuits (ICs) was competing with another company whose price was 10 cents less. The buyer asked for a price concession, noting that the competitor's product was obviously less expensive. Unbeknownst to the supplier, however, the buyer had already examined the value propositions of the two companies and determined that the higher-priced one was actually worth 12 cents more than the less expensive one, due to services offered. Thus, in reality, the buyer had already realized that the higher-priced one was actually less expensive in terms of value (12 cents more in value minus the 10 cents higher in price = 2 cents higher in value per IC). The higher-priced supplier caved in and gave the buyer a 10 cent reduction in price, costing his firm $500,000 (5 million units at 10 cents each) in potential profits! And the sad fact is that the buyer was already planning on going with the higher-priced supplier.[10]

Intangible features can also provide value that offsets price. Some of these features are services, company reputation, and the salesperson:

- Good service in the form of faster deliveries, technical advice, and field assistance is but one of the many intangibles that can spell value, savings, and profits to a customer. For example, one company cut its prices in response to buyers' demands. However, the company later found that what the customers really wanted was technical support. As the company cut its prices, it had only reinforced its image as low priced with little technical support.

- For a customer tempted to buy on price alone, salespeople can emphasize the importance of having a thoroughly reliable source of supply: the salesperson's company. It has been demonstrated time and again that quality is measured by the reputation of the company behind it.

- Customers value sales representatives who go out of their way to help with problems and promotions—salespeople who keep their word and follow through when they start something. These services are very valuable to customers.

USE COMMUNICATION TOOLS EFFECTIVELY

One pharmaceutical salesperson often hears that her company's drug for migraines is too expensive. Her response is to paint a word picture:[11]

> DOCTOR: How much does this product cost?
>
> SALESPERSON: It costs about $45.... There are 15 doses per bottle, so it ends up about $3 per dose.
>
> DOCTOR: That's too much money!
>
> SALESPERSON: Consider your patients who have to lie in the dark because their headaches are so bad they can't see straight, can't think straight, and are nauseated by migraine pain. A price of $3 is really inexpensive to relieve these patients' pain, wouldn't you agree?

Just telling customers about quality and value is not enough; they must be shown. Top salespeople use the communication tools discussed in Chapter 9 to describe more clearly the quality and value of their products. This process includes activities such as demonstrating the product, showing test results and quality control procedures, using case histories, and offering testimonials.

Salespeople must learn to deal with tough prospects and customers.

DEALING WITH TOUGH CUSTOMERS

Sellers need to maintain the positive attitude discussed earlier, even with rude, hard-to-get-along-with prospects. It's not easy, and it's not fun.

Sellers need to realize that we all have bad days. Maybe the buyer is having one. If the rudeness is quite blatant and the seller believes that this behavior is just due to the timing of the visit, the seller might say, "I'm sensing that this might not be the best time to talk. Should we reschedule for another time?"

If the buyer continues to communicate aggressively, being downright rude, you probably need to call attention to the fact.[12] After all, to develop a long-term win–win relationship and partnership, you both need to be on the same footing. Perhaps saying something like this will clear the air: "I'm sorry, Joe. I don't know quite how to say this. But it seems to me that you wish to argue more than learn about my products. I'll gladly continue if you think we can both approach this problem with professionalism and courtesy." By doing so, you are asserting yourself and confronting the issue head-on. At the same time, you are avoiding an emotional reaction of anger. Of course it is important to keep in mind the various personalities that buyers can have (see Chapter 5) and the adjustments suggested for each.

Also remember that the buyer's culture often dictates how he or she will respond to a seller. For example, Germans are known as being thorough, systematic, and well prepared, but they are also rather dogmatic and thus lack flexibility and the desire to compromise. As a result, sellers not accustomed to such a culture could have difficulty dealing with a German prospect who raises a price objection in a strong tone of voice.

Believe it or not, some of the toughest customers aren't those who are noisy and boisterous. Rather, they are often the passive ones, the quiet ones—the ones who don't object, don't question, and don't buy. What should a seller do? Be open, direct, and honest. Stop talking. Ask questions. Try your best to get the buyer involved. Establish trust so the buyer can feel confident enough to ask questions. If the buyer is still quiet, use a trial close. If this doesn't result in gaining commitment, ask the prospect what he or she would like to do at this point.

Believe it or not, the hardest prospects can be the quiet ones.

SELLING YOURSELF

Every day of your life, you will have objections. People love to tell me what isn't going to work or why I am wrong about things or why my product is all wrong for their business.

But when I get an objection from a friend about our weekend plans or I get questioned about whether I'm a good fit for the job during an interview or a doctor about why my product isn't going to work in his or her practice, the same techniques work. Listen to what the person is saying, ask good open-ended questions, keep the same pleasant demeanor, make note of what they are objecting to, and confidently educate the other person on why what you are telling them is the right answer!

Here's an example:

INTERVIEWER: You don't have a lot of experience in this field. Why should we consider you?

ME: Great question. You should hire me because I am trainable. I have a great background of different sales experiences, I'm well educated, and I am very coachable. You would be able to teach me any new process, and I will execute it exactly as you would like—unlike someone with already established "habits" that would come from having had experience in this field.

INTERVIEWER: Good point.

Objections can help you better understand people, situations, and life. Asking good open-ended questions always gives you an opportunity with any situation, to uncover the real need. If you don't take objections personally and learn how to make them into positives, you will be successful.

Source: Renee Miles; used with permission.

SUMMARY

Responding to objections is a vital part of a salesperson's responsibility. Objections may be offered at any time during the relationship between buyer and salesperson. They are to be expected, even welcomed, and they must be handled with skill and empathy.

Successful salespeople carefully prepare effective responses to buyers' concerns. Salespeople need to develop a positive attitude, commit to always telling the truth, refrain from interrupting, anticipate and forestall known objections, and learn how to evaluate objections.

Buyers object for many reasons. They may have no money, or they may not need the product. They may need more information or misunderstand some information already offered. They may be accustomed to another product, may not think the value exceeds the cost, or may not like the product's features. They may want to get rid of the salesperson or may not trust the salesperson or his or her company. They may want time to think or may object for many other reasons.

Effective methods of responding to objections are available, and their success has been proved. Methods exist both for concerns that are not true and for objections that either are true or are only the buyer's opinion. Sensitivity in choosing the right method is vital. Salespeople need to develop skill in responding to price objections and in dealing with tough customers. Nothing will substitute for developing skill in these areas.

KEY TERMS

acknowledge method   269
boomerang method   268
compensation method   266
direct denial   265
excuses   263
feel–felt–found method   268
forestall   260
friendly silent questioning stare   (FSQS) 264
indirect denial method   266
LAARC method   260

objection   254
pass-up method   269
pioneer selling   256
postpone method   270
probing method   264
referral method   268
revisit method   268
superior benefit method   267
third-party-testimony method   268
turnover (TO)   258

ETHICS PROBLEMS

1. Your product has become the victim of industry price erosion. To remain competitive, your company has decided to allow all sales reps to drop all prices by 25 percent. However, you have a number of clients who are paying the original prices and seem happy. Do you tell them about the 25 percent price reductions or keep prices the same for them?

2. One student in a selling class once said, "Why are we learning these objection-handling methods? These techniques are just to help us manipulate our buyers!" How would you respond?

QUESTIONS AND PROBLEMS

1. Categorize each of the following responses into the five basic types of objections. Then illustrate one way to handle each:

   a. After a sales presentation, the physician says, "You've made some good points, but your competitor's drug can do just about everything yours can do."

   b. After the salesperson answers an objection, the prospect remarks, "I guess your product is all right, but as I told you when you walked in, things are going pretty well for us right now without your product."

   c. After a thorough presentation, the prospect answers, "Are you kidding me? You want how much money for that thing?"

   d. The customer says, "I can buy that online for a lot less than what you're selling it for."

2. Marjorie Kemps spent considerable time working with a prospective buyer. She thought a good order would be forthcoming on her next call. A portion of her conversation with the buyer went as follows:

   BUYER: You know, I like what I hear about your scaffolding and aerial lift service. But how can I be sure it will be available on the days that we need it for our next project?

   MARJORIE: We've never had any real complaints before. I'm pretty sure they will be easily available.

   BUYER: You are sure of that?

   MARJORIE: Well, I've never heard of any problems that I can remember.

   BUYER: [appearing unconvinced and looking at some papers on his desk without glancing up]: I'll let you know later what I plan to do. Thanks for dropping by.

   How can you improve on Marjorie's answer to the buyer's concern?

3. Describe the differences between postponing an objection and forestalling an objection. Then provide a clear example of appropriate postponing for this objection: "This iPad is way too expensive. I can buy Google tablets much cheaper than buying your iPad!"

4. Occasionally a buyer will offer several objections at one time. How would you respond if a buyer made the following comments without pausing? "Say, how long does it take your lab to get the results back to us? And what if we need same-day service sometime? Are your technicians certified? That's important, you know!"

5. In "Building Partnerships 10.1," you learned that some buyers don't want to do business with you because the last seller in your position was not very good. Make a list of questions you could ask someone you might go to work for that will help you ascertain this before you work for them.

6. Choose a restaurant in your town. Assume that you work at that restaurant and are planning to make calls to campus club organizations. Assume that the restaurant has a private meeting room available that will seat 25 people. Your objective is to have officers of the clubs schedule their meetings at the restaurant.

   a. Make a list of objections you may expect to encounter.

   b. What can you do to meet these objections effectively? List the answers you would propose, and label the methods used.

7. In "From the Buyer's Seat 10.1," you learned about a number of complaints that food buyers

have for new food products. How would you respond to a buyer who said, "Your new product is way too spicy for me!"

8. You have been describing to a retail security officer and his boss a new security camera that your firm just introduced. The camera has tracking features that make it easier for security officers to review tapes. The security officer says, "I would really like that!" The boss says, "Well, if it's what you think we need, OK. How much does it cost?" At your reply, "This one is $2,498," the boss exclaims, "For that little thing?" What should you say or do?

9. For each of the following objections, provide answers that clearly demonstrate the direct denial and indirect denial methods. Assume each objection is not true:

a. My interior design customers wouldn't be impressed with the ability to see their proposed design plan in 3D. It's enough for me

to just explain it to them and show them two-dimensional drawings.

b. The cost of replacing the filter will be more than just buying a new unit.

c. I heard that the resins used in manufacturing your unit might cause cancer.

d. I can buy this cheaper online.

10. For each of the following objections, provide answers that clearly demonstrate the compensation method and referral method. Assume all the objections are either true or are the prospect's opinion:

a. Your repossession service costs a lot of money!

b. I don't think our customers will like the new fitness machines you're selling.

c. Your repair mechanics aren't certified by the ATSG.

d. My customers have never asked for this brand of recreational vehicle.

CASE PROBLEMS

case **10.1**

Zadro Inc. (Part B)

There are many harmful germs found in the home, in public places, and in hotels while traveling. The Programmable UV Sanitizing Wand, made by Zadro, can effectively kill up to 99.99 percent of germs and viruses in just 10 seconds. It can also kill dust mites in mattresses, pillows, and carpets. Since the wand is portable, it can travel with you wherever you travel, removing harmful substances regardless of where you are. The user simply waves the scanner within a quarter inch of the surface for 10 seconds to kill the substances.

The scanner is 1½ inches high × 20 inches wide × 1¾ inches deep and runs on three C batteries. An optional AC adapter is sold separately. The scanner includes an electronic child lock to prevent misuse. A stand is provided and is used to go over keyboards, butcher blocks, and so on for hands-free operation. The programmable unit can be set for 10-, 20-, 40-, and 60-second times as well as two to five minutes, depending on the surface area that needs to be scanned. The unit is not designed to be used on humans or animals. The scanner, which is laboratory certified and tested, retails for $99, and all units come with a 90-day limited warranty. Resellers are offered the units for $60, with a quantity discount of $50 for all units over 100 in a single order.

Assume that you are selling the Programmable UV Sanitizing Wand to Target Corporation for them to resell.

Questions

1. What objections could the buyer raise? Make any assumptions necessary to develop this list.

2. Provide a response to each objection you listed in question 1 (make any assumptions necessary to create your responses). Include the name of the method you recommend for each objection.

Source: http://www.zadroinc.com/health-solutions-nano-technology-c-43_44.html; discount information is for illustration purposes only.

case **10.2**

Hometown Focus
Newspaper

Hometown Focus is a small, locally owned and operated free weekly newspaper operated in Virginia, Minnesota. The paper was established in 2007 and is available in print and online. It is a community-driven newspaper that allows members in the community to share their stories, recipes, and photos. It is a small business that employs only nine people, but they do have over 400 contributors from 40 local communities. You can view more details about the paper at their Web site: http://www.hometownfocus.us.

Carlos Rivera is a salesperson for *Hometown Focus* and has made an appointment with Vijay Patel, a sales manager at Iron Trail Motors, a Chevrolet and Toyota dealership located in Virginia, Minnesota. Iron Trail offers quality new and preowned cars, trucks, and SUVs with a strong service department. Iron Trail already does advertising with a competing local newspaper called *Mesabi Daily News,* a daily, paid-subscription newspaper. Carlos is planning to discuss having Iron Trail Motors place ads in both its online and its print version of the paper.

Questions

1. List objections you think might occur during this first meeting with Vijay. Make any assumptions necessary to develop this list.
2. Describe how you would respond to each objection listed in question 1. Be sure to label the methods. Make any assumptions necessary to create your responses.

Sources: http://www.hometownfocus.us, http://www.virginiamn.com/site/forms/subscription_services, and http://www .irontrailchevrolet.com.

ROLE PLAY CASE

Today you will repeat your role play presentation from Chapter 9. (If you have not done role plays before, you will need to review the information about the various role play customers that can be found at the end of Chapter 3. If you didn't do the role play for Chapter 9, you will need to review that material also, which can be found at the end of Chapter 9.) When you act as the observer today, you should identify what objection-handling method the seller used and if it was done effectively. The professor will give you a sheet to use as a buyer, listing objections for you to use during the role play. When you sell, try to use a variety of objection-handling methods.

Note: For background information about these role plays, please see page 26.

To the instructor: Additional information needed to complete the role play is available in the Instructor's Manual.

ADDITIONAL REFERENCES

Boe, John. "Overcome Objections and Close the Sale." *American Salesman* 56, no. 8 (August 2011), pp. 10–14.

Bud, Peter Paul. *How to Be a Best Seller: 18 Simple and Proven Steps You Must Know to Succeed.* Raleigh, NC: Lulu, 2009.

Fisher, Leo D'Angelo. "Wind in the Sales." *BRW* 34, no. 1 (January 19, 2012), pp. 36–37.

Hunter, Mark. *High-Profit Selling: Win the Sale without Compromising on Price.* New York: AMACOM, 2012.

Kahle, Dave. "Preventing the Price Objection." *American Salesman* 54, no. 6 (June 2009), pp. 24–27.

McGaulley, Michael. *How to Sell: Face-to-Face Survival Guide.* New York: Champlain House Media, 2010.

Mulvey, Richard. *Handling Objections/Closing the Sale.* Durban, South Africa: Perception Business Skills, 2010.

Reilly, Tom. *Crush Price Objections: Sales Tactics for Holding Your Ground and Protecting Your Profit.* New York: McGraw-Hill, 2010.

Rutherford, Brian N., Nwamaka A. Anaza, and Adrienne Hall Phillips. "Predictors of Buyer-Seller Firm Conflict." *Journal of Marketing Theory and Practice* 20, no. 2 (Spring 2012), pp. 161–72.

Schiffman, Stephan. *25 Toughest Sales Objections—and How to Overcome Them.* New York: McGraw-Hill, 2011.

Shaltz, Gerry. *The DNA of Selling: What You Won't Learn in Business School.* Bloomington, IN: iUniverse, 2009.

Thull, Jeff. "The Three Traps of Selling." *American Salesman* 57, no. 9 (September 2012), pp. 15–19.

chapter **11**

OBTAINING COMMITMENT

SOME QUESTIONS ANSWERED IN THIS CHAPTER ARE

- How much emphasis should be placed on closing the sale?
- Why is obtaining commitment important?
- When is the best time to obtain commitment?
- Which methods of securing commitment are appropriate for developing partnerships?
- How should pricing be presented?
- What should a salesperson do when the prospect says yes? When the prospect says no?
- What causes difficulties in obtaining commitment, and how can these issues be overcome?

2
PART

PROFILE

PROFILE "What do you want to be when you grow up?" We've all heard that question. A doctor, a firefighter, or maybe even a prince. For me, the answer was always a vet. Growing up in Connecticut and being close to an aunt who lived on a farm, my childhood was filled with interesting animals: dogs, snakes, and even geckos. This love for animals led to seeking an education at Texas A&M, where I received a degree in biomedical science and then completed veterinary training. However, little did I know, sales would be where I found my true passion.

One summer afternoon before my senior year, a friend shared his experience he had in the sales world with me; I quickly became intrigued by how well he had done for himself and decided to get involved. Shortly after, I landed my first sales position with Vector Marketing. After that first sales job, I have found myself in the exciting, fast-paced world of selling and have never looked back since. While my degree may not have been in sales, I found that mastering the art of sales and performing veterinary surgeries were not all that different.

Both closing up a patient and closing a deal are important final steps to any surgery or sales meeting. One deal in particular taught me how to be effective at the close. A lucrative opportunity to help my company and a client arose early on in my career. After building a strong relationship with the director of operations, I felt confident I had an "in" with the company. Although my contact was not the final decision maker, I felt certain she would help make the deal happen. I felt assured that following her advice, her process, and her approach would seal the deal for me. I did follow her process, and when the time came to make the close, I *lost* the business!

Unfortunately, not following the sales process is an all-too-common mistake. I felt sure the relationship I had built would be enough for smooth sailing to the close, but regrettably it wasn't. Without earning the right to earn the prospect's business by following the sales approach, obtaining commitment at the close is nearly impossible. As I learned that day, following the sales process is an irreplaceable part of successfully closing a deal. Every step brings the buyer to the closing point, and skipping even one step can throw the process out of balance, leaving an unsatisfied customer and a confused salesperson. If you find yourself scratching your head in confusion when a deal that looked certain turns south, you may just have skipped a step in the process. The hardest part to gaining commitment from the prospect simply comes when one of the steps has been skipped.

I can relate to this situation. I know what it is like to get excited, inch to the edge of your seat, feel the enthusiasm from the buyer, and sense a close. At that point, it's easy to skip a step and jump to the end. But being patient and following *all* the steps is a road map to success at the close. The best part is when the process has been followed, the closing actually becomes automated—the buyer ultimately ends up asking *you* for the business!

Being honest and open is also critical to an effective close. Whether you call yourself a consultant, an advisor, or any other title, at the end of the day the prospect knows you're a salesperson. I find freedom in this. Being sincere, honest, and open to the prospect has allowed me to gain respect and trust from my clients. At the end of the day, I just want my prospects to know "I'm here to earn the right to earn your business."

Whether you're a veterinarian or a salesperson, following the right process is the key to a successful close. Just as a vet would never skip a step in a surgery, a salesperson should never skip a step in a sales meeting to be successful. Following the right process will ultimately lead to one happy dog owner and one happy customer.

Visit our Web site at:
www.kmbs.com

SECURING COMMITMENT TODAY •

Asking for the buyer's business, often called **closing,** has always received a great deal of emphasis in sales training. Hundreds of books, DVDs, CDs, and seminar speakers have touted the importance of closing—just Google "close sales" at Amazon, and over 8,000 book titles will appear. Almost all are devoted to a method or methods that will make the decision maker say yes.

Look a little closer at those titles, however, and you'll notice that most of them are old. Some of the books may even be older than your parents! Today's sales professionals recognize that securing a sale is the reason for their existence, but getting that sale should be due to the value created, not the technique used.

Rob Keeney, training director for Frosty Acres Brands, says this about closing:

I don't see good closers as being "pushy." Assertive, yes. Direct, yes. "Pushy" implies the customer being somehow compelled to do something they really don't want to do. By contrast, a good closer helps a customer make the decision they really want or need to make. And sooner rather than later.

Charles Cohon, president of Prime Devices and an influential speaker in the manufacturer's representation industry, agrees, saying,

Closing an order is not the end of a process, it is the beginning. Concentrate just on closing that order, and it will be the last order you get from that customer. Concentrate instead on developing a relationship with that customer that leads naturally to an order and you will earn not only that order, but also that customer's orders for many years to come.

Others also believe the traditional emphasis on getting the sale no matter what damages trust, insults the buyer's intelligence, and raises the possibility of losing commitment altogether. Customers make a buying decision, rather than the salesperson closing the sale. Buyers want to buy, not to be sold.

Solid research provides strong evidence that questions the value of closing techniques. The research, based on more than 35,000 sales calls over 12 years, has found that in a major sale, reliance on closing techniques actually reduces the chances of making a sale.[1] Further, salespeople who were specifically trained in closing actually closed fewer sales. For very low-priced products (as in door-to-door magazine sales), however, closing techniques may increase the chances of a sale.

So why even cover closing at all? Because there are nonmanipulative and trustworthy ways to gain commitment and because obtaining commitment is critical for the success of salespeople and their firms. Without a buyer's commitment, no sale takes place. As Dave Brock points out in "From the Buyer's Seat 11.1," salespeople who fail to gain the right commitment simply end up annoying the customer and failing to generate business. Also, buyers rarely volunteer to make a purchase even when that decision is obviously the right thing to do. This chapter covers the topic of obtaining commitment in a manner that is consistent with the theme of the book: developing and building long-term partnerships.

PART OF THE PROCESS

The process of obtaining commitment occurs throughout the natural, logical progression of any sales call. Recall from Chapter 3 that creeping commitment occurs when a customer becomes committed to a particular course of action throughout the buying process. Salespeople actually gain commitment repeatedly: when asking for an appointment, when checking to see whether the customer's entire needs have been identified, and when asking whether the prospect would like to see a demonstration or receive a proposal. Commitment, of course, is more than just

From the BUYER'S SEAT

SILLY ME, I THOUGHT SELLING WAS SUPPOSED TO GENERATE REVENUE!

I am president of Partners in Excellence, a company that consults with Fortune 500 clients in sales effectiveness. I have a keen eye in what to look for when I'm being sold to in my role as president, and I don't always like what I see.

I've always been under the impression that revenue generation (quota) was the key objective for salespeople. Therefore, I've always focused my time on finding customers that are interested in my solutions, who want to make a change, and who are willing to invest money in achieving the results they expect. That's a fundamental principle in qualifying. It's always seemed to be very important—I don't want to waste the customer's time, and, greedily, I don't want to waste my time.

Recently, however, I think I've been badly mistaken—at least based on the vast majority of sales calls I get. I always thought the goal was to find and qualify opportunities that could ultimately generate revenue, but that no longer seems to be the priority. I have to admit to being a little embarrassed. I try to keep at the forefront of best practices and emerging trends in sales effectiveness. However, I've missed this major new trend.

It seems the key goals for salespeople are (1) getting a customer to accept a piece of literature—a case study, a brochure, a catalog—and (2) getting a meeting, even if the prospect is not a fit in any possible scenario where they might buy a product.

I've been fielding a lot of prospecting calls from hopeful salespeople. They astound me! They must be on quota to send me a piece of literature. I've gotten calls from small businesses, from very large technology salespeople, various professional services organizations, and others. The salespeople are singular in their focus—"Can I send you [insert the right word—a cases study, a catalog, our brochure, etc.]?"

Most of the salespeople don't even ask questions. They have a well-rehearsed opening sentence (most of which have little meaning to me) culminating in "Can I send you

some information?" My response is, "Why would I even be interested in that?" Most are not able to handle the objection. Their usual response? "Well, it's free!"

A few ask me a questions about me and my business, then somehow it gets to "Can I send you some information?" I struggle in these conversations. I try to connect the dots. I think to myself, "We were talking about this and that, how did we get to 'Can I send you some information?'" I can never figure it out; I don't know how my responses to the questions led to needing a piece of literature. In fact, a few times, the next action might have been a meeting—I was more than casually interested in what they were offering, but rather than picking up on the "buying signal," they wanted to send me a piece of literature.

Then there are the others: "We're going to be in the neighborhood and would like to meet." When I respond, "We don't buy that stuff—that's never a requirement in our business," they come back, "Well we'd just like the opportunity to meet." I always go back with, "If I never intend to buy anything you sell, why do you want to meet? What's the purpose?" They can never answer this, but they persist: "Are you available next Monday or Tuesday?"

I think I've figured it out. I'm a little ashamed. I've missed the trend. Apparently, revenue is no longer a key metric for salespeople. In sales training sessions, they are told, "Ignore buying signals, ignore whether the customer is qualified, ignore whether they are even in our sweet spot—get the meeting! The more meetings you have, the more successful you will be! Make sure you find some excuse to get a meeting, everything will work out once you get the meeting!"

I have always been of the impression that we are most effective when our activities are purposeful and create value for the customer. I've thought it better to reduce the number of calls required to close—not increase them. I've thought it not good to waste the customer's time or my time on things that are meaningless.

Have I missed something?

securing an order. As Exhibit 11.1 illustrates, salespeople will attempt to obtain a commitment that is consistent with the objectives of the particular sales call.

Obtaining commitment is also important in moving the account through the relationship process. Once a sale is made, salespeople begin to plan for the next sale or for the next level of commitment that indicates a deepening relationship.

Exhibit 11.1
Examples of
Commitments
Salespeople May
Attempt to Obtain

Examples of Presale Commitments

- To have the prospect agree to come to the Atlanta branch office sometime during the next two weeks for a hands-on demonstration of the copier.
- To set up another appointment for one week from now, at which time the buyer will allow me to do a complete survey of her printing needs.
- To inform the doctor of the revolutionary anticlotting mechanism that has been incorporated into our new drug and have her agree to read the pamphlet I will leave.
- To have the buyer agree to pass my information along to the buying committee with his endorsement of my proposal.
- To have the prospect agree to call several references that I will provide to develop further confidence and trust in my office-cleaning business.
- To have the prospect agree on the first point (of our four-point program) and schedule another meeting in two days to discuss the second point.
- To have the prospect initiate the necessary paperwork to allow us to be considered as a future vendor.

Examples of Commitments That Consummate the Sale

- To have the prospect sign an order for 100 pairs of Levi's jeans.
- To schedule a co-op newspaper advertising program to be implemented in the next month.
- To have the prospect agree to use our brand of computer paper for a trial period of one month.
- To have the retailer agree to allow us space for an end-of-aisle display for the summer presentation of Raid insect repellent.

At the same time, commitment is a two-way street. Salespeople also make commitments to buyers when the sale is made.

THE IMPORTANCE OF SECURING COMMITMENT

Overall, gaining commitment tells the salesperson what to do next and defines the status of the client. For example, gaining a needs identification appointment may mean that you have a "suspect"; at the end of that call, gaining commitment for a demonstration means you have a prospect. Gain an order and you gain a customer. Without gaining commitment, the salesperson may waste time doing the wrong things.

Salespeople need to become proficient in obtaining commitment for several other good reasons. First, if they fail to obtain commitment, it will take longer (more sales calls) to obtain a sale, if a sale occurs at all. Taking more time with one sale means fewer sales overall because you lose time for prospecting and other important activities. Second, assuming the product truly satisfies the prospect's needs, the sooner the prospect buys, the sooner she or he can realize the benefits of the product or service. Third, the company's future success depends on goodwill and earning a profit. Finally, securing commitment results in financial rewards for the salesperson; in addition, meeting needs is also intrinsically rewarding for the seller.

One thing to remember is that if you have done your job well and you have a product that the buyer truly needs, then you deserve the sale. The buyer is not doing you a favor by buying, and he or she expects you to ask for the sale if you've

thinking **it** through   Think for a moment about a major purchase that you or a family member made, such as a new TV or a car. During the shopping process, what were some of the worst closes you experienced? What salesperson behavior really angers you when you try to shop for major purchases? What made the difference between those experiences and the ones you found satisfying?

done your work professionally. Not only is gaining commitment important for you and your company, it is the professional thing to do. What is not professional is a high-pressure close; typically, high-pressure closing is necessary (and inappropriate) when the salesperson has not done a good job throughout the entire process.[2]

Before we get into how to obtain commitment, some time should be spent on the importance of terms and conditions of the sale and how these influence the total cost. Sometimes terms are an important need and may be presented early in the call. But we present the credit terms here because often a buyer decides what to buy and then explores the financial terms that are available.

FINANCIAL TERMS AND CONDITIONS

Most salespeople try to hold off on presenting price until the end. Yet price is often the first question asked. The final price is really a function of the terms and conditions of the sale and depends on several factors.

Cash flow is an issue for many buyers and can stop a sale. No matter how badly they may want or need the product, not having the cash can delay or even prohibit a sale. Santosh Natarajan, of SSI-India, experienced such a challenge when developing a software application for Korcett. The company was growing so fast that all cash was being used up in production, leaving no cash for an important software upgrade. Santosh worked out a payment plan that matched his invoices to receipt of payments from customers. There was added risk for SSI-India, but it was worth it.

Factors that affect price are the use of quantity and other discounts, as well as credit and shipping terms. Figuring out the final actual price can be difficult, especially in situations with many options and packages rather than standardized products.

DISCOUNTS

Discounts are given for many reasons and may be based on the type of customer (such as wholesaler or retailer, senior citizen or younger adult), quantity purchased, or some other factor. The most common type of discount is the quantity discount.

Quantity discounts encourage large purchases by passing along savings resulting from reduced processing costs. Businesses offer two types of quantity discounts: (1) the single-order discount and (2) a cumulative discount. An office equipment company offering a 10 percent discount on a single order for five or more facsimile machines is an example of a single-order discount. When offering a **cumulative discount,** that same company might offer the 10 percent discount on all purchases over a one-year period, provided the customer purchases more than five fax machines. The customer may sign an agreement at the beginning of the year promising to buy five or more machines, in which case the customer will be billed for each order at the discounted price (10 percent off). If the customer fails to purchase five fax machines, a single bill will be sent at the end of the year for the amount of the discount (10 percent of the single-unit price times the number of fax machines actually purchased). Another method is to bill the customer at the full price and then rebate the discount at the end of the year, based on the actual number of fax machines purchased.

CREDIT TERMS

Most U.S. sales are made on a credit basis, with **cash discounts** allowed for early payment. These cash discounts are the last discount taken, meaning that if a

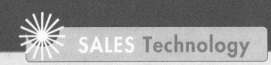

TECHNOLOGY THAT CLOSES THE SALE

Salespeople today are often involved in highly complex sales that involve customized solutions. Technology is often thought of as supporting customer contact management or supporting customer service, but there is also technology that helps close the deal, too.

For example, product configurators are solutions that help salespeople at the close. Anritsu, a company that makes highly technical communication devices, uses Configure One's Concept software to allow customers to configure their own products online. Salespeople can use the software, too, and the software frees salespeople to focus on selling, not on product configuration. Katherine van Diepen, Anritsu's marketing communications manager, estimates that this software saves salespeople about 45 minutes per configuration, or the equivalent of adding one sales call per day per salesperson. Increased accuracy in configuration also means more satisfied customers.

Similar software can aid salespeople in converting proposals into sales. These systems, such as Quotegine

(quotegine.com) and ProposalSoftware.com, help salespeople save and reuse components of successful sales proposals. Like product configurators, these systems also help manage complex purchases from the sales process into the implementation process. The same data used to generate the proposal become the data that are then input automatically into the accounting system to generate accurate invoices as well as put automatically into production systems so that the right solutions are built and then input into the customer service system so that service documentation can be created.

One extra sales call per day may not seem like a lot, but for some sales settings, that may mean a 10 percent increase in sales. These systems, in the right settings, can significantly improve a salesperson's performance!

Sources: Matt Moore and Keith De La Rue, "Closing the Deal with the Help of Knowledge," *Knowledge Management Review* 11, no. 3 (July/August 2008), pp. 14–19; "Anritsu Case Study," http://www.configureone.com/pdf/ConfigureOnecasestudy-Anritsu.pdf, accessed March 3, 2010.

quantity discount is also offered, the cash discount is calculated after the quantity discount is taken off. A common discount is 2/10, n/30, which means that the buyer can deduct 2 percent from the bill if it is paid within 10 days from the date of invoice. Otherwise the full amount must be paid in 30 days. Another common discount is 2/10, EOM, which means that the 10-day period begins at the end of the month. For example, if the customer receives $1,000 worth of supplies on February 15 with terms of 2/10, EOM and pays the bill on March 5, the customer would pay $980 (that is, $1,000 at 2% = $20 discount for paying cash; $1,000 − $20 = $980). But if the customer pays on March 11, the bill would be the full $1,000.

Credit terms can be very important in capital equipment sales. Capital purchases have long lives and cost more than a buyer can afford to pay all at once. For example, the HVAC (heating, ventilation, and air conditioning) industry relies heavily on financing to sell heating and cooling systems. Johnson Controls offered a six months with no interest plan, called "same as cash." "Most consumers need some type of bridge financing to handle an unplanned $8,000 HVAC expense. That is why we feel we've seen so much business in the same-as-cash programs."[3] Easy credit terms can help salespeople close sales, but sales aren't complete until the buyer takes delivery. One home builder noticed that buyers were willing to put contracts on houses that hadn't been built yet in order to fix their credit during the nine months it took to complete the homes. So many "buyers" were unable to actually get credit and canceled sales that he quit taking orders on prebuilt homes.[4]

SHIPPING COSTS

The terms and conditions of sale include shipping costs. Recall from Chapter 2 that the term *free on board (FOB)* is used to determine the point at which the buyer assumes responsibility for both the goods and the costs of shipping them. Thus, FOB destination means the buyer will take responsibility for the goods once they reach the buyer's location, and the seller will pay the freight.

Suppose Hormel quotes an FOB origin price. It will load the truck at its Chicago plant, but the buyer will pay for shipping. If Hormel sold a truckload of pepperoni to Coppoli's Deli under terms of FOB destination, Hormel would pay for shipping and would have the pepperoni delivered to Coppoli's Deli's warehouse, where warehouse personnel would unload the truck.

If Hormel quotes a price for pepperoni that's FOB origin, then Coppoli's Deli pays for shipping. If the price is FOB destination, then Hormel pays for shipping.

Another form of FOB is *FOB installed,* meaning that title and responsibility do not transfer until the equipment is installed and operating properly. In some instances FOB installed can also mean that operator training must be provided before title transfers. These are important terms because there are significant costs associated with the technical installation and operator training for many pieces of sophisticated equipment. Buyers want to know the total price and what it includes.

The terms and conditions of a sale, including but not limited to price, can often play as important a role as the product itself in determining what is purchased. Creative salespeople understand the terms and conditions they have to work with so they can meet the needs of their buyers while also meeting the profit objectives of their own companies.

PRESENTING PRICE

Price is often discussed at the end of the presentation simply because the salesperson may not know what that price will be until the final solution is agreed on. Because price is so important to the buyer, it is worth considering how price should be presented.

Most firms set prices after careful study of competitors' offerings, the value delivered by the product or service, and the cost of providing the product or service. For these reasons the price should represent a reasonable and fair picture of the product's or service's value. Therefore, never apologize for a price or present the price apologetically; rather, present it with confidence.

Bruce Culbert, now chief service officer with the Pedowitz Group, says that salespeople sometimes negotiate against themselves. When he was at IBM,

> I had an account manager who was under pressure to make quota for the quarter. In presenting a proposal to a prospective customer, the salesperson did as was agreed and sent the proposal via e-mail a full two weeks prior to quarter end because the client said they would be able to make a decision by the end of the month. If this deal closed, the salesperson would hit quota. Several days went by, and there was no response from the prospect. A follow-up e-mail and phone went unanswered. In a panic the salesperson began to submit revised proposals each time, lowering the price in an attempt to get the prospect to respond positively.

A week went by with no response. During the week two revised proposals had been submitted, each time lowering the price almost 10 percent. On the Tuesday before the quarter closed the client responded favorably to the original proposal with their apologies that they had not responded sooner but they were on vacation the past week and were just now catching up on e-mail. Needless to say the salesperson was ecstatic to learn of the good fortune just prior to quarter close. About 10 minutes later the salesperson received an additional e-mail from the client informing them to ignore the previous note and that they would like to accept proposal revision 2, which was almost 20 percent less than the original proposal.[5]

As Bruce says, here is a salesperson who panicked and lost the company 20 percent. Sometimes, companies can add to the pressure on salespeople, as you can see in Building Partnerships 11.1.

In addition to presenting the price with confidence, remember that price is not the focus of your presentation. The real issue is satisfying the needs of the buyer, of which budget is only one. True, a budget limitation can halt progress toward a sale. The real issue, though, is the total cost of ownership, which means the buyer should also factor in the value of the benefits delivered.

WHEN TO ATTEMPT TO OBTAIN COMMITMENT

Novice salespeople frequently ask themselves these questions: Is there a right time to obtain commitment? How will customers let me know they are ready to buy? Should I make more than one attempt? What should I do if my first attempt fails?

The right time to attempt to gain commitment is when the buyer appears ready, as evidenced by buying signals. Some salespeople say that one psychological moment in each sales presentation affords the best opportunity to obtain commitment, and if this opportunity is bypassed, securing commitment will be difficult or impossible. This belief is not true, however. Seldom does one psychological moment govern the complete success or failure of a sales presentation.

Most buyers will commit themselves only when they clearly understand the benefits and costs of such a decision. At times this point occurs early in the call. A commitment to purchase a large system, however, usually will not occur until a complete presentation and several calls have been made and all questions have been answered.

Buying signals, or indications that the buyer is ready to buy, can be evidenced both in the buyer's comments and nonverbally. Buying signals are also called **closing cues.**

BUYER COMMENTS

A customer's comments often are the best indication that he or she is considering commitment. A prospect will seldom say, "All right, I'm ready to endorse this product to our buying committee." Questions about the product or terms of sale and comments in the form of requirements or benefit statements signal readiness to buy, as do responses to trial closes.

Buyer Questions

Here are some examples of questions that signal readiness to buy:

If I agree to go with this cooperative advertising program, do you have any ads already developed that I could use?

BUILDING Partnerships   11.1

TIMING AND PRICING

What's it like to be closed—especially for a big deal? Steve Schlesinger is a sales guy who tells this story: "Just last week, we had a significant purchase to make, not just because it was an expensive or large purchase but because it represented a major change in strategy. Our strategy for information technology has been to build our own. In many ways, we were ahead of the market, and off-the-shelf programs did not fit our needs." His company reconsidered this approach when it came time to upgrade their customer management software. "Our first thought was that it was too expensive. Two years ago, we had looked at software for customer management, and it just didn't make sense."

He called a friend at Salesforce.com, and they went to work on a solution. "The development meeting was excellent, the integration piece was developed, and then they came back with a good cost/benefit analysis." But then the decision got tougher. "With offices across the United States and United Kingdom, we realized we needed everyone who works with clients would need access to the software. This decision increased our license from 10 users to 70 or 80. That raises the costs substantially, and suddenly, that cost/benefit analysis wasn't looking so good." But it was two days before the end of the fiscal year for Salesforce .com, so they slashed the price and got the deal done.

Steve says it wasn't a hard, aggressive sale. The Salesforce .com team was transparent, "they needed to get it done and told us, and they gave me the leeway in the terms that I needed. They were very professional." But Steve clearly believes he got a better deal because of the timing.

LeeAnne Pearson conducted a study for a company that asked for anonymity. During the study, salespeople complained that top management would slash prices at the end of each quarter in order to get sales up and look good on Wall Street. "These salespeople were frustrated that they were giving up margin and commission in order for top management to look good and stock prices to go up. Worse yet, they also said buyers recognized the practice and purposively timed purchases and negotiated fiercely, knowing they could get bargains by waiting until the end of the quarter." These are sales of half a million dollars or more—yet salespeople are under the same pressure to close deals that car salespeople face every month!

Sources: LeeAnne Pearson, "Sales Practices: A Comparison of Top and Bottom Salespeople," Research Paper 11-1, Baylor University's Center for Professional Selling (September 1, 2011); Steve Schlesinger's quotes are from personal interview, February 5, 2010.

Do you have any facilities for training our employees in the use of the product?

How soon would you be able to deliver the equipment?

Not all questions signal a readiness to buy. But if the question concerns implementing the purchase and points toward when, not if, the purchase is implemented, the prospect may be getting ready to buy.

Requirements

Requirements are conditions that have to be satisfied before a purchase can take place. For example:

We need a cash discount for a supply order like this.

We need to get this in weekly shipments.

Requirements that are stated near the end of the presentation are need statements that reflect a readiness to buy when they relate to how the purchase will be consummated. As the examples illustrate, requirements relating to financial terms or shipping indicate that the decision to buy the product has been made and now it is time to work out the details.

Benefit Statements

Sometimes prospects offer their own benefit statements, such as these:

> Oh, I like the way this equipment is serviced—it will make it much easier on my staff.

> Good, that color will match our office decor.

Such positive statements reflect strong feelings in support of the purchase—a sign that the buyer is ready.

Responses to Trial Closes

Salespeople can solicit such comments by continually taking the pulse of the situation with **trial closes,** which are questions regarding the prospect's readiness to buy (first discussed in Chapter 8). Throughout the presentation, the salesperson should be asking questions:

> How does this sound to you so far?

> Is there anything else you would like to know at this point?

> How does this compare with what you have seen of competing products?

Such questions are an important element of any sales process because trial closes serve several purposes, including identifying the customer's proximity to making the decision, gaining agreement on minor points, and creating a true dialogue in which the ultimate close is a natural conclusion. Note that these are more general questions than simply gaining agreement on benefits (discussed in Chapter 8), say as part of a FEBA.

One approach is to try a soft third-party trial close, such as by asking, "At this point, do you feel comfortable in recommending our product/service to others in your organization?" If you know that the buying process is likely to involve others, you can ask the question more specifically, such as, "Are you comfortable in bringing this to the [insert the appropriate title or name] attention?"

When a seller asks a trial close question, the buyer responds, thus creating a dialogue. Issues can be raised as objections or questions by the buyer, which tell the seller what to cover. Then, because the salesperson has been asking closing questions all along, the final close is just a natural part of the ongoing dialogue, as it should be.

NONVERBAL CUES

As in every phase of the presentation, nonverbal cues serve as important indicators of the customer's state of mind, as discussed in Chapter 4. While attempting to gain commitment, the salesperson should use the buyer's nonverbal signals to better identify areas of concern and see whether the buyer is ready to commit. Facial expressions most often indicate how ready the buyer is to make a commitment. Positive signals include eyes that are open and relaxed, face and mouth not covered with hands, a natural smile, and a relaxed forehead. The reverses of these signals indicate that the buyer is not yet ready to commit to the proposal.

Customers' actions also often indicate readiness to buy or make a commitment. For example, the prospective buyer of a fax machine may get a document and operate the machine or place the machine on the table where it will be used. The industrial buyer may refer to a catalog to compare specifications with competing products. A doctor, when told of a new drug, may pick up the pamphlet and begin carefully reading the indications and contraindications. A retailer considering whether to allow an end-of-aisle display may move to the end of an aisle and scan the layout. Any such actions may be signals for obtaining commitment; they should be viewed in the context of all available verbal and nonverbal cues.

Do the two buyers on the right look like they are ready to commit to a purchase?

HOW TO SUCCESSFULLY OBTAIN COMMITMENT

To obtain commitment in a nonmanipulative manner, salespeople need to follow several principles, including maintaining a positive attitude, letting the customer set the pace, being assertive instead of aggressive, and selling the right product in the right amounts.

MAINTAIN A POSITIVE ATTITUDE

Confidence is contagious. Customers like to deal with salespeople who have confidence in themselves, their products, and their companies. On the other hand, unnecessary fear can be a self-fulfilling prophecy. The student who fears essay exams usually does poorly; golfers who believe they will miss short putts usually do. So it is with salespeople: If they fear customers will not accept their proposals, the chances are good they will be right.

One manager related the example of a salesperson selling laundry detergent who unsuccessfully tried to convince a large discount chain to adopt a new liquid version of the product. When the rep's sales manager stopped by the account later in the week to follow up on a recent stockout problem, the buyer related his reasons for refusing the Liquid Tide: "Listen, I know you guys are sharp. You probably wouldn't come out with a new product unless you had tons of data to back up your decision. But honestly, the sales rep who calls on me is always so uptight and apprehensive that I was afraid to adopt the new product! Don't you guys teach them about having confidence?"

LET THE CUSTOMER SET THE PACE

Attempts to gain commitment must be geared to fit the varying reactions, needs, and personalities of each buyer. Thus, the sales representative needs to practice adaptive selling. (See Chapter 5 for a complete discussion of adaptive selling.)

Some buyers who react slowly may need plenty of time to assimilate the material presented. They may ask the same question several times or show they do not understand the importance of certain product features. In these circumstances the salesperson must deliver the presentation more slowly and may have to repeat certain parts. Trying to rush buyers is unwise when they show they are not yet ready to commit.

As we discussed earlier in the book, buyers' decision-making styles vary greatly. Japanese and Chinese buyers tend to move more slowly and cautiously when evaluating a proposition. In contrast, buyers working for *Fortune* 500 firms located in the largest U.S. cities often tend to move much more quickly. The successful salesperson recognizes such potential differences and acts accordingly.

BE ASSERTIVE, NOT AGGRESSIVE

Marvin Jolson has identified three types of salespeople: aggressive, submissive, and assertive.[6] Exhibit 11.2 summarizes the differences among assertive, aggressive, and submissive salespeople's handling of the sales interview. **Aggressive** salespeople control the sales interaction but often fail to gain commitment because they prejudge the customer's needs and fail to probe for information. Too busy talking to do much listening, they tend to push the buyer too soon, too often, and too vigorously. They might say, "I can't understand why you are hesitant," but they do not probe for reasons for the hesitancy. A recent study found that

Exhibit 11.2
How Aggressive, Submissive, and Assertive Salespeople Handle Sales Activities

Selling Activity	Selling Style		
	Aggressive	Submissive	Assertive
Defining customer needs	Believe they are the best judge of customer's needs.	Accept customer's definition of needs.	Probe for need-related information that customer may not have volunteered.
Controlling the presentation	Minimize participation by customer.	Permit customer to control presentation.	Encourage two-way communication and customer participation.
Closing the sale	Overwhelm customer; respond to objections without understanding.	Assume customers will buy when ready.	Respond to objections, leading to somewhat automatic close.

aggressive salespeople negatively impacted overall customer satisfaction, even when customers were satisfied with the product itself.[7]

Submissive salespeople often excel as socializers. With customers they spend a lot of time talking about families, restaurants, and movies. They establish rapport quite effectively. They accept the customers' statements of needs and problems but do not probe to uncover any latent needs or opportunities. Submissive salespeople rarely try to obtain commitment, perhaps because they may fear rejection too much.

Assertive salespeople, the third type, are self-confident and positive. They maintain the proper perspective by being responsive to customer needs. Rather than aggressively creating new "needs" in customers through persuasion, they look for buyers who truly need their products and then use questions to acquire information. Their presentations emphasize an exchange of information rather than a one-way presentation.

SELL THE RIGHT ITEM IN THE RIGHT AMOUNTS

The chance of obtaining commitment improves when the right product is sold in the right amount. Although this principle sounds obvious, it often is not followed. Sometimes salespeople try to get the biggest order they can. Customers have long memories, they will refuse to do business again with someone who oversells, and they may also lack confidence in someone who undersells.

ethics

For example, before attempting to sell two copiers, the office equipment sales representative must be sure that these two copiers, instead of only one copier or perhaps three, best fit the needs of the buyer's office. The chemical company sales representative selling to an industrial firm must know that one tank car of a chemical is more likely to fit the firm's needs than 10 55-gallon drums. The Johnson Wax sales rep who utilizes the firm's Sell to Potential program knows the importance of selling not too few units (the store will run out of stock during the promotion) and not too many units (the store will be stuck with excess inventory after the promotion). The chances to obtain commitment diminish rapidly when the salesperson tries to sell too many or too few units or the wrong grade or style of product.

Also, salespeople should not rely solely on trial orders. A **trial order** is a small order placed by a buyer to see if the product will work and should not be confused with a trial close. A trial order is no commitment, and all too often a buyer will agree to a trial just to get rid of the salesperson. Further, if any learning curve is necessary, a customer who agrees to a trial might be unwilling to invest the time necessary to fully learn the product and will not fully realize the benefits.

The product will be rejected often because customers don't have time to give fair trials. Trial orders can work well when the product is easy to implement (such as selling a new product to a retailer for resale) or when the benefits can be realized only by seeing the product in use.

EFFECTIVE METHODS

"If closing is seen by so many sales experts as manipulative and insulting, are effective methods those that are manipulative but not insulting?" asked one of our students. It is a fair question, and the answer has two elements. First, the salesperson's purpose is to sell the right product in the right amounts. If the prospect does not need what is being sold, the salesperson should walk to the next door and start again. Thus, there should never be a need for manipulation (review Chapter 2 for a discussion of manipulation). Second, in addition to selling only what the customer needs, the salesperson should also sell in a fashion consistent with the way the buyer prefers to buy. Therefore, the salesperson should gain commitment in a manner that will help the buyer make the choice, consistent with the principle of persuasion. We use the word *choice* here to mean that the buyer can say no. Salespeople do try to persuade buyers, but with persuasion, the choice remains with the buyer. Manipulative techniques are designed to reduce or eliminate choice; partnering methods are not.

Studying successful methods and techniques enables salespeople to help prospects buy a product or service they want or need. Buyers sometimes have a need or a want but still hesitate to buy the product or service that will satisfy it. For example, an industrial buyer for a candy manufacturer refused to commit to a change in sweeteners, even though she needed better raw material. Why? Because the sweetener rep had met with her on four separate occasions, and the buyer had difficulty remembering all that was said and agreed on. (Apparently this salesperson was not using a software program like NetSuite very effectively.) Had the salesperson used the appropriate method (the benefit summary method, discussed later in this section), commitment might have been obtained. This section describes several of the most important methods for gaining commitment.

DIRECT REQUEST

The most straightforward, effective method of obtaining commitment is simply to ask for it, called the **direct request method.** However, salespeople need to be wary of appearing overly aggressive when using this direct request method. Decisive customers, such as drivers, appreciate getting down to business and not wasting time. Here are some examples:

Can I put you down for 100 pairs of model 63?

Can we meet with your engineer next Thursday to discuss this further?

Will you come to the home office for a hands-on demonstration?

Can you call the meeting next week?

BENEFIT SUMMARY

Early in the interview salespeople discover or reiterate the needs and problems of the prospect. Then, throughout the presentation, they show how their product can meet those needs. They do this by turning product or service features into benefits specifically for that buyer. As they present each benefit, they ask if that benefit meets the need. When using this approach, called the **benefit summary method,** the salesperson simply reminds the prospect of the agreed-on benefits of the proposal. This nonmanipulative method helps the buyer synthesize points covered in the presentation to make a wise decision. For example, a salesperson attempting to obtain a buyer's commitment to recommend a proposal to a buying committee might say this:

> You stated early in my visit that you were looking for a product of the highest quality, a vendor that could provide quick delivery, and adequate engineering support. As I've mentioned, our fasteners have been rated by an independent laboratory as providing 20 percent higher tensile strength than the closest competitor, resulting in a life expectancy of more than four years. We also discussed the fact that my company can deliver fasteners to your location within 3 hours of your request and that this promise holds true 24 hours a day. Finally, I discussed the fact that we have four engineers on staff whose sole responsibility is to provide support and develop specifications for new fasteners for existing customers. Would you be willing to give the information we discussed to the buying committee along with your endorsement of the proposal?

One advantage of the benefit summary method over the direct request method is that the seller can help the buyer remember all the points discussed in the presentation. The summary becomes particularly important in long presentations and in selling situations involving several meetings prior to obtaining commitment. The salesperson cannot assume that the buyer will remember all the major points discussed in the presentation.

BALANCE SHEET METHOD

Sometimes referred to as the *Ben Franklin method* because Franklin described using it to make decisions, the **balance sheet method** aids prospects who cannot make a decision, even though no reason for their behavior is apparent. Such a prospect may be asked to join the salesperson in listing the pros and cons of buying now or buying later, of buying the salesperson's product or that of a competitor, or of buying the product or not buying it at all.

However, like many nonmanipulative sales techniques, this method can insult a buyer's intelligence if used inappropriately. The salesperson may start to obtain commitment with the following type of statement:

> You know, Mr. Thacker, Ben Franklin was like you, always determined to reach the right decisions and avoid the wrong ones. I suppose that's how you feel. Well, he suggested taking a piece of paper and writing all the reasons for deciding yes in one column and then listing the reasons for deciding no in a second column. He said that when you make this kind of graphic comparison, the correct decision becomes much more apparent.

That close may seem manipulative; it certainly sounds silly. A more effective start may be to simply draw a T on a plain piece of paper, place captions on each side of the crossbar, and leave space below for the insertion of specific benefits or sales points. Then ask the buyer to list pros and cons of making the purchase. For example, assume the product is National Adhesives' hot-melt adhesive used to attach paper labels to plastic Coke bottles. Coca-Cola is currently using a liquid adhesive made by Ajax Corporation. The top of the T might look like this:

Benefits of Adopting the National Adhesives Hot-Melt Method	Benefits of Staying with the Ajax Liquid Adhesives

The salesperson may say something like, "Making a decision like this is difficult. Let's see how many reasons we can think of for your going with the National

Adhesives system." The salesperson would write the benefits (not features) in which the customer has shown interest on the left side of the T. Next the salesperson would ask the customer to list reasons to stay with the Ajax adhesive on the right side. When completed, the T lists should accurately reflect all the pros and cons of each possible decision. At that point the buyer is asked, "Which method do you think is the wisest?"

When used properly, the balance sheet method can help hesitant buyers express their feelings about the decision in a manner similar to the multiattribute matrix (see the appendix of Chapter 3), which gives the salesperson an opportunity to deal with those feelings. It is especially appropriate for a buyer who is an analytical but would make less sense for an expressive. However, the balance sheet approach takes time and may appear "salesy," particularly if relatively unimportant benefits are considered to be equal to more important reasons not to buy. Also, the list of benefits of the product being sold will not always outnumber the list on the other side of the T.

PROBING METHOD

In the **probing method** sales representatives initially attempt to obtain commitment by another method, perhaps simply asking for it (the direct request method). If unsuccessful, the salesperson uses a series of probing questions designed to discover the reason for the hesitation. Once any reason becomes apparent, the salesperson asks a what-if question. (What if I could successfully resolve this concern? Would you be willing to commit?) An illustrative dialogue follows:

SALESPERSON: Could we make an appointment for next week, at which time I would come in and do a complete survey of your needs? It shouldn't take more than three hours.

PROSPECT: No, I don't think I am quite ready to take that step yet.

SALESPERSON: There must be some reason why you are hesitating to go ahead now. Do you mind if I ask what it is?

PROSPECT: I'm just not convinced that your firm is large enough to handle a customer of our size.

SALESPERSON: In addition to that, is there any other reason why you would not be willing to go ahead?

PROSPECT: No.

SALESPERSON: If I can resolve the issue of our size, then you would allow me to conduct a survey?

PROSPECT: Well, I wouldn't exactly say that.

SALESPERSON: Then there must be some other reason. May I ask what it is?

PROSPECT: Well, a friend of mine who uses your services told me that often your billing department sends him invoices for material he didn't want and didn't receive.

SALESPERSON: In addition to that, is there any other reason for not going ahead now?

PROSPECT: No, those are my two concerns.

SALESPERSON: If I could resolve those issues right now, would you be willing to set up an appointment for a survey?

PROSPECT: Sure.

This dialogue illustrates the importance of probing in obtaining commitment. The method attempts to bring to the table all issues of concern to the prospect. The salesperson does not claim to be able to resolve the issues but simply attempts to find out what the issues are. When probing has identified all the issues, the salesperson should attempt to resolve them as soon as possible. After successfully dealing with the concerns of the buyer, the salesperson should then ask for a commitment.

There are many modifications of the probing method. Another way to achieve the same results is the following:

SALESPERSON: Are you willing to buy this product today?

    PROSPECT: No, I don't think so.

SALESPERSON: I really would like to get a better feel of where you are. On a scale of 1 to 10, with 1 being absolutely no purchase and 10 being purchase, where would you say you are?

    PROSPECT: I would say I'm about a 6.

SALESPERSON: If you don't mind my asking, what would it take to move you from a 6 to a 10?

Also, it is important to always keep cultural differences in mind. For example, if a Japanese businesswoman wants to tell an American salesperson that she is not interested, she might state, "Your proposal would be very difficult," just to be polite. If the seller attempts to use the probing method, the Japanese businesswoman may consider the seller to be pushy or a poor listener. In the same way, an Arab businessperson will never say no directly, a custom that helps both sides avoid losing face.[8]

This Frosty Acres Brands salesperson is using the alternative choice close, giving the buyer an option between a name brand (Domino) and their own brand of sugar.

Photography by Lynn Conn, used with permission

ALTERNATIVE CHOICE

In many situations a salesperson may have multiple options to present to a buyer. For example, Teo Schaars sells diamonds directly from cutters in the Netherlands to consumers in the United States. When he started in sales, he would display several dozen diamonds on a purple damask–covered table. Sales were few until his father, a Dutch diamond broker, suggested that he limit his customers' choices; there were simply too many diamonds to choose from, overwhelming the buyer. Schaars found his father's comments to be wise advice. Now Schaars spends more time probing about budget and desires and then shows only two diamonds at a time, explaining the key characteristics of each. Then he allows the customer to express a preference. Schaars may have to show half a dozen or more diamonds before a customer makes the final decision, but he rarely shows more than two at a time (www.anschardiamonds.com).

TRIAL OFFERS

One strategy that can be effective but is also very tricky is the trial offer. This approach is also called "the puppy dog close," based on the idea that once you take a puppy home, you won't want to give it up. If your product is simple to use and the benefits are obvious only in use, a trial offer can be effective. If the product is complicated, however, prospects may not want to make the investment in learning how to use it and conclude it is too difficult to learn. A fear that some sales managers have is that salespeople will rely too much on the approach as a way to avoid actually asking for the order.

If you plan to use the approach, it's best to do the following:

- Set a specific time for training, if needed, and make sure the user is comfortable with the product.
- Document that the decision criteria are concrete—and that the trial is needed to achieve those criteria.
- Agree on when a decision will be made.

Some salespeople, such as in the car or office equipment business, find that prospects may use trials as a way to simply borrow the product and solve a short-term need. Setting proper expectations at the outset can aid in avoiding those situations.

OTHER METHODS

Literally hundreds of techniques and methods to obtain commitment have been tried. Exhibit 11.3 lists a number of traditional methods. Most of them, however, tend to be ineffective with sophisticated customers; nevertheless, many can be

Exhibit 11.3
Some Traditional Closing Methods

Method	How It Works	Remark
Minor-point close	The seller assumes it is easier to get the prospect to decide on a very trivial point than on the whole proposition: What color do you like, blue or red?	This method can upset a prospect who feels he or she is being manipulated or tricked into making a commitment. Even unsophisticated buyers easily spot this technique.
Continuous yes close	Throughout the presentation, the seller constantly asks questions for which the prospect most logically would answer yes. By the end of the discussion, the buyer is so accustomed to saying yes that when the order is requested, the natural response is yes.	This method is based on self-perception theory. As the presentation progresses, the buyer begins to perceive himself or herself as being agreeable. At the close, the buyer wants to maintain this self-image and almost unthinkingly says yes. Use of this method can destroy long-term relationships if the buyer later feels manipulated.
Assumptive close	The seller, without asking for the order, simply begins to write it up. A variation is to fill out the order form as the prospect answers questions.	This method does not even give the buyer the courtesy of agreeing. It can be perceived as being very pushy and manipulative.
Standing-room-only close	The seller attempts to obtain commitment by describing the negative consequences of waiting. For example, the seller may state, "If you can't decide now, I'll have to offer it to another customer."	This method can be effective if the statement is true. However, if the prospect really does need to act quickly, this deadline should probably be discussed earlier in the presentation to reduce possible mistrust and the feeling of being pushed.
Benefit-in-reserve close	First the seller attempts to obtain commitment by another method. If unsuccessful, the seller says, "Oh, if you order today I can offer you an additional 5 percent for your trade-in."	This method can backfire easily. The buyer tends to think, "If I had agreed to your first attempt to obtain commitment, I would not have learned about this new enticement. If I wait longer, how much better will your offer be?" The buyer may then seek additional concessions in every future sale attempt.
Emotional close	The seller appeals to the buyer's emotions to close the sale. For example, the seller may say, "This really is a good deal. To be honest with you, I desperately need to secure an order today. As you know, I work on a straight commission basis. My wife is going to have surgery next week, and our insurance just won't cover. . . ."	Many obvious problems arise with this method. It is an attempt to move away from focusing entirely on the buyer's personal needs. It does not develop trust or respect. Do not use this close!

used in a nonmanipulative manner if appropriate. For example, the minor-point close can be appropriate if there really is a need to make a choice between two options; the factor that makes the method manipulative is the assumption that the minor choice is the equivalent to making the sale.

No method of obtaining commitment will work if the buyer does not trust the salesperson, the company, and the product. Gaining commitment should not require the use of tricky techniques or methods to force buyers to do something they do not want to do or to manipulate them to buy something they do not need.

IF COMMITMENT IS OBTAINED

The salesperson's job is not over when commitment is obtained. In fact, in many ways the job is just beginning. This section describes the salesperson's responsibilities that accrue after the buyer says yes.

NO SURPRISES

Customers do not like surprises, so now is the time to go over any important information they will need to fully enjoy the benefits of the product or service. For example, if you are selling life insurance and a physical is required, give the customer as much detail as possible to prepare him or her for that experience. Or if a company is going to lease a piece of heavy equipment, let the customer know that delivery will occur after a credit check and how long that credit check will take. John Branton, president of Safe Harbor Financial, requires his salespeople to make sure the client understands how the product works and, if any negative consequences can occur, make sure the client is prepared for it. No customer wants to be surprised with a tax bill later, for example, even if the purchase was still the best choice available.[8]

CONFIRM THE CUSTOMER'S CHOICE

Customers like to believe they have chosen intelligently when they make a decision. After important decisions, they may feel a little insecure about whether the sacrifice is worth it. Such feelings are called **buyer's remorse** or **postpurchase dissonance.** Successful salespeople reassure customers that their choice was the right one. For example:

> I know you will enjoy using your new office machines. You can plan on many months of trouble-free service. I'll call on you in about two weeks to make sure everything is operating smoothly. Be sure to call me if you need any help before then. Or

> Congratulations, Mr. Jacobs. You are going to be glad you decided to use our service. There is no finer service available. Now let's make certain you get off to the right start. Your first bulletin will arrive on Tuesday, March 2.

> Or

> You've made an excellent choice. Other stores won't have a product like this for at least 30 days.

GET THE SIGNATURE

The buyer's signature often formalizes a commitment. Signing the order is a natural part of a well-planned procedure. The order blank should be accessible, and the signing should be treated as a routine matter. Ordinarily the customer has decided to buy before being asked to sign the order. In other words, the signature on the order blank merely confirms that an agreement has already been reached. The decision to buy or not to buy should not focus on a signature.

The salesperson needs to remember several important points: (1) Make the actual signing an easy, routine procedure; (2) fill out the order blank accurately and promptly; and (3) be careful not to exhibit any excess eagerness or excitement when the prospect is about to sign.

SHOW APPRECIATION

All buyers like to think that their business is appreciated even if they purchase only small quantities. Customers like to do business with salespeople who show that they want the business.

Salespeople may show appreciation by writing the purchaser a letter. This practice especially develops goodwill after large purchases and with new customers. In some situations a small gift, such as a pen with the selling company's name on it, may also be an effective thank-you. Salespeople should always thank the purchaser personally; the thanks should be genuine but not effusive.

Is an e-mail message adequate? Eleanor Brownell doesn't think so. She says, "It (a handwritten note) makes you memorable."[9]

CULTIVATE FOR FUTURE CALLS

In most fields of selling, obtaining commitment is not the end of a business transaction; rather, it is only one part of a mutually profitable business relationship. Obtaining commitment is successful only if it results in goodwill and future commitment. Keep in mind that research shows that it is how the salesperson treats the customer that is the biggest determinant of future sales. How the customer gets treated determines loyalty, which then influences repurchase.[10]

Customers like to do business with salespeople who do not lose interest immediately after securing commitment. What a salesperson does after achieving commitment is called **follow-up**. As Jeffrey Bailey, sales director for Oracle, recognizes, "Making the sale is only the beginning." After making the sale, the salesperson must follow up to make sure the product is delivered when promised, set up appropriately, and so forth. We talk more about follow-up in later chapters. The point here is that the sale does not end with the customer's signature on the order form. Research shows that the quality of follow-up service is an important contributing factor in perceptions of salesperson quality and long-term relationships.[11]

REVIEW THE ACTIONS TO BE TAKEN

An important step, particularly when commitment is next in the buying process, is to review what each party has agreed to do. In the case of a multiple-visit sales cycle, the salesperson must review not only what the client will do but also what the salesperson will do to prepare for the next meeting. To be welcomed on repeat calls, salespeople must be considerate of all the parties involved in buying or using the product. They must pronounce and spell all names correctly, explain and review the terms of the purchase so no misunderstandings will occur, and be sociable and cordial to subordinates as well as those in key positions. In addition, the buyer or user must get the service promised. The importance of this point cannot be overemphasized. Chapter 13 provides detailed information about how to service the account and build a partnership.

IF COMMITMENT IS NOT OBTAINED

When asking for commitment, salespeople can often encounter objections. One important consideration is to recognize that these objections are no different than any others; they just happen at a time when you might think they're more important because the process is near the end. One approach is to respond with a question that checks the importance of the objection. For example, if the buyer objects to price, ask, "If price weren't an issue, is there anything else preventing us from moving forward?" If the answer is yes, then you probe to determine what those issues are, as price was likely just a screen for the real concerns. If the answer is no, then you can explore financial terms and other financial options. Other objections can serve as excuses to screen the real one, but price is the most often used screen.

Naturally the salesperson does not always obtain the desired commitment. The salesperson should never take this situation personally (which is easier said than done). Doing everything right does not guarantee a sale. Situations change, and customers who may have really needed the product when everything started may find that other priorities make a purchase impossible.

Many times, when a buyer says no, the seller is wise to treat it as "No, not now" rather than "No, never." Kenneth Young, CEO of Tymco, once told a salesperson that he just didn't have the budget to make the decision now but that he'd consider it again the following year. "The salesperson stayed in touch, and when it came time to plan the budget, I made sure she was given a chance to give us all of the cost details so we could plan for the purchase."

thinking **it** through   Many students report that asking for the order is the hardest part of selling. Why is it difficult? Does the customer need you to ask for the sale? Have you ever needed a salesperson to ask you to buy? Why or why not?

This section describes some of the common reasons for failing to obtain commitment and offers practical suggestions for salespeople who encounter rejection.

SOME REASONS FOR LOST OPPORTUNITIES

In this discussion, we are assuming that the salesperson did an appropriate qualifying job and understood the buyer's needs. As you saw in "From the Buyer's Seat 11.1," some buyers are being asked to take a meeting or take the next step in the purchase process when no need is present. Clearly asking for commitment when there's no need is foolish. So why would you lose a sale if the customer clearly had a need? Here's a few reasons.

Wrong Attitudes

As discussed earlier in the chapter, salespeople need to have a positive attitude. A fear that obtaining commitment will be difficult may be impossible to hide. Inexperienced salespeople naturally will be concerned about their ability to obtain commitment; most of us have an innate fear of asking someone else to do anything. Some salespeople even fail to ask for the sale because if they never ask, they will never hear no. As a result, they always have more prospects but fewer customers than everyone else. But all salespeople know they need to focus on obtaining commitment to keep their jobs.

Some salespeople display unwarranted excitement when they see that prospects are ready to commit. Research suggests that nonverbals are very important cues and can signal trustworthiness or a lack thereof to buyers. A salesperson who appears excited or overly eager may display nonverbal cues that suggest dishonesty or a lack of empathy.[12] At this point wary buyers may change their minds and refuse to commit.

One of the main reasons for salespeople's improper attitudes toward obtaining commitment is the historical importance placed on closing the sale. Closing has often been viewed as a win–lose situation (if I get the order, I win; if I don't get the order, I lose). Until salespeople see obtaining commitment as a positive occurrence for the buyer, these attitudes will persist.

Poor Presentation

Prospects or customers who do not understand the presentation or see the benefits of the purchase cannot be expected to buy. The salesperson must use trial closes (see Chapter 8) and continually take the pulse of the interview.

A boring presentation can be one reason for failure to obtain commitment.

A poor presentation can also be caused by haste. The salesperson who tries to deliver a 60-minute presentation in 20 minutes may skim over or omit important sales points. Forgoing the presentation may be better than delivering it hastily. Further, a sales presentation given at the wrong time or under unfavorable conditions is likely to be ineffective.

Another reason for not obtaining commitment is lack of product knowledge. In fact, lack of product knowledge is often cited as an important barrier to obtaining commitment.[13] If the salesperson does not know what the product does, you can be certain the buyer will not be able to figure it out either.

Poor Habits and Skills

Obtaining commitment requires proper habits and some measure of skill. The habit of talking too much rather than listening often causes otherwise good presentations to fail. Knowing when to quit talking is just as important as knowing what to say. Some salespeople become so fascinated by the sound of their own voices that they talk themselves out of sales they have already made. A presentation that turns into a monologue is not likely to retain the buyer's interest.

DISCOVERING THE CAUSE

The real reasons for not obtaining commitment must be uncovered. Only then can salespeople proceed intelligently to eliminate the barriers. Some firms have developed sophisticated systems to follow up on lost sales. Sales software, such as NetSuite or salesforce.com, can also identify points in the selling process where a salesperson may be having difficulty. If the sales cycle involves a demonstration, for example, and the salesperson turns fewer leads into demonstrations, the fault may lie in the needs identification skills of that salesperson.

Dave Alexander, account executive for SGA, Inc., says his company does a postsale analysis whether it wins or loses the sale. This discipline causes the sales team to focus on the factors that really lead to success.[14] Dave Stein, author of *How Winners Sell*, says that all too often salespeople will lay the blame for failure on price or the product but will take personal credit for any successes.[15] Both Stein and Alexander agree, however, that an effective win/loss system forces the salesperson to examine the real causes and, if the sale was not won, consider personal strategies for improvement.

SUGGESTIONS FOR DEALING WITH REJECTION

Maintain the Proper Perspective

Probably the inexperienced salesperson's most important lesson is that when a buyer says no, the sales process has not necessarily ended. A no may mean

"Not now," "I need more information," "Don't hurry me," or "I don't understand." An answer of no should be a challenge to seek the reason behind the buyer's negative response.

In many fields of selling, most prospects do not buy. The ratio of orders achieved to sales presentations may be 1 to 3, 1 to 5, 1 to 10, or even 1 to 20. Salespeople may tend to eliminate nonbuyers from the prospect list after one unsuccessful call. This practice may be sound in some cases; however, many sales result on the second, third, fourth, or fifth call. Tim Pavlovich, sales executive for Dell, had one client require over 50 sales calls before closing. Of course, the sale was worth over $100 million annually, so it was pretty complicated. When an earlier visit has not resulted in commitment, careful preparation for succeeding calls becomes more crucial.

Another perspective is that when a buyer says no it is because the buyer is not yet fully informed; otherwise the buyer would have said yes. Consequently, if the buyer has given the salesperson the opportunity to make a presentation, the buyer recognizes that a need exists or is going to exist. What has not happened yet is that match between the offering and the need. At the same time, however, no does not mean "Sell me again right now." As we discussed earlier, "No" may mean "Sell me again later."

The salesperson should have a clear objective for each sales call. When commitment cannot be obtained to meet that objective, the salesperson will often attempt to obtain commitment for a reduced request (a secondary or minimum objective). For example, the salesperson may attempt to gain a trial order instead of an actual order, although, as we discussed earlier, this opportunity should be offered as a last resort.

Recommend Other Sources

A sales representative who uses the consultative selling philosophy (as described in Chapter 5) may recommend a competitor's product to solve the prospect's needs. When recommending other sources, the sales rep should explain why his or her product does not meet the prospect's needs and then provide the name of the competitive product. The goodwill generated by such a gesture should lead to future opportunities when the timing and needs are right.

After recommending other sources, the salesperson usually should ask the prospect for names of people who might be able to buy the seller's product. Also, the salesperson should emphasize the desire to maintain contact with the prospect in the event the seller's firm develops a competitive offering.

Good Manners Are Important

If obtaining commitment fails for any reason, the salesperson should react good-naturedly. Salespeople have to learn to accept no if they expect to call on prospects again. Even if salespeople do not obtain commitment, they should thank prospects for their time. Arguing or showing disappointment gains nothing. The salesperson may plan to keep in contact with these prospects through e-mail, an occasional phone call, a follow-up letter, or product literature mailings. One salesperson likes to make the following statement at the conclusion of any meeting that does not result in commitment: "I'll never annoy you, but if you don't mind, I'm going to keep in touch."

Many salespeople consider leaving something behind that will let the prospect contact the salesperson in the future. Some firms use promotional products, such as a pen with the company's name and phone number, as a gift after each call to remind the prospect of the salesperson's company. Others may simply use brochures and business cards.

BRINGING THE INTERVIEW TO A CLOSE

Few buyers are interested in a prolonged visit after they commit. Obviously the departure cannot be abrupt; the salesperson should complete the interview smoothly. But goodwill is never built by wasting the buyer's time after the business is concluded.

Remember that most sales take several calls to complete. If an order wasn't signed (and often getting an order isn't even the objective of the call; see Chapter 7) and the prospect wishes to continue considering the proposal, the salesperson should leave with a clear action plan for all parties. An example of the kind of dialogue the salesperson might pursue follows:

> SALESPERSON: When will you have had a chance to look over this proposal?
>
> BUYER: By the end of next week, probably.
>
> SALESPERSON: Great, I'll call on you in about 10 days, OK?
>
> BUYER: Sure, set up something with my secretary.
>
> SALESPERSON: Is there anything else I need to do for you before that next meeting?

The salesperson should always make sure the next step is clear for both parties. Therefore, review what you will do next, what the customer will do next, and when you will meet again.

Follow up promptly with a thank-you and reminder note after the sales call. If you are following up after a sales call in which you gained commitment for the next sales call, an e-mail message is not only sufficient but the best idea. For example, Bruce Culbert of the Pedowitz Group follows up each sales call with an e-mail that summarizes what happened, what each person promised to do (including what the buyer promised), and when the next meeting is. The sales cycle may take months, and such documentation is necessary to avoid losing momentum. Even when he is told no, his follow up e-mail includes a simple thank-you for the opportunity, along with a time frame for a follow-up. When he finally gets the sale, he'll follow up with a handwritten note and, in some cases, a "launch" dinner with the client to celebrate the new relationship.

Shirley Hunter, an account executive with Teradata, will follow up a sale with a handwritten thank-you note. She may also personally present a thank-you gift (her product costs half a million dollars, so a sale is worth celebrating). Her choice of a gift, though, will reflect the situation—a box of Lifesavers for the executive who got behind the purchase, a box of crayons for an architect, or something equally creative.

SELLING YOURSELF

When Carter Simon felt his fraternity needed a stronger recruiting program to attract new members, he had to gain the support of the senior leadership of the chapter. In addition, he had to convince the older members to take on a more active role with the recruiting process. "Getting someone to say they will do something is a lot easier than actually getting them to do it," says Simon.

Corey Bergstrom and others at Cabela's faced a similar challenge when they realized that the company needed a new direction in how it sold through technology. Corey presented his plan to the executive team, who then asked him to present it to the board of directors. Corey, who is an IT guy and not a salesperson, successfully proved his business case. A year later, the board is very happy with the results, as Corey's team has grown sales significantly. The stock market also likes the results, with stock prices up over 35 percent.

When selling internally, in your fraternity now or in your company later, gaining real commitment can mean the difference between a program's success or failure. Just because the choice seems obvious to you—"It's the best decision for our customer and our company!"—doesn't mean that others in the company see it the same way. Nor can someone always order an employee to do something and expect the task to be done well. Commitment skills when selling yourself are critical to a successful career, whether you go into sales or something else altogether.

As with external customers, though, understanding and selling to others' needs has to come first. If you are interested only in your own needs, no closing skills will carry you.

What's also important to remember is that when selling internally, you have to live with the consequences of the selling process much more intimately than when selling to a customer. Using pushy or cheesy techniques contributes to a reputation that makes future decisions or actions more difficult to secure.

Earlier we noted Shirley Hunter's perspective on thanking a customer for a sale. She also believes, though, that internal celebrations are necessary to say thank you to those who contributed either to a sale or to a successful customer implementation. Cultivating for future calls or decisions is also important. You may not win on this decision, but there will be other opportunities to use your closing skills when selling yourself.

SUMMARY

Commitment cannot be obtained by some magical or miraculous technique if the salesperson has failed to prepare the prospect to make this decision throughout the presentation. Salespeople should always attempt to gain commitment in a way that is consistent with the objectives of the meeting. Obtaining commitment begins with the salesperson's contact with the prospect. It can succeed only when all facets of the selling process fall into their proper place. All sellers need to keep in mind this old saying: "People don't buy products or services; they buy solutions to their problems!"

The process of obtaining commitment is the logical progression of any sales call. Commitment is important for the customer, the seller's firm, and the seller. Commitment should result in a win–win situation for all parties concerned.

Pricing is an important element of any sale and is usually presented at the time of closing. Quantity discounts, payment terms, and shipping terms can affect the final price charged to the buyer as well as influence the decision.

There is no one "right" time to obtain commitment. Salespeople should watch their prospects closely and recognize when to obtain commitment. Successful salespeople carefully monitor customer comments, their buyers' nonverbal cues and actions, and their responses to probes. Comments can be in the form of questions, requirements, benefits, and responses to trial closes.

To successfully obtain commitment, the salesperson needs to maintain a positive attitude, allow the customer to set the pace, be assertive rather than aggressive, and sell the right item in the right amounts. Engaging in these practices will result in a strong long-term relationship between buyer and seller.

No one method of obtaining commitment works best for all buyers. The direct request method is the simplest to use; however, the prospect often needs help in evaluating the proposal. In those instances other methods may be more appropriate, such as the alternative choice, the benefit summary, the balance sheet method, or the probing method. No method of obtaining commitment will work if a buyer does not trust the salesperson.

If commitment is obtained, the salesperson should immediately assure the buyer that the choice was judicious. The salesperson should show genuine appreciation as well as cultivate the relationship for future calls.

If commitment is not obtained, the salesperson should analyze the reasons. Difficulties in obtaining commitment can be directly traced to wrong attitudes, a poor presentation, and/or poor habits and skills. Even if no commitment is obtained, the salesperson should thank the prospect for his or her time.

KEY TERMS

aggressive 293
assertive 294
balance sheet method 296
benefit summary method 295
buyer's remorse 300
buying signals 290
cash discount 287
closing 284
closing cues 290

cumulative discount 287
direct request method 295
follow-up 301
postpurchase dissonance 300
probing method 297
requirements 291
submissive 294
trial close 292
trial order 294

ETHICS PROBLEMS

1. One buyer stated, "All closing methods are devious and self-serving! How can a salesperson use a technique but still keep my needs totally in mind?" Comment. Integrate into your discussion the concepts of persuasion versus manipulation.
2. A customer asked the salesperson, "How do you intend to solve my problem?" The salesperson told the customer his approach and provided a time line on when each step would be completed. When asked for the sale, the customer said, "Oh, I'll just do it myself." Now that she had the process spelled out for her, she felt that she no longer needed the salesperson. Was her behavior appropriate? Why or why not? And, whether appropriate or not, how can salespeople avoid such situations?

QUESTIONS AND PROBLEMS

1. Review Exhibit 11.3 and discuss which social style would be best suited to which method of closing. Note that some of the methods are appropriate for multiple styles if worded differently. Give an example of how you would word one differently to address two different styles.
2. "The ABCs of closing are 'Always be closing.'" Another version is "Close early—close often." What is your reaction to these time-honored statements?
3. Harold Bumpurs, a professional purchasing agent, says he has never noticed any tricky closes. His perception is due not to the smooth closing skills of the salespeople who call on him but to the total skill sets they have developed. Prioritize a list of selling skills, from most important to least. How much time should be spent improving commitment-gaining skills as opposed to developing other skills? Why?
4. You've made six sales calls over a month with one prospect, qualifying needs with three separate influencers, and you finally get through to the decision maker. You make your presentation and it seems to go well. All of the

influencers are there; they are all nodding yes, so as you wrap up, you ask when they'd like to get started. The decision maker replies, "I'd like to think this over." Two of the influencers look surprised while the third looks confused. "OK," you reply, "is next Tuesday OK to check back?" How could you improve on your answer? Be specific; what exactly would you say?

5. One sales manager who worked for a refrigeration equipment company taught his salespeople the following close: Ask questions that allow you to fill out the contract. Assume the sale is made and hand the contract to the buyer, along with a pen. If the buyer doesn't immediately take the pen, drop it and make the buyer pick it up. Once the buyer has the pen in hand, he or she is more likely to use it to sign the contract, so just wait silently until the buyer does.
   a. Would you label this seller as assertive or aggressive?
   b. Is this a trick (manipulative) or merely dramatization (persuasive)?
   c. How would you respond to this behavior if you were the buyer?

6. You've identified a process by which your company could recycle packaging material, saving the company about 10 percent of the packaging costs. But when you talk this over with the person in charge of shipping, he says, "You're just a sales rep! Go sell something and let me do my job!" What do you think is driving his reaction? How would you respond? What would you do next?

7. What makes a Mercedes-Benz worth more than a Volkswagen? How would you convince someone that it is worth more if she or he knew nothing about the various brands of cars? How would the buyer's lack of knowledge influence how you try to gain commitment?

8. Todd Pollock, while in ticket sales for the San Francisco 49ers, says he heard "no" at least 10 times for every "yes," sometimes 20 times. How do you deal with rejection? What strategies would you try if you were in Todd's situation?

9. What would you say to a friend to gain his or her commitment to go on a spring break trip? Describe exactly what you would say to your friend using each of the following methods (make any assumptions necessary):
   a. Alternative choice.
   b. Direct request.
   c. Benefit summary.
   d. Balance sheet.
   e. Probing.

10. A customer is willing to order 100 cases listed at $20 per case to get a 15 percent quantity discount. Terms are 2/10, n/30. The customer pays five days after receiving the invoice. How much did the customer pay?

CASE PROBLEMS

case **11.1**

Closing Euro_LED

Using radio frequency identification (RFID) technology, Matya manufactures inventory management and tracking systems. Used in any environment where tracking inventory location is important, these devices track movement of products within a warehouse, within a manufacturing facility, and even while on the truck or train. Patsy Moorman was calling on Dave Daugherty, senior purchasing director for Euro-LED, a company that makes low-energy lighting for commercial applications. Dave has global responsibility for purchasing standardization, and developing a common inventory management system across all of Euro-LED's 24 locations in eight countries is a task he has to complete this year. Patsy's primary call objective was to have Dave agree to set up an appointment in the next several weeks for Patsy to present to the supply chain committee that will review proposals and narrow the choices down to three systems.

PATSY: Our scanning systems can support the digital standards of both the United States and Europe, which means that, with some engineering changes in your computer network, your locations can use the same scanners.

DAVE: Patsy, I've really been thinking that the RFID scanners made by Alcatel are industry standard, and I'm concerned about our China plant. What has Matya done differently with these scanners?

PATSY: Quality is something we take very seriously at Matya, but having the best-built old product isn't enough, is it? So we've also built probably the finest engineering staff over the past five years that you'll find anywhere. The result is a product line that was just awarded the Dubai Engineering Innovation World Cup award only last month.

DAVE: That's impressive, and you're right. A well-built product using yesterday's technology is of no benefit to us. But how important is bicontinental use at the scanning level? It's not like we ship from our European plants to the States; seems to me we could use local-made products and just merge data later when we need to.

PATSY: Yes, you can, but that's really inconsistent with the overall strategy of minimizing the number of vendors and having global suppliers. How do you serve Latin America or Africa?

DAVE: Well, we don't have a lot of business in Africa, yet but it's growing. And in Latin America, we supply both from China and the United States, so I see your point.

PATSY: Then you may have seen a report issued by DataMark that indicates some users have had data problems that were difficult to identify until something goes horribly wrong. Just merging data from disparate systems isn't always the best option.

DAVE: I've seen that data from DataMark as well as an article in the last issue of *Supply Chain Management*. But we've had no plans for a global RFID process.

PATSY: Why is that?

DAVE: We don't know that it is necessary—we don't think we've got that many locations where scanning is a necessity.

PATSY: What would be considered a significant percentage—of your total sites, I mean?

DAVE: I would guess 50 percent would be acceptable. What are others experiencing?

PATSY: We've got several, maybe four, that have standardized with us globally and another group of about two dozen that use us in the United States or Europe. How does that sound?

DAVE: Intriguing, though we're not the same as others.

PATSY: I know. That's why I'd like to set up a meeting with your supply chain team in the near future. But we'll probably also need someone there from logistics, right?

DAVE: Yes, I suppose we would.

PATSY: Will I have your endorsement at the meeting?

DAVE: We'll have to wait and see. I'll need some documentation on the figures you've given me, and I'd like that before we set up the meeting.

Questions

1. What form of closing did Patsy use to gain Dave's commitment to the idea? Was that appropriate? Why or why not?

2. List how you would attempt to obtain commitment using three other methods of your choice. Write out exactly what you would say for each method (and be sure to identify the method).

3. Although you have been shown only a portion of the conversation, evaluate Patsy's performance in terms of the following:
  a. Selling benefits, not features
  b. Using trial closes
  c. Using communication aids to strengthen the presentation
  d. Responding to objections
  e. Attempting to gain commitment at the proper time

case **11.2**

Blue Onion

Blue Onion is a systems integrator, meaning that it helps companies integrate new software into the old systems and the customer's processes. So when a customer buys SAP software, for example, Blue Onion customizes the software to fit the customer's work processes and to work with the customer's old software.

Sean Thornton just joined the company as an account executive. After five years of systems analysis and sales support for Oracle, a major software provider, he wanted to earn a salesperson's living, so he made the switch. As part of his training he spent some time working with several experienced salespeople. One such salesperson was Mary Kate Danaher.

She filled him in on the client they were about to see as they entered a large office building. "They are buying a system called BOSS," she said. "This is going to be a massive change for them, and it looks like they'll implement in three phases over a two-year period."

"In other words, a big sale for us, right?" replied Sean.

"Yup. And I'm not going to let them get away. They are considering doing the integration on their own, using temporary employees, and that never works well. So I've already filled out a contract and today, when we meet with the CEO, we'll get it signed." The determination in her voice matched the purpose in her step as she strode to the bank of elevators in the center of the lobby.

Once in the CEO's office, sitting around a small conference table with the head of MIS and the CFO, Mary Kate reviewed the key points of the agreement, saying, "Shirley, you know that this is a critical implementation and you can't afford any mistakes. That's why you should rely on Blue Onion," and handed the contract to the CEO.

The head of MIS squirmed uncomfortably. Shirley looked at him, and he said, "Shirley, I really think we can do this ourselves and save a lot of money."

"With all due respect, Jack, my experience would say that you can't. Temporaries just don't care as much as your own people do, nor as much as our people do," said Mary Kate, with conviction.

Silence draped over the table. Sean could hear an antique clock ticking away on the shelf behind Shirley's desk. After what seemed like an hour but was probably only a few seconds, Shirley looked at the CFO, who nodded almost imperceptibly. She took out her pen, signed the contract, and handed it back to Mary Kate.

"Thank you, Shirley. I will personally see this project through to completion, on time and on budget, and at the end, you'll get all you hoped for and more," said Mary Kate.

The MIS director stood, looking at the CEO and then the CFO, then back to the CEO. Then he stuck out his hand, saying, "Congratulations, Mary Kate and good luck." Then he turned, and left the room.

An awkward pause was broken first by Mary Kate. "Shirley, I will set up a meeting with our engineering manager and Jack for next week so that we can lay out the plan for integration. I'm sure that Jack will enjoy meeting her." Small talk ensued, and within five minutes, Mary Kate and Sean were back in the lobby.

"Well, rookie, we got it!" exclaimed Mary Kate. They exchanged high fives and headed to the parking lot.

Questions

1. Assess Mary Kate's style. Is her style something Sean should emulate?
2. Blue Onion's implementation team will need to work very closely with Jack and his people, and it doesn't appear that Jack wants to be helpful. What could Mary Kate have done to avoid this situation? Assume this meeting was called by Shirley. How could Mary Kate have handled it differently?

ROLE PLAY CASE

Once again you will give your presentation to the same buyer (BancVue, GelTech, and High Point Solutions) that you did after Chapters 9 and 10 (if you did not do role plays after those chapters, review that material now). This time you will complete your presentation, first summarizing the needs and going all the way to asking for the sale. You will have an opportunity to work on presentation, objection handling, and closing skills.

If two people are involved in the sale (a seller and a buyer) while a third observes, the observer should do the following:

1. Identify any objection-handling methods used.

2. Determine whether the seller is focused on benefits or only features.

3. Note when trial closes are used.

4. Identify the closing method used.

The professor will pass out new buyer sheets.

ADDITIONAL REFERENCES

Agnihotri Raj, Adam Rapp, and Kevin Trainor. "Understanding the Role of Information Communication in the Buyer-Seller Exchange Process: Antecedents and Outcomes." *Journal of Business and Industrial Marketing* 24, no. 7 (2009), pp. 474–89.

Baumgarth, Carsten, and Lars Binckebanck. "Sales Force Impact on B-to-B Brand Equity: Conceptual Framework and Empirical Test." *Journal of Product and Brand Management* 20, no. 6 (2011), pp. 487–98.

Bradford, Kevin D., J. Michael Crant, and Joan M. Phillips. "How Suppliers Affect Trust with Their Customers: The Role of Salesperson Job Satisfaction and Perceived Customer Importance." *Journal of Marketing Theory and Practice* 17, no. 4 (Fall 2009), pp. 383–94.

Fu, Frank, Willy Bolander, and Eli Jones. "Managing the Drivers of Organizational Commitment and Salesperson Effort: An Application of Meyer and Allen's Three-Component Model." *Journal of Marketing Theory and Practice* 17, no. 4 (Fall 2009), pp. 335–50.

Gough, Orla, and Mohamed Nurullah. "Understanding What Drives the Purchase Decision in Pension and Investment Products." *Journal of Financial Services Marketing* 14, no. 2 (September 2009), pp. 152–72.

Pettijohn, Charles E., and Linda Pettijohn. "An Exploratory Analysis of Student Exposure to Personal Selling: An MBA Perspective." *Academy of Educational Leadership Journal* 14, special issue (2010), pp. 35–46.

Pinar, Musa, J. Russell Hardin, and Zeliha Eser. "Applicant Perceptions of the Gender Effect on the Selling Process and on Targeting Customers: Does Gender Matter?" *Academy of Marketing Studies Journal* 15, no. 1 (2011), pp. 107–24.

Rutherford, Brian N., James S. Boles, Hiram C. Barksdale Jr., and Julie T. Johnson. "Buyer's Relational Desire and Number of Suppliers Used: The Relationship between Perceived Commitment and Continuance." *Journal of Marketing Theory and Practice* 16, no. 3 (Summer 2008), pp. 247–57.

Singh, Ramendra, and Abraham Koshy. "Determinants of B2B Salespersons' Performance and Effectiveness. *Journal of Business and Industrial Marketing* 25, no. 7 (2010), pp. 535–46.

Turner, Roger, Christophe Lasserre, and Pascal Beauchet. "Marketing Metrics: Innovation in Field Force Bonuses: Enhancing Motivation through a Structured Process-Based Approach." *Journal of Medical Marketing* 7, no. 2 (2007), pp. 126–35.

Weber, John A. "Business Ethics Training: Insights from Learning Theory." *Journal of Business Ethics* 70, no. 1 (2007), pp. 61–85.

Zallocco, Ronald, Ellen Bolman Pullins, and Michael L. Mallin. "A Re-Examination of B2B Sales Performance. *Journal of Business and Industrial Marketing* 24, no. 8 (2009), pp. 598–614.

chapter **15**

MANAGING YOUR TIME AND TERRITORY

SOME QUESTIONS ANSWERED IN THIS CHAPTER ARE

- Why is time so valuable for salespeople?
- What can you do to "create" more selling time?
- What should you consider when devising a territory strategy?
- How does territory strategy relate to account strategy and building partnerships?
- How should you analyze your daily activities and sales calls?
- How can you evaluate your own performance so you can improve?

PROFILE

PROFILE Window seats, early check-ins, and upgrades to roomier seats are airline essentials any frequent business traveler craves. These are just some of the requests I make whenever possible when I am covering my territory—the western half of the United States.

I've held many sales roles for the 3M Infection Prevention Division since graduating from college seven years ago. I studied sales as an undergraduate and also completed an internship with 3M in the Infection Prevention Division. My division manufactures products used in operating room and clinic settings. Currently, I am a surgery center specialist managing our relationship with a vendor partner and their sales team. I also work on internal cross-functional marketing, sales management, and sales learning and development teams. With this much responsibility, the way I manage my territory and time is critical to my effectiveness.

I usually like to travel with my vendor reps at least twice a year in their respective territories for at least two days a week. We meet with customers and distribution partners, creating plans for how to grow their business. We also travel to many industry and customer trade shows throughout the year around the country in their territories. With these sales expectations and customer interactions, one has to develop an effective plan and tactics to receive the most value for their time. Here are a couple of my time and territory management tactics and tools I employ to be effective. I encourage you to develop your own tactics that are effective for you in your territory:

1. *You have to spend time on the opportunities that have the greatest potential.* We all have finite time in most instances with our customer. For example, when I make a trip to the western half of the United States to work with my sales team, I try to direct our efforts to our largest sales opportunities while I am in the territory. Of course, we do meet with our medium to small opportunities, but we just want to make sure we are maximizing our time in the field. In addition to meeting with these customers while I am out working in the West, I try to meet with my western distributor partners, product/clinical specialist, and regional sales directors from my organization. The more points we can touch, the more information and knowledge we can have to manage our time and territory better.

2. *Delegate items to your sales support team.* That team can include sales analyst, product specialist, contract specialist, and so on. These team players have specific skill sets and experience that will help you along the way in closing and completing the sales process. We love to employ our clinical specialists (who are nurses) to educate nurses like themselves on the benefits of using our products in the operating room. It lends great credibility to us, the sales reps, as well as our organization. Even if you don't have specific resources assigned to you, finding people who can help you is important. Teaming and delegation is essential in any sales process, as it will free you to spend your time where it will pay off the most.

3. *Use digital tools such as e-mail, text messages, product webinars, and instant messaging wisely.* These tools have allowed me to manage my territory virtually from anywhere. We most recently used a combination of webinars over three weeks to present a sterilization class to over 150 customers throughout the country. Because of these webinars, we were able to secure a nice amount of new business for Q3 without having to do as many individual presentations in someone's clinic or hospital. These are great easy-to-use applications, and I would advise you to add them to your repertoire to maximize your time and territory management.

I suspect these recommendations would apply in principle to many jobs, but you can see how you have to manage your territory as you embark on your sales career. The great thing about time and territory management is that you can personalize it to fit your and your customer's schedule. Time and territory management is an ever-evolving concept that I am quite sure will look different 10 years from now, and this makes sale roles exciting and makes for more progressive careers. Well, I have to go out check in for flight now, as I think I am running late!

Visit our Web site at:
www.3m.com

THE VALUE OF TIME

The old axiom "Time is money" certainly applies to selling. If you work 8 hours a day for 240 days of a year, you will work 1,920 hours that year. If you earn $50,000, each of those hours will be worth $26.05. An hour of time would be worth $31.25 if your earnings climb to $60,000. Looking at your time another way, you would have to sell $260 worth of product per hour to earn $50,000 if you earned a 10 percent commission!

The typical salesperson spends only 920 hours a year in front of customers. The other 1,000 hours are spent waiting, traveling, doing paperwork, or attending sales meetings. Thus, as a typical salesperson, you really have to be twice as good, selling $520 worth of products every hour to earn that $50,000 commission.

The lesson from this analysis is clear: Salespeople must make every hour count to be successful. Time is a resource that cannot be replaced if wasted. But time is just one resource, albeit a critical resource, at the salesperson's disposal.

Managing time and territory is often a question of how to allocate resources. Allocating resources such as time is a difficult management process, but when done well, it often spells the difference between stellar and average performance. Many times it is difficult to know what is really important and what only seems important. In this chapter we discuss how to manage your time. Building on what you have learned about the many activities of salespeople, we also provide strategies for allocating resources among accounts—that is, managing your territory.

Salespeople have to carefully allocate resources such as time. Although every job will occasionally require burning the midnight oil, carefully planning one's time can make for a more balanced and enjoyable life.

THE SELF-MANAGEMENT PROCESS

The self-management process in selling has four stages. The first stage is setting goals, or determining what is to be accomplished. The second stage is allocating resources and determining strategies to meet those goals. In the third stage the salesperson implements the time management strategies by making sales calls, sending e-mail or direct mail pieces, or executing whatever action the strategy calls for. In the fourth and final stage, the salesperson evaluates performance to determine whether the goals will be reached and the strategies are effective or whether the goals cannot be reached and the strategies must change. This process is illustrated in Exhibit 15.1 and will serve as an outline for this chapter.

Exhibit 15.1
The Self-Management
Process

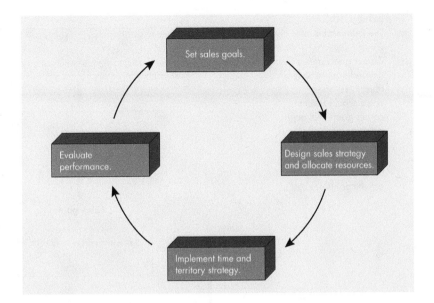

SETTING GOALS

THE NEED FOR GOALS

The first step in managing any worthwhile endeavor is to consider what makes it worthwhile and what you want to accomplish. Salespeople need to examine their careers in the same way. Career goals and objectives should reflect personal ambitions and desires so the individual can create the desired lifestyle, as illustrated in Exhibit 15.2. When career goals reflect personal ambitions, the salesperson is more committed to achieving those goals.

To achieve career objectives, salespeople must set sales goals. These sales goals provide some of the means for reaching personal objectives. Sales goals also guide the salesperson's decisions about which activities to perform, when to perform those activities, whom to see, and how to sell.

The salesperson lacking goals will drift around the territory, wasting time and energy. Sales calls will be unrelated to objectives and may be minimally productive or even harmful to the sales process. The result will be poor performance and, eventually, the need to find another job.

In Chapter 7 you learned that salespeople should set call objectives so the activities performed during the call will bring them closer to those objectives. The same can be said for setting sales goals: When sales goals are set properly and adhered to, the salesperson has a guide to direct his or her activities.

THE NATURE OF GOALS

As you read in Chapter 7, goals should be specific and measurable, achievable yet realistic, and time based (SMART). Goals should be specific and measurable so the salesperson knows when they have been met. For example, setting a goal of making better presentations is laudable, but how would the salesperson know if the presentations were better or worse? A more helpful goal would be to increase the number of sales resulting from those presentations. The best goal would be a specific increase, such as 10 percent. Then there would be no question about the achievement of the goal.

Exhibit 15.2

The Relationship of Goals
Career goals are devised from lifestyle objectives. Sales goals should reflect career goals. Although activities lead to sales, performance goals are usually set first. Then, using conversion goals, activity goals are set.

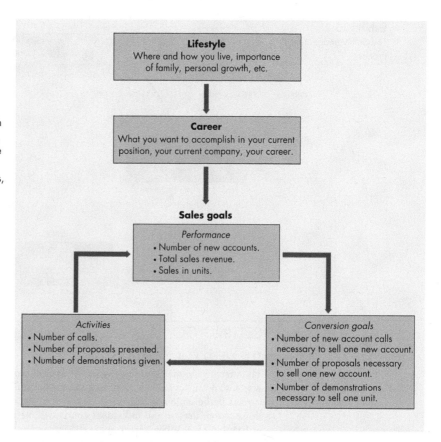

Lifestyle
Where and how you live, importance of family, personal growth, etc.

Career
What you want to accomplish in your current position, your current company, your career.

Sales goals

Performance
• Number of new accounts.
• Total sales revenue.
• Sales in units.

Activities
• Number of calls.
• Number of proposals presented.
• Number of demonstrations given.

Conversion goals
• Number of new account calls necessary to sell one new account.
• Number of proposals necessary to sell one new account.
• Number of demonstrations necessary to sell one unit.

Goals should also be reachable yet challenging. One purpose of setting personal goals is to motivate oneself. If goals are reached too easily, little has been accomplished. Challenging goals, then, are more motivating. But if the goals are too challenging or if they are unreachable, the salesperson may give up.

Goals should be time based; that is, goals should have deadlines. Putting a deadline on a goal provides more guidance for the salesperson and creates a sense of urgency that can be motivating. Without a deadline, the goal is not specific enough, and the salesperson may be able to drag on forever, never reaching the goal but thinking progress is being made. Imagine the motivational difference between setting a goal of a 10 percent increase in sales with no deadline and setting a goal of a 10 percent increase for the next month. The first instance lacks a sense of urgency, of needing to work toward that goal now. Without a deadline, the goal has little motivational value.

One problem some people have is periodically creating goals and then forgetting them. Goals should be written down and then posted. For

Some salespeople keep a reminder, like a photo of a new house, of their personal goals in front of them to help motivate themselves.

example, each month Will Pinkham has a goal for selling five new accounts (Will sells office equipment for Ikon Office Solutions). At the start of each month, he puts a new list on the wall over his desk, and as he sells each new account, he adds it to the list starting at the bottom. He starts the list at the bottom to remind him that his goal is to sell five, so when he sells one, his goal becomes four, and so forth. Probably not all goals should be posted in highly public areas, but the idea is to keep the goal in front of you so it continues to direct your activities.

thinking **it** through

What types of goals have you set for yourself in your college career? For specific classes? How would these goals meet the criteria of specific and measurable, reachable yet challenging, and time based? How do you keep these goals in front of you? What would you do differently now?

TYPES OF SALES GOALS

Salespeople need to set three types of sales goals: performance, activity, and conversions (refer back to Exhibit 15.2). Although many salespeople focus only on how many sales they get, setting all three types of goals is necessary to achieve the highest possible success.

Performance Goals

Goals relating to outcomes are **performance goals.** In sales, outcomes such as the size of a commission or bonus check, the amount of sales revenue generated or number of sales generated, and the number of prospects identified are common performance goals. For example, the salesperson in Exhibit 15.3 set a performance goal of $6,000 in commissions and another performance goal of eight sales. Revenue quotas are an example of goals set by the company, but each salesperson should also consider setting personally relevant goals. For example, you may want to set higher goals so you can achieve higher earnings. People are more committed to achieving goals they set themselves; that commitment makes achieving them more likely. Performance goals should be set first because attaining certain performance levels is of primary importance to both the organization and the salesperson.

Personal development goals, such as improving presentation skills, are important to long-term professional growth and are a form of performance goals. Every person, whether in sales or other fields, should have some personal development goals. Reaching those goals will not only improve overall job performance but also increase personal satisfaction. Like all performance goals, however, these goals should meet the criteria of being specific, challenging, and time based. Further, it helps to make these goals measurable. For example, if you set improving presentation skills as a performance goal, some outcome such as increased sales or fewer objections should occur that you can measure to determine if your skills are truly improving.

Exhibit 15.3
Goal Calculations

Monthly earnings goal (performance goal):	$6,000
Commission per sale:	$750
$6,000 earnings ÷ $750 per sale = 8 sales	
Monthly sales goal (performance goal):	8
Closings goal (conversion goal):	10%
8 sales × 10 prospects per sale = 80 prospects	
Monthly prospects goal (performance goal):	80
Prospects per calls goal (conversion goal):	1 in 3
80 prospects × 3 calls per prospect = 240 calls	
Monthly sales calls goal (activity goal):	240
240 calls × 20 working days per month = 12 calls	
Daily sales calls goal (activity goal):	12

Activity Goals

Salespeople also set activity goals. **Activity goals** are behavioral objectives: the number of calls made in a day, the number of demonstrations performed, and so on. Activity goals reflect how hard the salesperson wants to work. The company may set some activity goals for salespeople, such as a quota of sales calls to be made each week. Exhibit 15.3 lists two activity goals: 240 sales calls per month and 12 calls per day.

All activity goals are intermediate goals; that is, achieving them should ultimately translate into achievement of performance goals. As Teradata discovered by auditing sales performance, activity goals such as a specific number of telephone calls per day are needed for the salespeople to achieve the overall performance goals.[1] Activity goals help salespeople decide what to do each day, but those goals must ultimately be related to making sales.

However, activity goals and performance goals are not enough. For example, a salesperson may have goals of achieving 10 sales and making 150 calls in one month. The salesperson may get 10 sales but make 220 calls. That salesperson had to work much harder than someone who managed to get 10 sales in only 150 calls. What caused the difference? Answer that question and you, too, can work smarter rather than harder, but the answer presupposes that you first measured conversions and then set goals based on what should be achieved.

Conversion Goals

Conversion goals are measures of a salesperson's efficiency. Conversion goals reflect how efficiently the salesperson would like to work, or work smarter. Unlike performance goals, conversion goals express relative accomplishments, such as the number of sales relative to the number of calls made or the number of customers divided by the number of prospects. The higher the ratio, the more efficient the salesperson. Exhibit 15.3 lists two conversion goals: closing 10 percent of all prospects and finding one prospect for every three calls. In the preceding example, a rep earning 10 sales while making 150 calls could close 4 or 5 more sales by making 220 calls because that rep gains a sale every 15 calls.

Conversion goals are important because they reflect how efficiently the salesperson uses resources, such as time, to accomplish performance goals. For example, Freeman Exhibit Company builds custom trade show exhibits. Customers often ask for booth designs (called speculative designs) before making the purchase to evaluate the offerings of various competitors. Creating a custom booth design is a lot of work for a designer, and the cost can be high, but it does not guarantee a sale. If a salesperson has a low conversion rate for speculative designs, overall profits will be lower because the cost for the unsold designs must still be covered. If the rep can increase the conversion rate, the overall costs for unsold designs will be lower, hence increasing profits.

Working harder would show up as an increase in activity; working smarter should be reflected in conversion goals. For example, a salesperson may be performing at a conversion rate of 10 percent. Reaching a conversion goal of 12 percent (closing 1 out of 8 instead of 1 out of 10) would reflect some improvement in the way the salesperson operates—some method of working smarter.

Measuring conversions tells salespeople which activities work best. For example, suppose a salesperson has two sales strategies. If A generates 10 sales and B generates 8 sales, the salesperson may think A is the better strategy. But if A requires 30 sales calls and B only 20, the salesperson would be better off using strategy B. Thirty sales calls would have generated 12 sales with strategy B.

Comparing your performance with the best in your organization is a form of **benchmarking.**[2] Benchmarking can help you see where you are falling short. For example, if your conversion ratio of leads to appointments (the number of leads needed to get one appointment) is the same as that of the top seller but you are closing only half of your spec designs and that person is closing 80 percent, you know you are losing sales at the spec design stage. You can then examine what that person does to achieve the higher conversion ratio.

SETTING SALES GOALS

Performance and conversion goals are the basis for activity goals. Suppose a sale is worth $500 in commission. A person who wants to earn $4,000 per month (a performance goal) needs to make eight sales each month. If the salesperson sees closing 1 out of 10 prospects as a realistic conversion goal, a second performance goal results: The rep must identify 80 prospects to yield eight closings. If the rep can identify one prospect for every three sales calls (another conversion goal), 240 sales calls (an activity goal) must be made. Assuming 20 working days in a month, the rep must make 12 sales calls each day (another activity goal). Thus, activity goals need to be the last type of goals set because they will be determined by the desired level of performance at a certain rate of conversion.

Even though the conversion analysis results in a goal of 12 calls each day, that conversion rate is affected by the strategy the salesperson employs. A better strategy results in a higher conversion rate and better allocation of time, one of many important resources that must be allocated properly to achieve sales goals. We discuss how to allocate resources in the next section.

ALLOCATING RESOURCES

The second stage of the time and territory management process is to develop a strategy that allocates resources properly. These resources are allocated to different sales strategies used with different types of accounts with the purpose of achieving sales goals in the most effective and efficient manner possible.

RESOURCES TO BE ALLOCATED

Salespeople manage many resources. Some of these are physical resources, such as free samples, demonstration products, trial products, brochures, direct mail budgets, and other marketing resources. Each of these physical resources represents a cost to the company, but to the salesperson they are investments. Salespeople consider physical resources as investments because resources must be managed wisely to generate the best possible return. Whereas financial investments may return dividends or price increases, the salesperson's investments should yield sales.

A key resource that salespeople manage is time. Time is limited, and not all of a salesperson's work time can be spent making sales calls. Some time must be spent attending meetings, learning new products, preparing reports for management, traveling to sales calls, and handling other nonselling duties; in fact, nonselling activities can take up to 70 percent of a salesperson's time. Thus, being able to manage time wisely is important. As we discuss in the next chapter, salespeople also coordinate many of the company's other departments to serve customers well. Salespeople must learn how to allocate these resources in ways that generate the greatest level of sales.

WHERE TO ALLOCATE RESOURCES

For salespeople the allocation of resources is often a question of finding the customers or companies that are most likely to buy and then allocating selling resources to maximize the opportunities they offer. As you may have learned in your principles of marketing course, some market segments are more profitable than others. And just as the company's marketing executive tries to determine which segments are most profitable so that marketing plans can be directed toward those segments, salespeople examine their markets to allocate their selling resources.

Maximizing the opportunity means finding profitable ways to satisfy the greatest number of customers, but not necessarily everybody. One study of services customers found that only 44 percent were profitable; the rest cost the company money.[3] In the following section we discuss how to analyze the market to identify potential customers that are most likely to buy so resources will be allocated properly.

ACCOUNT CLASSIFICATION AND RESOURCE ALLOCATION

Not all customers have the same buying potential, just as not all sales activities produce the same results. The salesperson has to concentrate on the most profitable customers and minimize effort spent with customers that offer little opportunity for profitable sales. The proportion of unprofitable accounts is usually greater than one would think. As a rule, 80 percent of the sales in a territory come from only 20 percent of the customers. Therefore, salespeople should classify customers on the basis of their sales potential to avoid spending too much time and other resources with low-potential accounts, thus helping to achieve sales goals.

Customer management is not just a time management issue. Managing customers includes allocating all the resources at the salesperson's disposal in the most productive manner. Time may be the most important of these resources, but salespeople also manage sample and demonstration inventories, entertainment and travel budgets, printed materials, and other resources.

ABC Analysis

The simplest classification scheme, called **ABC analysis,** ranks accounts by sales potential. The idea is that the accounts with the greatest sales potential deserve the most attention. Using the 80/20 rule, the salesperson identifies the 20 percent of accounts that (could) buy the most and calls those A accounts. The other 80 percent are B accounts, and noncustomers (or accounts with low potential for sales) are C accounts. Eli Lilly (a pharmaceuticals company) classifies physicians and SC Johnson Wax classifies retail stores this way. One use is planning sales calls; so for example, A accounts could be seen every two weeks, B accounts every six weeks, and C accounts only if there is nothing else to do. An example of an account analysis appears in Exhibit 15.4. As you can see, Sam Thompson has used estimated potential to classify accounts so he can allocate sales calls to accounts with the greatest potential.

ABC classification schemes work well only in industries that require regular contact with the same accounts, such as consumer packaged goods and pharmaceuticals. Some industries (plant equipment, medical equipment, and other capital products) may require numerous sales calls until the product is sold. After that sale, another sale may be unlikely for several years, and the number of sales calls may diminish. Then the A, B, and C classification may not be helpful.

Salespeople in some industries find grid and customer relationship analysis methods more useful than ABC analysis. They have learned that simply allocating sales activities on the basis of sales potential may lead to inefficiencies. For example, to maximize great potential, satisfied customers may need fewer calls than accounts of equal potential that are loyal to a competitor.

Grid Analysis

The **sales call allocation grid** classifies accounts on the basis of the company's competitive position with an account, along with the account's sales potential. As with ABC analysis, the purpose of classifying accounts through grid analysis is to determine which accounts should receive more resources. By this method, each

Exhibit 15.4
Account Classification

Salesperson: Sam Thompson A. Analysis of Call Pattern: 2011					
Customer Type	Number of Customers Contacted	Number of Calls	Average Calls per Customer	Sales Volume	Average Sales per Call
A	15	121	8.1	$212,515	$1,756
B	21	154	7.3	115,451	756
C	32	226	7.0	78,010	345
D	59	320	5.4	53,882	168
Total	127	821		$460,859	561

B. Annual Territory Sales Plan (dollars in thousands)

Account	Actual Sales			2012 Estimated Potential Sales	Forecast	Number of Calls Allocated	Classification
	2009	2010	2011				
Allied Foods	$100	$110	$150	$250	$150	48	A
Pic N-Save	75	75	90	300	115	48	A
Wright Grocers	40	50	60	175	90	24	B
H.E.B.	20	30	30	150	30	24	B
Piggly Wiggly	10	10	25	100	55	18	C
Sal's Superstore	0	0	30	100	80	18	C
Buy-Rite	0	0	0	80	75	18	C
Tom Thumb	0	10	20	75	70	18	C
Apple Tree	0	5	12	60	60	12	D
Buy Lo	0	0	10	60	50	12	D
Whyte's Family Foods	10	8	9	50	40	12	D

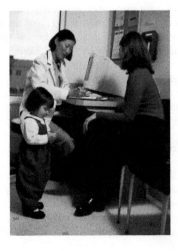

Although Dr. Liu's practice may appear smaller than that of the clinic on the right, the astute salesperson would determine each business's sales potential before classifying either as an A, B, or C account.

Exhibit 15.5
Sales Call Allocation
Grid

		Strength of Position	
		Strong	**Weak**
Account Opportunity	**High**	*Segment 1* Attractiveness: Accounts are very attractive because they offer high opportunity, and the sales organization has a strong position. Sales call strategy: Accounts should receive a high level of sales calls because they are the sales organization's most attractive accounts.	*Segment 2* Attractiveness: Accounts are potentially attractive because they offer high opportunity, but the sales organization currently has a weak position with accounts. Sales call strategy: Accounts should receive a high level of sales calls to strengthen the sales organization's position.
	Low	*Segment 3* Attractiveness: Accounts are somewhat attractive because the sales organization has a strong position, but future opportunity is limited. Sales call strategy: Accounts should receive a moderate level of sales calls to maintain the current strength of the sales organization's position.	*Segment 4* Attractiveness: Accounts are very unattractive because they offer low opportunity, and the sales organization has a weak position. Sales call strategy: Accounts should receive a minimal level of sales calls, and efforts should be made to selectively eliminate or replace personal sales calls with telephone sales calls, direct mail, etc.

Source: Raymond W. LaForge, Clifford E. Young, and B. Curtis Hamm, "Increasing Sales Productivity through Improved Sales Call Allocation Strategies," *Journal of Personal Selling and Sales Management*, November 1983, pp. 53–59.

account in a salesperson's territory falls into one of the four segments shown in Exhibit 15.5. The classification is determined by the salesperson's evaluation of the account on the following two dimensions.

First, the **account opportunity** dimension indicates how much the customer needs the product and whether the customer is able to buy the product. Some factors the salesperson can consider when determining account opportunity are the account's sales potential, growth rate, and financial condition. This rating is similar to the ABC analysis and is a measure of total sales potential. Again, the idea is that accounts with the greatest opportunity deserve the greatest resources.

Second, the **strength of position** dimension indicates how strong the salesperson and company are in selling the account. Some factors that determine strength of position are the present share of the account's purchases of the product, the attitude of the account toward the company and the salesperson, and the relationship between the salesperson and the key decision makers in the account. The strength of position helps the salesperson understand what level of sales is likely in the account. The account opportunity may be tremendous—say, $1 million. But if the account has always purchased another brand, the salesperson's strength of position is weak, and his or her real potential is something much less than $1 million.

Global accounts represent a difficult challenge in terms of determining potential and position. Position may be strong in one location and weak in another; potential may also vary. Marvin Wagner, an engineer with John Deere, has been working with Deere engineers and suppliers to Deere to standardize products globally. He's had to help suppliers negotiate with buying centers involving engineers in as many as four different countries, all with different expectations and preferences for different vendors. What may be preferred by engineers at the Arc-les-Gray plant in France may not even be considered by engineers in Ottumwa, Iowa.

The appropriate sales call strategy depends on the grid segment into which the account falls. Accounts with high potential and a strong position are very attractive because the salesperson should be able to sell large amounts relatively easily. Thus, these attractive accounts should receive the highest level of sales calls. For example, if you have an account that likes your product and has established a budget for it, and you know that the customer needs 300 units per year, you may consider that customer to be a segment 1 account (assuming 300 units is a high number) and plan to allocate more calls to that account. But if a competitor has a three-year contract with the account, you might be better off spending less time there. The account may buy 3,000 units per year, but you have little chance of getting any of that business. By classifying the account as a segment 2, you would recognize that the most appropriate strategy is to strengthen your position in the account. The sales call allocation grid, then, aids salespeople in determining where, by account, to spend time in order to meet sales goals.

THE GRID AND CURRENT CUSTOMERS The sales call allocation grid is a great tool for analyzing current customers. Recall the value of a customer that was discussed in Chapter 13; many businesses experience little or no profit in the first year of a customer's life. But over time profit grows if the salesperson can increase sales in the account, find ways to reduce the cost to serve the account (for example, shipping more can lower shipping costs), and so on.

In a landmark study of the paper and plastics industry, the key to a company's profit was found to be customer share, not market share. **Customer share,** also called **account share,** is the average percentage of business received from a company's accounts in a particular category. A similar term is **share of wallet,** which is the same thing but usually for an individual consumer. Over 15 years ago, an analysis of companies in that industry indicated that even if a company was the dominant supplier to a group of buyers, another company could be more profitable if it served fewer customers but had all their business.[4] Since that study, numerous studies have found similar insights. As a result, many companies are looking for how to increase account share, rather than the number of accounts.[5]

INVESTING IN ACCOUNTS

Planning based on customer analysis should result in more effective use of the opportunities presented by accounts. This improvement relates to better use of time, which is allocated to the appropriate accounts (see From the Buyer's Seat 15.1). But developing good strategies entails more than developing good time use plans; strategies require the use of other resources as well.

Salespeople invest time, free samples or trials, customer training, displays, and other resources in their customers. Companies such as IBM use predictive modeling to determine which accounts are likely to be more productive. This knowledge helps salespeople determine where to invest resources—time, samples, displays, and so forth. Sales costs, or costs associated with the use of such resources, are not always costs in the traditional sense but rather are investments in the asset called customers. This asset generates nearly all of a firm's revenue. Viewed from this perspective, formulating a strategy to allocate resources to maintaining or developing customers becomes vitally important.

Salespeople must determine not only which customers require sales effort, but also what activities should occur. CRM software can assist through

From the BUYER'S SEAT

SALES ACCORDING TO WOODY ALLEN

Woody Allen, the famous movie director, says that 80 percent of success is just showing up. Paul Tepfenhart, vice president of e-commerce for the grocer HEB, agrees. As one who has bought many technology solutions for HEB and formerly for Walmart.com, Paul has had a great deal of experience observing whether salespeople show up.

"There is no substitute for personal interaction," says Paul. He notes that "companies sell very little in the B2B environment. People buy from people." During the sales process, he emphasizes the importance of judging how a salesperson will take care of him after the sale by what happens during the sale. "Nothing damages credibility as a lack of dependability. Not showing up, being late, being unprepared are all symptoms of what might be poor execution later, something no buyer can afford. In sales, showing up, being prepared, optimistic, personable, and engaged is essential. It is the price of entry. It overcomes many other shortfalls. A successful start to a sales career begins with making an unwavering commitment to show up."

Greg May agrees. Greg is one of Honda's top dealers and chairs the company's dealer committee for technology. "I was looking at making a purchase of a technology platform to serve my customers more effectively and had scheduled an introductory call with a salesperson from an agency that would not only provide me the technology, they would also create the applications and campaigns

using the technology. But then the salesperson stood me up for the call—no notice, no follow-up for 24 hours. I can't trust my customers' well-being and my business to someone who can't even answer the phone when they say they will."

Paul offers a more positive example. "A more recent one involved Sarah who worked for a CPG (consumer package goods) company for about three years. She was always on time and prepared with her company's view of the category and how we were performing versus our competitors. Her philosophy came across as 'I am here to help you win by growing your category relative to your competitors.'" Paul recognizes that "she wanted to grow her branded items and finding a common objective made it a shared mission between me (her buyer) and her." Paul says the door opened for her when her competitor failed to meet his commitments. "Because Sarah was diligent and dependable and showed up, she grew her shelf space, achieved better placement on the shelf, and got the promotion (to feature her product) she had presented repeatedly. Beating the competition is not always having the better offer, but it always is consistently being there and doing exactly what you commit. Sarah has double-digit growth, and her competitor is scrambling to make up for his lack of dependability."

Woody Allen was right—opportunities are there only for those who show up.

pipeline analysis: a process for identifying and managing sales opportunities, also known as *opportunity management*. Recall that in Chapter 6 we discussed how accounts can move through stages from lead to prospect to customer. NetSuite, for example, can complete a pipeline analysis, telling the salesperson how well she is moving accounts from one stage to the next. In addition to being useful in determining conversion ratios and ensuring that a salesperson is creating enough opportunities to reach sales goals, pipeline analysis requires identifying which stage an account is in. Recognizing the account's stage in the pipeline is useful to determine what steps are appropriate. You don't want to try to do a spec design with a prospect for whom you haven't finished identifying needs, for example.

IMPLEMENTING THE TIME MANAGEMENT STRATEGY

Time is a limited resource. Once spent, it cannot be regained. How salespeople choose to use their time often means the difference between superstar success and average performance. Susan Flaviano, a sales manager for Lonseal, offers the

SALES Technology   15.1

PRESALE TECHNOLOGY

There's no doubt that the last few minutes of the sales process are critical. That moment when the account goes from prospect to customer is a moment to enjoy, to savor, to celebrate. But so much leads up to that moment, and much of that presale effort is supported by technology.

The effects of technology are felt even before there is a territory! A sales territory can be optimally created using software such as GeoMetrx (www.geomtrx.com), just one of many that combine data on potential customers with mapping capabilities to create balanced and optimized sales territories. Centrix Pharmaceuticals, for example, uses the software not only to create sales territories but also to help salespeople generate call patterns that minimize time wasted driving from one doctor to the next.

Another important presale technology is lead nurturing software, also called marketing automation. Aprimo (www.aprimo.com), for example, is one program that allows marketers to communicate with leads before they are prospects. Because so many purchases now start with research on the Web, software helps sellers identify those who are browsing

on the company's Web site. The same software can then apply marketing automation tools to "talk" via e-mail, chat, text, or any other digital channel to potential buyers early in the research process. Then, when the potential buyer has signaled sufficient interest, the lead is passed on to the salesperson. United Rentals (the largest construction equipment rental company in the world) uses Aprimo to follow browsers, offer additional material to help them make decisions, and then, when the time is right, introduce the salesperson.

Together, these two technologies mean more sales calls on higher probability accounts, resulting in more sales per salesperson. Most salespeople, though, are not even aware that their company uses such software. The Dwyer Group, for example, uses Eloqua (an Oracle product) for marketing automation, but the salespeople know only that their leads have already gotten certain information about the company's offerings and what information the leads have shared online. This above-the-funnel interaction means a lot fewer cold calls and more time spent with people who are ready to buy.

following tips for managing your time as a salesperson; keep these in mind as you read through this section:

- Start early. Get a jump start to the day before anyone else. Then you control the day without the day controlling you.
- Manage responsiveness. Although responsiveness is key to being successful, you cannot let customer calls, e-mail messages, and voice mail consume your day. We now have the ability to respond immediately, but it is important to choose specific times during the day to reply to correspondence.
- Schedule in advance. I set most of my appointments one week in advance, which helps me stay on target. Usually, if there is not a set commitment, it is easy to justify staying in the office to get caught up on paperwork.
- Use downtime wisely. If you have a canceled appointment or extra time over lunch, or you arrive to an appointment early, use this time to plan or follow up. With our laptops and sophisticated project tracking tools, you can use this time anywhere and reduce the amount of time spent in your office or at home on Saturday catching up on paperwork![6]

Remember that your time is worth $30 to $40 an hour, but only if you use it to sell. Your company has invested a great deal to get prospects ready to see you (see Sales Technology 15.1) but all of that goes for nought if no sales call is made. Use your time to hone a golf game or spruce up the yard, and opportunities to sell disappear. Although no manager really knows how a salesperson uses time, when the results are posted, accurate conclusions can be drawn.

How do you plan your time now? Do you use a computer to help you manage your time? How much of your time is planned by others, and how much of it are you free to allocate? What do you do to make sure you use your time wisely?

DAILY ACTIVITY PLANNING

To be effective time planners, salespeople must have a good understanding of their own work habits. For example, some people tend to procrastinate in getting the day started, whereas others may want to knock off early. If you are a late riser, you may want to schedule early appointments to force yourself to get started. On the other hand, if your problem is heading for home too early, schedule late appointments so you work a full day.

Many salespeople have the opposite problem—they never seem to stop working. One study found that 81 percent of salespeople felt like they had to be available to their customers 24/7.[7] The iPad, iPhone, and other similar products make the Internet and phone ubiquitous, but that is no excuse for failing to plan adequately. Susan Flaviano, now a sales manager for Lonseal, believed quantity of calls was the most important thing. But after a while, she realized she had no personal life and, more importantly, no more success than anyone else. She backed off the quantity of calls and began to spend more time planning her activities; the result was an increase in both sales and personal time.[8]

GUIDELINES

Salespeople need to include time for prospecting and customer care in their daily activities. Some minimize the time for such activities because they think sales do not occur on such calls, but prospects and happy customers feed future sales. Ikon, an office equipment dealer, requires salespeople to handle customer care calls before 9 a.m. and after 4 p.m. and to schedule prospecting activities between 10 a.m. and noon and between 2 p.m. and 3 p.m. Scheduled appointments are worked in when customers require them. The company bases these guidelines on its experience with buyers and when they are available.

Such planning guides are designed to maximize **prime selling time**—the time of day at which a salesperson is most likely to see a buyer. One salesperson, Lee Brubaker with Sandler Systems, calls this "pay time."[9] Prime selling time depends on the buyer's industry. For example, a good time to call on bankers is late afternoon, after the bank has closed to customers. However, late afternoon is a bad time to call on physicians, who are then making rounds at the hospital or trying to catch up on a full day's schedule of patients. Prime selling time should be devoted to sales calls, with the rest of the day used for nonselling activities such as servicing accounts, doing paperwork, or getting information from the home office.

Prime selling time varies from country to country. In the United States prime selling time is usually 9 a.m. to 4 p.m. with the noon hour off for lunch. In Mexico lunch starts and ends later, generally from 12:30 to 2:00 p.m.; offices may not close until 7 p.m. or later. In Great Britain prime selling time starts later; a British Telecom rep may not begin making calls until 10 a.m.

PLANNING PROCESS

A process exists to help you plan your daily activities, with or without the aid of planning guides. This process can even help you now, as a student, take more control of your time and use it effectively.

As Exhibit 15.6 shows, you begin by making a to-do list. Then you determine the priority of each activity on your list. Many executives rank activities as A, B,

Exhibit 15.6
Activities Planning
Process

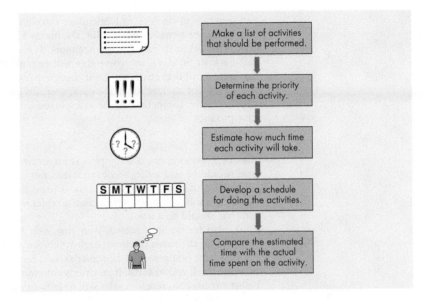

Make a list of activities that should be performed.

Determine the priority of each activity.

Estimate how much time each activity will take.

Develop a schedule for doing the activities.

Compare the estimated time with the actual time spent on the activity.

or C, with A activities requiring immediate action, B activities being of secondary importance, and C activities being done only if time allows. You can correlate these A, B, and C activities with the A, B, and C accounts discussed earlier, as well as activities such as paperwork and training. Prioritizing activities helps you choose which activities to perform first.

Note the difference between activities that seem urgent and activities that truly are important. For example, when the phone rings, most people stop whatever they are doing to answer it. The ringing phone seems urgent. Activities such as requests from managers or even customers may have that same sense of urgency; the desire to drop everything else to handle the request is called the "tyranny of the urgent." And the "urgent" can get overwhelming: The average businessperson receives 274 personal e-mail messages and 304 business e-mail messages weekly, and according to another study, that number will grow as marketers increase their use of e-mail marketing.[10] Of course these statistics do not include telephone requests from customers. Yet, like most phone calls, even requests from customers may be less important than other tasks. Successful businesspeople learn to recognize what is truly urgent and prioritize those activities first.

The next step in the planning process is to estimate the time required for each activity. In sales, as we mentioned earlier, time must be set aside for customer care and prospecting. The amount of time depends on the activity goals set earlier and on how long each call should take. However, salespeople often have unique activities, such as special sales calls, demonstrations, customer training, and sales meetings, to plan for as well. Time must also be set aside for planning and paperwork.

The next step, developing an effective schedule, requires estimating the amount of time such activities will require. As follow-up, be sure to compare how long an activity actually took with how long you thought it would take. Comparing actual time to planned time with the aid of calendaring tools in software systems like NetSuite can help you plan more accurately in the future.

Using the Computer for Planning

Many of the same customer management programs that salespeople use to identify and analyze accounts incorporate time-planning elements. This software can generate to-do lists and calendars through a tickler file or by listing certain customer types. A **tickler file** is a file or calendar that salespeople use to remember when to call specific accounts. For example, if customer A says to call back in 90 days, the computer will remind ("tickle") the salesperson in 90 days to call that customer. Or if the company just introduced a product that can knock out competitor B, the computer can generate a list of prospects with products from competitor B; the salesperson then has a list of prospects for the new product.

Need for Flexibility

Although working out a daily plan is important, occasions will arise when the plan should be laid aside. You cannot accurately judge the time needed for each sales call, and hastily concluding a sales presentation just to stick to a schedule would be foolish. If more time at one account will mean better sales results, the schedule should be revised.

To plan for the unexpected, your first visit of the day should be to a prime prospect (in the terms discussed earlier, this would be an A account or activity); then the next best potential customer should be visited (provided the travel time is reasonable); and so forth. If an emergency causes a change of plans, at least the calls most likely to result in sales will have been made.

MAKING MORE CALLS

Making daily plans and developing efficient routes are important steps toward better time use. But suppose you could make just one more call per day. Using our analysis from the beginning of this chapter and Exhibit 15.3, this change would mean 240 more calls per year, which is like adding one month to the year!

Some salespeople develop an "out Tuesday, back Friday" complex. They can offer many reasons why they need to be back in the office or at home on Monday and Friday afternoons. Such a behavior pattern means the salesperson makes 20 to 30 percent fewer calls than a salesperson who works a full week. John Plott, with DG Vault, got one large sale by working the full week. He was making cold calls on a Friday afternoon, trying to set up appointments for the following week, when he reached an attorney whose current vendor was unable to meet a deadline. The attorney said if he could get the software set up that afternoon, he could have the business. The result was a $30,000 account and $4,500 in commission.[11]

To get the most out of a territory, the sales representative must make full use of all available days. For example, the days before or after holidays are often seen as bad selling days. Hence, while the competition takes those extra days off, the salesperson can be working and making sales calls he or she would otherwise miss. The same reasoning applies to bad weather: Bad weather reduces competition and makes things easier for the salesperson who doesn't find excuses to take it easy. On the other hand, good weather can tempt the salesperson to the golf course, doing yard work, or otherwise avoiding the job. No matter the weather, the professional salesperson continues to work.

Salespeople can use certain techniques to increase the time they spend in front of customers selling instead of traveling. We mentioned Susan Flaviano's (Lonseal sales manager) challenges in managing her time earlier. One of her solutions, in addition to planning her time more effectively, was to use GPS routing software to help her plan her travel time more efficiently. Using routing techniques means she spends less time in the car and more time in front of customers.[12]

Salespeople who make calls in bad weather often find that their competition has taken the day off, leaving the field wide open for those who want to succeed.

Routing

Routing is a method of planning sales calls in a specific order to minimize travel time. Two types of sales call patterns, routine and variable, can be more efficient with effective routing. Using **routine call patterns,** a salesperson sees the same customers regularly. For example, Eli Lilly pharmaceutical salespeople's call plans enable them to see all important doctors in their territory at least once every six weeks. Some doctors (those who see large numbers of certain types of patients) are visited every two weeks. The salesperson repeats the pattern every six weeks, ensuring the proper call level.

Variable call patterns occur when the salesperson must call on accounts in an irregular order. In this situation the salesperson would not routinely call on each account within a specified period. Routing techniques are useful, but the salesperson may not repeat the call plan on a cyclical basis.

The four types of routing plans, **circular routing, leapfrog routing, straight-line routing,** and **cloverleaf routing,** are illustrated in Exhibit 15.7. If an Eli Lilly

Exhibit 15.7

Types of Routing Plans

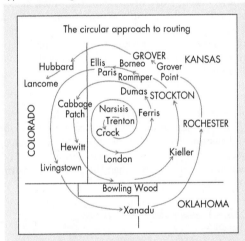

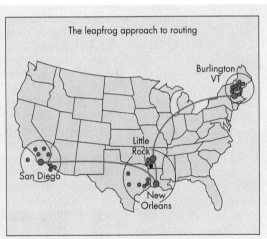

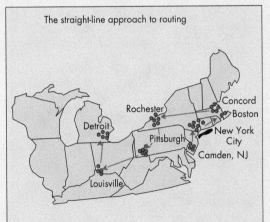

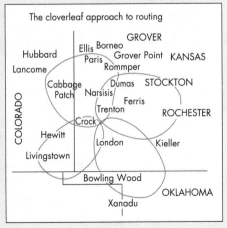

salesperson used the cloverleaf method (with six leaves instead of four) for a routine call pattern, every sixth Tuesday would find that salesperson in the same spot. But a salesperson with variable call patterns could use the cloverleaf method to plan sales calls for an upcoming week and then use the straight-line method the next week. The pattern would vary depending on the demands of the customers and the salesperson's ability to schedule calls at convenient times.

Zoning

Zoning means dividing the territory into zones, based on ease of travel and concentration of customers, to minimize travel time. First, the salesperson locates concentrations of accounts on a map. For example, an office supply salesperson may find that many accounts are located downtown, with other concentrations around the airport, in an industrial park, and in a part of town where two highways cross near a rail line. Each area is the center of a zone. The salesperson then plans to spend a day, for example, in each zone. In a territory zoned like the one in Exhibit 15.8, the salesperson might spend Monday in zone 1, Tuesday in zone 2, and so forth.

Zoning works best for compact territories or for situations in which salespeople do not call regularly on the same accounts. (In a large territory, such as the entire Midwest, a salesperson is more likely to use leapfrog routes, but the principle is similar.) Calling on customers that are in a relatively small area minimizes travel time between calls.

Salespeople can also combine zoning with routing, using a circular approach within a zone, for example. When zones are designed properly, travel time between accounts should be minimal.

Using E-Mail and Telephone

Customer contacts should not always be in-person sales calls—the phone or e-mail can be effective. For example, some customer care calls can be handled by simply sending the customer an e-mail message asking whether everything is OK. The customer may appreciate the e-mail more than a personal visit because it can be read and responded to when the customer has time and

Exhibit 15.8
Zoning a Sales Territory
A salesperson may work in zone 1 on Monday, zone 2 on Tuesday, and so forth.

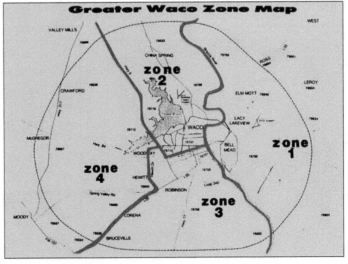

Source: *Waco Tribune Herald.*

doesn't interfere with other pressing responsibilities. The salesperson may be able to make more customer care calls by e-mail, increasing the number of contacts with customers. Keep in mind, though, that not all customer care activities should be handled by e-mail or phone. Recall from Chapter 14 that there are many reasons, such as reorders and cross-selling, to continue to make sales calls in person to current customers. For example, Sandra Kennedy, account executive for Spherion, has one account that she visits weekly. "It's my largest and most complicated account, and it just takes face time to make sure everything is going smoothly."[13]

Similarly, the telephone and direct mail can be used profitably for prospecting, as we discussed in Chapter 6. More calls, or customer contacts, can be made equally effectively with judicious use of e-mail and the telephone.

HANDLING PAPERWORK AND REPORTS

Every sales job requires preparing reports for management. All salespeople complain about such paperwork, but it is important. As we discuss later, paperwork can provide information that helps a salesperson determine what should be improved. The information also helps management decide what types of marketing plans work and should be used again. Therefore, every salesperson should learn to handle paperwork efficiently.

Paperwork time is less productive than time spent selling to customers, so completing it quickly is important. Salespeople can do several things to minimize the impact of paperwork on their prime selling time.

First, salespeople should think positively about paperwork. Although less productive than selling, it can increase their productivity and the productivity of the company's marketing programs by facilitating a detailed review of selling activities and marketing programs.

Second, salespeople should not let paperwork accumulate. We once knew of a salesperson who never did expense reports. He finally offered a summer intern 10 percent if she would complete his expense reports for the previous 12 months. This deal cost him $600; in addition, he was essentially lending the company $500 per month, interest free.

Routine reports should be completed daily. Nonproductive time (like time spent waiting for a customer) can be used for paperwork. Call reports and account records should be updated immediately after the calls so that important points are remembered and any follow-up actions can be planned.

Finally, salespeople should set aside a block of nonselling time for paperwork. The quickest way to do this job is to concentrate on it and avoid interruptions. Setting aside a small amount of time at the beginning or end of each day for writing thank-you and follow-up notes and completing reports saves prime selling time for selling activities while ensuring that the salesperson keeps up with paperwork.

Using the Computer to Handle Paperwork and Communications

Many companies, such as McGraw-Hill, give their salespeople pad, laptop, or notebook computers. These computers can be hooked up to the company's network to access customer information and process other paperwork automatically. Salespeople who

Many companies now provide their salespeople with wireless notebook or pad computers so they can access customer information and complete paperwork in the field, sometimes even in a customer's office.

travel can thus complete their paperwork while in a hotel, an airport waiting area, and other places. Voice recognition systems enable salespeople to do paperwork without any paper. Companies such as Giant Eagle, a grocery distributor, use such systems to enable salespeople to call orders in and handle other paperwork from their cell phones.[14]

Salespeople calling on overseas accounts can also file reports or check the status of orders, even though the home office in another time zone may be closed for the night. Computers can help international selling organizations operate smoothly by reducing communication barriers between the field and the home office. Computers and fax machines enable salespeople to communicate with colleagues and customers all around the world, despite significant time differences.

Some customer relationship management packages, like NetSuite, include territory management capabilities. These packages allow salespeople to track their performance by calculating conversion rates, commissions, expenses, and other important figures. Such technology enables salespeople to file reports quickly. Salespeople for J&K Sales Associates (Manchester, New Hampshire) input detailed call information into a simple Outlook file. The detail includes the buyer's stage in the buying cycle (J&K uses five stages, from introduction to postsale follow-up) based on the purpose of the sales call. The company has seen greater than 20 percent productivity improvement throughout the organization simply because all company members, from the purchasing department to customer billing, have the information they need at their computers.[15]

To manage your time wisely, you must exploit a scarce resource in the most effective manner possible. Your objective is to make as many quality calls as possible by reserving prime selling time for selling activities. Routing, zoning, goal setting, and other methods of planning and scheduling time will help you maximize your prime selling time.

EVALUATING PERFORMANCE

Success in sales is a result of how hard and how smart a salesperson works. Unlike many other workers, salespeople have a great deal of control over both how hard and how smart they work. Evaluating performance is the component of self-management that provides direction for how hard the salesperson should be working as well as an opportunity to determine which strategies work best. Salespeople should evaluate each sales call individually but also look at which activity leads to desired outcomes and at what rate. Tom Jud expresses his perspective on evaluating performance in Building Partnerships 15.1, and the importance of recognizing what's important through self-evaluation. Let's examine each component in more detail.

POSTCALL ANALYSIS

At the end of each call, many salespeople take a moment to write down what occurred and what needs to be done, perhaps using a printed form or entering the information into a territory management program such as NetSuite. Information such as the customer's purchase volume, key people in the decision process, and current vendors is important to have, but so is personal information such as the fact that the buyer's three children play soccer. The salesperson can use that information when preparing for the next call.

Remember the plan you made for each sales call? That plan included one or more objectives. Postcall analysis should include reflecting on whether those objectives were reached. The professional salesperson not only looks for specific areas to improve but also evaluates the success of the overall sales call.

BUILDING Partnerships

15.1

URGENT VERSUS IMPORTANT—NOT ALWAYS THE SAME

"We have a tendency to focus on the *urgent* things in life. But the more time we spend doing the *important* things, the greater success we can have," says Tom Jud, VP of inside sales at CA Technologies. Tom refers often to Dr. Stephen R. Covey, a highly recognized author and business consultant, who illustrates the difference between these two through his creation of the urgent-versus-important matrix. Urgent things are those crises, emergencies, and deadlines that monopolize our time. But the truth is that while these things seem so critically important, they really steal our attention away from the value activities that drive our businesses, like planning, prospecting, and meeting with customers. Learning to *manage* the urgent things and *focus* on the important things leads to greater efficiency and success.

Tom has been in sales and sales management for 16 years. Throughout those years he has seen how time management really can make or break a successful salesperson. He determined early on in his career that he would focus on the important things and manage time well, even if that meant doing administrative and clerical work during lunch or after hours. And many times it did. "I didn't want to waste a minute on anything that did not add value if I could be in front of a customer or prospect." He had witnessed how seemingly urgent activities could eat up a salesperson's day. "In sales, there is only a limited amount of time during a workday to connect and visit with your prospects and customers.

If you are not in front of them, your competition will be. Yet we let countless other things clog up our days and occupy our time. A lot of time we feel like we're being efficient and productive, but at the end of the day, we drive home from work wondering 'what did I even accomplish today?'"

Tom explains that this feeling of regret is a result of focusing on the urgent things during the day rather than the important activities. Forms may have been filled out, contracts drawn up, and e-mails replied to. These activities make us feel busy and productive, but did any of them really drive value creation or further long-term goals? Most likely not.

"Understanding that you only have a limited time to create value and do important things can revolutionize the way you work." Tom urges his salespeople to focus on the important things, like reaching customers during critical hours, planning sales call, and prospecting, to create value. He tells his salespeople, "When you manage the urgent things and focus on the important things, you'll quickly climb to the top. The drive home will no longer be filled with unsettling questions about productivity but rather, feelings of accomplishment and excitement."

"We are all given the same amount of time. We can't buy or add any minutes, hours, or days to our lives. But what we do with it and how we use that time is up to us."

Source: Brooke Borgias; used with permission.

ACTIVITY ANALYSIS

When planning their time, salespeople set certain activity goals. They use these goals not only as guidelines but also to evaluate their own performance. At the end of each day, week, and month, salespeople should review their activities in relation to the goals they set. Goals are written down or entered into NetSuite when they are set—say, Sunday evening when planning the following week. Then, on Friday evening, the actual activities from each day would be tallied and totaled for the week and compared to the goals. The salesperson could then evaluate whether more calls of a certain type are needed in the following week.

Merrill Lynch, for example, recommends that new brokers make 100 telephone calls each day (calls count even if no one answers). Frank Baugh, a new broker in central Texas, made 7,544 calls in his first 92 working days, or 82 calls per day. His goal is now 120 calls per day to bring his average up to 100 in the next quarter.

PERFORMANCE ANALYSIS

Salespeople also need to evaluate performance relative to performance goals set earlier. For example, they often evaluate sales performance in terms of percentage

Exhibit 15.9
Sales Evaluation
Measures

Evaluation Measure	Calculation	How to Use It
Conversion rate For total performance By customer type By product type	$\dfrac{\text{Number of sales}}{\text{Number of calls}}$	Are your strategies effective? Do you need to improve by working smarter (i.e., a better strategy to improve your hit rate)? Compare yours to your company and/or industry average.
Sales achievement	$\dfrac{\$ \text{ Actual sales}}{\$ \text{ Sales goal}}$	Is your overall performance where you believe it should be? Are you meeting your goals? Your company's goals?
Commission	$\dfrac{\$ \text{ Actual commission}}{\$ \text{ Earnings goal}}$	
Sales volume (in dollars) By customer type		Where are you most effective? Do you need help with a customer type?
By product category		Are you selling the whole line?
By market share		How are you doing relative to your competition?
By new customers		Are you building new business?
By old customers		Are you servicing your accounts properly?
Sales calls Prospecting calls Account calls Sales presentations Call frequency by customer type		Are your efforts in the right place?

of quota achieved. Of course a commission or a bonus check also tells the salesperson if the earnings goal was met.

An earnings goal can be an effective check for overall performance, but salespeople also need to evaluate sales by product type, as outlined in Exhibit 15.9. Salespeople who sell only part of the product line may be missing opportunities for cross-selling or full-line selling, which means they have to work harder to achieve the same level of sales as the salesperson who successfully integrates cross-selling and full-line selling in the sales strategy.

PRODUCTIVITY ANALYSIS

Salespeople also need to identify which strategies work. For example, if using a certain strategy improved the ratio of appointments to cold calls made, that approach should be continued. Otherwise the salesperson should change it or go back to a previous approach. Frank Baugh, the Merrill Lynch broker, tried several approaches before settling on one that works well for him. Of course Baugh keeps good records, so he knows what works and what does not.

The **conversion ratio,** or number of sales per calls, is an important measure of effectiveness. Conversion ratios should also be calculated by account type; for example, a conversion ratio for type A accounts should be determined. Other conversion ratios can also pinpoint effective strategies and areas that need improvement.

Conversion ratios can also be calculated for each step of the sales cycle. Profiles International, for example, calculates the conversion ratio of leads to prospects to determine which marketing activities generate the highest number of qualified sales leads. These leads can be tracked all the way to the close, too, telling Dario Parolo, vice president of marketing, where to invest his marketing activities.

SELLING YOURSELF

A theme for this chapter is self-analysis to improve performance. As a student, engaging in self-analysis is important so you repeat activities that are successful (lead to good grades) and avoid those that are not. Did pulling an all-nighter improve your exam performance? Or did you do better when you studied for shorter periods each day beginning a week ahead?

Similarly, if you are in an organization and examine the organization's recruiting practices, you'll find that some methods work better than others. What method of finding leads worked best—posting a flyer in the dorms or posting an e-vite on Facebook? What events attracted the largest crowds, and which events provided the best prospective members? By applying what you've learned in this chapter to organizational recruiting (or fund-raising or other activities that mimic the sales process), you'll be able to improve your organization's performance.

But what about you? Do you set goals for your academic performance each semester? Do you track your progress toward those goals and keep the goals visible as a way to motivate yourself? Paul Lushin, a noted sales trainer based in Indianapolis, says, "Over the years, I've come to know myself very well: what makes me work harder and what I have to do to make myself do things I really don't want to do so that I can enjoy the performance I seek. I find that teaching this concept of knowing yourself is one of the most important things that can help salespeople succeed."[16] While he was talking about salespeople, the concept applies to students, too.

SUMMARY

A sales territory can be viewed as a small business. Territory salespeople have the freedom to establish programs and strategies. They manage a number of resources, including physical resources such as sample inventory, displays, demonstration equipment, and perhaps a company vehicle. More important, they manage their time, their customers, and their skills.

Managing a territory involves setting performance, activity, and conversion goals. Salespeople use these goals to allocate time to various activities and to manage customers.

To manage customers well, the salesperson must analyze their potential. Accounts can be classified using the ABC method or the sales call allocation grid. These analyses tell how much effort should be put into each account. Some organizations use CRM software to conduct these analyses on the entire customer database, which helps identify patterns within a territory. Salespeople can use these patterns to develop account sales strategies.

More calls (working harder) can be accomplished by moving nonselling activities, such as paperwork, to nonselling time. Also, selling time can be used more efficiently (working smarter). For example, routing and zoning techniques enable the salesperson to spend more prime selling time in front of customers instead of behind the steering wheel of a car.

Effective planning of the salesperson's day requires setting aside time for important activities such as prospecting and still making the appropriate number of sales appointments. Using the full workweek and employing technology such as telephones, computers, and fax machines can help the salesperson stay ahead of the competition.

Finally, salespeople must manage their skills. Managing skills involves choosing how to make sales calls and improving the way one sells. Improvement requires that salespeople first understand what they do well and what needs improvement. Evaluating their performance can provide them with that insight.

KEY TERMS

ABC analysis   404
account opportunity   406
account share   407
activity goals   402
benchmarking   402
circular routing   413
cloverleaf routing   413
conversion goals   402
conversion ratio   418
customer share   407
leapfrog routing   413
performance goals   401

pipeline analysis   408
prime selling time   410
routine call patterns   413
routing   413
sales call allocation grid   404
share of wallet   407
straight-line routing   413
strength of position   406
tickler file   412
variable call patterns   413
zoning   414

ETHICS PROBLEMS

1. A sales manager schedules all sales training and sales meetings on the weekend so salespeople lose no selling time. Is this ethical? Does your answer depend on how they get paid—straight salary, salary plus commission, or straight commission?
2. One company's culture is "flashy," meaning salespeople are expected to wear custom-tailored clothing, flaunt expensive jewelry and watches, and drive expensive cars. Assume you are about to graduate and go to work for this company. Consider this culture and relate it to your goals—how might this culture influence your goals? Is that influence healthy? Why or why not?

QUESTIONS AND PROBLEMS

1. Reread the chapter-opening profile, "From the Buyer's Seat 15.1," and "Building Partnerships 15.1". What themes run through all three essays?
2. Mike Rocker, Susan Flaviano, and many other salespeople work out of their homes. Rocker and Flaviano both recognize how tempting it is to work longer and to put off paperwork until the weekends because it is so convenient. What problems might succumbing to such temptation cause? What safeguards can they put into place?
3. Compare and contrast the special problems of self-management for Mike Rocker (this chapter's opening profile) and John Tanner (he was profiled in Chapter 14). Both work in health care sales, but one travels the western half of the United States and works out of his home, and the other manages a territory consisting of one small city and works out of the office.

4. Shakespeare wrote, "To thine own self be true." How would you apply this statement to your planning and development activities?
5. Which factors are important for classifying customers? Why? How would these factors change depending on the industry?
6. Distinguish between routing and scheduling and between routing and zoning. Explain how routing and scheduling can interact to complement the planning of an efficient day's work.
7. How might a pharmaceutical salesperson increase the number of calls made per day? A financial services representative selling pension plans to companies? A financial services representative selling retirement plans to consumers? A representative who sells golf clubs to retailers and pro shops?

8. One sales manager said, "Sales is a numbers game. To make more sales, make more sales calls." Should sales managers encourage salespeople to continually increase the number of calls made each week? Explain your answer. Reread "From the Buyer's Seat 15.1." How does this essay relate to your answer?

9. One recruiter told a class that students are used to getting feedback on how they are doing every couple of months, but salespeople do not get a "final grade" until a year has gone by. He claims that students have a hard time making that adjustment when they enter the work world.

What do salespeople do to know where they stand at any given time? What do you do now that helps you know where you stand in your classes? Why is such knowledge important?

10. How would you use the sales call allocation grid to determine a prospecting plan? Be specific, and number each step of the process you would use.

11. All semester so far, you've been selling Netsuite in practice role plays. List three benefits that Netsuite provides salespeople in self-management and three benefits for sales managers in supporting the sales team's time and territory management efforts.

CASE PROBLEMS

case 15.1

MicroDyne

When Bill Maguire saw the headline that Micro-Automation and Dynamic Tools merged, he almost passed out. MicroDyne, the new company, would be his account, but what kind of account would it be?

Two years ago Bill landed the Dynamic Tools business after a hard-fought negotiation and sales process. First, the company had been using Bill's strongest competitor, Target Supply, for almost 10 years. Although some minor issues had arisen, overall Dynamic Tools was pretty satisfied. The director of manufacturing, Jack Reilly, really liked the Target Supply rep and fought hard against Bill. In one meeting Jack not only shouted at Bill, he told the head of purchasing that he resented Bill's company even getting a chance to bid! But in the end Bill's lower price and several customer testimonials, including one from a good friend of the CFO, won the business.

Over the two years since, Bill made a lot of progress in strengthening the relationship, except with Jack. But then, six months ago, Jack left Dynamic to take a position with Micro-Automation, also one of Bill's accounts. The first thing he did was call Bill. "Well, guess what, Bill. I'm canceling all outstanding orders with your company as of now. And that pallet of sweepers you sent yesterday? You can come get it. I switched all our business to Target."

Micro-Automation's business for Bill was much smaller than that of Dynamic, so the loss wasn't so bad. But Micro-Automation is bigger overall, and Dynamic Tool was acquired by Micro. Jack was back, as the movie promos say, "bigger and badder than ever."

Suddenly Bill's cell phone rang. The caller ID showed MicroDyne. Was Jack calling to cancel already?

Questions

1. Assess the new MicroDyne account in terms of the sales call allocation grid.

2. Assume the call is not from Jack but from the former Dynamic Tool CFO. She tells you that she is the new CFO, and they will be reviewing all vendors. You ask about Jack's responsibility and job title, and she laughs. "I know what you're thinking. But don't worry. You've done a great job for us. We just want to consolidate all purchases so we know we're getting the best deal." How should Bill respond? What should he do?

case **15.2**

TriQual Systems

In January, Kevin Ludlum took over the sales team at TriQual Systems (TQS), a company that serves the cable TV industry. TQS installs cable TV equipment at apartment buildings, dorms, and similar high-intensity multitenant dwellings, then provides technical support service to the tenants.

At lunch on Kevin's first day, CEO Dave Dougherty said, "I want the company to expand significantly, but cash is tight, so hiring more salespeople isn't an option. But keep in mind we have a patented technology that our competitors can't match, so continuing our high growth rate seems likely."

"I think the first thing is to assess where we are with our top accounts," Kevin replied. "We don't have 100 percent penetration with any account, do we?" David shook his head no, then said, "We've not been able to get an exclusive agreement except with ACH; they'll use us in all of their new projects and any refurbishing projects. But elsewhere, each new complex is determined by a bid process."

David began to tick off names and discuss the top accounts. "With the exclusive agreement, ACH will be our largest customer by the end of the year. Next will be The Orchard." The Orchard is a company that owns and operates apartments near colleges and universities across the country. There are currently 32 such complexes, with 20 on the books to be built in the coming year. Of those 32, 14 were acquired, and the rest were built by Orchard; half of those built are served by TQS and the others by two other vendors. Of the 14 acquired sites, all were served by various other vendors, but TQS has expressed an interest in upgrading to new equipment over the next two years. "How quickly they refurbish," said David, "will be determined by how well they are able to build the new units within budget, but I'd like to get an exclusive with them because of the growth. But they seem reluctant to put all their eggs in one basket."

Third on the list was Pinetree Properties, a company that owns 64 properties across the South. "They've got us in five of their newer complexes, all of which serve colleges and universities. Our systems are best suited to the high data demands students put on their Internet cable systems. The company has seven older university properties and plans to refurbish two each year. I think we'll win that, as they really see our benefits in that environment. Where we've struggled with them is in their family properties because they don't think it's worth the price premium to get the higher-quality product."

Young & Family was fourth. This family-owned business operates a dozen apartment complexes in Florida, with four in Miami. "Frank Young loves us. He's totally bought into our system of billing and will use us in any new properties they build. Right now, they're looking at two smallish complexes, both in Miami. They put us in the last three properties they built."

Last on the list of top five is The Franklin Group, which owns 32 properties in the Pacific Northwest. "Like Young, they like us a lot, but their growth rate has slowed. We're also in their last three properties, and our best shot there is probably refurbishing the older properties. They should be doing a complete makeover in the next five years, but getting them to make that investment has been tough," said David. Kevin asked why, and David replied that the operations VP was in favor of it but the CFO was not. "Maybe we just need to find some new companies to work with."

Questions

1. Where would you place these accounts on the sales effort allocation grid? Justify your responses.
2. What is your sales strategy for each one? What is the order of priority?
3. If you were to look for new companies to work with, use the information from these descriptions and design the perfect prospect.

ROLE PLAY CASE

Six months ago, you went through your accounts and determined that how you've allocated your effort is not consistent with the potential of each account and your relative position. In one instance, National Barns, you've got a great relationship with the CIO (chief information officer or head of information technology) and have called on National Barns once or twice a month. There are, however, only 24 salespeople there, and the company isn't growing, so there isn't much opportunity. You decided that this is an account you no longer plan to visit in person but will check by phone.

Another account, Maguire Manufacturing, merited more calling. It had 34 salespeople six months ago and has 44 now. Because it continues to grow and has indicated that it may grow through acquisition of other companies, you've decided to visit it once or twice a month.

Grafton Gifts, a distributor of gifts and greeting cards, has been a tough account to understand. Its 120 salespeople who call on retailers around the country use a paper-based system to keep track of their accounts. Orders are placed on special handheld computers that are downloaded at night. The VP of sales says that's all the company needs, but the VP of marketing wants more information so a CRM marketing strategy can be used. Today you will visit the VP of marketing to determine whether you want to continue with this account.

Your professor will give you buyer sheets for your turn as a buyer.

ADDITIONAL REFERENCES

Berry, Julian. "How Should Goals for 'Contact Optimisation' Be Set, and How Should Contact Optimisation Be Managed in a Multi-Channel Inbound and Outbound Environment?" *Journal of Database Marketing and Customer Strategy Management* 16, no. 4 (2009), pp. 241–46.

Cespedes, Frank V., James P. Dougherty, and Ben S. Skinner III. "How to Identify the Best Customers for Your Business." *MIT Sloan Management Review* 54, no. 2 (Winter 2013), pp. 53–59.

Christ, Paul, and Rolph Anderson. "The Impact of Technology on Evolving Roles of Salespeople." *Journal of Historical Research in Marketing* 3, no. 2 (2011), pp. 173–93.

Eggert, Andreas, and Murat Serdaroglu. "Exploring the Impact of Sales Technology on Salesperson Performance: A Task-Based Approach." *Journal of Marketing Theory and Practice* 19, no. 2 (Spring 2011), pp. 169–85.

Eggert, Andreas, Wolfgang Ulaga, and Sabine Hollmann. "Benchmarking the Impact of Customer Share in Key-Supplier Relationships." *Journal of Business and Industrial Marketing* 24, no. 3/4 (2009), pp. 154–69.

Fleischer, Mark. "Key Account Management in the Managed Markets: Visibility and Collaboration for Greater Effectiveness." *Journal of Medical Marketing* 10, no. 1 (January 2010), pp. 53–60.

Hartmann, Nathaniel, N., Brian N. Rutherford, G. Alexander Hamwi, and Scott B. Friend. "The Effects of Mentoring on Salesperson Commitment." *Journal of Business Research* (forthcoming).

Koller, Monika, and Thomas Salzberger. "Benchmarking in Service Marketing: A Longitudinal Analysis of the Customer." *Benchmarking* 16, no. 3 (2009), pp. 401–20.

Lambert, Douglas M. "Customer Relationship Management as a Business Process." *Journal of Business and Industrial Marketing* 25, no. 1 (2010), pp. 4–17.

Sweet, Catherine, Tim Sweet, Beth Rogers, Valerie Heritage, and Mike Turner. "Developing a Benchmark for Company-Wide Sales Capability." *Industrial and Commercial Training* 39, no. 1 (2007), pp. 18–28.

Zallacco, Ronald, Ellen Bolman Pullins, and Michael L. Mallin. "A Re-Examination of B2B Sales Performance." *Journal of Business and Industrial Marketing* 24, no. 8 (2009), 598–611.